DEATH OF A HERO

ANSWERING THE CALL OF MIDLIFE

BIRTH OF THE SOUL

JOHN C. ROBINSON, PH.D.

Tzedakah Publications
Sacramento, California

For information, address
Tzedakah Publications
P.O. Box 221097
Sacramento, CA 95822
1-800-316-1824

Robinson, John C., 1946 –
Death of a hero, birth of the soul : answering the call of
midlife / by John C. Robinson. – 1st ed.
p.   cm.
Includes bibliographical references.
ISBN 0-929999-09-6 : $16.95
1. Midlife crisis. 2. Midlife crisis – Religious aspects. 3. Middle
aged men – Psychology. I. Title.
BF724.65.M53R63   1995   94-47528
155.6'6'081 – dc20   CIP

10   9   8   7   6   5   4   3   2   1

"Dr. Robinson has written a book from his heart. It is about what happens at midlife, what it really means to be a man, and how men can return to sacred ground in the second half of life."

Robert A. Johnson
Author of *Femininity Lost and Regained* **and** *He*

"A powerful contribution to men's literature — synthesizing folk tales, poetry, psychology, and personal experiences in a refreshing and novel way. Robinson offers a breathtaking vision of the depths and heights of the masculine, and a clear, practical account of the paths that lead men safely through this wild and forgotten land."

Allan Chinen, M.D.
Author of *Beyond the Hero* **and** *Once Upon a Midlife*

"For any man willing to look in the most important direction inside himself, this book can be an excellent guide."

Dr. Bernie Siegel
Author of *Love, Medicine & Miracles*

"There's much in John Robinson's work helpful to men who find themselves wanting to live. I like especially the emphasis on poetry here and on the emotional expressive side of men."

Robert Bly
Author of *Iron John*

"Portraying the depths of his soul journey, John Robinson maps the midlife masculine experience in its raw pain and evolving beauty. His alternative to the 'compulsive warrior,' model of man strikes joy in my feminist heart."

Nina Boyd Krebs, Ed.D.
Author of *Changing Woman, Changing Work*

"A thoughtful, sensitive, soulful, and insightful look at men's lives that is full of wisdom about how to bring healing to them."

Aaron Kipnis
Author of *Knights Without Armor* **and**
co-author of *Gender War, Gender Peace*

CONTENTS

Part 4. Return to Sacred Ground: The Mystical Experience in the Transformation of Men

Part 5. Beyond the Story of Everyman

DEDICATION

*To Mallow, my wife, for weeks of work tracking down and securing
permissions, many hours of editorial feedback, and what was most priceless,
her steady love, patience, support, and belief in this project.*

*To my children, Amy, Chip, Adam, and Nikki, for showing me
that the journey begins anew with each and every generation, and for their
unquestioned faith that this book would see the light of day.*

*To Aggie and Robbie, my parents, who lit this path years ago
with their lives and their values long before I even knew I was on it.*

*To my brothers Nick, Hugh, Jim, and Lewis, for being my brothers
along the way and for teaching me about the brotherhood of men.*

*To David and Laurie Cawthorn, my publisher and his wife, for convincing
me that this work was truly worth publishing and for their friendship.*

FOREWORD

Little is known about the developmental tasks and opportunities of life's second half yet our population wave is racing into this "new age" in record numbers. Men in particular seem to lack a vision for the gifts, tasks, and deep purposes that arrive at midlife and will continue through their elder years. Few men, in fact, would even consider the process of aging to be one of the great opportunities for personal, social, and spiritual growth. Fewer still grasp the inner work necessary to recover the original story of their lives, to find the work of their souls, and then to grow into the kind of elders our world needs. *Death of a Hero, Birth of the Soul* provides this vision. It argues that the midlife and aging of man, rather than being grim and barren times, represent instead the birth of the soul and the beginning of the new spiritual journey.

Dr. Robinson has taken on the very interesting challenge of integrating the psychology of midlife, the new and vigorous voices of the men's movement, and the timeless teachings of mysticism into a single story. It is his own story, the story of "everyman," and the potential story of our collective future. It takes the reader from the security of the known into the vast possibilities of the unknown, yet in such gradual steps that one arrives filled with hope, joy, gratitude, and courage.

John Robinson has written a book from the heart. It is about what happens at midlife, what it really means to be a man, and how men can return to sacred ground in the second half of life. He writes eloquently about the search for meaning, beauty, ecstasy, and service. He writes about what mature men — men who have had the courage to face the great developmental tasks of midlife — can offer a world aching for love, compassion, and mature guidance. Full of surprises and ancient wisdom, personal and transpersonal lessons, and the richness of story and poetry, Dr. Robinson's work fills and nourishes the male psyche.

This is a work that must be read and savored, and then read again. More than a book, it is a story, a meditation, a celebration and map of the potential transformation of men in the middle and later years. A man will find himself in this book and he will find much more. It is obvious that this writer understands and cares for men.

— *Robert A. Johnson*

PREFACE

❧ This is the book I always wanted to read but never found among the countless bookstore shelves I browsed all my life. It is the book I always wanted to write but was too young and insecure to conceive. For years I ignored my own voice, thinking wisdom was out there someplace. Until now. This book has been waiting for me to grow old enough to grasp what I already "knew." It is about what men need to understand at midlife and about what life asks of them in the second half of the journey.

This book began nearly forty years ago in connection with my father. "Robbie," as he liked to be called, was a man who lost his psychological bearings at midlife and, unable to understand the quicksand of his own unfaced childhood wounding, found himself pulled inexorably into sadness, depression, and alcoholism. Sitting morosely at the family dinner table, too many drinks later, he would challenge us, his family, or dinner guests, with paradoxical questions such as, "What is the meaning of life?" "What is its purpose?" "What is the role of a man?" and "What is the role of a father?" Neither my mother nor my four brothers nor any of the guests could successfully solve these tragic koans, though I — the future psychologist — tried to over and over again, as if some kind of 10-year-old wisdom just might reach him through the fog and pull him back to us. It was not to be.

The questions my father asked, however, haunted me, and as my midlife approached, I sensed the profound importance of facing what he had not — the reality of childhood pain and the dual responsibility we bear to our personality and to our soul. This book is an effort to answer my father's questions for myself and, perhaps belatedly, for him. It is also my attempt to honor him, for as I puzzled over my father's riddles, I came to renew my respect and affection for this often intoxicated and inadvertent Zen master, this unadmitted shaman who spouted "crazy wisdom" with a trickster glint in his eye. He was a tragic figure, but he was also teaching me something I would not understand for three decades. In this way, he was an elder and spiritual teacher for me. I did not realize it until my own midlife passage was completed.

Death of a Hero, Birth of the Soul grew from my own experience of getting older and arriving tired and empty at midlife. My heroic and ambitious "young man's" goals of conquest, knowledge, and status in life were dissolving into the reality of a relentless midlife burnout. Unable to push any longer, all I could do was enter my exhaustion and examine its origin, nature, and meaning. As I did, my father's midlife questions began confronting me insistently from within: "What is the meaning of life?" "What is its purpose?" "What is the role of a man and father?" I asked further, "What is the teaching in this exhaustion?" "What does it want from me?" "What does it show me about how a man finds the real work of his soul?" I realized later that these were questions fundamental to the midlife passage, questions all men secretly ask as they cross into the second half. With the death of my own heroic strivings, I had to go deep into the realm of grief and ashes to find the wellspring of soul lost when the hero was born.

Called into the haunting mist of these urgent midlife questions, I began a search that would change my life. First, I studied the literature on the midlife years looking for answers and comparing its teachings to my own personal experience. Then, I found myself profoundly drawn into the hybrid field of depth psychology and the developing men's movement. Men's gatherings, full of myth, poetry, Jungian psychology, and the language of soul, pulled me ever more deeply into the swirling energies of masculine grief, male relationships, and the archetypal restoration of manhood at every level: personal, fraternal, communal, and universal. I kept going deeper and gradually experienced contact with a kind of masculinity long forgotten by modern "civilized" society, one I had never imagined. The awakening of an ancient maleness, old and dark like a primordial forest, took place in me. A preformed but buried masculinity also taught me that there are powerful imperatives stored in the male psyche that we must learn to feel, know, and respect to truly become men. Such imperatives arise from our spiritual core. I needed to learn more about them and about this core.

Then, quite by surprise, my post-midlife journey brought me full circle to a mystical awareness forgotten since early childhood. Here was the final missing piece. I began researching the spontaneously occurring mystic vision and the absolutely remarkable teachings hidden inside it. I learned that this vision was not reserved for ancient prophets only. It is still happening in the world today — to average people.

Because the insights and understandings explored in this book erupted first and foremost out of personal experience, I will be sharing my own story along the way. Because so much of what I learned was also tested against the experiences of my patients, male friends, and colleagues, I will also be sharing what I have learned from their stories. The material in this book has also been "tested" in numerous presentations, including men's gatherings, men's groups, classes, psychiatric grand rounds, professional conferences, and the powerful forge of individual psychotherapy with men. The model has been worked and reworked in my life and in the lives of the men I have shared it with.

This book also owes a tremendous debt to the psychological, theoretical, and philosophical writings of those who came before me. It is an emergent and inductive work that erupted from within but also drew upon many other men's lives. Understanding like this is truly cumulative and incremental. I honor these preceding voices by referring frequently to their invaluable gifts. Rather than being a single man's theory, logic, or science, this is a blending of voices into a chorus of surprises and realizations that were never planned or expected. But it is rich and powerful, and I believe it provides a vision that can shake and open your heart. If you, too, have become tired, it may renew your journey.

It may seem to you that I am sometimes mixing "psychobabble" with paradox and pirated Zen. Perhaps I am a little guilty of such excess, for I cannot reduce life's sacred mysteries to a formula, and they are too important to trivialize as an everyone-can-do-it self-improvement psychology. But bear with me. The ideas will be spelled out extensively in the coming chapters. And if these words excite something in your interior, then I encourage you to "hang in" here with me so that this book may ignite the unique chemistry that bubbles in your life's second half.

Finally, in the course of writing this book, or letting it write me, I realized that one does not do this kind of work for the outcome. One does it because one has to, because it is the work of soul. It is the work my life has been leading to all along. May it guide you safely through the death of *your* hero and the birth of *your* soul. ⚜

INTRODUCTION

❧ What is this time called *midlife* all about? Some call it a time of confusion, despair, even crisis. Others insist it is characterized by challenge, transition, and renewal. It is both.

Death of a Hero, Birth of the Soul describes the profound psychological and spiritual changes that men experience crossing the meridian into life's second half. The great majority of men, however, misunderstand or deny these changes. Their struggle for healing and renewal is instead unconsciously played out in risky romantic or business ventures, in work problems or burnout, illness or accidents, or is simply mired in stagnation. And, too often, society also conspires against a man, trivializing or mocking these problems as merely "midlife crazies," or berating him to stop whining and "be a man." But it is a grave mistake to minimize and betray this calling.

Where do we begin? When we look deeply at psychology, mythology, and religion, a universal male story emerges. I have called it the "Story of Everyman." It narrates the journey each man takes through the seasons of life — from the earliest dawning of consciousness to the final completion of his life's opus. In the pages that follow, this story is told in its personal, psychological, mythological, and spiritual forms. Each version adds to our understanding of life's meaning and purpose. As the story's hidden essence is revealed, we will begin to appreciate the unrealized tasks and possibilities of midlife, as well as the altogether new adventure of life's second half.

The land of aging has been a relatively uncharted territory until recently, for the vast majority of men throughout history simply did not live long enough to thoroughly explore it and report back on their discoveries. Carrying the "Story of Everyman" as a map to guide our souls on this perilous adventure, we reach midlife, the gateway into a new world. It is an age when biological, social, vocational, and marital forces all conspire to turn a man's life inside out.

What has been called the "men's movement" in America is heavily populated by midlife males coming together to face the midlife truths of stressful lives: personal isolation; numbing addictions; hidden emotional wounds; and confusion about manhood, money, and happiness. What is missing in their lives cannot be filled with more status, income, or sex. They are seeking the healing balm of genuine male friendship and deep masculinity. If they look closely, men at midlife discover that the male soul has been imprisoned in a dungeon of gladiator competition for years.

A more authentic masculinity, however, can be discovered and nourished. It is a masculinity that is restorative, vital, positive, and energizing. Found in the rich soil of honest and non-competitive male relationships, it grows in male friendships, men's groups and gatherings, and male community. The men's movement has renewed these original forms of masculine association, providing an alternative to the "compulsive warrior" and an opening into the realm of male soul.

Male aging, rather than representing inevitable decline, truly offers a vast new horizon of possibilities for self, soul, love, renewal, work, mature masculinity, and male friendship. Men whose quest is still the heroic vision of unlimited achievement and implicit immortality may not find the doorway into this archetypal realm. It is an older man's threshold, and crossing it, he can look forward to new male roles, becoming an initiator, mentor, teacher, or elder. A man has much to give back when he has truly taken this journey.

In the heart of each man, in each ancient masculine soul, is also a longing for some kind of significant contact with the sacred. Spiritual interests arise naturally with aging. As the personal specter of death looms toward a man at midlife, his spiritual core and its quest are activated. In this sense, each man becomes a "mystic" in his own way, and returning to the realm of spirit becomes the natural destination of The Story of Everyman.

Some people, however, have particularly intense and life-transforming mystical experiences. They are not crazy, nor are they fanatics or saints. Rather, they are usually everyday people who suddenly find themselves open to something so extraordinary and so undeniably real that they are profoundly changed. As we will see, mystical experiences are happening in the world today and have much to teach us about the sacred nature and purposes of life.

As our population and our leaders age in unprecedented numbers, and in this aging have the opportunity to ripen spiritually through the restructuring phases of midlife and archetypal masculinity, a gradual transformation of civilization can happen. Our culture's current patriarchal consciousness is itself going through a kind of midlife. It is breaking down in ways analogous to the male midlife passage. Though disruptive, such change offers the chance for a profound reordering of our social forms toward a rebalanced, regenerative, and non-destructive interplay of masculine and feminine, matter and spirit, order and love. This evolution may cultivate a new kind of man — one far more open to the brotherhood of all men and to the singular spirit of life.

Finally, I have attempted to explore the central themes in this book from a multidimensional format. Weaving psychology and personal experience with the strands of myth, story, poetry, song, and spirituality, I have tried to make a whole cloth — for life is, in its essential nature, already whole. It is our vision that needs restoring. Each of these strands also embodies our title, *Death of a Hero, Birth of the Soul*, in its own unique way, touching the reader in many ways that, I hope, will evoke new and ever more meaningful personal insights. My purpose is to reach all parts of you and to get deep enough to truly make a difference.

Not all men go as far as this model reaches. Just as the great visionaries throughout the ages have shown us what is possible though not yet commonly attainable in our lives, this is a model of potentials and possibilities. Because the journey cannot be controlled, this is more of a guide book than a detailed itinerary. We are on a pilgrimage, not a trip. Keep in mind that the journey is as important as the destination. The experiences along the way are the teaching and the means of growing consciousness, self, and soul.

A Note to Women: This is a book for and about men. I wrote it because I am a man and sense that I know men best, most intimately. I also wrote about men because I agree with the feminists who argue that women should write books about women, not men. But that does not mean that women should not read this book or learn from it. This is not a secret book. It is not woman bashing or a ploy to "get the upper hand" in relationships or in the world. Quite the contrary, it is my hope that you will benefit in the following ways from reading it.

- ✗ First, I hope these ideas will help you understand your men a little better. Whether they are lovers, husbands, sons, brothers, friends, fathers, grandfathers, grandsons, or nephews, manhood, with all its hidden trials and stages, is their common experience and collective destiny. Their midlife struggles, their need for other men, and their search for soul and spiritual values as they age — these common male issues are as important as they are confusing. Your understanding will make this journey easier for both you and the men in your life.

- ✗ Secondly, midlife is not just for men. It happens to women too! While some gender-based issues differ, the stages and life-transforming purposes of this process are identical, and it is useful to have a map of the territory. Indeed, men are the reflection of your own masculine side, a side that you will become increasingly familiar with in the second half of life.

- ✗ Third, few books seem to address the transformative and spiritual potentials of the human midlife, which I believe is one of its central thrusts. The spiritual journey, of course, includes us all irrespective of gender, and offers universally important teachings. If spirituality is important in your life, if it is growing more important as you age, then this book will have much to offer.

- ✗ Fourth, and perhaps most important, this book is about dismantling the rigid patriarchy that has injured you and me, women and men, and our world. It is about how midlife and new male relationships can, for many men, be the inception of real and significant emotional change. In this admittedly painful evolution, men rework their masculinity to become more natural, loving, and trustworthy. This process of change is for all of us and it is ultimately good. Understanding it will make the transitions a little more bearable.

ſ Fifth, women in our culture, insofar as they emulate the model of the "Compulsive Warrior" I describe in Part 3, also need to examine its personal, collective, and spiritual costs. Unfortunately, more and more women are adopting this standard, believing that success depends on competing with men in the contest of false masculinity. This abandonment of the feminine is a great tragedy in its own right. If you can understand and support men without surrendering yourself, the rewards for you and your men will be well worth it.

ſ Finally, I have come to appreciate how deeply and pervasively women are afraid of men. They are afraid of men's violence, exploitation, abandonment, and apparent insensitivity. Our individual and collective histories teach that sometimes they have good reason to be afraid. But men too are afraid of men for the same painful reasons. The men we are afraid of are false men, wounded and hardened men, men acting blindly from their own pain and abusive conditioning. On the other hand, when women see men who can cry, dance, and embrace one another, their fears are softened by perceptions of beauty, appreciation, love, and vulnerability. These are the men you really wanted in the first place. They are afraid too. Support their birth and growth toward a deeply centered masculinity that honors women, children, nature, self, other men, and other cultures. Thank you.

How to Use This Book: Each section of this book can be read by itself. So can the poetry. The material can be read sequentially or in any order you like; each part can stand alone. Skip what you don't want to read. If poetry or fairy tales don't interest you, that's okay. You won't lose the message of the book. However, reading the final part — Beyond the Story of Man — probably won't make too much sense unless you have understood what led up to it. I recommend you read it last.

Approach this book in any way that works for you. Read whatever really grabs you, what you need to read, what jumps out at you. Analyze it, make it a meditation, read the poems out loud, take it on a trip into nature. You will find a way that is your own. And take your time. There is too much here to digest in a single reading. It needs to work on you. I recommend you read it slowly. Then ask yourself why you are responding to it the way you are. If you keep exploring these kinds of questions throughout the book, I believe that your own answers, and the plan for your life, will become more clear. ☙

PART I

The Story of Everyman

Full circle, from the tomb of the womb to the womb of the tomb, we come: an ambiguous, enigmatical incursion into the world of solid matter that is soon to melt from us, like the substance of a dream. And, looking back at what had promised to be our own unique, unpredictable, and dangerous adventure, all we find in the end is such a series of standard metamorphoses as men and women have undergone in every quarter of the world, in all recorded centuries, and under every odd disguise of civilization.
(Campbell, 1968, pp. 12-13)

DEATH: Almighty God, I am here at Thy will, Thy commandment to fulfil.

GOD: Go thou to Everyman, and show him in my name a pilgrimage he must on him take, which he in no wise may escape; And that he bring with him a sure reckoning without delay or any tarrying.

DEATH: Lo, yonder I see Everyman walking; Full little he thinketh on my coming. His mind is on fleshly lusts and treasure, and great pain it shall cause him to endure before the Lord, heaven's King. Everyman, stand still! Whither art thou going thus gaily? Hast thou thy maker forgot?
(*Everyman*, in Gassner, 1987, p. 209)

CHAPTER 1

The Timeless Story

❧ When one looks back from a vantage point late in life and examines the twists and turns of his own biography, it all seems so personal and individual. I had these parents, these things happened to me, I did the best I could with my life. I had children, a career, fate blessed or cursed me, I got older and slowed down, soon I will retire and will face the end the best I can. It's just what I did. Was it valuable? Was there really any purpose to all this? We wonder, sometimes sadly, what it has meant, if anything. But when we look at the recurrent psychological themes common to all our individual stories, a more general developmental pattern also begins to appear across the lifespan. It is a pattern that both steers and gives definition to our lives.

Science and Story: Two Ways of "Knowing"

We can understand this developmental pattern in two ways: through science and story. The goal of scientific research is to describe objectively the behaviors, attitudes, tasks, and processes typically associated with each stage and then create theories to explain them. Psychologists have extensively studied the normal stages of child development, and our culture is relatively familiar with this information. We know a lot about the cognitive and behavioral characteristics of infancy, preschool, and grade school ages, adolescence, and so forth. In more recent years, the psychological stages of adult life have also been mapped. Interestingly, our knowledge of adult development is still relatively new; that is, it has not yet been fully integrated into our culture as common and everyday information. Most adults still don't realize that there are, in fact, fairly predictable phases, emotional tasks, and even crises common to each age.

The unfolding of human development through the lifespan has also been captured by the imaginal language of the world's myths, legends, fairy tales, parables, fables, and religions. Here developmental knowledge is woven into stories that symbolize the stages and tasks of life. The medium of information storage and communication is the language of symbol, image, metaphor, and allegory. This imaging ability is innate to the human mind and probably preceded the development of speech. It is essentially the same language we see in dreams, where pictorial symbols encode meaning in condensed and cryptic ways. Because of their symbolic nature, stories can hold a tremendous amount of information, for as we will see, symbols seem to be an almost inexhaustible source of meanings, personal and universal. And, of course, we still use stories to encode and share information. Everyday we recount our everyday lives or problems to each other, and we do so in the form of stories.

Story and Psychology: Ancient Wisdom

In mythology and fairy tales, the stages and issues of life are represented as heroic journeys filled with seemingly impossible challenges, supernatural characters, and fateful clashes between the forces of good and evil. All cultures have them. They are stories that "explain" in secret symbolic language what life and its problems are all about and why we are here. They are, in effect, cosmologies that give meaning to our existence, especially in times of crisis, change, and suffering. Thus, our stories encode our psychology! What an amazing way to do it.

The cross-cultural study of stories and myths reveals the presence of many universal themes and patterns, suggesting that mankind has been organizing its intuitive developmental psychology in this way from the beginning of time. Carl Jung and Joseph Campbell, among others, demonstrated the existence of constantly recurring motifs, beliefs, and patterns in man's mythology and showed us how to open them to symbolic interpretation. Jung also hypothesized that a common psychic ground, the collective unconscious, was responsible for these worldwide similarities. He viewed it as a deep psychological substrata that stored and structured the basic experience of all peoples, independent of geography, race, or culture. The collective unconsciousness may be likened to a common encyclopedia from which we all draw our ultimate knowledge, or to a magnetic field that invisibly orders all the electrical activity in its reach. Or, expressed somewhat differently, we might argue that there is simply one basic developmental sequence stored in our cellular DNA that takes us from birth to death. Our stories are simply the way we use imagination to encode what this sequence means to us.

Whatever the explanation, it can be seen that pre-scientific man had his own way of understanding and capturing the developmental significance of his life journey. He put this information into symbolic stories. Handed down generation to generation, a tribe or culture's stories and myths carry their most important psychological and sacred teachings. All the wisdom man has progressively accumulated about himself over the eons is unconsciously stored in his stories, and they have served him for millions of years. Later we will explore several stories and learn how to understand this ancient knowledge.

One more surprise. In the final analysis, mankind's basic life experience and its profound psychological and spiritual meaning can actually be summarized in one ageless and universal symbolic story. It is a made up of countless individual variations and splinters, but put them all together and the pattern can be seen in its complete form. Campbell has called this story *The Hero's Journey* (Campbell, 1968). George Lucas used it as the basis of his enormously successful *Star Wars* movies. (Lucas, in *Cousineau*, 1990, p. 180) It is the infrastructure of all great novels and movies. We easily and readily identify with the epic journeys they portray because they speak to the same unconscious experience and wisdom stored in each of us. It is this great story that we will be exploring in Part 1.

Opening to the Story

When we seek to understand ourselves, both approaches — the objective approach of science and the symbolic way of story and myth — are useful. For example, to better understand his own experience in any particular stage of life, a man might wish to review psychological research concerning the stresses and issues most common to that stage. He might read about midlife, for example, and see if his own experience fits the psychologist's research findings. This approach appeals to our logical, left-brained analytic style of comprehension and gives scientific order, orientation, and perspective to our confusion. Exploring the symbolism of story and myth, on the other hand, engages our right-brain language of metaphor, picture, and emotion. Here we can find rich symbols and metaphors that imaginatively portray the drama of our lives, revealing its hidden psychological meaning and purpose. Each approach has value, and we will be going back and forth between both modes as we move through the sections and chapters of this book.

Understanding the wisdom hidden in stories, however, has two particular advantages over the scientific approach. The imagination and emotion evoked by a good tale expands and enriches our inner perspective. The images seem to elaborate themselves and unfold spontaneously like a movie, taking our imagination beyond the rigid boundaries created by fixed logical and conceptual thinking. Suddenly, as if drawn into a magic theater, we "see" the story hidden in our struggles and it begins to move on its own. Secondly, when we tell our own story, we are drawn into that unconscious layer that stores mankind's universal drama as well as eons of learning about it. In this realm of archetypal imagination, symbols and images arise spontaneously within us that carry all the ultimate meanings in life. Opening our mythic imagination, therefore, offers a relationship to the universal unconscious that is creative and instructive. It affirms life as meaningful and sacred. Struggling and suffering in this dimension can find larger significance, value, and dignity.

Until you have had the experience of finding and opening your own story, these ideas may seem intellectual and dry. So it is useful to retell this universal story in a way that invites you into your own personal version and begins the magic process of moving you into its hidden meanings, depths, and inherent strivings. So as you read this universal story, see how it connects to your own. Find the thread that your life follows in this larger tapestry and search for new insights along the way. Finally, make an exercise of this process. In other words, write your story as it is re-stimulated here and let it tell you what it wants from you, what your life has really been about up to now. We will be returning to your story and the universal story over and over again in the pages to come.

The Story of Everyman

Everyman is a late fifteenth century English morality play. In it, God sends the character of Death to tell the Everyman (who of course represents each of us) that it is time for the final pilgrimage from this world of sensual pleasures to the grave. In his fear and loneliness, Everyman cries out for company to the characters of Fellowship, Cousin, Kindred, Goods, Good Deeds, Strength, Discretion, Five-Wits, Beauty, Knowledge, and Confession. Ultimately, all abandon him at the grave except Good Deeds, who will accompany him to the final reckoning. Though perhaps simplistic, this play was nonetheless meant to represent an epic journey, a drama confronting everyone with the ultimate questions of life. I incorporated this play's title into the central theme of Part I of this book because of its value as a collective reference. The Story of Everyman portrays the equally profound journey that all men must take in this adventure called *life*.

My version of the Story of Everyman will be told three times in the course of this book. The first time is a psychological version. It is a subjective and purely experiential characterization of the unfolding and progressive transformations of the male self through the seasons of life. The second telling is a mythological one, symbolizing our universal male wounds and the symbolic journey we take to heal these deep but necessary psychic injuries. The final version of the Story of Everyman is the spiritual one. It frames the sacred issues and tasks of a man's life. This last telling also takes us to the ending of the story and to the "ending of time" so frequently described in man's prophetic religious literature and experience. Interestingly, this final story has a surprise ending!

Finally, keep in mind that these three versions actually comprise one whole story with endless variations. Though each version has its own unique level of meaning and implication, they are simply different ways of looking at the one great human experience. My experience — our experience — your experience. ❧

CHAPTER 2

"The Seasons of a Man's Life"

>> The metaphor I like best for describing the story of man's developmental stages is that of *seasons*. This ancient and eternal symbol holds two especially appropriate connotations: first, our lives go through natural cycles, as do all living organisms on earth, reconnecting us with the harmony of the earth and universe, and second, entering the imaginative realm of this metaphor can be an especially valuable way to comprehend our life journey. Daniel Levinson penned *The Seasons of A Man's Life* as the title for his classic book on men's development (Levinson, 1978), but remained primarily interested in the more objective psychological and scientific sphere. I borrow his title for its subjective and symbolic power, that is, as means of activating the reader's memory and imagination. It is through his imagination that a man's biographical story can be brought to life, not merely as a collection of facts, but as a living and dynamic story with its own intrinsic validity, desire, and destiny. Reliving this story in the magic theater of imagery will tell us so much more than we knew before. What it tells us may correct years of misunderstanding and renew our courage to hear its call.

The Story of Everyman is a story of seasons, each with its own essential energies, strivings, experiences, tasks, meanings, and outcomes. The transitions between seasons are also important times that can be described and appreciated. As we come to understand how each season and transitional period forms our life experience and moves it along even in the face of our ignorance or defiance we can begin to honor the greatness of this underlying story and the secret purposes of its seasonal nature.

This *Great Story*, as Jean Houston called it (Houston, 1987), hints at a deep and universal symbolic underground of our lives, a pre-established and powerful archetypal form that seeks and engages us for its own purposes. The tasks of each season provide a kind of structuring or calling that moves us along this journey from childhood to death. It is my deepening conviction that the experience of life has meaning and purpose beyond material success or emotional gratification, beyond even individual or species survival. That the stages of our life's unfolding are neither accidental nor simply biological. We as men need to better understand the ultimate tasks secreted in this story in order to focus our love and our work in truly meaningful and conscious ways.

Our analysis of the story will also reveal that, rather than living life, we are, far more than we know, lived by life. The stages, forms, issues, and passages are already within the seed. Moreover, the most profound decisions and turning

points in our lives are not as rational or calculated as we would like to believe —
they happen to us. We rationalize them later, we explain our motives, but in fact
we are carried relentlessly along by the forces and dynamics operating in the
unfolding unconscious. We travel in a small boat on a powerful river of change.
How we handle this voyage affects our lives, our families, our destiny, and the
world itself. We can know about these forces in time, we can gradually learn to
discern their direction and power, but we are, ultimately, not in charge. It is only
as we understand this reality that we can meaningfully participate in our personal and cultural evolution. Ultimately the destination and the transformative experiences of this journey are magnificent. Along the way, however, are many doubts,
trials, and necessary sufferings.

For our purposes, Spring is defined as the period from birth to emancipation
from family. Summer then takes a man to midlife, which serves as a transition
into the Fall. Winter comprises the final years of his life, which now often begins
after the transition to retirement and lasts into his seventies and eighties. When
the average man's life span was much shorter, less than forty years for example,
such seasonal demarcations still existed but with far less experiential depth and
symbolic richness.

Within each of the four seasons, we can also find a cycle of mini-seasons; that
is, a similar pattern of Spring, Summer, Fall, and Winter. For example, even
though Winter represents the final season of life, it often begins with a time of
freedom from the stress and drudgery of work that feels a bit like a new beginning. This "springtime" feeling may develop into an "Indian summer" which may
go on comfortably and productively for years. Then a man again feels the biological clock of age acting on his body beginning a Fall-like mini-season of reflection and preparation preceding Winter's last substage with its final snows.

The summary I present here is an overview, almost an allegory. It is a mytho-
psychological parable that seeks the essential individual and collective meaning of
each critical stage of development. The brush strokes are broad, experiential, sometimes whimsical or idealized, with inherent ambiguities that will be explained later.
Finally, this story is not meant to be taken as a precise script for men for there are
wide variations in individual experiences of male development. But try to look for
what is true to your experience. Each journey still involves the same powerful energies and emotions, events and passages, purposes and potentials. However disguised by culture, era, and fashion, it is the inner story of the male spirit.

Here, then, are the seasons of a man's life. Let your memory wander back and
discover what this story wants you to remember and understand. Then, as the
story moves beyond your chronological age, let your imagination take you into a
future already inside you. Grow your story rich and full. It seeks something from
you. Find it.

Springtime

Original Wonder. Our story naturally begins in the Spring. For many men, it is difficult to recall this time of original and pristine awareness. A young boy's consciousness awakens and organizes itself amidst a kaleidoscopic chaos of light, vivid color, crystal clear sounds, and the amazing experiences of movement, temperature, skin, and smell. All this is pure perception without the filtering functions of belief, expectation, and knowledge. Everything is new, and a boy is open, innocent, trusting, full of wonder and awe. Can you remember that time — how the grass felt on your bare feet, the shade of summer, the sound of crickets or lightning, the taste of rain? Parents were so big then. So was the world. This is the original experience of the garden of Eden before expulsion.

What arises next is even more wondrous. In this original world, a boy begins to feel the remarkable stirrings of his own nature. An energy comes from his very being that excites and moves him. It is sometimes quiet, sometimes eruptive, sometimes fierce, sometimes joyous. The world of thoughts and images, too, is discovered, and the adult boundary between "real" and "imaginary" is pretty loose. It is an endless present filled with magic, monsters, vivid dreams, and unbounded imagination. What an amazing experience! Can you remember those times? Picture that boy the way he was, naturally, without any effort, and the way he might have developed before the adult world decided he "needed" correction.

A Natural Self. There was, in the beginning, a natural self, a magic child, born already full of his own spontaneous energies, interests, talents, appetites, and internal order. How did you feel special as a child? Were you a sensitive, quiet child full of thought or intuition; a rambunctious, wild or exploring child, a leader or follower, a dreamer or mechanic, a questioner or conqueror? This original self, before it was challenged by the expectations and judgments of the adult world, is tremendously important. It has always wanted to shine through and did so in various ways as you were growing up. It is this essential and potential self, born from its own nature, that gives our life its hunger, its urging and initiative. It is this always-emerging self, with its inborn, unique but still hidden gift, that carries us into life. Because this original self seems to coalesce magically from the unbounded domain pre-existing life energies, it seems to hint at transcendent origins. This original self holds a secret connection to the sacred that we will experience and draw upon over and over again in life.

Inevitable Wounds. But the story is not so simple or kind. Always, it seems, this original self is hurt, betrayed, or shattered in our dealings with our parents, siblings, and the older generation. For each of us, there will be one or more "Great Wounds," that is, an event, a parent, or a circumstance that injures, violates, or suppresses this young and tender self. You may remember such woundings: times of criticism, neglect, rejection, abandonment, shame or violence — and the pain that comes with them. It is as if we must inevitably sustain such a wound, and then keep it buried inside for years. Much later we will find that this subterranean wound seems to have a purpose: eventually it will draw us down into the deepest contents of self and soul.

Before the "Great Wound," however, our individual stories are magical and inspired. They take us into that vast and boundless realm of imagination that draws so richly upon the mythic consciousness. It is a wonderful, boundless land, like the great American West at the time of Lewis and Clark, and we wish we could explore it forever. But, alas, our early mythic consciousness will in time be conquered and domesticated. Parental and social prescriptions inherited from the surrounding culture are superimposed on our joyous adventures and soon the province of soul is closed to us.

...Of the Mother. The mother wound occurs in many ways. Each boy, sometime in early childhood, falls in love with his mother. She is the source of his life and his happiness. Some mothers belittle, withhold, or exploit this first love to shape the boy to fit her requirements. In the rejection of his natural self, a boy feels ashamed. Or perhaps his mother is overwhelmed with her own life problems or demands, and has no time to nourish and mirror his personhood, or worse, vents her own unbearable emotions on him. Sometimes, too, a woman cannot view her son's masculinity in a positive way, and ridicules or implicitly devalues his gender. Unspoken disappointment with her own father or husband may fuel this criticism. Whatever its source, her attitude tells her son that his maleness is defective, ugly, or evil.

However the mother wound occurs, it acts as a prohibition, a statement forbidding him to express the offending qualities of self or gender. Mythically speaking, the great and powerful mother, the archetypal mother, "steals" or "imprisons" his soul and the boy, trapped in his emotional and physical dependency, must give it up to survive.

...Of the Father. The father wound occurs in similar ways when a man is unable to acknowledge and value his son's personhood or masculinity. This happens when the father is disinterested, remote, absent, critical, or abusive. Perhaps he is threatened by his son's emerging manhood or special talent. Or, the father, himself, may be psychologically deadened or twisted due to alcoholism, drugs, depression, or unresolved childhood wounding. This wound may also occur when the father, rejecting his own emotional need for love as a sign of weakness, secretly resents his son as competition for his wife's attention. Often the father wounds his son as he himself was once wounded.

Whatever way it occurs, a boy feels as if he has been pierced or "killed" inside by his father's words or actions. Without a father's blessing, a boy's individuality and personhood are not finished. He feels unseen, inferior, unacknowledged, and uninitiated. He is unfinished. And it is in the nature of masculine development that most boys do not get their father's blessing.

...Of Siblings, Peers, and Gender. Sibling wounds arise either by comparison, direct or implied, or by attack. Comparison wounds occur when a higher value is placed on one child than another by parental messages or by the boy himself who believes he holds an inferior position in the family. Peer wounds similarly contrast one boy with another or with whatever popular norms of masculinity exist, again causing him to devalue himself. Finally, wounds from the opposite sex arise when a boy feels judged as an inferior male by girls. What these wounding processes have in common is the attachment of shame and unworthiness to a boy's intrinsic experience, a contamination that is deeply injurious to his ability to feel, value, and activate that unique and invaluable self forming within him.

The Plan: Fixing (but not healing) the Wounds. Whenever there is a wound, there is a struggle to overcome it. Each boy takes his secret wound and strives desperately to restore his former self or, at the very least, somehow cover or compensate for his perceived inferiority. He asks himself, "What do I have to do to be wanted, loved, or valued again?" It may be working hard, being tough, making money, being nice, having friends, seducing girls, making good grades, competing in sports, caring for his parents or siblings, getting even, stealing cars, or saving mankind. Whatever it is, it becomes his quest. As he succeeds, the sum total of his effort becomes the character he shows the world, his mask, his armor. Sometimes it is with him for a lifetime.

A New Energy: The Eruption of Masculinity. Before Spring is completed, however, one more great and portentous development occurs in the boy's life: adolescence. The time of adolescence, with its bodily transforming growth, newly activated sex hormones, and the awakening of the brain's developing frontal lobes, is a time of unparalleled metamorphosis. It is as if the great and eternal myths of power and immortality, of Olympian gods and Superheroes who stole his pre-teen imagination, now flood and arouse every cell. He finds his body, mind, and soul all expanding as if by magic. Initially moody and self-conscious, the developing adolescent soon discovers the god-like wonders of sexual arousal, the powerful warrior energy stored in his capacity for physical aggression, and the far reaching capacity of his mind's abstraction and idealization. It is here, too, where a young man momentarily glimpses some piece of his own gift, an intuition of something he wants more than anything else to be or do. In this cosmic and alchemical mixture of fresh new ingredients, the boy and his world are transformed.

Glimpses of Love. A man can usually recall the name of that first girl who moved his heart. She was a symbol of the love, beauty, and divinity stored inside him. Teenage boys, however, don't know much about their interior nor can they admit such bliss is their own. So it is played out in the drama of the "princess." She is everything he could ever imagine wanting. Having her love would not only make his life complete, it would empower him to pursue any heroic quest no matter how hard or perilous. What potent nectar is this love's firstblush.

Finding the Power: The Need for Initiation. A young woman stays in this love phase much longer. For a young man it is a potent and urgent experience, but also episodic. His search for the princess is repeatedly interrupted by something else: an instinctive hunger for an evoked manhood and for a heroic quest. He needs to find out who he is, what he is really capable of doing, and why he is here. This need for the initiative experiences of competition, testing, or adventure pounds at his adolescent soul.

This is the time in tribal culture for initiation, when the boys are taken from the world of mothers and women into the world of fathers and men. This is when they are given the chance to be warriors! As a man from the African Maasai people recalls, "We were supposed to be brave, brilliant, great lovers, fearless, athletic, arrogant, wise, and above all, concerned with the well-being of our comrades and of the Maasai community as a whole. We realized that we were totally trusted by our community for protection, and we tried to live up to their expectations." (Saitoti, 1993, p.109)

Late Spring, then, is a time when the explosive energies of the young warrior need to be forged and fashioned in the fires of combat, competition, risk, confrontation, and final tests. These tests and this kind of recognition teach the youth what manhood is and what being a warrior brings to his community. These need not be solely physical tests. A warrior is one who can tough it out in pursuit of any rugged quest, whether for grades, musical skill, or automotive knowledge. Often this quest links up with the boy's earlier plan, and the two sets of needs combine to produce tremendous effort. When this powerful forge is neglected or trivialized, however, boys will nonetheless continue to look for initiation in risk-taking behaviors, territorial confrontation, and physical testing of one another. Young men without tutelage will spill each other's blood, sometimes in gangs, sometimes in alcohol-ignited explosions. Others will go the opposite direction, overcontrolling their energy, forcing themselves to conform to conventional definitions of masculine success. Still others will become depressed, lost, or passive.

Naming the Gift. Ideally, the object of initiation is to recognize and name the young man's gift. The tests are meant to reveal it to the boy. It is the medicine he was born to bring into the tribe. When it is found, he can be a true warrior serving not war but the community and the sacred world. This is the core of a boy's initiation into true manhood. Modern man has forgotten its urgency.

However incomplete the actual initiatory process may be, it is nonetheless in adolescence that a young man begins to sense and experience his own possibilities, to feel that calling of his nature that predicts his life's work. This is his vision, and he must find ways to follow it for his soul to grow. This gift is his true love and he will follow her anywhere, and does, and should.

Women honor boys, too. To have his emerging manliness, maturity, or still-hidden gift noticed and admired by a woman in a nonsexual way is wonderful for a boy. He feels so full of the possible in himself. For a moment, he can admire himself, and this kind of narcissism is an empowering and priceless offering. When his manliness is admired as sexually exciting to a woman, however, a boy feels the same confusion and exploitation experienced by girls when they are reduced to sex objects rather than valued as wonderfully flowering young women. The sexual initiation of a boy by an older woman is not the gift our culture fantasizes; it is usually a rationalized and injurious form of molestation.

Suppressing Wounds, Forging Competencies. Springtime, then, is a time of both incredible growth and secret wounds. Each additional wound breaches a boy's very soul, but most, rather than being healed, must lie dormant, waiting for midlife. A young man simply does not have the luxury of spending much time on these hurts. The armor forged from his quest must be stretched, strengthened, and hardened, and he must develop the cognitive, emotional, and social competencies described in every book on child development. All this represents the building of a personality strong enough to face the tasks of adulthood, one of which will be returning to these wounds at midlife.

Growing Up. Each boy must become a man by the end of Spring. Each does this growing up in his own way, and some boys grow up faster than others. Growing up happens when you have to be responsible for yourself, when you're it, when you are not let off the hook any more, either because it's now expected or because survival now depends on you alone. In farm country or wilderness, in non-industrial places, boys grow up sooner. They have to. In the city, where so much is provided, it takes longer (unless a boy is abandoned). When a boy's family environment is not secure, he has to grow up much too early. Growing up too soon in this manner is part of the "Great Wound." Sometimes boys never grow up.

Although these soul wounds continue to bleed psychologically inside, a boy gradually learns to cover them with education, pretension, cultural gender patterns, identity, and whatever other coping patterns he discovers. Some cope aggressively, some through compliance, others in social popularity or withdrawal, each according to his individual temperament.

Leaving Home. Carrying these hidden wounds a young man is forced to leave home. Now he must find his own way and his own nature as a separate entity. Whether it is to his first apartment, first real job, first lion hunt, first semester of college, or off to the military, an odyssey to Europe, the Peace Corps, or a missionary assignment, he leaves home. He leaves to meet his fate. He cannot know the enormous changes he will experience.

Usually a young man leaves home alone. Sometimes, however, he leaves taking with him his first adult love relationship. In this way, he makes a small transitional nest to give him comfort and support in the hard adult world. These early relationships can help a young man into this first stage of emancipated adulthood, but they cannot last in their original form, for the unforeseen pressures of change, inner and outer, will be enormous in the years to come. Fortunately and unfortunately, neither he nor his princess can know this yet.

Birth of the Hero. Springtime ends as the youth strives to wear a "man's" identity and takes his newly constellated warrior self into the adult world. Homesickness and secret self-doubts must be shielded with bravado. The young man must become heroic, and this "hero complex," which has been rehearsed during earlier years, worshipping brave and invincible athletes or masculine movie stars and then practiced in adolescent competition, must be strong enough to carry him into his own life. Though older men forget, entering the hierarchical world of adults, particularly older males and posturing peers is secretly terrifying for young men. To suppress this terror, denial of the still fragile and uncertain self must be rigid, uncompromising, and grandiose. On the other hand, the hero complex also carries a "medicine bag" of remarkable contents: the young man's inborn gift, his secret woundings, his true self, and his capacity to love. These contents will be opened as life asks for them.

Summer

The Endless Quest. The Summer of a man's life often seems to be endless. There is no real mortality, at least not for him. His journey is forever onward and upward, driven by the masculine motive for competency, status, power and independence, and climbing toward idealized visions released from his deep psyche. In Summer, this outer world of adventure, conquest, and determination takes total precedence, and a young man strives with relentless energy to build an adult life. He can withstand almost anything in these years with this amazing masculine energy. Even his victories in work and love are left behind for the new quests that seem forever on the horizon. The hero is busy in the Summer.

Hidden Wounds, Secret Problems. Hidden far beneath all this questing is a developmental issue the young man cannot see but at the same time cannot escape. He is destined to repeat his childhood wounds in his first attempts at adulthood. In fact, the whole family drama surrounding his original wounding will simply be repeated in his own adult life. For example, a man from an emotionally distant family will find himself psychologically or geographically distant from others, even within his own family. A man from an enmeshed and entangled family system will often not get very far from home at all. If he left with anger, he will find himself in angry relationships, with depression in depressing relationships, with immaturity in immature relationships. Or, if consciously fearing such a repetition, he chooses an opposite scenario. It still turns into the past. For the first half of summer, however, all this is nicely forgotten. Still the clock is silently ticking.

Whatever his secret problems, the young man must carry them alone, for his parents can no longer help him even if they could recognize what was being repeated, for to help him is a return to parental dependency. If he does not break these bonds, he will slide into a progressively darkening morass of passivity, ambivalence, resentment, or defiant failure — until he hits bottom. If bottom comes too soon — for example, in drug or alcohol abuse or prolonged dependency, the adult competencies he needs for life will never develop, and he will find himself severely crippled. What looks like a man will be only a pretense.

Search for a Mentor. The fortunate man during this great Summer is the one who finds a mentor. A man still carries the gifts of his soul inside, but often he cannot see them. He needs the help of an external mirror, and he finds this mirror in an older man who has, to some significant degree, expressed the same kind of gift. When a young man's mentor sees his gift in potential form, and when he "blesses" it with his attention, interest, or guidance, then the young man feels empowered. He is initiated. This is the blessing he couldn't get from his own father and only partially received in whatever initiatory experiences took place during adolescence. Now he, too, can recognize his gift, and he can fulfill it.

Every man sooner or later outgrows his mentor. Complicating this special relationship, many mentors, because of their own unfaced wounding, try to mold the younger man in ways that violate him, and the relation ends in bitterness and conflict.

Marriage: A New Alliance. Sometimes a man feels he has found his princess. He courts her actively, works for her love, and if it takes, they marry. Lust, infatuation, need, dependency, control, necessity, security, standing, looks, values, and love are all intermingled in the new bond.

Often ambivalent about love, men wrestle with their criteria and standards for the "good enough" woman. Is she attractive enough, sexy enough? Is she bright enough? Is she going to be good with children? What do other men think of her, what will his own parents think of her? Never completely satisfied, the ambivalent man tests his woman's tolerance with delays and distance until she finally tests him back again: settle down with me or I'm leaving. Most men are so much more attached by this time than they realize that they capitulate to this threat because they are not yet psychologically complete in themselves.

Most men do not marry the princess. Somehow she invariably got away. Instead they marry someone with whom they have become emotionally intermingled and attached, or sometimes with a woman they believe will fit their larger aspirations. Some never marry or, upon one or more failed marriages, settle into bachelorhood.

With his choice of mate settled, a man starts a family. Typically, his wife carries the emotional and interdependent side of the relationship, which he again sets aside in his heroic quest. Although these gender differences often appear blurred by changing social values and work patterns, they still permeate and order our lives.

Moving Forward and Settling Down. Whatever their hidden problems and wounds, most men do move forward in life. As the years go by in this seemingly endless Summer, a man progressively tests and develops his adult competencies. He is learning more and more about himself, about what he is and isn't, what he excels at and what he loves, and about how the world really operates. This is an experimental process that eventually allows him to find an adult life more or less consistent and compatible with his gifts and talents. Over the years, much is accomplished. By his mid thirties, he begins to feel that he has made it, or will, or knows what making it means, and he begins to congratulate himself for all he has accomplished.

Children of the Quest. A man's relationship to his children also evolves over the years of Summer. Their birth is a miracle, their presence is a joy, but still the demands of his quest and of his economic role in supporting the family often take precedent over time with them. He tries to be with them through activities such as coaching, homework, and family vacations, and through whatever initiations his culture provides, but it almost seems as if something "out there," out in the world of big dramas, or masculine responsibility keeps pulling him away from the intimate family relationships at home. Again, it is the quest. His children are left to find fathering where they can, but this too is not as unusual as it may sound. Rather, it happens all around the world, for in addition to biological fathers, sons must find psychological and spiritual fathers to bless them — and they are rarely the same.

As Summer draws to an end, however, a man senses that he has missed something vital in this quest. He missed time with his little ones who are now not so little, but who now have little time for him. By late Summer, his children are being swept into the powerful currents of their adolescent world, which rapidly becomes even more important than Dad. They are preparing to leave home just when their father is preparing to come home.

And Then Disillusionment. By the end of Summer, a man's wife or partner has grown weary of his increasing moodiness or inattention. The heroic quest has taken its toll on the relationship. The typical complaints: he doesn't share his feelings, the relationship has lost its romance, he is disinterested in the family. These complaints too often carry bitter thorns of truth. Disillusionment has come into the marriage. Each has wanted from the other what a parent never gave them. This wound of childhood cannot be healed by putting something else in its place. To heal, the original wound must be felt — consciously.

By midlife, a man's marital pain has begun to expose his childhood wound. Still entranced by the romantic belief that someone "out there" could heal his pain, a man resists the wound. Marital strife intensifies as each partner tries to get the other to change. Sometimes one or the other is so unhappy in the marriage that divorce ensues. Sometimes the strife is denied, forbidden, or frozen by fear. Whether it is his original or subsequent marriage, a murky darkness envelopes the relationship.

Growing Tired. With or without the help of a mentor, a man moves on in his career. Up the ladder he goes. Whatever field a man is in, he works hard to fashion his skills, develop his mastery, and build real confidence. Summer becomes a time of accumulation: possessions, house and property, children, furniture, debts, skills and education, work duties, expanding roles, and expanding responsibilities. It is empire building, and this empire is usually built up around his marriage. But in this sometimes combative and competitive climb, men sooner or later confuse success for soul. He conquers his world, but forgets what he was after originally. Something profound is felt to be missing. What is missing is the original wonder of life, the natural self he once knew long ago, the wounds he buried along the way, and the gifts he is here to realize. He is missing his soul.

Disintegration. This theme of disintegration is happening everywhere as Summer ends. Though his social disguise may look normal and well-adjusted, close inspection reveals a flawed personality that has produced an equally flawed life structure. Looking back on this period, a man with insight will come to realize that the injuries he had in childhood had to be re-enacted in his marriage, work, and life in order bring them into awareness. It is pain that forces the unfinished issues of his development into consciousness. It may be put off, denied, explained, or trivialized, but it won't go away. Instead, his pain builds until it cannot be put off, denied, explained, or trivialized any longer. As if the suffocation of a lost soul were not enough, a man finds his marriage filled with rage and impotence until it too is at risk. Everything is at risk. Everything he thought he had in nice order now begins to unravel.

Midlife: Transition Between Summer and Fall

Wilderness: Midlife is the time when the clock's hands begin to run the wrong way. It is the time when nothing works because what was constructed by the determined and questing young warrior now lacks soul, love, and life. As morning turns to afternoon, as Summer's warm days give way to Autumn's coolness and its hint of what is to come, whatever a man has been doing now feels false. He loses his way.

Crisis One. The hero is tired, but he feels he cannot stop, so a healing crisis must ensue not just to lessen his pain, but far more importantly, to recover and restore his true self and make room for its next stage of growth. This is the task of the midlife crisis. The pain and strife of this transition are the hard labor and birth of his soul as it cracks through the hardened armor of character back into consciousness. This opening is critical. The self can no longer be harnessed to ambition without costs to the soul. Even more importantly, without this renewal of self, a man will not meet the developmental tasks of the Fall and Winter.

Grief and Descent. The hero dies at midlife. He must give up his outer quest. His task now is to face the cruel wounds of childhood and confront the road of self-betrayal he took in building his character armor. Ironically, the healing, he will find, is in the pain itself and, for a while, in going backward rather than forward. These are the paradoxes of midlife and without a map most men become lost. Routinely, midlife involves a painful descent from the lofty heights of aspiration to the bankrupt depths of sorrow. But in this falling, something else vastly more important can be revealed: a larger story and purpose to life. This is the recovery of soul and the renewal of the real journey. The pain endured and the subsequent strengthening was one of the central tasks of Summer. The ex-hero must use all the masculine strengths and competencies he acquired in the long years of summer to deal with the despair he now finds at midlife.

Opening to the Feminine Within. One of the new elements of a man's story at midlife is the call of his own feminine side. But he must struggle to free the feminine, for his capacity to love has been buried, stifled, or rejected as unmanly. To know his own feminine side, a man usually needs contact with a variety of actual women with whom he can experience these interior potentials (e.g., soulmate, erotic lover, or friend) and he may be tempted to believe they really exist in the world, leading to infatuations or affairs. He does so in order to make the inner figures conscious, for if they remain unconsciously imprisoned in his psyche, he will never come to know their teachings and revivifying energies.

Crisis Two: The Pain of Marriage. By midlife, the idealized and sexualized feminine images have often been excluded from his primary relationship, so they begin to appear outside the marriage, which has become dominated by the wounded, dominating, or caretaking images. Tension and conflict mount between positive and negative figures in order to bring the realm of the imprisoned and splintered feminine to the surface. The whole purpose of this struggle is to teach a man how to feel love again and to restore his soul. It is no longer his role to fix things, least of all his partner's pain. It is his role to let feeling and truth find their own way. Moreover, the gifts and aptitudes symbolized by these women are exactly the skills a man will need to deal with the issues of life's second half.

Crossing Paths. Gender paths tend to cross at midlife. As men and women let each other go free, each gender seeks to develop the side they had suppressed in the first half of life. Discovering the women within, men often become more tender, nurturing, and interdependent. They yearn to love. Feelings matter more. Gender styles, however, do not just switch. Men express the feminine the way men do it, and women express the masculine the way women do it. And each individual's style is colored further by their unique temperament, personality, and life experience. It is a marvelous interweaving, this gender dance, especially as we learn to liberate its energy with acceptance, support, respect, and love.

Ultimate Questions. As these complexities suggest, it is not easy growing up and becoming really conscious. It is the work of a lifetime. Midlife is a particularly complex time. All the rules and goals seem to have changed. Yet at the same time it is one of man's most important developmental stages, for it poses his ultimate questions: Who am I really? Why am I here? What has become of my soul? How do I face the world when the hero is dead? What does it mean to love?

The Work of Midlife. If a man can find the support, courage, and perspective to enter this transformative wilderness in a conscious, steady, and deliberate way; if he can understand what is symbolized in its common pitfalls (e.g., affairs, precipitous life changes, stagnation, illness, or resignation), then he may be able to navigate his way into a land of new and unimaginable possibilities of soul. The masculine social facade and its grandiose story can fall away to reveal a man's original though deeply injured self. This true self, as it is healed and nourished, releases so much that is new: seemingly inexhaustible creative energies, a new vision of life, his own unique and wondrous gift, and the capacity for a new kind of love which holds the divine in its center. With the grateful release of the heroic quest, he discovers the deepest work of his soul; a natural capacity for love replaces his former romanticized version. He returns to his family as a primary source of happiness and meaning, and he realizes that life itself is holy. This stage takes a man right through the archetypes of death and rebirth, and changes him forever.

Finding Male Community. If a man is lucky, he will also discover his need for other men at midlife. Men to talk to, to share life with. He needs to replenish himself with forms of male spirit and community that were totally absent in the competitive quest for status. Exiting the damaging wasteland of warrior conformity, a man begins to search for something more authentic, something he lost along the way. But what is it and how can he find it? Certainly it cannot be found in the old masculinity of logic, rugged individualism, solitary achievement, and competition. A man at midlife is like a horse who was domesticated so early in life that he has forgotten his instincts and is unable to feel the untamed energy in his body. It is the purpose of a mature and authentic male community to restore this energy.

When men join together in the kind of mature emotional space that invites honest and thoughtful talk, the kind that recognizes a man's inherent brotherhood and the wisdom of elders, and that speaks respectively and reverently of the sacred, then a deeper kind of masculinity begins to be felt. This kind of masculinity has been forming recently in the small groups and gatherings found in the men's movement. Straight talk, sharing one's story, or joining activities such as drumming, dance, music, song, poetry, story, invocation, grief, ceremony, and ritual — all these ancient forms of masculinity stir something long forgotten in a man and, suddenly, the overly domesticated horse finds some of the energy with which he was born.

This male energy is the key, and the energy at midlife is a broad spectrum — it consists of play, zaniness, grief, confrontation, laughter, song, and honesty. Often this energy will move toward the sacred. Then a man's masculinity takes on new and renewing modes of connection. Some are spontaneous acts of worship that break from his soul, some are rituals he learns or relearns that offer rich forms for the expression of his religious image and impulse. Uniquely personal yet somehow universal, all these forms can give a man the value orientation he is seeking.

The Question of Spirituality. Given the central archetypes of death and rebirth, it is not surprising that the harsh realization of life's inevitable ending should visit a man at midlife. He will die. This fact is becoming real now. It asks him to clarify his values and life purpose. It also invites him to confront other even more ultimate questions, such as: What happens at death? What is the spiritual purpose of life? What is my relationship to God? In a world of constant change and strife, a world in which his confidence is being shaken daily, the midlife man longs to find values that are timeless, universal, and generous. These are the deeper values he hopes will comfort him. Most of all, he knows that he must replace serving the ego with serving something more real, authentic, loving, and sacred. He must learn what this higher reality is.

Renewal: A Life of Soul. For the man who successfully confronts the great tasks of midlife, the unbearable frustration and restlessness felt earlier are finally replaced with a sense of rebirth and renewal, changed purposes, and trust in his own longings. His wild and restless energies now dissipated, he lets down and settles into the stream of life again. His work has become the work of his soul. He is hungry again, this time for ultimate things. For the man who does not successfully confront the great tasks of this period, life goes on, but his unresolved conflicts and disappointments, the unfinished work of self and soul, have a way of multiplying or ensnaring him.

Fall

The Work of Soul. It is a bittersweet time, the Fall. A man still has a lot of vitality left, but it is measured now. He has learned some profound lessons about love and life, yet he also notes the subtle and sometimes not so subtle limitations of his energy, memory, bodily resilience, and health that portend its gradual and eventual disintegration. He knows how to love with less physical passion, but more sensuality and tenderness. He is more patient and forgiving, recognizing with increasing insight and regret the kinds of mistakes he has already made. Personal ambitions in the world are not as important now as they were. He senses lessons in all these changes and wonders what these lessons are. And still there is a kind of impatience — for the work of his soul is unfinished and he struggles to understand what that work must be.

Letting Go: Finding the Nature of Being. A man learns in the Fall to let go; to let go of his children, his questing, his fantasy of control over life, his athletic mastery, his omnipotence, his real and symbolic virility. This aging process is attended by a growing sense of humility — about his limitations, failures, and future. Some additional melancholy and regret are necessary parts of this letting go process, constituting another kind of grief. The gift of this release is a new kind of freedom — the freedom to simply be and to accept what the real nature of "being" is.

When a man cannot let go, when he has never felt the joy in his true nature, then bitterness, control, and stagnation become his lot. The possessiveness, greed, and emptiness of the false self seep into such a man's character, rigidifying it and tragically alienating him from the life-renewing mystery of soul. This is the kind of man who cannot release or bless his children, love his wife, forgive his wounds and errors, be generous with his wealth, or face death with understanding. He is atrophied or already dead inside. So it is that the emotional work a man does in midlife has profound consequences later in life — for himself, his family, his community, and the world.

Accepting the Teachings of Loss and Hardship. As life goes on, the losses accumulate and some, such as death of loved ones, personal failure, or disability, can seem unbearable. The great achievements of character in the Fall and Winter often come not from the natural growth of personality, but from catastrophic tragedies that tear open the psyche to reveal life's heretofore hidden spiritual tasks and dimensions, if a man is willing and capable of looking into the mirror of hardship. Here is true heroism — quiet and humble — but heroism nonetheless that allows him to see the world through spiritual eyes and to find the gifts secreted in an attitude of simple gratitude, renunciation, acceptance, and love. The growth of a soul does not stop until a man sets his own limits; that is, until he closes himself off to any further evolution. Thereafter, the body must bear the change, often expressing somatically what cannot be tolerated consciously.

A New Marriage. A man in the Fall will find his marriage changing further if it is to remain a living and authentic relationship. Man and wife now shed relationship roles previously defined solely by social expectation, children, or emotional needs, to explore their own separate forms of creativity, individuality, or adventure. The respective journeys of each partner, however great or difficult, feed the relationship, and the relationship, in turn, feeds the journeys.

Changing Places. An altogether new and different generational niche often forms for a man at this time, intermediate between his aging parents and the arrival of his grandchildren. His relationship to each has unexpected teachings, opportunities, and pain. He finds his parents to be increasingly vulnerable, dependent, helpless, and sometimes foolish as they struggle to preserve their dignity and autonomy against the regression of aging bodies. With the archetype of the parent disappearing before his eyes, a man sees his mother or father as simply persons now, as individuals with their own personalities, values, and needs, who happened by luck or fate to have been in his life. They are no longer powerful authority figures. They are people who are old now. It is a remarkable transformation.

Forgiveness. As his parents literally change in front of his eyes, residual feelings of resentment or disappointment often melt away. It is also time to care for these people, his parents, without violating the dignity or autonomy central to their integrity, for age will assault that integrity soon enough. It is time, then, for love and understanding, for saying his thanks and goodbyes, perhaps subtly at first, but then, as the final days appear, as clearly as he possibly can. It is his own unconditional love and forgiveness that completes the healing with his parents. Then he finally sees his parents as instances of "everyman" and "everywoman." Ironically, this is often the time when a man's own children are confronting him with his responsibility for their early wounds.

Grandfathering. At the other end of the spectrum, a man's relationship with his grandchildren, who often arrive in mid to late Fall, bring other surprises, roles, and concerns. Grandfathers and younger grandchildren share an extremely important secret and a temporary alliance based on it: the seriousness of life emphasized by the children's parents isn't really so serious. The grandfather gave up his heroic quest for success years ago, and his grandchildren haven't yet been hooked by it.

So grandfathers secretly communicate to their grandchildren: "Don't worry too much yet. You don't have to be so serious. Hang onto your youth and play. Your mom and dad are just stressed out." And grandfathers, freed from their responsibilities, join in the play.

As grandchildren get older, as the masculine and feminine energies and archetypes of adolescence and young adulthood steal them from both their parents and grandparents, a grandfather's role as elder and consultant moves to the fore. With the wisdom of age and distance, he can see what has to happen; that is, why the children have to leave or betray the family as they do. So he helps the parents understand.

Grandfathers worry for their grandchildren's chances in a world of ever increasing uncertainty and for the fate of the world these children are entering. Grandfathers also secretly cheer them on, rooting especially for those grandchildren who seem to carry on the spark they knew in their own soul. These are the reasons grandfathers are so important and why they have a special mission with their young proteges.

Accepting Death. The reality of death continues to disturb a man in the Fall, and he occasionally waxes melancholy about old age and the futility of life. Moodiness in the middle-aged man is actually doing the emotional work of accepting his personal mortality — not all the way, and not consciously, but enough for him to put it in proper perspective and then move on.

Becoming an Elder. A man with seniority can use his authority to teach, guide, and serve others. But it is not his primary identity. If a man has worked on himself, that is, if he has truly suffered the real depths of his wounds, then his true self can be found to be a flowing source of love and creativity. In this way, with less ego and more soul, a man can become a real elder as Fall moves toward Winter.

Becoming an elder should be marked and blessed by ritual. It is passage into a new and important life stage and role for a man and his community. An older man carries so much wisdom. When he is asked to share what he has learned about life, a man will discover that he knows more than he realizes and that younger men really want to hear his "sage" advice. His willingness to assume this role with dignity and generosity blesses both the young men and himself.

Ripening and Harvesting. By late Fall, a man has ripened. He harvests a spiritual fruit now — the deepening knowledge of what life is all about. He does this in preparation for the Winter and the final journey into darkness, a time when he, himself, will be harvested by the great cycle of life.

Opening to the Sacred. Once upon a time, men devoted themselves to learning and teaching sacred things in secret rituals or societies. They knew the importance of learning to see again, to see what they had each forgotten in early childhood and what culture forgets in its own self-fascination. In the Fall, a man can learn to see what shamans, mystics, and prophets have always known. He can see that the world and everything in it is a spiritual process and place, saturated with the sacred, and that his purpose is to know and serve this reality. He realizes that there is nothing intrinsically wrong with life or the world, nothing for him to fix or achieve.

Yet Living in the World: Survival and Responsibility. Despite the many gifts of aging, a mature and creative man finds that, in the Fall, issues of survival and responsibility always cycle back to test him further. Job loss or demotion, illness, deaths, and financial mismanagement are particularly frightening possibilities when he can no longer call on the Hero's energy, denial, grandiosity, and blind determination to survive. As his resources falter, he is frightened in a new way. He is frightened that he will not be able to maintain control or depend on his own resources to make it through. So a man must still be responsible for life's new and continuing problems. He can do so, however, with new resources: humility — he doesn't have to have it all or be number one any more; experience — he can respond more flexibly with tools learned over a lifetime; interdependence — he can call on others for support and help; and spirituality — he sees life's hurdles now as spiritual lessons, opportunities for ultimate growth and understanding. And he discovers in the mystical realm new kinds of help and solutions. Finally, unconditional love is seen as a responsibility, his ultimate responsibility. A man later in life increasingly realizes he has an obligation to love and to open his heart to all that he has been given.

Duality: Holding the Opposites. The world is full of opposites: life and death, joy and suffering, success and failure, good and evil, meaning and despair, transcendence and embodiment. An older man learns to bear these opposites, not attempt to fix or overcome them, for they cannot be fixed or overcome. Holding these opposites is each man's burden and one of his greatest accomplishments. It is an index of maturity.

Winter

"Indian Summer." Winter often begins with an "Indian Summer" of fertile and wondrous learning. Free from the pressures of work and family, a man has more time to explore and savor his new role and the new reality he found in the Fall. Still healthy and with morbid preoccupation about death behind him, a man can use this freedom to follow his soul wherever it may call him, for he trusts himself so much more now. Men in these years often have no shortage of interests.

Activity, Creativity, Productivity, and Generativity: Medicine for the Myth of Aging. Life goes on until the end. If a man retires from life itself, he will suffer premature psychological death. It is the task of Winter's good years to create an experience of aging that defies the current cultural myths of uselessness and deterioration. A man who remains active, creative, and productive finds that his body and mood stay healthy. More importantly, a man will find that self and spirit are, in fact, ageless, and that Winter can be a time of harvesting the wisdom of a lifetime.

Return to Original Wonder. Without an indefinite future, in fact, without any guaranteed future, a man in Winter is returned profoundly to the present. Time has almost run out. For the mature man who has worked consciously on his story and on the growth of consciousness through the seasons, this realization can have profound impact. Eternity is here, now. With this discovery, the lens of perception clears more and more. Consciousness, unclouded by fantasies of ego and future, glimpses the world again in all its pristine, crystalline brightness.

Everything in life becomes precious, for now is literally all he has. This is all there is and when he really looks, he sees that the world is miraculous. It is enough. It includes now what he saw once, a lifetime ago, before the Great Wound. A man thus returns to the beginning of his story. In fact, the story ends in this consciousness. It was leading here all along. A man, if he can trust this new seeing, returns to an awareness of paradise. Here love, service, joy, and learning are all that matter.

This is also a time of endings. A man loses aging friends and family, leaves his career far behind, even the world he knew (or thought he knew, or once knew) is no longer the same. It is no longer his world. A man may feel like a relic in the Winter, forgotten by the community he fought so hard to join. One of the deepest losses may be his partner — that person who has been friend, lover, adversary, mother, family, and companion for so many years — virtually his life structure itself. Sometimes the ache of these losses is unbearable and a man wills his own death in one way or another. Still, for those willing, able, and prepared to stay and to notice, what has fallen away now reveals even more clearly the sacred garden of earth and man. Now even the tiny confines of a patio or backyard reveal the light and resplendent beauty of eternity that was always there, but overlooked in the rush of life. The old sit, pensively, sleepily, in the garden's warm sunlight, perhaps not realizing all that they see, yet seeing still the shimmering, living, divine reality that surrounds and sustains them always.

Final Preparations. With advancing old age, a man returns for the last time to the reality of his death in a profound, poignant, immediate, and inescapable way. Now the reality of death is the Winter's arctic air, the darkening days, and the barren trees. Now there is the realization that even the compass of self, that inner reference that had always provided a sense of identity and orientation, is undergoing a process of dissolution, disorganization, and death, even as his body is moving toward mortality. He is preparing for something else.

A man may temporarily fight against this night, again seeking to reassert his former personality or control, but again he will be defeated. For many, this final confrontation is too uncomfortable and disturbing to face. Some retreat into bodily preoccupation, memory failure, increased dependency, garrulousness, sickness, or manipulation. The dark side of a man's personality may gain control as he fights against his fear and defeat. And many, who arrested their growth long ago, simply continue with the same personality problems they have always had, and wait nervously, unconsciously, for the end.

Transparency and Transcendence. Winter need not be only darkness. This last leg of the journey, if it is consciously and courageously experienced, can also serve a man's final spiritual realization. Ego, personality, identity, competence, and social status become paper thin, and through these previously impenetrable walls that served to separate his psyche from the ultimate, come intuitions of the other side, of immortality, and of being in Being. Wisdom is born of this transparency and transcendence, for as his vision clears between the worlds, a man sees the relativity of death, the shallowness of ego, and the infinite presence, timelessness, and preciousness of the life principle in the world. He sees the passions of youth and the whole play of life as itself remarkable and wondrous. And he will ultimately be capable of releasing himself and his body into the cosmos knowing that something far more wondrous will greet him and flood his consciousness in this final passage.

Remembrances. There is one more piece of soul work a man does deep in the Winter darkness. Dreamily, vividly, he sorts out his life memories. Some good, some bad, more and more lucid now than ever before, they come back asking for him to feel and know each one again. He needs to experience his story one last time, and discover perhaps for the first time what the really important parts were. He will find in them the stepping stones of his life, what it was really all about, and how poignantly beautiful it was.

His story wants to be known as a whole now, and perhaps, as holy. What has it all meant? What did he learn? With melancholy and joy, he sees just how much he loved this life of his, how much he missed, how good it was, and, more than he ever knew, how much he still loves it, and even loves his memory of it. This time, by the fire, alone, he tells his story secretly to himself so he can now see just how sweet it was. His life, and the wonder of it all.

Going Home. Then, at the end, each man relaxes into the soft velour darkness, back into the comfort of nightfall, and in the vast blackness waits instinctively for the light. Perhaps a pinprick at first, but as soon as he sees and longs for it with his original knowing, he is swept into its brilliance and a new world is born to him. Or so the timeless story has always told. ❊

CHAPTER 3

The Timeless Story
in Myth and Fairy Tale

Whether we listen with aloof amusement to the dreamlike mumbo jumbo of some red-eyed witch doctor of the Congo, or read with cultivated rapture thin translations from the sonnets of the mystic Lao-Tse; now and again crack the hard nutshell of an argument of Aquinas, or catch suddenly the shining meaning of a bizarre Eskimo fairy tale: it will be always the one, shape-shifting yet marvelously constant story that we find, together with a challengingly persistent suggestion of more remaining to be experienced than will ever be known or told. (Campbell, 1968, p.3)

The myth of the hero is the most common and the best known myth in the world. We find it in the classical mythology of Greece and Rome, in the Middle Ages, in the Far East, and among contemporary primitive tribes. It also appears in our dreams. It has an obvious dramatic appeal, and a less obvious, but nonetheless profound, psychological importance. These hero myths vary enormously in detail, but the more closely one examines them the more one sees that structurally they are very similar. They have, that is to say, a universal pattern. (Joseph Henderson, 1964, p.110)

» As described earlier, myths and fairy tales reveal the universal pattern of our human journey in symbols, images, metaphors, and stories. They tell essentially the same story we have just reviewed, but from a mythical perspective, and present it anew in wonderfully varied though sometimes enigmatic ways. Like dreams, these tales encode all the hidden stages, secret purposes, transformative crises, and ever repeating meanings of man's pilgrimage through life.

This chapter presents three tales filled with lessons from this Story of Everyman. Expressed in the magic of mythic imagery, their teachings reaffirm the psychological story told in the previous chapter and speak not only to our intellects but, more importantly, to our hearts as only ancient words and symbols can. They sketch the basic childhood woundings all men experience and then they take us into the deep and challenging emotional work of healing those wounds. As we will see, much of this healing is done at midlife.

The Crystal Ball

Our first story is a deep, powerful, and painful one adapted from *Grimm's Fairy Tales* (Colum & Campbell, 1972, pp. 798-801). It is an ancient story, probably thousands of years old, passed down in the oral tradition that preceded the printing press. Arising in this manner from the collective experience of mankind, it is a story of male development that has meaning for the Everyman in each of us.

The *Crystal Ball* is a dark story of the Mother Wound. It contains difficult psychic material that men must face if they are to liberate themselves from the regressive power of this inevitable childhood injury. As you read it, try to let go of your conventional intellect and instead experience the story with your old mind, that part of you that intuits the ancient symbolic language of myth and fairy tale. Let the images become vivid and alive inside. Finally, keep in mind that these stories are not meant to be condemnations of our parents — rather, they are symbolic representations of basic developmental challenges all men face, generation after generation, in their struggle for mature adulthood. Women have their stories and woundings as well. Each gender and each generation takes its turn as victim and perpetrator in the timeless cycle. For whatever reason, this is one of the deep ways we learn its lessons.

Our story will be told in four parts. I suggest you read them slowly, and observe how each image and each event takes form in your inner theater, and how its symbols speak secretly and personally to you. Ponder also what these images and symbols may want from you; that is, what memories, recognitions, new directions, or life decisions come into awareness asking for your attention. Keep in mind that the most important story is the one being evoked in you along the way. So, pay attention to both versions, the universal and deeply personal, and listen for the meanings or teachings whispered just to you.

As you read this tale, open your inner vision to the imaginal world that comes alive in the timeless oral tradition of story telling. See how clearly you can actually see and hear and smell and touch the world created by this story in your imagination, just as our fathers did listening to the radio before the days of television, and their fathers did before them, listening to the stories of their tribal history.

Grow quiet and move inward now. Imagine the curtains opening on the screen of your inner theater and get ready as the light flickers from the projector. We are leaving the twentieth century of TVs, computers, mortgages, and sports. Coming through the fog of time, we find ourselves entering into a mythic land of castles, curses, quests, and mighty soul-shaking confrontations. The story begins in the springtime of life.

Springtime

There was once an enchantress, who had three sons who loved each other as brothers, but the old woman did not trust them, and thought they wanted to steal her power from her. So she changed the eldest into an eagle which was forced to dwell in the rocky mountains and was often seen flying in great circles in the sky. The second she changed into a whale which lived in the deep sea, and all that was seen of it was that it sometimes spouted up a great jet of water in the air. Each brother bore his human form for only two hours daily. The third son, afraid his mother might change him into a raging wild beast — a bear perhaps or a wolf — fled in secret.

Now the third son had heard that a King's daughter, who was bewitched, was imprisoned in the Castle of the Golden Sun, and was waiting to be set free. Those who tried to free her did so only at great peril. Three-and-twenty youths had already died a horrible death, and now only one other might make the attempt, after which no more would be allowed to try. Despite the danger, the young boy's heart was without fear. He made up his mind to seek out the Castle of the Golden Sun. And so he left home to begin his journey.

Discussion: The Mother Wound

This story begins by immediately posing dark and disturbing questions: What power does a mother possess during a boy's earliest years that seemingly allows her to control his very life force and destiny? How does she wound or control her son by using it? And why? These are questions we are not used to asking about our mothers, for we wish to see them through sentimental eyes as perfect and loving figures. We may feel guilty or afraid even considering them. But there are universal themes at work here, themes that can ultimately determine a man's fate. We need to have the courage to face them.

In the mythic consciousness of a young boy, a mother can seem like an enchantress, a witch, a sustainer, or a devourer. She holds the magic powers of love: attention, affection, tenderness, comfort, and life itself. But she also wields darker forces when this same love is withheld or angrily withdrawn: rage, disapproval, control, disinterest, neglect, coldness, rejection, abandonment, and physical pain. A mother's awesome powers seem to emanate from her very nature, and in early childhood it feels as if she can create either a garden of loving happiness or a wretched wasteland of despair, emptiness, pain, and emotional starvation.

These images and their associated emotions actually reside in the boy, though he cannot know it for years. Latent in the theater of his own psyche, they are conjured up by his mother's presence, energy, and behavior. They are so powerful because they derive from an accumulated storehouse of images from millions of years of harsh and unforgiving evolution when a boy's very survival was literally at risk. Is it any surprise, then, that these images are the stuff of fairy tales and nightmares? To master and dissipate the power of these images, however, a man needs to understand their nature, origin, and operation in his life.

Let us begin with the power of being able to change a boy into an animal. How is it that a boy can lose his human form and become an animal? This is a symbolic transformation. A child can be made to feel ugly, defective, even "less than human" by a parent's angry face, contemptuous remarks, or implied distrust. He automatically feels subhuman when he believes that his natural human form is unwanted or unloved. So it is in this story, for the mother does not value her sons just as they are. For some reason, she thinks they want to steal her power.

Power in this tale symbolizes the life force and natural energy of being human. A child's life force is expressed in his inborn temperament, his enthusiasm, creativity, and spontaneity. This is the living power of the world, of spirit, of Being as it manifests in individual form. When we have control of our own power, we don't need to control anybody else. We joyfully feel and express this energy of self and soul naturally, until someone forbids or seeks to control it. When you cannot be yourself, when you have to give up that self to survive or be loved, your connection with this power is severed. This is a deeply painful experience because you lose who you really are.

Why would a mother fear that her children would steal her life force, her power? There are usually two kinds of reasons. First, when a mother feels overwhelmed by the stresses of adult life, drained by her own personal problems, or distracted by interests other than her family, she may resent a child's needs or lack the energy to cope with his energetic life force. At such times, a boy's exuberance may be crushed by the irritability of a frustrated mother.

But there is also a deeper and more pernicious reason for a mother fearing that her children will steal her power: someone in her own past already took her power — permanently. Someone in her childhood forbade her to be herself. She correctly realizes that her child has something that she was forbidden — a true and spontaneous self. He has taken the power she lost, and she fears he will grow even more powerful. Driven by the pain of an empty self, a mother's need for power can become a dark and evil quest to control others, particularly her family. She may believe that stealing their power will restore hers. She may also believe that they are similarly motivated to steal hers, so she must act first. Whatever its particular form, the result of this twisted logic is always the same: the boy is robbed of his personhood and his soul, and whoever steals it in this manner is mythically imaged in terrible ways: as a witch, monster, or devil.

Fairy tales can be cruel in their symbolism. Though seemingly fictional, the mother in this story is, in some measure, representative of "Everymother." All mothers struggle with both overload and personal loss of power. The vast majority of mothers are not bad people, but they are, like all of us, wounded people whose personal conflicts do, at times, interfere with childrearing. They too had parents who were overwhelmed or compromised. Fathers suffer the same struggles. It is simply the cycle of things, which continues generation after generation. To see and heal this cycle, both genders need to look beyond sentimental beliefs and discover whatever truth lies within.

Returning to the story, we see that the sons of the enchantress had to take animal forms to survive. These animals symbolize parts of a man's own psyche and temperament that help him cope during desperate or painful times. The eagle represents the emotionally distant, judgmental intellect that scrutinizes the world while flying high above the pain. The whale symbolizes the ability to dive deep into the sorrow-numbing darkness of unconsciousness and hide there. And the raging wild beast represents the red hot explosion of uncontrollable anger that feels too big for our young egos to contain. All of us use these kinds of coping mechanisms to survive the customary, though devastating wounds and losses of childhood. Do you have a sense of what kind of mythic animal forms you took in order to get through?

There is more to the animal symbolism in this story. In myths and fairy tales and in the spirituality of indigenous peoples, animals are not considered less than human beings. Ancient man knew that animals hold magic, wisdom and intelligence, that they often function as intermediaries or visitors from the spiritual world, that they are equal to or above man in their importance to the living planet, and that they can and do befriend man in times of crisis. To become an animal means to tap into these kinds of spiritual abilities and intuitions. Our story also suggests that we could learn much from taking on the symbolic form of animals, especially if we entered their realm with humility, respect, and receptivity.

The mother wound also contributes to the way in which we leave home. The third son in this tale represents the *conscious self* seeking a way to cope with the pain and damage of his wound. Permitted to be himself only minimally (that is, "only two hours daily") and terrified of his own rage at this unbearable injustice, a boy comes of age when he finally leaves the home of his mother's personality to seek his own wholeness. In doing so, he begins a long journey into the world searching for this lost, forbidden, or damaged self. Although there are certainly many other reasons for sons to leave home, this story simply tells us that one of them is the developmental imperative of healing this wound of the mother.

The story tells us next that the mother wound is somehow connected to a bewitched King's daughter who is imprisoned in the Castle of the Golden Sun. This association suggests that when a man's relationship to his mother is damaged, so too is his relationship to the inner feminine, his capacity to feel, love, and relate intimately with others. More to the point of this story, this feminine image is also, as Jung brilliantly discovered, a symbol for a man's own soul. His soul has been imprisoned.

The story also tells us that a young man must search for the Castle of the Golden Sun, where his soul and capacity to love are imprisoned. What does this mean? It means he must confront and pass through the rigid masculine walls he erected to fend off his mother, for they have become walls that now confine his soul. When he has done so, he can free his love. Young men don't realize that a significant part of their outward journey in the springtime of life is really a search to recover the capacity to love damaged by the mother wound. Instead they search for reflections of their imprisoned soul in the outer world of actual women. This journey will take him into the realms of love and romance, marriage and children, idealization and disillusionment, until finally, it will lead to the recovery of his soul, the soul that was taken long ago by the enchantress.

What does it mean for a man to lose his life trying to free the King's daughter? And why have so many men died trying? Over and over in a man's childhood and adult love relationships, he strives to free the imprisoned self by seeking the love of his mother or mother substitutes. That is, the various women in his life. But what he wants cannot ultimately come from another. The cure, he must learn, comes with experiencing the deep grief of the original wound rather than coercing women to love him the way his mother didn't. So men find themselves "killed" again and again in conflicts with women, who are themselves trying to work out a reciprocal process with men. At this point in the story, the third son, that part of us that is still not injured beyond repair, sets out to solve this riddle.

Summer

Now we return to our story. As you will recall, the third son left home secretly to avoid being changed into a raging wild beast by his mother and began looking for the Castle of the Golden Sun. As we join him, the young man had already traveled about for a long time without being able to find the castle when he came by chance into a great forest and did not know the way out of it. Suddenly he saw two giants who made a sign to him with their hands, and when he came to them, they said: "We are quarreling about a cap, and which of us it is to belong to, and as we are equally strong, neither of us can get the better of the other. The small men are more clever than we are, so we will leave the decision to you." The youth responded, "How can you dispute about an old cap?" The giants answered, "You do not know what properties it has! It is a wishing-cap; whosoever puts it on can wish himself away wherever he likes, and in an instant he will be there." "Give me the cap," said the youth, "I will go a short distance off and when I call you, you must run a race and the cap shall belong to the one who gets first to me." He put on the cap and went away. At length he forgot about the giants and, thinking of the King's daughter, sighed from the very bottom of his heart and cried, "Ah, if I were but at the Castle of the Golden Sun." And hardly had the words passed his lips than he was standing on a high mountain before the gate of the castle.

Discussion: Running the Race in Adulthood

What does it mean to "travel about for a long time" looking for the Castle of the Golden Sun? As suggested earlier, a man seems to know unconsciously that he must find this castle with the bewitched princess, but he has no idea what that really means or how to proceed. So he travels about during the long Summer of his life looking for the princess and, at the same time, fighting for a successful niche in the world of men. His search for love, and the relationship struggles that ensue, represent unconscious attempts at healing his mother wound. But they don't work because they are outward substitutes for the real healing within. Eventually a man becomes lost in "a great forest," that is, a time of darkness, confusion, and disorientation. Distracted by work and real world relationships, he has forgotten the quest of his soul. By midlife, nothing is working very well and he has no idea how to escape his predicament.

The giants can be seen as the huge, powerful, combative, and competitive energies of masculinity that fill a man in the early Summer of his life. Rooted largely in the body, they are powerful and aggressive, but not too intelligent. They do, however, hold something very big — the capacity to wish. By the time a man reaches midlife, however, these huge, ram-like energies have usually been reduced to futile fussing and quarreling for they are no longer connected to the longings of his heart. Worldly combat holds no benefit now and our protagonist is smart enough not to get entangled with more "giant" battles. Instead he appeals to his own intelligence to confront the problem, and indeed solves it brilliantly by simply naming it — a race. "Calling it like it is" identifies the true form of a problem and for men, Summer is indeed a race. When you name something correctly, it often arrests or deflates the energy involved, and allows one to move on. Freed from the masculine need to prove himself, our hero is drawn to the very thing the conflict was really about — the wishing cap — which is a wonderful symbol for his unrequited longing. He suddenly remembers the original purpose of his journey, and because his heart's wish has finally returned to consciousness, the hero finds himself where he was headed all along: at the gates of his imprisoned soul.

Entering Midlife

As you will recall, we left the third son standing on a high mountain before the gate of the Castle of the Golden Sun. He entered and went through all the rooms, until in the last he found the King's daughter. But how shocked he was when he saw her. She had an ashen-gray face full of wrinkles, bleary eyes, and unkempt red hair. "Are you the King's daughter, whose beauty the whole world praises?" cried he. "Ah," she answered, "this is not my form; human eyes can only see me in this state of ugliness, but that you may know what I am like, look in the mirror — it does not let itself be misled. It will show you my image as it is in truth."

She gave him the mirror and he saw therein the likeness of the most beautiful maiden on earth, and saw too how the tears were rolling down her cheeks with grief. Then the youth said: "How can you be set free? I fear no danger." The maiden answered, "He who gets the crystal ball, and holds it before the enchanter, will destroy his power with it, and I shall resume my true shape. But," she added, "so many have already gone to meet death for this, and you are so young; I grieve that you should encounter such great danger."

"Nothing can keep me from doing it," said he, "but tell me what I must do." The King's daughter replied: "You shall know everything. When you descend the mountain on which the castle stands, a wild bull will stand below by a spring and you must fight with it, and if you have the luck to kill it, a fiery bird will spring out of it, which bears in its body a red-hot egg, and in the egg the crystal ball lies as its yolk. The bird, however, will not let the egg fall until forced to do so, and if it falls on the ground, it will flame up and burn everything that is near, and even the egg itself will melt, and with it the crystal ball, and then all your trouble will have been in vain."

And so the youth begins his downward journey.

Discussion: The Midlife Descent into the Soul's Despair

The young man has now entered the prison of his own wounded soul. The references to castle, the king, and the sun suggest we are dealing with the masculine psyche. It is in the fortress of the male persona, in its most armored and rigidified form, that the boy's soul became imprisoned. The boy had to be tough, he had to deny his pain in order to take this perilous journey away from his mother into unknown lands of the psyche. But he became trapped in his heroic strength.

Finding the King's daughter ugly and ashen symbolizes the true state of the middle aged man's inner feminine and inner life. His soul, his ability to love, and his imagination have become ill and shriveled, both because of the original wound and because of the years he neglected them running the competitive race. But the story goes on to tell us something even more amazing: that this alienated and atrophied self holds the very wisdom necessary for curing the wound. The princess gives him a mirror, which symbolizes the work of looking inward. Insight! He sees then the potential beauty of his soul and knows the deep grief of betrayal and abandonment it has experienced. The fact that the feminine soul tells the man how to heal her is important in another way. It indicates that the masculine analytic consciousness, that problem-solving style which seeks to fix things by dissection, rationality and will power, cannot heal this wound. Facing, not fixing, the wound must be the first step.

Finally, the story contains another symbol for the soul — the crystal ball — and says that it must be recovered from its captor for healing to take place. In other words, only when a man recovers his true self, that self which was forbidden in the original mother wound, will he destroy the power of the enchantress, the dark mother, as well as the power of the maiden's enchanter, the controlling masculinity of the inner King that continued her imprisonment. The story seems to be saying that recovering the soul, the true self, is the great work of midlife.

The prescription given by the maiden for this great and life saving work may at first glance appear mysterious and virtually impossible. When we understand this story in symbolic terms, however, we can see that it involves first descending into one's own inner depths and conquering the wild, intense, and uncontrolled rage at the mother (the wild bull) which stands at the very source of the self (the inner spring). Then one must face the equally intense urge to escape the pain of the mother wound (the fiery bird). Finally, the story tells us that trapped within these masculine symbols is the feminine principle symbolized as an egg. In the center of this egg lies the crystal ball of soul. A man has to enter this germinal center of self and life, he must be touched by the feminine consciousness, to recover the crystal ball of his soul!

The story also reminds us that this is a dangerous mission, that anger, arrogance and impatience can obstruct the journey and destroy the soul before it is recovered. These, then, are the psychological challenges and dangers a man must face and overcome in the recovery and healing of his true self.

The Work of Midlife

Move your consciousness once again into the mythic interior of soul and back to our story. As you will recall, our hero was descending the hill from the Castle to face the first of several seemingly impossible tasks: killing the ferocious bull that stood by the spring.

The youth went down to the spring, where the bull snorted and bellowed at him. After a long struggle, he plunged his sword in the animal's body, and it fell down. Instantly a fiery bird arose from it, and was about to fly away, but the young man's brother, the eagle, who was passing between the clouds, swooped down, carried it away to the sea, and struck it with his beak until, in its desperation, the bird let the egg fall. The egg, however, did not fall into the sea, but on a fisherman's hut which stood on the shore. At once the hut began to smoke and was about to break out in flames. Then waves as high as a house streamed over the hut and subdued the fire. The other brother, the whale, had come swimming by and had driven the water up on high. When the fire was extinguished, the youth sought the egg and happily found it. The egg was not yet melted, but the shell was broken from being so suddenly cooled with the water, and the boy could take out the crystal ball — unhurt!

When the youth went to the enchanter and held the crystal ball before him, the latter said, "My power is destroyed, and from this time forth you are the King of the Castle of the Golden Sun. With this can you likewise return your brothers to their human form. Then the youth hastened to the King's daughter, and when he entered the room, she was standing there in the full splendor of her beauty. Joyfully, they exchanged rings with each other. And

so it was that the curse was lifted, the three sons regained their rightful forms, the king's
daughter was healed, and harmony was restored to all the kingdom.

Discussion: The Final Healing

The youth begins this great and hazardous mission of rescuing his captive soul by "killing" his blind, bull-like aggression. Then he encounters some very interesting surprises. His brothers, those self-protective parts of himself that saved him at the time of the original wounding, come again to his aid. The eagle, the soaring intellect, can now confront and arrest his pain-driven escape tendencies, whatever their form (e.g., drugs, workaholism, intellectualization, narcissism).

The soul, still burning in pain, then falls onto a fisherman's hut. The fisherman symbolizes balance. He lives on the shores of the great unconscious sea, drawing sustenance from its bounty, but also respecting its power and staying grounded. The hut represents the humble yet sturdy life structure we build in Summer that is strong enough to can catch and bear, at least temporarily, this red hot, burning, falling, out-of-control pain. Now before this part, too, is burned, the whale adaptation of a man's struggle, that part of him that has learned to live in hidden sorrow, returns to put out the flames with the waters of grief. The soul is released undamaged.

Finally, the male enchanter is confronted. He was the dark King, the domineering male, the false masculine, in other words, the part of a man that needed to control or idealize women in order to hide the terrible pain and shame of his mother wound. Having recovered his soul, the rule of the false masculine can end and the true self can become king. The hero's brothers, those split off parts of his own personality, are also restored to their rightful form so that the personality can be whole. Now a man may become his own king. He can cease controlling his own soul, set her free, and most importantly, have an ongoing relationship with her. It is the marriage of the masculine and feminine sides of his own nature, where neither is subjugated to the other. The wedding ring, a circular representation of wholeness, symbolizes the final fulfillment of self.

The Three Languages

Our first story ended with the recovery of the soul and the union of the psyche. We saw the treacherous psychological journey a man must take to heal his mother wound and restore his soul. This healing is part of the great work of midlife, but it is not the whole story. A man must also take a similar journey to face the wound of his father.

This next story is about the universal father wound. Also adapted from *Grimm's Fairy Tales* (Colum & Campbell, 1972, pp. 169-71), it symbolizes three of the central maturational stages common to all men. Like the crystal ball, it takes him again on a deep descent into grief and back again, but also goes a step further. The story tells about a man's journey into spirituality as well.

Springtime

Picture a medieval countryside with green fields and meandering streams and a palace in the distance. As we travel up the dirt road and finally approach the castle, we find a count and his only son in angry discussion. The older man, viewing his son as stupid and incapable of learning anything of the world, grows increasingly impatient with him and finally says: "Hark you, my son, try as I will I can get nothing into your head. You must go from hence. I will give you into the care of a celebrated master who shall see what he can do with you." The son was to be sent away.

The youth traveled by horseback to a strange and distant town. There he remained a whole year with a wise and perceptive master. Finally, at the end of this time, the son returned home. Upon arriving, his father asked sternly, "Now, my son, what have you learnt?" His son enthusiastically answered, "Father, I have learnt what the dogs say when they bark." Disgusted and furious, his father replied, "Lord have mercy on us! Is that all you have learnt? I will send you into another town to another master."

The youth was then taken to another strange and distant town. He stayed there a whole year with this master who was also wise and perceptive. Finally when the teaching was completed, the son returned home. When he came back the father again asked sternly, "My son, what have you learnt?" and his son again enthusiastically replied, "Father, I have learnt what the birds say." Falling into a rage, the Count cried, "Oh, you lost man, you have spent this precious time and learnt nothing. Are you not ashamed to appear before my eyes? I will send you to a third master, but if you learn nothing this time also, I will no longer be your father."

So the youth traveled to yet another strange and distant town. There he remained another year with this third master. When the year was up, he came home again and his father sternly inquired, "My son, what have you learnt?" "Dear father," his son responded, "I have this year learnt what it is that the frogs croak." Well, as you can imagine, the father fell into the worst and most furious rage, whereafter he leapt to his feet, assembled his court, and pronounced with great disgust, "This man is no longer my son. I cannot bear his stupidity and foolishness. I drive him forth and command you to take him out into the forest and kill him."

The count's henchmen took the youth into the woods as ordered, but when they reached the place where he was to be killed, they could not proceed for pity, and let him go. Instead, they cut out the eyes and the tongue of a deer that they might carry them to the old man as a token and proof of their accomplished deed.

Discussion: The Father Wound

This father is angry, impatient, and critical. Increasingly fed up with his son, his remarks are sharp, punctuated with disgust. Though perhaps harsher than most, this painful beginning nonetheless sets the stage for a journey every son must take to heal a wound every son must incur. Why is this pattern so pervasive?

James Hillman explains that fathers and sons almost always grow from different "spiritual trees." (Hillman, 1990) By this metaphor he means that fathers are typically so different in temperament from their sons that they are unable to see them clearly. Their own values and personalities get in the way and they cannot truly recognize and celebrate their son's unique gifts. The blessing that a boy really wants from his father, the accurate acknowledgement of his own soul, is lost in these father-son differences.

As suggested in the Story of Everyman, fathers also invariably wound their sons. One may be threatened by the emerging manhood or special talents of his son. Another may fear his son will challenge the prideful achievements of his own life; or that he will be eclipsed by his son's accomplishments or forgotten by his disinterest. Yet a third may be so stuck in his own compulsive work ethic that he has no time for children or views their youthful experimentation as irresponsibility. Sometimes a father's own personal wound, character flaws, or life stresses leave him with little to give. However it happens, sooner or later a father will cut his son with criticism, comparisons, shaming, or disinterest.

The story next hints at the compensatory role other men can play in this drama of the father wound. Often there are other men who can see in a boy what his father cannot. Although a father often can't help his son directly, he can help him get to men who can. Think back: in your own case, who were your "celebrated masters," those wonderful people who were able to recognize and celebrate your potential worth and talent as you were growing up (e.g., neighbors, teachers, scoutmasters, coaches, older men, father surrogates)? How did they bless your uniqueness with their interest and recognition?

Whether or not one receives the kind of dramatic father wound portrayed in this story, myths and fairy tales around the world agree that sooner or later each man is somehow betrayed, wounded, or abandoned by the father. It may be large or small, obvious or subtle, but it is a parting of the ways. A young man must then leave the security of home and his father's values to set off on a personal journey of self-discovery. He must find out of what he is really made and what his own destiny will be. Often it is this break with the father that sets him on his own way.

What is the meaning of the henchmen freeing the count's son? A boy typically internalizes his father's words and actions. If they are cruel, he may leave home sentenced by his father's judgments, creating a psychological pattern of self-hatred and failure that can last a lifetime. The henchmen's decision not to kill the boy represents a decision not to carry out his father's condemnation. A young man needs this leniency and understanding, from himself most of all. The healing balm offered by other men's kindness is also important; men who counterbalance a father's angry excesses.

Summer and Midlife

As you will recall, the count's son was freed in a forest by sympathetic henchmen after his father's furious order that he be killed. The youth could not go home again, so instead he wandered on through the medieval countryside passing haystacks and cottages, woods, and meadows. Finally, after this extended wandering, the youth came upon a fortress, looming darkly in the distance, gloomy and somehow cursed and troubled. There he begged for a night's lodging from the lord of the castle.

"Sire," he asked, "I have traveled long and far from my homeland. May I stay the night in your fortress?" "Yes, you can stay here," the lord of the castle replied, "but only if you pass the night down in the old dungeon. Go there. But I warn you, it is at the peril of your life, for it is full of wild dogs that bark and howl without stopping. At certain hours, a man must be given to them whom they at once devour."

The whole countryside was disturbed by these tormented and insatiable dogs, yet no one had been able to stop them. Apprehension, sorrow, and dismay filled the fortress and surrounding lands. Our youth, however, was without fear and said bravely, "Let me go down to the barking dogs, and give me something that I can throw to them. They will do nothing to harm me."

As the youth himself would have it so, the lord of the castle gave him some food for the wild animals and led him down to the dark and cursed dungeon. When he went inside, however, the dogs did not bark at him, but wagged their tails quite amicably around him, ate what he set before them, and did not hurt one hair of his head. Next morning, to the astonishment of everyone, he came out again safe and unharmed, and said to the lord of the castle, "The dogs have revealed to me, in their own language, why they dwell there, and bring evil on the land. They are bewitched and are obliged to watch over a great treasure which is below in the dungeon, and they can have no rest until it is taken away. And I have likewise learnt from their discourse how it is to be done."

Then all who heard this rejoiced and the lord of the castle said: "I will adopt you as my own son if you can indeed accomplish this task." So the youth went down again into the dungeon and, as he knew what he had to do, he did it thoroughly, and brought a chest full of gold out with him. The howling of the wild dogs was henceforth heard no more. They had disappeared, and the country was freed from the curse.

Discussion: Healing the Father's Curse

After one leaves the outer father, that man involved in our actual wounding, separation, and journey into the world, it eventually becomes necessary to find, face, and heal the wound of the inner father. When a father steals or shames his son's beauty, a dark, painful yet often silent wailing begins deep in his son's soul. No matter where a man goes, that wound will go with him and affect all his actions. The land of his psyche will be disturbed until this hidden torment is healed. Like *The Crystal Ball*, this story tells us that a man must go deep into the haunted dungeon of his soul to find that wound, that this descent is perilous, and that the wound is filled with pain and suffering. Moreover, the story suggests that it is this unfaced inner sorrow that blocks contact with his own deeply buried treasure, that special gift secreted in the imprisoned psyche.

At first, the inner journey is frightening. It is a journey into the dark unknown. Before dogs were domesticated and became identified as man's best friend, they were seen as guardians of the underworld. The wild dogs in this story represent the fear or loathing that turns men back from the dark underworld of their buried wounds. They may be insatiable, capable of consuming a man's consciousness. When the images of our unconscious are hated or feared in this way, they appear as hateful or terrifying. Our attitude blends with the image. However, when approached without fear, when valued, honored, and respected, these very same images become friendly and generous. In the story, the boy did not fear the howling dogs — and they did not kill him. Rather, they explained in the language of symbols the nature of his soul's curse.

As we saw in the previous story, the castle symbolizes the hard masculine ego that surrounds the wounded self. It is the outer fortress of persona, the tough compensatory wall a man erects to protect the deeply wounded self and help him stand strong in the world. The dungeon is his own inner depths where his true self lies injured. He must descend into the castle dungeon to find and heal the wounded self. Healing this self opens the way for him to realize its treasure. If the youth had chosen instead to avoid this descent and deaden or obliterate his pain (e.g., with alcohol or drugs, workaholic compulsivity, aggrandizing a false self, rigid social conformity) his healing could not take place and the gift of self would have been forever lost.

A mentor also appears in this story. He is the Lord of the Castle, who took the young man in for the night and showed him what he must do to lift the curse. This older male figure helps by posing the problem that must be solved and pointing to the path of its solution. He is the boss, teacher, older friend, psychotherapist, spiritual guide, or elder who reveals and encourages the healing journey. Notice, too, that the mentor can show the way but he can't do the healing himself. Each man must do that for himself.

In your own life, did you find (or do you still need to find) guidance and support for your healing from an older man? Do you have a sense of what the inner treasure, guarded by the father wound pain, may be for you? What is your gift of self that longs to find expression? It is in midlife that we become so restless to find this gift and we will see how midlife shakes it free for us.

Fall

Now, the concluding chapter of our story. We left off with the count's son having broken the dungeon's curse and relieved the countryside of its despair and suffering. He did not, however, remain with the king. Instead he thought to himself: "It is time for me to begin my own travels, and I think I shall go to Rome."

The son left right away and soon passed by a marsh where a number of frogs were croaking. He stopped and listened carefully, and when he became aware of what they were saying, he grew thoughtful and sad. And he said to himself, "I hear and understand this message. It is indeed a sad one, and I must hurry on to Rome."

At last the son arrived in the great and ancient city of Rome and soon found his way to its main cathedral. There, in its echoing halls, he heard hushed, worried murmurings that confirmed the frogs' message, "The Pope has died. Who shall succeed him? How will we recognize his true successor? We must await a divine and miraculous sign." Then, just as the youth entered, two snow-white doves descended onto his shoulders and remained there. The Cardinals, astonished and joyous, recognized therein the divine sign from above. "Praise unto Heaven! Here is our Pope! Yes, he must be the one! Dear man, will you be our next pontiff?" they begged. "Oh my," thought the son, "I am undecided. Is it possible that I, a wandering stranger, am truly worthy of this great responsibility? How shall I know?" Immediately, the doves answered and the youth understood and accepted their counsel: "Yes, I will accept your calling for this is His will," replied the son.

The youth was then anointed and consecrated, and thus was fulfilled the prophesy he heard from the frogs on his way to Rome — that he was to be His Holiness the Pope. Then he was asked to sing a mass, though he knew not a word of it. Still, it did not matter, for the doves stayed on his shoulders and whispered it in his ears.

Thus ends our story.

Discussion: Mature Masculinity and Journey of Spirituality

The story tells us that the young man chose not to be "adopted" by his mentor, the lord of the castle. He had come to him for guidance in healing his soul and discovering its treasure, and the guidance had been invaluable. Once he finds the treasure of self, however, a man no longer needs such guidance. He must eventually leave the older man in order to actualize his own expression of the treasure. He must become the Lord of his own castle; that is, the owner, master, or overseer of his own life. If he stays in another man's castle, that is, in another man's value system, he will never become his own king and realize the great gift of his own soul.

Unlike *The Crystal Ball*, this story does not end with the healing of the personality. It teaches that the male maturational journey proceeds onward after these inner wounds are healed, leading ultimately to a sense of spirituality and spiritual responsibility. As a man ages, and as much of his inner pain has been eased, he may begin to hear the quiet inner calling of the spirit, an intuition that there is something else he must do to complete the inborn purpose and destiny of his life. The story hints that such spiritual realization cannot fully occur until the true self has been restored. At midlife the heroic, self-centered masculinity "dies" and is replaced by transcendent purposes and the work of one's soul.

We still haven't penetrated all of the symbolism in our story. As suggested in the preceding tale, animals in myths and fairy tales often symbolize messengers from the "other" world, which may be interpreted as either the unconscious or the transcendent. They bring us information unknown by our conscious ego. Dogs, being mammals and hence closest to man, may reflect something of his own emotional nature. In this case, they faithfully stand guard over the young man's inner pain, howling for attention. Frogs are symbols of transformation as they themselves are transformed from tadpoles to four legged creatures capable of living in and out of water. When frogs appear, whether from the individual unconscious in dreams or the collective unconscious in fairy tales, you know that some kind of transformation is about to happen. Finally, birds, especially white doves, symbolize messengers from above; that is, from heaven.

The symbolism in the story's title can now be addressed. The young man in this tale trusted his intuition. Despite his father's repeated ridicule, and though it took years to master, the youth learned the language of intuition. He was able to "hear" the messages from his psyche and the transcendent world. Had our youth not trusted and responded to the voices of his spiritual calling, he would never have journeyed to Rome, the religious center of the medieval world, and would not have fulfilled his destiny. It was his intuitive capacity that gave him the direction and the courage to proceed through the difficult steps and stages of his own individuation process, particularly at times when those around him were advising wrongly. We must, the story suggests, trust these voices of our own intuition and then take the risks necessary to heed their counsel.

Finally, the Pope in our story symbolizes the opportunity for mature holiness and wholeness available later in life. In pre-Christian versions of this story, he might have been a shaman, great elder, or even a spirit. A spiritual archetype, the Pope represents a universal symbol of the possible fulfillment of the mature masculine potential of teacher, wisdom figure, steward, or elder. Although the role could be exploited for fame or power, the archetype itself indicates a profoundly humble and living connection to the sacred and a commitment to serve others. The "Pope" within can, without grandiosity or control, see and bless the divineness of others, care for the world without selfish motives, and take a genuinely mature leadership role in the community of man. The story suggests that a man fulfills these developmental tasks in later life.

This story completes the journey of the male midlife and introduces some of the spiritual themes of the Fall. After a man's soul has been recovered in the hard psychological work of the midlife passage, he finds himself drawn into the holiness of life itself, sensing that there are yet further stages of spiritual transformation and responsibility along the path. We will be exploring these themes in depth later on. For now, however, there is one more secret of this developmental process and one more story to reveal it.

The Man Who Didn't Believe

This last story is from the Cochiti Pueblo near Santa Fe, New Mexico, adapted from *Pueblo Stories and Story Tellers* by Mark Bahti. It is a folktale about man's right relationship to the spiritual dimension of the world. As you read the story, imagine that you are a member of this village and that what happens to this man can happen to anyone.

A man died in the village. This man had never believed in the ceremonies or in living again after death. He never believed there was Shipap, where people come from or where they return after death. He never danced or took part in the ceremonies or helped in any way. Whenever he saw an insect, he crushed it. He tore down the nests of birds and then ate the eggs. He threw rocks at snakes and killed them.

One day he found some eggs in a nest. He made holes in the ends and sucked them dry. When he came back to the village he sat outside his house, resting after his meal. The people suddenly heard a great sound. Like a whip, a snake flew through the air and into the man's mouth. He had eaten the snake's eggs! The man fell over, and everyone ran away. The snake came out of his mouth, carrying its eggs and slithered away. When the people of the village came back, the man was dead.

This man arrogantly and selfishly desecrates the sacred world. Without giving thanks or blessing, he sucks dry the very beginnings of life. One day he goes too far. He makes the mistake of sucking out the snake's babies. It is a big mistake because the snake is a very powerful deity. This man has violated the sacred order and offended the great mother. She returns to recover her babies. And he is dead.

The people prepared to bury him. The priest of the Shipap knew of this man and knew of his death. He immediately sent messengers to bring the dead man's spirit to Shipap. The messengers took his spirit and returned along the road they had come. As they went, the man's spirit marveled at how clear the road was. He saw how beautiful the fields were, filled with green corn, yellow melons, and young green plants. "How is it that these places we pass have come to be this beautiful?" the man asked. "It is because the people who care for the fields and use the roads to bring the water believe and have good hearts," replied the messengers.

Presently they arrived at Shipap. The man was taken to a room. The headmen were all there, and they were very sad. They were sad for all the things that this man had done and for what he had not done. Sorrow lay on their hearts because this man had not believed nor lived with a good heart. The man's spirit saw this and wept. The head man told him he could go back to his body, that it was not too late if he hurried. But, they counseled, "You must believe in everything!"

To this he readily agreed with all his heart. The messengers hurried him back to the village and hurled him back into his body. When the man awoke, he embraced his father and he embraced his mother and they were very happy. He told them what the headmen had told him, and what he was instructed to do. "They told me not to harm snakes or insects or birds or any of our brothers. They told me that when I am hunting I must respect the spirits of those that let themselves be taken. They told me to believe in the katsinas and the medicine men. They told me to believe in everything." And he always did after that, and he grew very old and he became a cacique who served the people well.

Discussion: Seeing with Spiritual Eyes

So the man who would not believe returns a believer. He learns not to harm anything, for all life is his brother. To take life for sustenance, he learns, is itself a sacred act that must be performed respectfully. And he learns to believe in his religion, including the katsinas (katchinas) and medicine men. Living in rightful harmony with his mother earth, the man grows old gracefully in a life of service.

This story speaks to Western Man as well, for he, too, robs the earth, taking her minerals, her animals, and her plants without humility or thanks. And too often, he neither believes in nor participates in the sacred rituals of life. He kills things just to kill them. He does not ask permission. His religion ignores such sacrilege. He is sucking the life out of his mother the earth. She will have revenge. More importantly, Western Man will one day see how much pain he has caused the living things of earth. Somehow, before it is too late, he must visit the other side, learn to "believe in everything" again, and return to this world with reverence and service for all life.

Prior to midlife, a man often believes he is like a hero who can act with spiritual impunity, that he can do whatever he thinks is right, take as much as he wants, use others to his advantage, and violate the natural order of body and life without having to pay a price. This is the hero in each of us that must die sooner or later so that we might give birth to a more soulful vision. Midlife is like a near death experience. A man suddenly realizes he will not live forever, that his children will not live forever, that the earth may not live forever, and that preparation for the world of the spirit is far more important than he ever realized. Learning to see with spiritual eyes becomes a new calling in the later years, one that can lead to a more loving, generous, and service-oriented way of life.

It is remarkable how many of mankind's fundamental questions and ultimate developmental experiences are symbolized in these kinds of stories. Naturally, many themes and issues remain only partially understood, for the land of the psyche and its images cannot be entirely reduced to rigid interpretative formulae. The purpose of telling these stories, however, is to give symbolic form to this journey, so that we might better understand what it is really all about. We will be exploring this metaphorical landscape further as we examine what the death of the hero and the birth of the soul really mean to a man's final maturation. ❊

CHAPTER 4

The Second Half of Life:
A New Wilderness

≫ The journey into the second half of a man's life, from his early forties to his death, represents the entry into an entirely new land, with unfamiliar terrain, unexpected emotional and spiritual weather, and challenges unforeseen in life's earlier days. It is a new time and place with deceptive new rules very unlike those mastered earlier. The stories presented in the last chapter took us up to midlife, with only a hint of what lies in the uncharted wilderness beyond. As Allan Chinen noted in his search for *Elder Tales*, there are very few stories in the world's mythology that give us a mapping of this realm (Chinen, 1989, p. 3). In fact, this lack of maps is really part of the experience itself, for the maps fail, the trail runs out, and what you find now must come from yourself. This is a time when outer signposts and directions will not guide a man's journey nor the development of his soul. Now only soul itself can lead the way.

Though this new land may sometimes look familiar, and even seem to yield at first to the authority of our former viewpoint, values, or problem-solving abilities, this yielding is illusory. A man can cruise along for a while in the second half believing that whatever happens will eventually submit to his logic and analysis, and be overcome. But the very nature of the problems encountered in this realm will sooner or later defeat this arrogance. It is very humbling territory. It is humbling because it is meant to defeat us, and defeat us it will, for there are no "solutions" to the problems found here. How do you solve the problems of aging, deterioration, illness, and death? What happens to a man's sense of confidence and mastery when he begins to realize that world hunger, population, warfare, and suffering will not be handled neatly by his arrogant logic or the certainty of science in his lifetime, or very possibly ever? All the tools, accomplishments, possessions, and power acquired in the first half will not only fail us as we go deep into this realm, they will get in our way. In the end, they represent only a desperate clinging of the failing ego and a refusal to let go. They will not serve the opening of the soul.

As we will see in more detail later on, one of the most important tasks of life's second half is to surrender the goals of mastery and control, and enter instead into the mysterious flow of unfolding existence. What a jolt this is after the heady accomplishments of Summer! This idea is so radically different than what we would have expected from our mature years. But radical it is, and also inevitable.

A man's energy, nature, and purpose move from the more traditionally masculine, goal-oriented doing (i.e., questing, striving, toughening, asserting, competing, boundary making, fixing, conquering, and accumulating) to a less goal-oriented doing (i.e., yielding, accepting, softening, opening, surrendering, merging, releasing, sharing, and nurturing). This biological and archetypally structured shift requires the death of the heroic male self and the birth of a deeper real self, which in time opens into the experience of soul with its vast possibilities of love, intuition, compassion, joy, and mystical realization. This shift is the beginning of an altogether new second life for a man. The old one he knew well; this new one he knows not at all.

It is not surprising that midlife, that point between these vastly different energy systems, should be such a jolting experience. Men are so identified with the traditionally masculine identity and mode of existence that giving it up without any guarantee of success feels like stepping off a cliff. Unless they have developed enough consciousness, enough contact with the wisdom and value of their inner lives, and enough self-confidence to trust this letting go process, their midlife transition and aging will be a bumpy ride. But yield the heroic they must, for it will eventually be taken anyway — by illness, retirement, loss, divorce, career dead ends, competition from younger men, and the economics of the workplace, to name just a few of the thieves along the way. Moreover, resisting these new energies will only lead to emptiness, sterility, deterioration, exhaustion, or illness, for their purpose is to fill a man's life with a whole new reality and destiny. Accepting and opening to them, however, can bring profound personal transformation; that is, an entire reworking of his relationships, his work, and his future. It is a renewal of the great adventure and a preparation for life's ultimate transformation.

Thus, this great divide, the borderland known as the midlife passage, must be traversed and its lessons steadfastly integrated for a man to confront the calling of life's second half. Similarly, the culture of men at this millennial divide, the ending of the twentieth century, must likewise be challenged to yield its heroic model of tough, isolated, and compulsive "warrior" masculinity and discover in its place the soulful capacity of intimacy, compassion, community, mentoring, and love. These new values can provide a regenerative and healing paradigm for mankind's second half. Selfless and non-heroic caring for the world will replenish man's tired soul and the beauty of his culture. For some, the men's movement has been a womb for these changes.

These changes go even further. In yielding the heroic posture, Western Man has the opportunity of returning to the sacred; that is, to the immediate awareness of existence as a divine mystery. Men hunger for the spirit when they grow tired of the hero's mission. This hunger is awakened not only by the hero's psychological death, but more fundamentally, by the deep realization of his forthcoming biological death, because in that realization hides a subtle and ancient knowing — that there is something more than death. No longer consumed by questing and no longer mired in old wounds, an older man can listen for the soft voice of spirit calling him to a new destiny, as it called our protagonist in *The Three Languages*. Now a man becomes capable of a more mystical apprehension: a realization that existence and the world itself are divine, pervaded by an infinite and loving consciousness that sustains him far more than he ever realized. In this existence, man has a new place.

The wilderness after midlife comes alive with the beauty and power of the sacred when it is mystically appreciated. Time and story seem to end here in a fresh and untrained capacity for wonder. A new world is born in the eyes of a man who can see. Such direct mystical apprehension is the core of every religion. Its life-affirming insights can be gleaned from the experiences of mystics themselves. Like the far reaching scouts from the old west, mystics are those visionaries who have journeyed across one more great divide, the divide of duality, and returned with a radically new perception of life. It is a vision that mankind needs in its second half to guide and nourish not only individual man, but also the coming world. ❊

CHAPTER 5

Telling One's Story at Midlife

≫ So far in this section we have been discussing the universal story common to all men. There comes a time, however, when a man must tell his own story, his own unique, personal, yet infinitely precious variation of the archetypal one. By story, I don't mean merely a factual biography with dates, places, degrees, and so forth. To tell one's story means to tell the inner tale of what really happened growing up, how it really was, and how one dealt with the all the personal challenges, losses, and problems of adulthood. Our stories can be told in our journals, to each other, to therapists, to men's groups and gatherings, or to any community of people where truth and compassion are the most highly valued.

The reasons for telling our stories are numerous and include the following:

ƒ *Finding out what the story actually says.* A man needs to tell his story first to learn what actually happened. For many men, the factual parts of their stories are missing or incomplete and must be researched to fill in the gaps. Gaps may be for facts (e.g., How long did I live in that house? How old was I when we moved?), meanings (e.g., Why did we move? Why did you divorce my mother? Why was my father fired?), or secrets (e.g., What really happened when my brother died? Was Dad an alcoholic? What were my sister's behavioral problems really all about?). The more of this story that we know, the more we finally understand ourself and our life so far.

ƒ *Finding out how one feels about the story.* When a man tells his story, he begins to discover how he feels about what happened. Stories come alive when feelings are evoked, for then the meaning and impact of all the big events in his life become real and understandable. Often men don't even know how they feel about their lives. Telling one's story is like finally listening to a piece of music after studying it in written form. It comes alive and one feels so much more of its rhythm and power.

ƒ *Healing the pain.* Telling his story also triggers the wounded feelings that will lead a man back to the pain of his lost and betrayed self. We enter it not to fix it, analyze it, reduce it to ideas, interpret it away, or minimize it. We enter our pain in order to feel it so that the wounds of self can be honestly faced and finally resolved. When we feel this self, the deepest healing occurs. Finding the pain also brings a man to his original self that must be located, understood, revalued, and nourished for his life to be renewed.

ƒ *Finding one's voice.* In telling his story, a man will eventually find his own voice; that is to say, he finds an ability to tell the truth, to "tell it like it is," and stand behind what he says without being compromised by shame or fear. This voice is particularly important for it reveals the truths buried in feelings, truths he often does not know himself until he expresses them. To be able to say the unthinkable, unacceptable, or forbidden is a tremendously liberating experience, for it restores the capacity for knowing and telling one's truth.

ƒ *Letting others know us.* When a man tells his story, he lets others in, lets them know who he really is. We are each essentially alone until we tell our stories in this way. When others actually understand and value our story, all of it, then we feel accepted and acknowledged in profoundly validating ways.

ƒ *Building and continuing relationships.* Because telling their stories fosters trust, closeness, and understanding between men, it grows their relationships. And, since the story goes on even as it is being told, and as men stay in relationships with one another for years, their stories weave a fabric of long-lasting friendship. When men do this with a collection of other men over the years, community forms as well.

ƒ *Becoming more fully human.* Our stories, as we have seen, are really universal. Personal stories are individual examples of the timeless story; single notes in a universal symphony. To the discerning eye, the events of our individual stories reveal the same symbols and tasks found in myths and fairy tales. Making these connections between personal and transpersonal themes then allows men to contact the deeper and universal meanings moving in their lives. These insights make us all more fully human, for we all share the themes of Everyman.

ƒ *Moving the Story Along.* In telling his story, a man discovers that the pen is still writing and the tale continues to unfold. In the mythic consciousness, fate, chance, and tragedy are found to be more than we thought, and recognizing their meaning connects us to the larger, unseen story, that has been guiding our journey all along. Feeling the power and urge of this universal story can activate and intensify its stages, energies, and possibilities. Such experiential insight actually stimulates and moves the story along and teaches a man how he can participate actively in this movement. He discovers decisions he didn't know existed, possibilities hidden in even the smallest moment, and new meanings that can serve his awakening even more. ❦

CHAPTER 6

The Value of Knowing

» Naive and unconscious movement through the second half of life permits little if any genuine growth of consciousness or self. Unawakened, we grow old with a certain emptiness and melancholy. More tragically, we grow old without knowing who we really are, what we might have been, what mysteries are hidden in our souls, and what the miracle of life — our own unique life — was actually all about. Consciously entering midlife, telling our story, letting the old identity die, facing the pain, surrendering to rebirth, and growing a new life allows us to know so much more about the story our life is telling. We enter a dimension unavailable to those who do not value this work of knowing.

Before midlife, our stories are childhood-centered, focused on how we were shaped, hurt, or influenced on the journey into adulthood. They are young and look backwards. The healing that occurs in going back into our personal past and facing the old pain is incalculable. At midlife and beyond, however, we become more reflective and start to understand our stories from a larger, older, and more detached perspective. There is so much to be learned from this looking back. First, we can better see the particular script and characters that organize our lives, how certain subplots keep repeating, what our larger life story may still want from us, and how we continue to get stuck. Looking back when our life's novel is two-thirds or more done also helps us take stock and clarify what we want most to happen in the time remaining. Third, looking back very often teaches that life had its own desires and plans for us, and that we were not (thankfully) really as in charge as we had assumed. We can then forgive ourselves, laugh at ourselves, accept ourselves in ways never before possible. Finally, we may ask ourselves about the spiritual threads and purposes woven into our stories. In his autobiography, Jung describes how he searched for the myth he was living; that is, the larger story that shaped his consciousness and destiny (Jung, 1964). This larger myth is, in its hidden content and purposes, ultimately spiritual. Learning its teaching can allow us to appreciate our life and our death in an entirely new way.

Jung also argued that we have an essentially ethical responsibility for the development of our personalities. Speaking of fantasies and dreams, Jung states, "It is equally a grave mistake to think that it is enough to gain some understanding of the images, and that knowledge of them can make them halt. Insight into them must be converted into an ethical obligation...The images of the unconscious place a great responsibility upon a man. Failure to understand them, or a shirking of ethical responsibility, deprives him of his wholeness and imposes a painful fragmentariness on his life." (Jung, 1961, p. 193). Phrased a little differently, we may assert that the psyche is a living process. It is like a garden. Untended, uncared for, it will not grow all it is capable of growing. Its soil may become hard and dry, its possibilities unrealized. Tender, thoughtful, and loving yet disciplined attention to this fertile ground, on the other hand, will stimulate and cultivate its unrealized growth. We are the gardener and we have so much to grow, so much fruit to taste, to become, and to share. This is the value of knowing. We are the stewards of this beautiful process and must take this responsibility seriously. We must do it consciously. ❊

PART 2

Birth of the Soul:
The Male Midlife Passage

"The nearer we approach to the middle of life, and the better we have succeeded in entrenching our personal attitude and social positions, the more it appears as if we had discovered the right course and the right ideals and principles of behavior. For this reason, we suppose them to be eternally valid, and make a virtue of unchangeably clinging to them... (but) we overlook the essential fact that the social goal is attained only at the cost of a diminution of personality...We see in this phase of life — between 35 and 40 — an important change in the human psyche is in preparation... Thoroughly unprepared, we take the step into the afternoon of life; worse still, we take this step with the false assumption that our truths and ideals will serve us hitherto. But we cannot live the afternoon of life according to the programme of life's morning; for what was great in the morning will be little at evening, and what in the morning was true will at evening have become a lie... Whoever carries over into the afternoon the law of the morning... must pay for it with damage to his soul..."
(Campbell, 1971, pp. 12-13)

"When the soul awakens at midlife and presents its gifts, life is permanently marked by the inclusion of them. Taken in, they become the hallmark of your life, the core of your uniqueness. Refused, they can haunt your days and undermine all your toiling."
(Stein, 1983, pp. 5-6)

CHAPTER 7

Introduction
to the Midlife Passage

» Midlife is a deeply important and often stressful phase of adult development. It typically occurs between the ages of forty and forty-five though it can begin in the late thirties or be delayed well into the fifties. Just like adolescence, it represents and involves a major reorganization of an individual's identity, personality, and value system. Its purpose seems to be that of dismantling old, increasingly rigid, and self-betraying personality structures so that new growth can appear in preparation for the profound and altogether different tasks of the second half of adult life.

The stress and instability experienced in this passage are precipitated by a mixture of social, physical, and internal psychological changes occurring in the forties that disrupt our lives in numerous and usually unexpected ways. None of us are prepared for this upheaval. The distress associated with these changes, however, is real, valid, unavoidable and, for the most part, healthy. Less healthy, however, is the way this passage tends to be denied, mislabeled, trivialized, somaticized, or pathologized in our society. And, without a map to guide and authenticate this process, men erroneously attribute their distress to one or more of the symptoms of the passage, such as marital or job problems, and miss its deeper nature and purpose.

To really understand and appreciate this turmoil, we have to try to get inside the experience and explore the feelings, urges, images, and conflicts involved. Gail Sheehy coined the term "midlife passage" for this transition (Sheehy, 1974). It is a more appropriate term for this experience than "crisis" because it suggests that we must take a journey across difficult and tumultuous psychological waters to reach another shore.

The midlife passage is also a process of inner-directed personality development. By its very nature, it is ancient, archetypal, and fundamental to the experience of adult life. Constituting the breakthrough of powerful instinctive drives for self-realization and spirituality, its goal is the birth of the soul and the radical restructuring of a man's life. At this time, the unfinished seeds of self and soul buried deeply in a man's psyche are powerfully and urgently activated. It is the unlived self, this no-longer-sleeping giant, this arising Neptune, that agitates a man in his core at midlife. A universal process of awakening, the midlife passage is powered by the themes common to myth, religion, and psychotherapy that speak of a journey of awakening and transformation, a journey whose impulse lies in the spiritual core of the personality itself. «

CHAPTER 8

Early symptoms
of the Midlife "Dis-ease"

» Let's get practical. How do you know when you are entering the midlife passage? What does it feel like initially, and what do its symptoms mean? Like puberty and adolescence, there is a cluster of inter-related symptoms welcoming us to this profound and deeply etched life stage. Understanding them will allow you to grasp the powerful forces beginning to take hold in your life. You may recognize only some of these experiences in the beginning; some you will recognize only in looking back; some of them will be more easily recognized by those around you.

ƒ *The Personal Realization of Death:* Perhaps most central to the midlife passage is the gut-level realization that life is finite and death will in fact be the ending of the story. This realization begins to creep into a man's consciousness as his fortieth birthday approaches and he senses that he is, after all, entering what Jung calls the "afternoon of life." So at the very same time as he seems to be reaching his peak professionally, a man also senses that this time of fulfillment is limited, for beyond it is aging and death. Death does not happen just to other people, it is not just an abstraction. It will happen to him. This first symptom is rarely conscious at first. More like the underground pressure on faults before the quake, it occurs without our clear awareness. Nonetheless, deep in our souls we sense things are changing.

ƒ *Time Urgency:* With the recognition that time is running out comes a vague but increasingly intense feeling of urgency. Urgency about what? As Levinson and Sheehy emphasize so poignantly, this urgency of time most commonly grips a man's deepest dreams and longings — whatever it was that he wanted most to do with his life. The often hidden (or forgotten) dream of success, accomplishment, recognition, self-expression, wealth, love, power, or contribution that was established sometime in childhood or adolescence now comes back as if to haunt him. A voice in the night, he suddenly awakens with a start — is it already too late? So he begins to measure time not in terms of how old he is now, but how much of this precious commodity is left with which to work. This symptom of time urgency is not easily verbalized early in the midlife passage. It is, rather, like a silent alarm that subtly shocks our attention and troubles our soul without telling us why.

✦ **Restlessness and Irritability:** Following naturally from this disquieting sense of time urgency is a restlessness to get on with whatever it was that one always wanted to do. Again a man may not initially know or remember what that original dream was, but still it begins to shake him like an insistent giant. Unaware of what calls them from inside, men at midlife are more likely to experience this symptom as a feeling of being trapped or strangled by their lives. Not surprisingly, this is a time when escape fantasies abound (e.g., sailing around the world, starting a new career, retiring in Mexico, finding a soul mate). It is also a time when anger and irritability erupt. Similarly, because the dream agitating in his depths may still be vague and unrecognized, a man may for a time pursue other enterprises with this displaced urgency, mistaking current tasks for the work of soul.

✦ **Boredom and Stagnation:** Losing interest in what they have already created, men at midlife begin to experience feelings of boredom and stagnation. What they have done is fine but now is increasingly experienced as repetitive and overly familiar. Doing the same thing for the rest of their lives now feels incredibly soul killing.

✦ **Loss of Creativity:** Hitching to boredom and stagnation is a feeling that creativity has been lost. Men feel as if they have lost their connection to the creative center of personality that had previously stirred their life quests and achievements. Creativity and self-expression feel stifled, smothered, stale, or dried up. Doing nothing new, stimulating, or meaningful, it feels like one's very soul is dying.

✦ **"Meaning of Life" Questions:** Dying inside and aware of death's inevitability, men at midlife begin to find themselves asking questions about life's ultimate purpose and meaning. "Why am I here?" "Is this all there is?" goes one song's refrain. What does it mean that we grow old and die? Why is there so much suffering in the world? Why do we all live like this? Fame and fortune, we soberly realize, will not solve these problems. Feeling disconnected from deep and inborn sources of motivation, feeling disoriented in our life's journey and now unsure what material success really means, men at midlife begin a search for their own answers, digging deep in the soil of self to find them.

ſ **Bodily Preoccupation:** As a result of his unconscious preoccupation with death, concerns about the body, aging, illness, mortality, and obituaries increase. Sometimes a bit of hypochondriasis may arise. Aches and pains could be something more. Men begin to feel older. Physical work and exercise take more of a toll. Men experience narcissistic wounds, too, as their muscle tone, appearance and strength begin to wane. Some men at midlife throw themselves into exercise regimes, hoping to forestall age forever. Preoccupation with the youthful bodies of women accompanies this denial of aging.

ſ **Depression, Anxiety, Explosions, and Collapse:** Some men begin to feel depression, despair, mood swings, and even feelings of hopelessness during this period. Often they can't locate any specific cause. Anxiety, vague but sometimes turning to panic, can also be stirred without apparent reason. Explosions of rage or grief may be triggered by the smallest problem, or all problems may seem huge. Everything is wrong! These are all symptoms telling men that something deep and important is changing in the psyche. When there are hidden pre-existing personality problems and vulnerabilities, the passage into midlife can trigger even more serious forms of emotional breakdown or disorganization. Midlife is a time when a man cannot stand what he has built. And something is leaving inside, something he does not yet understand. These realizations can make him feel crazy, hopeless, furious, or desperate, and the very inexplicability of these moods adds to his confusion.

ſ **Relationship Upheaval:** Not surprisingly, all of this inner turmoil leads to problems on the home front. Men may begin to feel an inner and unexpectedly strong urge to break free from their marital and family relationships, obligations, and duties. Matrimonial bonds may feel more like chains and years of unacknowledged disagreements; resentments and irritations can intensify into eruptive conflict, affairs, sexual promiscuity, or abrupt decisions to divorce and marry that younger secretary or "soulmate." As we will see, some of this acting out is really done to avoid the underlying issues of midlife and some is done to bring important marital problems out into the open. Whatever the case, fueled by the emotional storms rising in the male psyche, this relationship upheaval can be disorienting and upsetting.

ſ **Secrecy and Withdrawal:** Needing to change without even knowing how, the midlife male often becomes increasingly introverted, self-absorbed, and secretive. A man's hunger for a different or renewed self meets with his own profound self-doubts: Can I change? Will my family accept the changes I need to make? How can I get out of the financial and vocational obligations that now imprison me? What if what I need turns out to be stupid or foolish — or worse, fails? A man may also fear criticism from family members who may indeed feel threatened by the emerging stranger they see. So these inner changes, these new and desperate longings, are often denied in the beginning. This denial, however, may simply confuse, alienate, or frighten spouse and family even further. Just when a man most needs the support and love of his wife, she sees that her once-strong man has apparently become irritable, indecisive, and distant. This often causes her to back away, both physically and emotionally, which exacerbates the whole problem. Both husband and wife know something big is changing, but no one is talking about it directly and openly.

✔ **Driven or Impulsive Work Behavior:** Feeling an incessant sense of urgency in the face of the inescapable timetable of aging and death, fearing that their dreams are turning to dust, men at midlife sometimes displace this internal pressure. They do this by pushing themselves to work ever harder to meet their grandiose aspirations, or by starting new and even more unrealistic goals. This grandiosity is a symptom temporarily substituting for the underlying dream, a defense against grieving its failure. Workaholism, career burnout, stress-related illness, and risky job decisions can result from this renewed and even more self-abusing male heroism. Punctuating this risk, Sheehy cites the powerful example of F. Scott Fitzgerald, who at thirty-nine wrote, "I began to realize that for two years in my life I had been drawing on resources that I did not possess, that I had been mortgaging myself physically and spiritually up to the hilt." She adds, "Five years later he was dead." (Sheehy, 1974, p. 256)

✔ **Unusual Behaviors:** Sudden changes in clothing, hairstyle, exercise, sleep, obsessive new interests, and erratic decision making may similarly reflect the deep changes forming in the male psyche as midlife advances. Desperate for renewal yet unwilling to face the reality of aging and death, these behaviors are again symptomatic of denial and displacement, representing last minute "end runs" around this ominous undercurrent of change. ❦

CHAPTER 9

Causes of the Midlife Passage

⧉ When closely examined, the symptoms of distress described in the previous chapter are found to be surface reflections of a major life transition. Innumerable events and processes, small and large, conspire around this time to upset whatever neat world order a man has achieved in his life. Subterranean archetypes, like hidden tectonic plates, now shift somewhere deep in the underground of a man's psyche, a shift so profound that it will forever affect the course, meaning, and search of his life. Moving into the midlife years, most men are utterly unprepared for the sudden, painful, and life-disrupting changes constellated in their lives and psyches. With an emotional intensity forgotten since adolescence, there arises an intensity of personal unhappiness and an aching for personal freedom that can clash with all the life commitments and compromises previously made in the name of ambition, success, marriage, family, and security. Three main age-related categories of change can be readily distinguished during this crisis: changes in the external world, changes in our bodies, and changes in the internal world.

Changes in the External World

ƒ *Career Disillusionment:* A man's career summit, whatever lofty peak his masculine ambition had for years called him to climb, seems to be increasingly distant or unattainable as he moves into the middle years. The idealized goal a man found in his own soul, that heroic myth of deep personal significance and energy formed in the wondrous, unlimited, and grandiose days of adolescence, encounters a cold reality at this time; there are only so many top spots and the chances of getting there are frankly limited or beyond reach. Because identity and self-esteem are so closely tied to occupation for men, when career falters or fails, a deeply painful and unsettling personal crisis may develop. A man's underlying fears of failure, unworthiness, or meaninglessness may produce an urgent "all or nothing" reaction, a feeling that he will either fulfill his dream completely or fail abysmally.

ƒ *Relationship Disillusionment:* In previous generations, midlife was a time when a man's wife finished her domestic duties of child and home and moved outward, often going to work to pursue her own career interests or contribute to family finances. When this occurred, marital roles would change dramatically, requiring both a redistribution of responsibilities and an acceptance of new rules and identities. For many men, the increased independence, assertiveness, and reduced availability of their wives threatened long standing and comfortable patterns of practical and emotional dependency. When she is no longer "there" for him, a man may feel an emotional loss or deprivation he cannot quite define or is forbidden by the rules of manhood to voice. This kind of "traditional" marital restructuring still occurs at midlife, though it may be obscured by today's dual career family lives. Even when both partners work outside the home, women in the early years still tend more frequently to fulfill the nurturing roles in the family and postpone or sacrifice career dreams for family needs. As the children leave home and a woman finally begins to look inward at her own wants, long suppressed desires for freedom and independence often emerge. She no longer wants a hero.

Another common experience for couples in midlife is the normal disappointment and disillusionment of marriage itself. Each finds the other to be not-so-perfect, not always as desirable, cooperative, or attractive as before. Now there are power struggles and communication problems. Kids, chores, dual careers, and budget demands constantly limit relationship time. In short, romance is just not what it used to be. The prince and princess are gone. For some, disillusionment may shake the marriage to its foundations in midlife as the hidden but cumulative strains in the relationship crack the bond or illusion of marital harmony. One spouse or the other may for a time leave the marital boundary for the excitement of an affair or the freedom of separation.

For couples who stay together (and most do) and really work on these problems, the opportunity for real personal and relational growth is tremendous. Love, friendship, and intimacy can return to the marriage and be the reward for struggling through these midlife years. For people who stay married but do not work on their relationship problems, the cost may be a sterile and empty facade of marriage, a soul-less, unspoken, and resentment-ridden contract of "quiet desperation" that simply expresses all the same problems in repeating symptoms.

ƒ *Changing Relationships with Children*: Around the time of midlife, a man's children are frequently moving into adolescence and separating emotionally and physically from home and parents. This emancipation results in a loss of the active roles of parenting. For men, this is often a time when they begin to feel a need for greater intimacy with their children. Having put career first, they missed much along the way.

For a growing minority of midlife men, another dilemma presents itself: starting new families. Some men marry for the first time at midlife, others remarry and share their new wife's desire to create a new family. This is a complex undertaking, for a man knows he will be in his sixties when his children become teenagers. Will he have the energy and stamina to keep up? Will he resent the loss of freedom through his mature years? With tenderness and sensitivity that is beautiful to behold, many midlife men, now free from the ambitions of youth, embrace childrearing with great success. Other men with children remarry women with children, blending the "broken" parts of previous units into new stepfamilies. However he proceeds, a man's developmental sequence and his life script are both forever changed with the introduction of children at midlife.

ƒ *Aging and Dying Parents:* Also disorienting and difficult at this time are the aging or loss of a man's parents. Roles change as his parents become increasingly dependent. Gradually, sometimes suddenly, a man becomes the parent and caretaker, especially with the arrival of physical incapacitation or financial problems. Then, with the death of a parent, especially the death of the last remaining parent, a man senses that he has moved into another generation. This shift often feels disorienting at first and indeed it is, for his identity has changed without his consent. No longer the child, he is the aging parent, the older generation and soon even the grandparent. There is no denying the march of time, the reality of death, and the necessity of new responsibilities. He is different. His life is different.

ƒ *Changing Gender Needs:* As suggested earlier, men in midlife often find themselves becoming less ambitious and aggressive, seeking instead to replace the dream of unlimited career success with opportunities for nurturing, mentoring, and friendship. Traditionally masculine strivings often become tiresome now. Watching her husband's ambitious masculine side giving way to an increased capacity for tenderness and emotionality may be a wonderful experience for women. It can also be a disconcerting experience for the woman who has come to depend on him for identity and strength. This softening may be disconcerting for other men as well, men who are frightened by male emotion and view it as weakness or failure. An opposite pattern may occur for women who find themselves moved increasingly by a surprising new sense of ambition, independence, and accomplishment. They begin to integrate the unfinished masculine energies of their personalities.

Changes In Our Bodies

All through childhood, adolescence, and young adulthood, men expect their bodies to grow stronger, and better, and to carry them in spite of the abuses imposed by injurious sports, long work hours, or the excesses of eating, drinking, smoking, or addiction. By midlife, this is no longer the case.

ſ *Undeniable Bodily Changes:* With the coming of midlife, men begin to notice physical changes in their bodies. They have gray or thinning hair. It's harder to lose weight and stay trim and fit. Some may need glasses for the first time or require new lenses. Hearing may be less acute. Strength and vitality are not as diminished as in old age, but for the first time in our lives we notice that time itself is affecting our bodies whether we like it or not.

Women's bodies are also changing, and men no longer can expect their spouses to meet this culture's youth-oriented standards of beauty and fitness. A man finds himself married to a woman he would have ignored in the past, a middle aged woman far different than the sexy image fostered in the Summer of his life. Women see this change too. Neither gender can find pride in bodies that no longer match the ideal — yet another midlife loss.

ſ *Sexual Changes:* Sexual function also changes by midlife. It is well know that men reach their biologically determined sexual peak around the age of eighteen or twenty. By the mid to late forties, a man may lose his capacity for multiple orgasms in a single love making session. Occasional impotence may occur especially under conditions of fatigue, inebriation, stress, preoccupation, or marital conflict. Focused so much on performance, men struggle with this perceived failure of their anatomy, as if erections were athletic competitions and measures of manhood. Some men even become sexually disinterested to hide their unresolved fears of failure. Hidden and long unmanaged intimacy problems also cause men to cease sexual activity with their mates, for sexuality now involves far more emotional contact and relating. Men with such conflicts use aging as an excuse to rationalize their apparent lack of sexual arousal, arguing that the instinctual drive has simply faded.

Changes In The Internal World

At midlife, a man also finds his interior world shifting in unsettling and unfamiliar ways. Motivation, emotion, desire, and self now betray him from the inside and he can't seem to be what he used to be, what he wanted to be, or what he has been accustomed to being. Conventional social wisdom likens midlife to a "second adolescence" and indeed it can feel like one.

✒ *Disillusionment:* We have already seen the kinds of disillusionment a man experiences in response to specific occupational, familial, and physical disappointments. But the disillusionment referred to here goes even deeper; it is a loss of hope so deep that it can steal motivation, identity, and desire. This disillusionment is, as Levinson and Sheehy documented, intimately related to the loss of a man's life dream, for whatever his dream had been, by midlife it is typically deflated, unrealistic, or hopelessly flawed.

During late Spring and early Summer, a young man's dream usually undergoes some degree of sublimation and socialization; that is, it is externalized into specific desirable outer goals or accomplishments. Society and fantasy shape it into a reality he can see and pursue directly. But because it is actually symbolic of an inner potential, achieving the outer goal will paradoxically produce disappointment and disillusionment. Until a man can recognize and grieve this mistake, which is one of the key tasks of midlife, he will be unable to resume his soul's journey.

The dream-based disillusionment a man faces in midlife can take four principal forms. The first type arrives when a man realizes that his reality goal is beyond reach. He will never become a Fortune 500 CEO, professional baseball player, or millionaire. The second type occurs when his goal is in fact achieved, but found to be disappointing; it does not match his fantasy. Perhaps he does publish a book or head a company, but it never yields the success and happiness he imagined. In the third form, he reaches the dreamed of goal, attains considerable success, acclaim, or wealth — and then what? How does he go on after bright lights of fame dim and the externalized mission is seemingly complete? The last and perhaps most painful scenario happens when a man succeeds at a dream that is not truly his own. He buys into someone else's dream, usually that of a parent, boss, or mentor, and becomes what they want instead of pursuing his own path. When a man loses his dream, he experiences despair of the soul. He has been chasing a mirage. He has given so many years of his life, put aside so many other things, even betrayed his love and his family for this urgent goal, only to find it tarnished. It did not eradicate his great wound, actualize his lost self, or present the world with his soul's gift. A deep, confusing, and fathomless sorrow seeps everywhere into his life.

✒ *The Despair of Unconquerable Realities:* A man's sorrow grows deeper as he recognizes how little control he actually has over those forces that will eventually defeat all his efforts and take his life. The recognition of aging, death, poverty, insoluble world problems, and the perennial reality of suffering itself can bring a man into yet another deep cavern of despair. Heretofore, the dream of unlimited success and accomplishment protected him from these harsh realities. In fact, the dream served as the symbolic equivalent and guarantee of immortality and self-worth. In midlife, with the unconquerable everywhere, even inside, a man begins to ask formidable questions about life's purpose and meaning. And he should ask these questions, for throughout the ages, deep and honest suffering has always preceded the genuinely great works men have produced — works of soul. Personal and archetypal answers to these ultimate and painful questions are eventually found in the depths of a man's psyche when he works deeply enough with the grieving process. He can, after this "dark night" is done, crown his life with the work of his soul. The achievement of this pain is, in fact, the dream reborn. It helps locate the gift he originally intuited for his life, and the legacy he will bequeath his children and the world.

The realization that stimulates this search, jolting a man into a despair deep enough to make him feel he is losing his grasp on life, is a single but multifaceted awareness of death's ultimate victory. Though actual death may seem far away, its sobering presence now presses against his heart (albeit unconsciously at first). The midlife symptoms described earlier can all be seen as emotional signs symbolizing a realization of impending death. It is this core realization, this awareness that his plan won't work, that no fairy tale life will protect him from losing everything, that no amount of hard work or luck will save him from the ultimate failure of his life dream, that turns him inside out. It is not surprising, therefore, that men should go through all the stages Kubler-Ross described in dying people: shock, denial, anger, bargaining, depression, and acceptance. These stages are just another way to describe his loss of a "forever" mentality. The message of midlife is that nothing lasts forever. You can't get out alive. Whatever you do, it won't work because it won't last. The fairy tale is only pretend and the hero must die. No wonder midlife produces so much upheaval.

ƒ The Wounds of the Past: The disillusionment and despair a man encounters in midlife then takes him into the buried wounds of his past. The great wound, long hidden behind great goals, now becomes exposed. This opening occurs not only because the compensatory defenses organized by his dream (i.e., his fantasies of ambition, conquest, invincibility) unravel, but also because the original circumstances of the wound have, surreptitiously and unconsciously, been recreated in his life and now demand to be re-experienced.

As midlife approaches, men typically find themselves back where they started: in relationships that increasingly repeat their early parental conflicts and woundings, and in careers or life situations that don't make up for the early feelings of shame and inferiority buried inside. If a man will look inward (often with the help of a therapist), he will see that the core and cyclical problems in his marriage or intimate relationships are recreations. It is axiomatic in psychology and psychotherapy: we recreate our historical personality wounds and related interpersonal problems in our adult lives. This "repetition compulsion," as Freud called it, arises because these problems are unfinished and because they are unconsciously familiar to us. It has been stored inside for all this time. Childhood themes and issues now seep everywhere into his life. No matter how mature he may picture himself, a man at midlife is still trying to heal the pain of these early relationship hurts and get the love missed in those early years. To do so, he has been attracted to people with the same traits as his parents, or he evokes those traits from his loved ones to replicate past woundings. Either way, the pain returns usually disguised as marital problems.

We cannot truly become individuals until we can re-experience the early losses or wounds directly instead of trying to get other people to make up for them. Getting someone to love us in order to heal the original wounds doesn't work. Such efforts merely distract, numb, or plaster over the hurt for a while. At midlife, the plaster cracks. The adolescent fantasy of true and unconditional love was actually a defense against the old pain, and as such, it is a fertile ground for addictive relationships or endless conflict. Similarly, feelings of inferiority and shame are not healed by narcissistic postures of superiority or by great accomplishments. Old pain must be healed by directly being experienced as it really was. Then it is completed. Happiness, men eventually learn, does not come from the other person or the big achievement, it comes from completing the pain and then experiencing one's intrinsic capacity to feel, love, and live his own life. We probe this process more deeply in the next chapter.

⨍ **Understanding the Inner Feminine:** As suggested in the Story of Everyman, midlife is also the time for a man to understand his own inner feminine and her many faces. Each represents a basic feminine image and potential. A man typically becomes conscious of these inner figures through the real women in his life, who serve as mirrors.

Typically, the themes and images of a man's inner feminine fall into a handful of basic categories. First, he needs to experience that woman who can see, reflect, validate, encourage, and love his own authentic self and its natural gift. Usually she carries the same gift, and her love for his gift feels like the love he always needed from his mother. This woman often comes to a man at midlife when he most needs his unlived self to be awakened. At long last, here is the warm, nurturing soulmate he has always wanted, the one who sees and believes in him.

A second image is the wounded woman, sometimes pictured more as a girl in pain or sorrow. Like the bewitched princess in *The Crystal Ball* she represents the wounded nature of his own femininity. A man under her spell will be drawn to care for women with hidden wounds, often for many years. In time, she becomes a deep drain on his psyche.

The third image ignites a man's capacity for erotic sexuality, exciting his physical libido, dulled by work and marital routine. A major presence in the Spring and early Summer of his life, this image draws heavily on themes of lust, risk, wildness, fantasy, and visual stimulation.

A fourth inner woman is the limiting, controlling, dominating, manipulating, or rejecting one. This is a painful image reflecting the negative side of his mother. She may seem demonic to a man and evoke a deep fear of her rage and soul possession. Sometimes by midlife a man has come to project this image onto his wife, creating distance, resentment, and misunderstanding. She becomes his jailor.

A fifth theme is the caretaker or responsible woman, the internalization of that side of his mother. With this woman, a man may become too passive and depend on her to do too much of the shared work of their life (e.g., chores, child care, etc.).

A sixth image is that of friend. Up until midlife, many men find it easier to make female friends than male friends. Afraid of masculine competition and belittlement, they seek the more comfortable intimacy women often have naturally.

The last feminine image that commonly arises, although unconsciously, is that of the archetypal mother. This is the deep capacity to love and hold the world symbolized by the Great Mother.

Each feminine image has a gift or task for a man at midlife. The soulmate helps him to see and revalue his own gift, and to love that original self trying again to take shape within him. The wounded woman eventually teaches him that he must release the endless burden of protection and permit the pain she symbolizes to be felt directly, for this is both his own inner wounded feminine and whatever pain is carried by the actual woman he has chosen. The burden will not be lifted until he and his partner can separately feel their own pain. The erotic image evokes a man's instinctual sexuality, providing a recharging of his physical energy and excitement at this otherwise deadened time in his life. The jailor forces a man to establish and defend his boundaries and tolerate conflict. The caretaker challenges him to move from boyhood dependency to manhood; that is, to take more direct responsibility for his family and its problems. The friend teaches him about sensitive nonsexual intimacy, and sharing. He will need these skills to develop real male friendships, as well as a genuine and lasting friendship with his wife. Finally, the maternal image teaches a man to be a "male mother," to love, with the feminine energy, tenderly, unconditionally, deeply.

Typically, one or more of these images is projected onto his spouse at various times in their relationship. This mixture of images explains why a man can feel so many different emotions with his wife, and view her in so many contradictory ways: as his soul mate, his lusty lover, his burden, his jailer, his caretaker, and his friend. This also explains the lure of midlife infatuations and affairs. Only when he has withdrawn all these projections can he see his real woman and his own capacity for love.

ſ *The Search for the True Self:* The quest for what matters most in life is often a search for the true self and its transformative core. Within each of us there exists a conflict between the true self, what we most deeply and potentially are, and a false overlay of prescribed values and hidden self-betrayal. This false self can gradually and progressively rob our life of its natural vitality, direction, creativity, and joy. Sometime in the midlife passage we begin to hunger for this deeper, more personal, and truer self. We feel an urgency to live more authentically, which means according to the real and essential nature of this self. If we can do so, our life may begin to take on renewed meaning, inspiration, and excitement, and when this occurs we are drawn to begin a journey of our own unfolding and realization. This internal pressure to live one's own life is one of the most powerful forces operating in the midlife transition.

ſ *The Blessing of a Mentor:* Often this search for the true self brings men in search of a mentor. Hillman, drawing on Levinson's concept of mentor, explains, "The longing for a father is really the longing for a mentor." (Hillman, 1990). The father's role, he clarifies, is to provide materially for the family. It is not realistically possible for him to recognize and bless each child's uniqueness and value. Usually, because of differences in personality, the demands of providing, and his own personal problems, the father simply cannot perform this blessing. He lacks the time and aptitude to really see into his son and affirm his soul's true nature. Yet each son longs for this blessing and affirmation, and repeatedly seeks it from his father to feel confident and empowered. But this seeking is futile and disappointing. As we saw in *The Three Languages* (the story where the father sends away his son, and the youth meets all his challenges and eventually becomes Pope) fathers inevitably fail their sons. The son's hunger then drives his journey in search of a mentor.

In order to reclaim his true self and the gift it bears, a man begins an unconscious search for older man who has realized the same kind of gift.

In this search, he is actually looking for someone who can mirror and validate something inside himself that he only dimly intuits; the dormant potential of his true self. In this relationship, the younger man receives a profoundly important blessing of his own nature, arousing the hope that he, too, can develop and express his unique form of this gift.

In the end, as Levinson points out, the mentor often disappoints the younger man, a wounding experience based on the mentor's own insecurities, limits, or narcissism. He may fear the younger man exceeding his own achievements or perceive him going off in directions he cannot understand or approve. The mentor eventually imposes his own life as the template for the apprentice. In effect, it is the mentor's life that he wants the younger man to live. But the younger man must be true to his own destiny. In blessing him, the mentor facilitates the midlife birth of the younger man's true self. But the young man must become his own king.

ƒ The Need to Mentor Others: As a man rediscovers, reclaims, heals, and restores his original self with the support of a mentor, he intuitively comes to understand that role and is drawn to provide the mentoring function for other young men. Playing the part of the spiritual father or wisdom figure, an older man then takes his turn in the initiating and blessing of those in whom he sees parts of himself and the struggles he had. Mentoring is itself a very satisfying and fulfilling experience that nurtures both men and reaffirms an older man's value and commitments. In some respects, the mentoring need derives from the gender shift that occurs at midlife. Men, tired of questing, competing, and conquering, find themselves nourished instead by more culturally feminine roles. Expressing the warmth, affiliation, and caring he has heretofore projected into women, a man grows his own other half, and it is this nourishing capacity that allows him to mentor others.

ƒ The Awakening of the Soul: The discovery of the original self and its revitalizing energies now takes a man deeply into the center of his personality — the soul. The awakening and opening of the soul represents a new development for a man, a realization that within his center is a portal to the infinite, through which symbols, images, understandings, and divine consciousness, itself, can emerge to guide and direct his life. As we saw in *The Three Languages*, and *The Man Who Didn't Believe* learning to listen to the whisper of soul and restore its sacred vision, become deeply religious tasks at midlife that call a man to learn new skills and take new risks. The calling of one's soul is more important now than any kind of fame or achievement. ❧

CHAPTER 10

The Journey of Individuation

≫ In the midlife passage we increasingly dismantle and disorganize that which is false in our self in order to rediscover and reclaim a deeper and more authentic sense of who we are. This searching process activates the deeper inborn potentials of the true self and culminates at long last in a gradual reorganization of our energy, direction, and values. There are three stages in the midlife passage. During the journey through these stages, a man's life is typically marked by alternating periods of exhilaration and despair, and numerous wrong turns and false starts, as he contacts, loses, and recontacts his own transformative center. The three core stages of this passage are:

1. The Gradual Death and Dismantling of the False Self: As described earlier, the man entering midlife typically finds himself feeling trapped in a narrow, confining, inflexible, and compromised identity and life situation, or one that is being undone by unwelcome and unexpected life changes such as divorce, career problems, or illness. In either case, he learns that he is not really living the life he wants and the script he has been living feels increasingly empty.

If he looks deeply and honestly within, a man will see that he gave up, betrayed, or repressed important parts of his personality during childhood and early adult development in order to adjust or succeed socially, financially, or occupationally in the world. As a result of these concessions, he lost something of who and what he really is. At midlife, these compromises come back to haunt him.

To reverse this betrayal, the false self and false script have to be gradually dismantled in order for the true self to be intuited, rediscovered, and finally integrated into life. Though it seems simple enough, this recovery process frequently takes three years to five years to complete. When this dismantling occurs suddenly or impulsively, or when it is precipitated through unanticipated life crises, a man can feel overwhelmed and frightened. It is not easy to let go of commitments so tied in with his security and self-esteem; yet forcing himself to continue in the soul-emptying repetitive tasks of his old life feels even worse. A man at this crossroads has no choice. Like an oak sapling pushing up through the barren cement of drudgery and conformity, a man's urgency for the life of his own soul will fracture whatever is left after the changing events of his outer life do their work. It takes strength, courage, wisdom, and sometimes external guidance to survive and thrive during this incredible time.

2. Healing the Wounded Self: In the pain, suffering, and despair that opens in this midlife unraveling, a man can recontact his original wounded self. His emotional pain gradually brings a man back to his original pain, and to the Great Wounds that caused it. This pain also locates true self, that is, the person he really is, what he really feels, his central truths, values, and nature. A man must renew his relationship to this genuine center of personality in order for it to be restored. It takes time, patience, guidance, and support to recontact this living center of the psyche, and in so doing, learn to nourish its creative, self-motivating, and spontaneous nature. Then in time, it will change and evolve him.

Not surprisingly, finding the wounded self requires a backward search in time. We have to explore personal and family memories to locate and understand what caused us to compromise, betray, or surrender our true feelings, nature, and course.

A child's need for security, safety, and approval from parents is so powerful that most children are willing to sacrifice any part of themselves rather than risk these primary bonds. Recovering these lost parts is one of the central tasks of the midlife passage, for without finding the true self, there is no renewal. And when the wounds of childhood are deep enough, we may need psychotherapeutic help to face and resolve them before genuine personality growth can occur again.

The injuries we sustain in childhood range from times of disinterest or neglect to more frank rejection, abandonment, and abuse. Whether physical or psychological, these wounds have left emotional scars that will not heal until they have resurfaced. The struggles of midlife force them to the surface. They are first experienced as work, relationship, or other emotional problems. In time, we can discover these problems are re-enactments of the original parental woundings.

A man may go through several stages of understanding these wounds. In early childhood, his parents or older siblings were idealized. No matter what they did, they were right. When bad things happened, he saw himself as wrong and searched for ways to recover their love and attention. When he first begins to look back, a man often has to confront this defense of parental idealization, and realize how it serves to hide his pain. Feeling this pain may cause him to view his parents more negatively. He sees them as unfeeling, cruel, or unloving. Sometimes he sees them as monsters and hates them.

In the process of midlife healing, the painful wounds and perceptions associated with childhood trauma have to be re-experienced and confronted. A man must come face to face with the injurious parent images he has internalized and face the pain of his parents' unbearable behavior. Recovering and feeling these buried emotions is itself the healing process. A man must open compassionately to the sorrow only he can truly understand, and grieve. In doing so, the wounded self is finally heard, held, accepted, and loved. Slowly it heals.

With time and age, a man slowly recognizes that his parents, too, were injured and, if possible, he begins to empathically understand their inner pain. He can see his parents as ordinary human beings limited by their own history of wounding. The final healing arrives when a man can understand, forgive, love, and accept these people — not as his parents, but just as they are.

Midlife is the stage where a man must face and heal his soul's injuries. As we saw in the first folk tale, *The Crystal Ball*, he must resist acting out his rage (symbolized by the wild bull), confront the defensive behaviors by which he has heretofore escaped his hurt (the eagle and the whale), hold this burning pain and open to its hidden grief, and then recover the crystal ball of self. Here, too, is the descent pictured in *The Three Languages*, where a man must face the howling and tormented pain (the wild dogs in the dungeon) within his hardened masculine persona, the pain of old injuries that now blocks access to the underlying gifts of self and soul.

3. Renewal: After the pain, deep self-absorption, and internal healing of the last phase, a reactivated self-structure emerges. Here is the crystal ball of soul ready to release all its teaching images. The injured self heals and comes back to life. It awakens with a new yet natural energy. After such a deep and personally transforming evolution, a man begins to reshape his life in accordance with the values, goals, and strivings discovered from within. This rebuilding process, too, is a slow one. It must be trusted. When it is nourished with patience and love, however, changes emerge steadily, continuously, wondrously, in their own timing. Requiring neither intentional effort nor specific plan, a new life flowers.

The journey of individuation has begun. From here on, a man finds himself moved by the unique vision and energy of his true self. He increasingly expresses his soul in his work, his family, and his world. We will see later how this recovery of self and soul affects his masculinity and his relationship to the sacred. ❦

CHAPTER 11

The Journey's Mythic Nature

Every man in the Midlife Transition starts to see that the hero of the fairy tale does not enter a life of eternal, simple happiness. He sees, indeed, that the hero is a youth who must die or be transformed as early adulthood comes to an end. A man must begin to grieve and accept the symbolic death of the youthful hero within himself. (Levinson, 1978, p. 215)

≫ As we saw earlier, the process of self-transformation involved in midlife passages is an ancient one and has been symbolized for centuries in myth, legend, dreams, religion, and fairy tales. These spontaneous productions of the collective unconscious symbolize the quest for wholeness and renewal that has been called *The Hero's Journey* by Joseph Campbell and *The Great Story* by Jean Houston.

In their endless variations, these stories tell us that life is a transformative journey, a quest for healing, wisdom, personal growth, and ultimately for spiritual realization. Symbolically, this journey pivots around the central theme of death and rebirth, that is, the death of the false self, and in its place, the birth of the original self and its essentially divine nature. This transformative process is not really under our control for if we could dominate it, we would simply maintain the egocentric goals and rules already established for our lives. We would bend this process to fit our goals rather than surrender to its purposes. Midlife is that time when this great and ancient transformative journey ignites. The specific events of midlife are not chosen; rather the whole process seems to erupt within our psyches and then in our lives. In so doing, it asks each man to search honestly for his own truth and personhood.

To further illuminate this universal journey of midlife, an example of a midlife fairy tale is in order and I am indebted to Allan Chinen for this one. *Fortune and the Woodcutter*, a tale from Asia Minor, was adapted from *In The Ever After* (Chinen, 1989, pp. 9-11) It is a story that symbolizes many of the problems, mysteries, and magic embedded in the midlife passage. Like all myths, it is a storehouse of wisdom and information. But like an iceberg, it is mostly beneath the surface of consciousness, and so we will again seek access to its underlying form and meaning.

Read this story with your imagination and see if you can sense what it might be saying to you individually. Once again, open your inner vision to the imaginal world of story telling and picture the scenes created just as your medieval ancestors did listening to traveling medieval troubadours, or your ancient ancestors did around the fire hearing tales of great shamanic journeys. Are you ready? We are now leaving this twentieth century frenzy and returning to a mythic world of mysterious forests, magicians, treasures, and surprise endings.

Fortune and the Woodcutter

Once upon a time, there lived an old woodcutter with his wife. He labored each day in the forest, from dawn to dusk, cutting wood to sell in the village. But no matter how hard he struggled, he could not succeed in life, for what he earned in the day, he and his family ate up at night.

Now soon two sons grew to brighten his hearth, and they worked by his side. Father and sons cut three times the wood and earned three times the money, but they also ate three times the food, and so the woodcutter was no better off than before. Finally, after many years, the young men left home to seek their own fortunes.

So after twenty years, the old man finally had had enough. "I've worked for Fortune all my life," he exclaimed to his wife, "and she has given us little enough for it. From now on," the old man swore, "if Fortune wants to give us anything, she will have to come looking for me." And the woodcutter vowed to work no more.

"Good Heavens," his wife cried out, "if you don't work, we won't eat! And what are you saying? Fortune visits great sultans, not poor folks like us!" But no matter how much she tried to persuade him — and she reasoned, cried, and yelled — the old woodcutter refused to work. In fact, he decided to stay in bed!

Discussion: Putting the Old Self to Bed

As we have seen, myths and fairy tales are very much like dreams, and can be interpreted similarly, that is, as symbolic mirror of the inner workings, complexes, and conflicts of the personality. The psyche itself is purposeful, and in stories like this, sequences of events are not just accidental, but reflective of the psyche's deeper intentionality and wisdom. The main character in this story may be seen as our conscious self, with all our customary attitudes of consciousness. The other characters in the story represent split off and unconscious parts of our personality; that is, other attitudes, subpersonalities, and resources in the psyche.

We know that this story is about midlife because the woodcutter's sons have grown to adulthood and left home. Under normal circumstances this would place him near the age of forty. We also see that his behavior for the first twenty years of his adult life was typical of the pre-midlife male, characterized by the heroic striving for success and material prosperity. Just like the midlife male, the woodcutter was unable to achieve what he wanted, and he is now beginning to burn out. His life will not change unless he gives up this traditionally masculine, task-oriented mode of life so that something new can come from the psyche. So our woodcutter goes to bed, an act symbolizing the surrender of this compulsivity. All effort ceases.

In his analysis of this story, Chinen emphasizes the woodcutter's poverty and views it as a symbol of the deprivation, losses, and depression associated with aging. I like and agree with this interpretation and would extend it to the emotional poverty of the exhausted heroic ego at midlife. It is the emptiness inside the driven "Type A" personality, the "workaholic" male, and it cannot be filled by more material things or healed with more effort. The only real alternative is to let go, to surrender, and collapse. The woodcutter seems to know that this is just what he must do, and his decisiveness in going to bed despite his wife's laments sets the stage for what will come next. As Chinen points out, this inactivity "clears the way for something new to emerge in his life." (Chinen, 1989, p.13). Stated slightly differently, it prepares room for the deep psyche to respond, space that would not have been there if he continued with his driven personality.

The distress of the woodcutter's wife represents practical concerns of other family members triggered when the midlife male begins to talk of quitting his job, running away, giving up, or collapsing. This talk scares them. It also symbolizes a man's own anxiety, that voice of nagging self-doubt within. When he first starts thinking about making real changes in his life, a man may hear this voice of doubt and accusation, the one that says giving up the heroic model of masculinity will be a terrible mistake. Compulsive work has, after all, supported him and his family all these years. Is he crazy?

The Stranger

As you will recall, we left our story with the old woodcutter steadfastly lounging in bed. He was a real midlife dropout and his wife had given up on ever rousing him.

Now later that same day, a stranger came knocking at the door and asked if he could borrow the old man's mules for a few hours. The stranger explained that he had some work to do in the forest, and that he noticed the woodcutter was not using his mules. The old man agreed. He simply asked the stranger to feed and water the two animals.

The stranger then took the mules deep into the forest. This was no ordinary man, but a magician, and through his arts, he had learned where a great treasure lay. So he went to the spot and dug up heaps of gold and jewels, loading the booty on the two mules.

Now just as the magician prepared to leave, gloating over his new wealth, soldiers came marching down the road. The magician became frightened. He knew that if the soldiers found him with the treasure, they would ask questions. His sorcery would be discovered and he would be condemned to death. So the stranger fled into the forest and was never seen or heard from again.

Discussion: "The Return of Magic"

As anticipated above, when the heroic compulsive part of oneself "goes to sleep" at midlife, that is, becomes temporarily unconscious, something else does indeed happen. With the controlling ego no longer in charge of the psyche, the creative unconscious yields something new, something magical. It comes first in the form of a stranger. Actually, this stranger is a part of ourselves, but aptly named for he is a stranger to our conscious ego. He is that part of us that has not forgotten the treasure of self hidden deep in our center. Jungians argue that in midlife, the Hero archetype gives way to the Magician archetype, and this story seems to confirm that premise.

The magician is that part of a man that understands the secret ways of the psyche. He is the alchemist, sorcerer, or wizard within who knows the principles of transformation. Naturally he goes directly to the source of the problem — the forgotten treasure of self. This is the magic. In fact, Chinen views "The Return of Magic" as the central teaching of this story and one of the great gifts of midlife. This magic renewal at midlife comes only when the compulsive side is put to bed.

A word of warning. Putting compulsivity to rest does not rationalize magical thinking or irresponsibility at midlife (or any other time, for that matter). "Going to bed" is a symbol for putting the directive, goal-oriented ego to rest for awhile. It is not a literal prescription for dropping out. A man who takes this fairy tale to mean that he can just "wait for his ship to come in" or forget his everyday responsibilities misses its point. He will find himself in darker waters. Only the truly productive man can give up compulsivity at midlife. The lazy man has no compulsivity to release, hence nothing to gain by resting. The lazy man never achieved all the woodcutter did.

In fairy tales, the forest, like the sea, often symbolizes the unconscious. Like an unexplored medieval forest, it is dark, mysterious, uncharted, and unknown. In midlife, one must go deep into this dark wood to find the gold and jewels buried there. This treasure, of course, represents the gift of self buried in the center of the psyche. It is our gold. The magician must go deep within to help us locate it.

But the magician begins to gloat. He becomes grandiose with premature visions of grandeur. He seems to forget the real purpose of this treasure, and wants to exploit it for purposes of ego inflation rather than personal growth. As he gets puffed up and conceited in this way, the army comes marching by. What is this army? It may symbolize that such greed can evoke a dark, compulsive power that could steal the precious treasure of soul, through either insatiable avarice or rigid regimentation. The army may also reflect his own stern conscience which could charge him with such moral wrongdoing. He is, after all, stealing something precious for the wrong reasons. A third possibility is that it represents the collective jealously that represents people who find their success

too easily. Lastly, the army's presence might just be enforcing the fact th_
magician cannot be allowed to take over the story. In other words, the woodc_
ter, representing a man's ego, must eventually resume its rightful place as the carrier of consciousness. If another complex in the psyche were to take over the
story, we would have a personality change so dramatic that there would be no
continuity of self. Any or all of these possibilities may be true. There may be
other meanings as well. One merely needs to ask which insight would be true in
your psyche. Whatever the answer, the story also tells us that the work of the
magician is done and he is no longer necessary, so it is appropriate for him to
recede back into the unconscious.

Bringing Home the Gold

*Do you remember where our story left off? The woodcutter was still in bed. The magi-
cian, who had gone deep into the forest to find buried treasure, had run off as soldiers
approached, leaving the mules standing in the woods alone. As our story resumes, the soldiers march past the mules and notice nothing unusual. The two mules waited undis-
turbed in the forest. After many hours, they started for home on their own, following the
trails they have used with the woodcutter for many years.*

*When the mules arrived at the woodcutter's home, his wife saw the poor animals. She
ran upstairs. "Dear husband," she cried out, "come quickly. You must unload the mules
before they collapse!" The husband yawned and turned over in bed. "If I've told you once,
I've told you a thousand times, I'm not working anymore." The poor woman hurried
downstairs, thought for a second, and then fetched a kitchen knife. (No, it wasn't for stab-
bing her husband.) She ran to the mules and slashed the bags on their backs to lighten
the load. Gold and jewels poured out, flashing in the sun.*

*"Gold! Jewels!" she exclaimed. In a flash her husband was downstairs. He stared in
astonishment at the treasure spilling into their yard. Then he grabbed his wife and they
danced deliriously. "Fortune did come to us after all!" he exulted.*

*The story ends even more happily. The old man and his wife gave half their treasure
to their sons and half of the remainder to the poor, and they were still as rich as could be
and (naturally) lived happily ever after.*

Discussion: Building a New Life

Having "scared off" the motive of greed and exploitation, the soldiers become
benign and do not disturb the mules. Again we see this as a new midlife way of
solving problems. The solution comes not from masculine effort, such as fighting
or defending ourselves, but from letting go of control. We see that the main character is still asleep; that is, the active and instrumental part is still not trying to figure anything out or complete some job. This release of the task-centered ego

er "solutions" to occur naturally and spontaneously; in other
p and purposeful psyche.
story, as Chinen observes, symbolize the man's long and honest
efited from his ability to work and that benefit was not gone; it was
he will and the deeper purpose of his work. The mules now carry
unconscious ego. Again, without effort or conscious intent, something has happened. The woodcutter's gift and his capacity to work have been united
without any effort on his part. His work capacity can now carry his deepest gift and he
will "awaken" with renewed energy. This energy we see is not egocentric ambition, but
the natural vitality of the inner self. Now it is possible to grow something really new.

The woodcutter's wife, who still symbolizes the concern for the practical side,
sees that some action now does need to be taken, and it is she who reveals the
arrival of the woodcutter's good fortune by opening the bags. And when the sad-
dlebags were opened, the woodcutter roared joyfully back to life. He is more than
glad to wake up now. Having integrated both the practical and magical sides of the
psyche, a new synthesis and new life have been born. Both sides now dance together happily. The proof that something really new and ego-transcending has
occurred in this tale comes in the end. There is no hoarding, conceit, or greed here.
Instead, we see generosity, openness, and trust. The woodcutter "shares the
wealth" of his transformation by recognizing the larger oneness of mankind and
happily supporting the growth of others.

The resolution of the midlife burden and burnout has occurred, as we can see,
by trusting the psyche rather than by trying to fix it or manipulate it. It does not
happen when we attempt to coerce or motivate ourselves, or seek to be fixed by
medicine, hypnosis, or exercise. Surrender, magic, practicality, and generosity
must all cooperate in this passage for life to be renewed. Thus, rather than end
in hopelessness and desolation, growing older can open the door of freedom, creativity, and transformation. One of the keys to this door, however, is giving up the
ego-driven life, for its motives lead only to emptiness, distrust, isolation, and fear
in old age.

Allegories like this one of the transformative midlife passage are not hard to
find in drama and literature. The recent movie, *The Fisher King*, for example, is a
powerful story of the midlife collapse of the empty inflated ego. T. S. Eliot's poem
The Wasteland speaks of this same kind of bankruptcy. On the other hand, midlife
and elder tales about the second half, as Allan Chinen discovered, are rare
(Chinen, 1989, 1992). It would seem that man has simply not had as much experience with the wisdom of aging as it has had with the tasks of early adulthood.
Perhaps this is because conscious aging is such a new territory. It has only been
encountered as a common human experience in the last 100 years. We are all finding our way in the forest of this great new adventure of consciousness. ❦

CHAPTER 12

Carl Jung: An Example of the Confronted Midlife

≫ Jung himself is a most powerful example of the pain and the transformative potential found in the midlife passage. He experienced the midlife upheaval in the years after his break with Freud. Those familiar with their relationship will recall that Jung was selected by Freud to be his heir to the throne of psycho-analysis. Freud was clearly Jung's mentor. But the mentor relationship had gone sour. Freud disapproved of Jung's views on the collective unconscious and would not hear of them. For Jung, the cost of any continuing association with Freud would have to be submission to this more dominant personality and the submersion of his own deeply felt views on the nature of man. Both were untenable.

In his autobiography, Jung recalls, "Under the impress of Freud's personality, I had, as far as possible, cast aside my own judgments and repressed my criticisms. That was the pre-requisite for collaborating with him." (Jung, 1965, p. 164) But as Jung was working on his book, *Symbols of Transformation*, an apt title for his own impending midlife metamorphosis, and writing the chapter entitled "The Sacrifice," he recognized that his work, which represented a shift from the Freudian biographical approach to a fundamentally transpersonal and mytholog-ical one, would come at a great cost. And indeed it did. It cost him his relation-ship with Freud and sentenced him to years of painful professional isolation and denigration. Jung recalls, "After the break with Freud, all my friends and acquaintances dropped away. My book was declared rubbish; I was a mystic, and that settled the matter." (Jung, 1961, p. 167)

Jung then entered a period of profound darkness and disorientation which he later called "Confrontations with the Unconscious." (Jung, 1965) In this several year period, he voluntarily immersed himself in the immense distress and disor-ganization emerging from his own unconscious. He explored whatever surfaced, even when it seemed foolish, bizarre, or outrageous. All manner of phenomena were admitted and confronted, including professional paralysis (he was unable to read a scientific book or appear in public for three years), intensely painful emo-tions and withdrawal, childlike sand play (he built a little village of sticks and stones on a lake shore near his home), the expression through automatic writing of unconscious archetypal themes (equivalent to today's channeling), and numer-ous strange and paranormal events. Looking back at this cataclysmic time, Jung summarized, "I therefore felt that I was confronted with the choice of either continuing my academic career, or following the laws of my own inner personality, and forging ahead with this curious task of mine, this experiment in confrontation with the unconscious. But until it was completed, I could not appear for the public. Consciously, deliberately, then, I abandoned my academic career. For I felt something great was happening to me...I knew that it would fill my life, and for the sake of that goal I was ready to take any kind of risk." (Jung, 1961, pp. 193-4)

The gift of Jung's inward journey was enormous. Late in his life he observed, "It has taken me forty-five years to distill within the vessel of my scientific work the things I experienced and wrote down at that time. As a young man my goal had been to accomplish something in my science. But then I hit upon this stream of lava, and the heat of its fire reshaped my life...The years when I was pursuing my inner images were the most important in my life — in them everything essential was decided. It all began then; the later details are only supplements and clarifications of the material that burst forth from the unconscious and at first swamped me. It was the prima materia for a lifetime's work." (Jung, 1961, p. 199)

For men, the break with the mentor is not infrequently the gateway into the dramatic, earth shaking cataclysms of the midlife passage. Here is the father wound again, for leaving this guide is like leaving home. Now he is truly on his own for there are no more experts. For the individual willing to embrace this chaos and confusion, the treasure will indeed be great. ❧

CHAPTER 13

The Awakening
of Soul at Midlife

≫ One morning, early in my own midlife passage, the following piece of writing exploded into consciousness. It seemed to emerge full blown and complete, needing virtually no editing. To me, it speaks of the core intrapsychic pressure of midlife: the urgency of the unlived self to recover its own deep, powerful and independent voice, and the reality of the prefigured archetypal structure of that self, which cannot be dominated by the ego without irreparable damage to its inborn purpose and to its cargo and origin, the soul. This is the urgency that grabbed my life at forty. It is a voice that still urges me to take the risk to be what I am most fully, completely, deeply.

"To the unsuspecting and uninitiated, there is nothing more painful and disruptive than the awakening and rebirth of the soul at midlife. Aching for its own reality and destiny, the soul is heard as an insistent voice crying out for authenticity in the personal wasteland of conforming outward existence. The ego's shell, hard of substance and hard won in the early contests of life, too often becomes ossified as a barrier that must be cracked for the awakening soul to feel itself born. Ego becomes soul as the shackles of the false self are loosened and the inner light of eternity activates an urgency for genuinely felt truths.

"As this awakening and living process intensifies, the soul quickens its search for the heartfelt path. What has been secretly developing through lifetimes of experience now must come out into the world. Fragile, hidden, and distrusted through the first half of life, the soul now forms its own unique constellation of meaning and desire. And there is nothing more painful than the labor and birth of a soul that has been completely obliterated in life's early contests, and lost, forgotten, or crushed under the tyranny of false standards, imposed material objectives and self-alien values. For even when the false self is successful, what is the worth of fame, power, or wealth when the soul itself has slipped through your fingers?

"An urgent need to know and express one's self, one's true and essential nature, wells up in this midlife process as powerfully, painfully, and inescapably as an animal's instinct or the sexual awakening of the adolescent. Agitated and soul-hungry, this inner driven transformative process erupts inwardly like a volcano and then threatens to uproot and disorganize the entire predictable, secure, and well-manicured landscape of everyday life. Attempts at self-denial and renewed conformity are inwardly felt as crushing, smothering, and unbearably oppressive. Yet equally unbearable is the distrust of still unformed truths and the fear that they will be stillborn.

"Be who you are going to be! Get on with it now. Time gives up on those who postpone or betray their destiny.' Such a voice confronts the soul with increasing rancor. Shaken by unseen arms and battered by torrents of feeling, a life in the throes of such cataclysmic upheaval is like a puppet in the hands of an angry child, and the child is one's self. 'Who am I, what am I here for, and at what cost comes the answer? I cannot wait for someday and I cannot go on being somebody I am not.'

"Soon the false shell of the other-directed personality caves in and with the internal collapse of false strivings comes an exhaustion and despair that rots will and ambition. All activity originating from the false center of the personality becomes tiresome, empty, and anguished. But in the ruins of this shattered fraudulence, the soul can yet be found, and it can be nourished and revived with tenderness and love. To heal the injured soul, the real self must finally be intuited, awakened, and welcomed as the authentic center of personality and as a living presence that resides within. The return of the soul then releases creative and spontaneous energies that reshape both the inner and the outer life. And no one can dictate the purpose and course of these energies — neither the individual, his loved ones, the experts, nor society. This is the mysterious birth of the truly individuated life."

As this piece implies, the eruption of midlife is not something you choose — it's something that chooses you. ❦

CHAPTER 14

Poetry at Midlife

❧ At first glance, selecting poems to describe the midlife passage may seem as strange as did our earlier excursion into mythology. Why introduce poetry? Do poets, like ancient mythologists, also have access to dimensions of experience that regular folk or trained scientists miss? The answer, of course, is yes, and it follows from many of the same reasons previously discussed.

Good poetry and lyrical prose combine intuitive, emotional, symbolic, and sensory forms of knowing the world into word pictures. Some are Zen-like in their clarity, giving us glimpses of ordinary reality in fresh, deeper, and sometimes startling new ways. Like a sorcerer, the poet's words have the power to change our perception, showing us that extraordinary events are happening all around us. Poetry is also the sentimental language of feeling and soul. The poet describes what we all feel and experience, the fundamental matters of life, love, aging and death. Coming from the heart, however, his words have the power to enter our hearts in ways that dry, discursive reasoning misses. And, like dreams, poetic symbols often carry many levels of meaning, inviting us to search for their deeper and more profound significance. In this regard, poetry is very often about the significance and meaning of life itself.

Because poetry evokes meaning, imagination, and feeling, it literally acts on us. It interrupts our thoughts, sharpens our perceptions, triggers personal memories, and awakens archetypal images deeply embedded in the collective psyche and soma. A weatherman can factually describe a winter day, but the poet's words trigger immediate sensations of winter's hard, cold, barren ground and gray skies, the warm fireplace that envelopes us in the early darkness, and our primordial experience of the dying year, the cycle of life, and our own necessary mortality. In this way, poetic images are seditious, confronting us with realizations we customarily avoid. They are powerful because they undermine the routinized habits of perception that deaden our senses and the taken-for-granted cultural assumptions that mold what we believe, desire, and expect. Poetry, like midlife, can unmask a man and challenge him to the truth of his own experience.

The poetry that follows was written in this way. It wants to challenge and awaken us. Shaking our indolent complacency, it asks us to look at the deeper order of the psyche and the world. This archetypal order still operates in us like a giant clock whose hands at midlife tell us it is time to change. Not surprisingly, midlife poems tend to fall into the following familiar categories: The

Realization of Death, Confronting Falseness, The Necessity of Change, A New Kind of Love, Opening to Spirit, and Return of the Unfinished Self.

The Realization of Death: As we saw in Part 1, the Summer of young adulthood ends in the midlife realization of death. This poem speaks of that stark, cold, disenchanting, and impersonal truth. It enters the psyche subtly at first, sneaking in as a vague agitation, a disturbance of consciousness, a knowing that the larger forces of the universe cannot be denied or postponed.

End of Summer
Stanley Kunitz

An agitation of the air,
A perturbation of the light
Admonished me the unloved year
Would turn on its hinge that night.

I stood in the disenchanted field
Amid the stubble and the stones,
Amazed, while a small worm lisped to me
The song of my marrow-bones.

Blue poured into summer blue,
A hawk broke from his cloudless tower,
The roof of the silo blazed, and I knew
That part of my life was over.

Already the iron door of the north
Clangs open: birds, leaves, snows
Order their populations forth,
And a cruel wind blows.

Confronting the Falseness: In this poem, William Stafford asks us to confront the rigid disguise of character that masks who we really are, and serves to defend us against old wounds. At around thirty-five, this posture, like modeling clay, is starting to set. Like a developing print, it fixes and then will not change. The implicit message seems to be: look at the specific way you hold and control yourself. This is your character. It is also how you deny your secret wounds. Your character is a defense. If you hang onto this fixed posture, it will indeed be who you are forever. Excuses will not change it. Can you let it go?

An Archival Print
William Stafford

God snaps your picture — don't look away —
this room right now, your face tilted
exactly as it is before you can think
or control it. Go ahead, let it betray
all the secret emergencies and still hold
that partial disguise you call your character.

Even your lip, they say, the way it curves
or doesn't, or can't decide, will deliver
bales of evidence. The camera, wide open,
stands ready; the exposure is thirty-five years
or so — after that you have become
whatever the veneer is, all the way through.

Now you want to explain. Your mother
was a certain — how to express it? — influence.
Yes. And your father whatever he was,
you couldn't change that. No. And your town
of course had its limits. Go on, keep talking —
Hold it. Don't move. That's you forever.

The Necessity of Change: This next poem by Robert Bly captures for me the profound midlife recognition that the old ways, the ways of living and aspiring which are active before the midlife meridian, the ways that have become dead and false, really cannot go any further. It is as if the poem were about a man and his family at midlife. Social pretenses can no longer contain the family's false image of itself. Much has died here, including his relationships with his wife, his son, and his spirituality. This annihilation exposes for a moment the emptiness of his universe. So the man in black, in grieving, must reverse his path and go no further in the direction of falseness. He must change his course for reasons hidden in his own soul that no one else can see.

Snowbanks North of the House
Robert Bly

Those great sweeps of snow that stop suddenly six
    feet from the house...
Thoughts that go so far.
The boy gets out of high school and reads no more
    books;

the son stops calling home.
The mother puts down her rolling pin and makes no
more bread.
And the wife looks at her husband one night at a
party, and loves him no more.
The energy leaves the wine, and the minister falls
leaving the church.
It will not come closer —
the one inside moves back, and the hands touch
nothing, and are safe.

The father grieves for the son, and will not leave the
room where the coffin stands.
He turns away from his wife, and she sleeps alone.

And the sea lifts and falls all night, the moon goes on
through the unattached heavens alone.
The toe of the shoe pivots
in the dust...
And the man in the black coat turns, and goes back
down the hill.
No one knows why he came, or why he turned away,
and did not climb the hill.

A New Kind of Love: The world of love, too, is transformed by the great wave of midlife. The unrestrainable, passionate fire of the young man diminishes in time and, if he can surrender to this ebbing tide, a far different love is revealed. This is a love made of gentleness, natural rhythms, clarity, patience, and appreciation. It is a love tempered and mellowed by aging. What a gift midlife has left us! See if you can feel its velvet comfort in this poem by Erica Jong.

Living Happily Ever After
Erica Jong

We used to strike sparks
off each other.
Our eyes would meet
or our hands,
and the blue lightning of love
would sear the air.

Now we are soft.
We loll

in the same sleepy bed,
skin of my skin,
hair of my head,
sweat of my sweat —
you are kin,
brother & mother
all in one,
husband, lover,
muse & comforter;
I love you even better
without the sparks.

We are pebbles in the tide
rolling against each other.
The surf crashes above us;
the irregular pulse
of the ocean
drives our blood,
but we are growing smooth
against each other.

Are we living happily ever after?
What will happen
to my love of cataclysms?
My love of sparks & fire,
my love of ice?

Fellow pebble,
let us roll
against each other.
Perhaps the sparks are clearer
under water.

Opening to Spirit: Though the old ways must die, as the law of each seasonal round commands, and though we seem to lose all bearing and perspective in Summer's demise and our lonely fall from certainty, still, in the falling itself can be found a great mystic realization: that all of this is held in the patient and living consciousness of a single loving intelligence.

Autumn
Rainer Maria Rilke

The leaves are falling, falling as if from far up,
as if orchards were dying high in space.
Each leaf falls as if it were motioning "no."

And tonight the heavy earth is falling
away from all the other stars in the loneliness.

We're all falling. This hand here is falling.
And look at the other one....It's in them all.

And yet there is Someone, whose hands
infinitely calm, hold up all this falling.

Return to the Unfinished Self: This next piece by Charlotte Gray tells the story of every family man. When a man becomes a father, he puts aside a part of himself to shepherd the great and sacred project of bringing new life into the universe. When it's done, however, a man can return to the rooms of soul long ignored in this interim, and discover again the song still echoing inside. Then a man can return to the still-youthful and unfinished work of his soul.

Untitled
Charlotte Gray

At twenty he had put on this costume of fatherhood, padded the shoulders, added to his height, deepened his voice to fit the part. I never saw the greasepaint or the wig line as I clasped his hand.

Only when I had grown and had come to know everything myself, did I see the fraud. A well intentioned man, but not the man I thought him. A little man. A man who blurred into the small suburban landscape, his friends as nondescript and kind as he, his work respectable, ambition long since burned away. I saw him so till now, but suddenly I find him changed. Years and indifference have made him careless. He forsook the padding and the heels somewhere along the way, but how could this diminish his reality? He is I see, himself. Not shrunken, but the man he was before we came. His voice has lifted. His eyes are more alert, no longer speaking of preoccupations with children's shoes and adolescent brushes with the Law.

He has taken up again the things we interrupted, the skills we crowded to the edges of his life. He is no longer obliged to steal time for himself. We are his companions now, his friends, rather than demanding voices always at his elbow.

He has not grown young again. I see now that he was never old. The painted

wrinkles that he still retains, the careful silver streaks, no longer fool us. My dad's
a man as young as any of his children.
  Perhaps a little younger.

The poetry and prose of midlife teach us about its inner dimensions and possibilities, its journey of sorrow and renewal. But there is so much to deal with! How does a man navigate this crossing without drowning? The next chapter returns to the practical realm of coping with midlife. ❦

CHAPTER 15

Coping with Change

≫ In light of the numerous and highly disrupting pressures associated with the midlife passage, it is not surprising that men experience coping difficulties. They very often react to these pressures in maladaptive and self-defeating ways, some of which can be deeply painful, and some even disastrous. Given the many dangers of this tumultuous passage, we need to look closely at the kinds of navigational mistakes that can take our ship onto the rocks.

Maladaptive Responses:

Maladaptive responses are the most frequently cited behaviors behind what we colloquially describe as the "midlife crazies." Three variations are common.

ſ **Denial:** Fearing the eruptive and disorganizing forces of midlife that threaten his secure life structure, and fearing the despair growing in his soul, a man may cling to the old ambitious plans of early adulthood. He tries to deny what is going on and resist the passage, especially in the beginning. Denial may take several forms for a man, including:
- Criticizing himself for not achieving the dream in order to keep striving for it.
- Trivializing his emotional pain and need to change.
- Burying feelings of fatigue, depression, or despair under compulsive hard work, despite the cost to self, family, and health.
- Using chemicals, food, or distractions to avoid awareness.
- Blaming his midlife distress on something else such as lack of exercise or boredom.

Denial is also abetted by our societal blindness and devaluation of the midlife experience. Have you been told, for example, there really is no such thing as the midlife crisis, this is just an excuse for your own weakness? Or, "You're making too much of it, get more exercise?" Or, "Stop complaining, there's nothing wrong with your life?" Or even, "You're sick, you need to see a psychiatrist?"

In the face of such societal denial, ignorance, and depreciation, and without any socially valued model to guide and validate this passage, men are often utterly unable to realize its potential. Instead they feel more shame, inferiority, and inadequacy. In hiding their distress, they tragically abort a life-renewing process.

ʃ *Acting-out:* Caught up in the urgency of time, some men act impulsively in the desperate search for more authentic experience. They mistake excitement for youth and renewal. Throwing all caution to the wind, they abruptly and precipitously change careers, start affairs, file for divorce, or sail around the world.

Also in midlife, enamored by the transformative images and symbols of the unconscious (e.g., finding a true love or soulmate, the lure of freedom), men can fall under the spell of their fantasy, project it out into the world like a movie, and then pursue the projection. Eventually this spell breaks and the fantasy deflates; the affair was not true love, the sailboat has a major leak, you still have to support yourself, and you miss your family.

Actually, some acting out is useful in creating the crises that bring a man's attention back to the real tasks of midlife. For men in emotionally blocked or sterile marriages, a romantic infatuation may be the catalyst they need to provoke an "air-clearing" marital crisis where long-standing issues are finally addressed. Similarly, erupting angrily at work pressures may help a man see how tense or unhappy he has become.

ʃ *Resignation, Deterioration, Collapse, and Cynicism:* Under this heading come all the unhealthy forms of giving up common to an aborted midlife passage. Feeling that his life's deepest longings are beyond his reach or viewing himself as unable to risk change, a man may become resigned to unfulfillment. His life may then deteriorate into meaningless work, repetitive marital or parent-child squabbles, cynical or whining responses to hardship, chronic low grade depression, or illness. Alcohol or distraction may numb and mask this collapse into hopelessness, but it does not go away.

Healthy Responses:

Though not well publicized or supported by our culture, a wide range of genuinely healthy responses can ease the pain, nourish, and protect the developing embryonic self, and guide a man through the turmoil of midlife toward renewal of self and soul. Such healthy responses include:

ʃ *Permission to Feel Confusion and Pain:* It is imperative for men to give themselves permission to feel lost, confused, and troubled without belittling, condemning, or judging themselves. Then they can listen for the meaning of their plight and its deep connection to the real but wounded self. We need to remind ourselves that the emotional distress of midlife is necessary, valid, healthy, and unavoidable. It is only in accepting and paying attention to our experience of pain that the true self is located, healed, and reactivated.

✦ *Permission to Let Go:* Letting go means allowing life to be the way it is without trying to control or force it to fit our personal script. Letting go is trusting life to find its own way and appreciating that life's unfolding has a wisdom we cannot know ahead of time.

✦ *Supporting the Unfolding Process:* Even though it seems like all compass points and familiar bearings have been lost and that one must be crazy to go on, it is nonetheless important to support what is trying to happen. A man needs to make time to reflect on his life, meditate, walk alone along quiet wooded paths, and listen to the wants and desires of his gradually thawing self. Maintaining rigid and compulsive routines at work or home literally prevents this process from unfolding and chains the individual to the very life structure that has been strangling him.

✦ *Mourning:* Midlife is a time of grief, disillusionment, and sorrow. It takes time, patience, and compassion to truly mourn the hopes and grandiose dreams of the young man, to accept the passing of youth itself, and to grieve mortality. Try not to be afraid of the amount of grief that wells up, for what is felt now will leave less to feel later, and one day the mourning will be over.

✦ *Re-Assessing the Dream:* Levinson and Sheehy repeatedly stress that central to the process of midlife renewal is re-assessing one's life dream. Does it still make sense? Is it what you want after all? Ask yourself whether you are being liberated or dominated by the dream. Is it now a source of joy, energy, and inspiration, or of frustration, fatigue, and burden. New dreams can form only as old ones are allowed to die.

✦ *Re-Assessing Career Objectives:* Releasing oneself from the tyranny of a career ambition that no longer fits does not have to mean throwing your career away. After all, what most men have achieved by midlife may provide important security and creature comforts. Reducing the demand for career advancement, however, may allow a man to explore those work activities that are genuinely enjoyable, including the high degree of expertise and mastery already achieved, the honor of seniority and respect, and the pleasure of social bonds and mentoring at work.

✦ *Stimulating Spontaneity and Playful Creativity:* Learning to relax, have fun, play, and be creative again stirs the core of the original self. Find those activities that seem most naturally pleasurable and expressive for you. Especially important in this process is finding ways to mirror, symbolize, or express your interior experience in concrete external form through creative activities such as art, music, and writing. In this way, you create a record of the stepping stones of your soul's new journey. The act of mirroring back these changes stimulates the process further. As a result of this dialogue between you and your creativity, a relationship is begun with your inner source of growth.

ƒ **Evolving Your Primary Relationships:** Despite (and sometimes because of) the relationship turmoil associated with midlife individuation, this can be a time of healthy growth in men's primary relationships. Marriages, like individuals, have developmental stages through their life spans. They move from early romanticized symbiosis to the disillusionment and the conflict of separate individuation paths, then to the withdrawal of distorting positive or negative projections, and eventually to the rapprochement of mature love.

The process of reworking the relationship, while frightening at first, can also be the most invigorating and renewing experience of the marriage.

ƒ **Developing a Healthy Relationship with Your Body:** In the narcissism and seeming invulnerability of youth, we come to expect endless and tireless service from our bodies no matter how we abuse them. Begin instead to listen to your body, and care for it with tenderness and love. Pay attention to your physical symptoms, whatever they may be, and learn to interpret their hidden psychological language. What is your body trying to say to you?

Open your senses and learn new ways to experience pleasure in touch, smell, movement, sex, and everyday activity. Finally, reduce stress, because it is increasingly clear that intense or prolonged distress causes and exacerbates illness and depression. Stress kills body and soul.

ƒ **Taking Personal or Career Risks:** When you have really exhausted your alternatives in your marriage or career, and you are still unhappy or burning out, look toward your life structure. To take risks, you will need to analyze the obstacles in your path. When you honestly identify and confront your barriers, however, you will find that most reside inside you. External problems are frequently used to rationalize the fear of change. To overcome such barriers, share your struggle with family or close friends, admit your fears, and start making small but definite changes. Small steps might include taking a sabbatical or leave of absence, cutting back at work, making time to really explore another path, structuring a separation from your relationship to see how it feels, starting a second career as a part time job. Avoid the big, precarious, and irreversible changes at first, and test your ideas in small but meaningful ways.

ʄ *Searching for Ultimate Meanings:* As discussed earlier, in the afternoon of life, men begin to search for religious or spiritual understanding. Whether this is through formal religious doctrine or personal mysticism, the longing for a meaningful relationship with the transcendent becomes increasingly important. Failure to deepen our relationship to the sacred as we grow older is frequently associated with a deep sense of loss, insecurity, or distrust in the meaning of life and the order of the universe.

ʄ *Seeking Professional Help:* There are times when the midlife passage becomes too frightening, distressing, or depressing. This occurs when our adjustive resources are blocked, drained, or crippled by overwhelming stress or historical personality wounds. At such times, it makes sense to get professional help. Primitive man structured this universal symbolic journey in sacred rituals. There were initiation ceremonies and rites of passage directed by the tribal elders or shamans to guide the young man into adult roles and sacred wisdom. It falls, then, on the shoulders of psychotherapists, clergy, and other wisdom figures to provide this teaching. Sadly, few of them have taken their own journey sufficiently to really understand the risks and dynamics involved. Though helpers are frequently flawed, do not give up your search for guidance when you feel it is necessary. The right guide can be of great psychological value. Also keep in mind that you may need to have several guides over time as the sequential lessons of life are learned. ❦

CHAPTER 16

Emergence: A New
Orientation to Life

Dedications, Pledges, Commitments
William Stafford

For the past.
For my own path.
For surprises.

For mistakes that worked so well.
For tomorrow if I'm there.
For the next real thing.

Then for carrying it all
through whatever is necessary.
For following the little god who speaks only to me.

✻ The midlife passage marks the very birth of the individuating life journey. Its inner activated energies, encompassing all the inborn potentials of development, rise at this time to give our life its ultimate purpose, thrust, meaning, and destiny. If this awakening is ignored, belittled, denied, trivialized, or pathologized, then something infinitely beautiful, infinitely precious, and infinitely important is lost — possibly forever. If it is lived without insight, on the other hand, allowing the individual to blindly act out his urgent and restive impulses, then the myriad disasters of the midlife seen by the psychologist may occur. In essence, midlife distress is not a condition to be cured, but an invitation to embark on a deeply important journey of wholeness and self-realization. Most men betray this calling and hence most never know what might have happened had their soul's longing for authenticity been enacted.

This is the challenge of midlife: to consciously exchange security for awakening, to permit your life to be reshaped by the forces inherent in your own essential unfolding nature, and to give back to life whatever authentic truth or accomplishment this transformative process brings through you. For the ultimate message contained in this critical developmental transition seems to be this: that in the depth of our being resides an apparently purposeful and intelligent maturational force that pushes from within to expand and evolve the individual self. This mysterious inner realm of energy and purpose holds dormant the stages, workings, and secret teleology of our individual and collective evolution. Accepted and welcomed, this awakening of soul leads to life's highest attainments; betrayed, this individuating force may atrophy steadily for years leading at best to a barren but conforming life and at worst to depression, meaninglessness, and the multiple forms of tragedy and wasted potential a man can experience in his final years.

When the midlife passage is successfully and creatively traversed, a new era of life arrives. In the first half of life we grow ego, in the second half we grow soul. This second half opens new vistas for the man who has allowed the ambitious, materialistically motivated hero to die, and who has presided over the birth to a creative new self. In this renewal, a man may be able to identify the timeless work of his own soul amidst the universal tasks and teachings of the Fall and Winter seasons of life. A man's own work, his heart and soul work, really cannot begin until the personal truths of this passage are realized and allowed to radically transform him. Midlife, then, is a play of epic meaning and significance in the movement of the individuating self.

So far, the male midlife has been characterized primarily as an individual journey. And it is. But the male midlife is also part of something larger, an ongoing cultural change process, with numerous social and transpersonal themes, and ancient roots. In the passage through midlife, men need to heal their collective wounds and unearth an archetypal experience of masculinity that can restore the masculine soul. This is the topic of Part 3. ❦

PART 3

Masculinity 2000:
The Collective Issues
of Men at the Birth of the
Twenty-First Century

I still remember my first men's gathering led by Michael Meade, James Hillman, Robert Bly. One hundred or so men arriving with drums and journals up in the Santa Barbara hills. Everywhere there was a palpable, electric feeling of male energy, of something about to happen. Would it be dangerous? And then the surprise: a time not of competitive posturing and conflict, but of men sitting together listening to poetry and myth, speaking of timeless issues and their own woundings of men. Here were men talking of their personal lives, crying, hugging, even drumming and dancing together, challenging all the one dimensional stereotypes of men in a colorful and bold display of manhood — all in one room held together by teachers with real vision.

One hundred or so men's faces, all different, yet all men. Men galvanized as one in emotion, life experience, conflict. Men telling the truth to each other in pairs, small groups, and in the community. Men breaking down about being broken. And then the same men coming back to life, with more life radiating from them than when they arrived. Men drumming with rhythms that rivet the mind, lift consciousness, and then explode the illusion of separation as the drummers themselves are drummed by their drums and the dancers themselves are danced by their dance, and it all becomes a blur and celebration of the universal beauty of being male. Much more than rationality, this intense force, male spirit, color, ritual, contact, voice, and sound seemed almost to change my molecular vibration until, without having to understand why, a wondrous new male energy flooded me, and I soared alive and free at last.

I knew then that I loved men, could trust them, and that I was in turn loved by them. I had finally found my home. Here were men talking a language I could recognize, language I had hungered for all my life, a language of soul. A man I had worked with for fifteen years turned to me and said "I love you." And I answered, "I know that. I have always known that. And I love you, too." All this is the experience of being a man. This experience is itself initiation, for I knew I was different afterwards, and after each such gathering, and I knew I was more of my whole self each time. I was part of a vibrant male oneness that forever and without the need for justification or explanation answered the question of what it means to be a man.

This section is dedicated with deep respect, admiration, and appreciation to these men and especially to Michael Mead, James Hillman, and Robert Bly — three brilliant and renegade geniuses of the male soul.

CHAPTER 17

Introduction to the "Men's Movement"

※ Agreement on what it means to be a man has been eroding steadily in America over the past decade. Traditional models of masculinity — the tough, competitive, hard-driving, emotionally invulnerable warrior and tireless family provider — are being re-examined by wounded middle-aged men no longer willing to pay the price of workaholism, family estrangement, shortened life spans, and the betrayal of themselves and other men fostered by the prevailing social model of manhood. Men at midlife are collectively changing. They are looking under their Superman costumes, exposing their pain and confusion, and asking penetrating questions. But men are also uncertain how to change, what they really want, or what it even means to be a man. In this great confusion, many have begun to search; for themselves, for each other, for their real fathers, and for life-affirming models of masculinity. For these men, a quest for truth and soul has replaced the quest for success.

Born from the hunger of men to heal old wounds and know their deeper nature and purpose in life has been a spontaneous and loosely organized "men's movement." It has been an historic outpouring of pain, dissatisfaction, and honesty flowing contrary to all the prevailing social currents of masculinity. Championed quietly over the past ten to fifteen years by remarkable and far-seeing men, including Robert Bly, a dissident and challenging poet; James Hillman, an iconoclastic and unconventional Jungian analyst; and Michael Mead, a drumming storyteller from the streets of New York. It has grown steadily to include men from all walks of life. Always open to men of all backgrounds, it has been a truly amazing blending of voices.

Attending weekend and week-long conferences, small men's groups, and other male gatherings, men began coming together to share their struggle to understand what manhood really is and what it asks of them. The emerging and still tentative answers now create a richly dynamic, varied, and sometimes controversial collage filled with the ancient wisdom of myth and story, the living experience of male spirit evoked in dance, drumming, and poetry, and the insights of depth psychology, science, indigenous cultures, and countless individual male voices.

This is a movement of implicit male initiation. Simply being together in this new and honest dialogue, in a more and more experiential ground of manhood, can bring a man in touch with a different vitality of maleness and, even more importantly, with the energy and form of his own unique masculinity. In this process, a kind of male seasoning takes place. Somehow, invisibly, sooner or later, a man can find himself knowing his own masculine energy, its intrinsic value, and the birthright to be who he really is. For hundreds of years, and increasingly since the Industrial Revolution, men have hungered for this renewal.

The men's movement was born primarily from midlife males, men who have grown weary of the warrior model of masculinity. They are tired of competition, ambition, and the expectation of male combat. Younger men still moved by the heroic Summer of life have, not surprisingly, been far less involved with this movement. Their turn for this work will come with their midlife years, for this work of "soul-making" is the task of midlife and beyond. Thus, this coming together of men has been a movement of older males, aging men, men who have knowingly or unknowingly been changed by the midlife experience described in Part I of this book. For only when the compulsive hero in them dies can they finally meet what lies underneath: their souls. These are men who now need to find and share their personal stories and dig into the common, human ground of masculinity.

There are many tasks of this midlife journey into the realm of masculinity, and they are as heroic as any achieved in the earlier years of questing, conquering, and empire building. These tasks include dismantling our false and damaging posture of manhood, facing and healing the underlying wounds of male combat, revisioning the lost beauty of men, growing a more honest, inclusive, and life-nurturing value system, and restoring a relationship to the sacred that will yield new purposes to life. Like midlife itself, this is a developmental process, moving from personal injuries to collective ones, from competitive isolation to mature community, from the unborn self to a male-nourished and male-activated soul.

The term "men's work" has often been used in the men's movement to refer to the individual and collective emotional work men must now do to heal themselves and male community. More than a social movement, it is a moral imperative, a metaphor, and a blueprint for the emotional work all men are called to do in the middle years to part the curtain of defensive male invincibility. It implies that our "work" as men goes beyond the basic tenants of "providing and protecting" to include coming together to heal the wounded maleness in ourselves and other men, awakening the inherent joy and blessing of life, finding and cultivating the deep work stored in each man's soul. Finally "men's work" implies emotionally and spiritually joining our families and communities, not in the false, detached or ego-serving way of the old "patriarchy," but in ways that are authentic and life embracing. But, until men have recovered their deep instinctual connection to self and soul, and have done the deep healing work involved, their participation in family and community will miss the ultimate dimension — love —

this undivided, unconditional, and unselfish experience that forms the ground of self, family, and the intrinsic purpose of life.

In Part 3 we explore the nature and themes of the men's movement and its relationship to the midlife dynamics described in Part I. For as a man works to review his individual life, he inevitably comes to larger questions such as, "What does it really mean to be a man?" "What kind of men were my father, my grandfather, my male ancestors?" "What do we stand for?" "What is our nature?" These are not foolish questions. Rather they belie an intuitive longing to live a larger life open to the skies and the sacred, wild cosmos, a life already encoded and pulsing in our cells. Free from the deadening crush of compulsive work, it is a life of masculine energy, vitality, and community.

It is the contention of this book that a man discovers this kind of masculinity as he confronts the common tasks of the midlife passage with other men, and that both midlife and men's work operate in concert to initiate men into an altogether new life. It is argued further that men's work is, in this historical epoch, a process of cultural midlife, a profound metamorphosis of society itself. Like the false and inflated armor of masculinity that individual men can no longer carry, the ossified patriarchal rules of society are collapsing in this transitional, millennial time. With so many men passing through the middle years now, the world will have increasing numbers of older men, many of whom will have done the soul work of midlife. This potential for mature leadership and real wisdom is a hopeful development in a world so desperately awaiting it.

There is a growing body of literature now from the men's movement. It is written by articulate and gutsy men breaking the silence of conformity and challenging all our previously unquestioned assumptions about masculinity and the meaning of heroes, success, love, sex, relationships, power, and manhood. If a man is to grow beyond midlife, he must face these questions.

This section of the book owes an incalculable debt to each man cited and to countless others who have contributed to this general pool of male knowledge. A book like this is, by its very nature and genesis, a collective one with a collective debt. Finally, each of us who talk and write about male psychology in this way packages his ideas a little differently, usually emphasizing what is most personal and important to him. Each man tells a piece of his own story and what that story has taught him about manhood. Certainly that is what I have done. ❧

CHAPTER 18

The Lost Beauty of Men: Before the Fall

≫ It would seem that whenever we hear about men in the media or from social commentators, we hear what's wrong with them. We hear terrible stories of their cruelty, violence, or greed. It is so easy to criticize men, and men in my generation have become guilt-ridden, demoralized, or defensive about this criticism. So I want to start, instead, with the beauty of men. This chapter focuses on that beauty. Women are equally beautiful and a chapter like this could be written for them, but this chapter is devoted to the beauty of men.

Men are beautiful — incredibly so. So much more beautiful than we realize. We have virtually no grasp of this original beauty. We have lost the capacity to see it. And it is this ignorance and blindness, our collective failure to know ourselves, that leaves men feeling sad, ashamed, betrayed, and sometimes violent.

What is beautiful about men? To answer this question, wipe clean the lens of perception, this lens so over-colored by societal labels, acrimonious gender conflict, and internalized shame, and see what is original, real, and always here before us. Look with a clean eye. Even better, look with a loving eye. What is beautiful about men? Their bodies. Standing, moving, breathing, reaching, holding, running, pushing, straining, lifting, dancing, loving, sexing. Fingers, eyes, torsos, expressions, reactions. Seeing, hearing, touching, smelling, tasting the world. Look at a male body as if you had never seen one before, as if you were looking directly at a living work of God. What a marvel! Look, too, at laughter, song, twinkling eyes, imagination, foolishness, genius, camaraderie, heartbreak, bravery, wonder, sorrow, determination, self-sacrifice, wisdom, and hardship. Marvel at the extraordinary transformations experienced by the male body and personality through the life span. If we were not so accustomed to this reality, we would be transfixed in perennial awe at the miracle of masculinity.

Don't get caught up in judgment in this viewing. Don't get stuck in morality, responsibility, occupation, appearance, status, sexism, ageism, or comparisons of any kind. Avoid comparisons. Look just at what you see and regard it as an expression of divinity. Old bodies, new bodies, fat bodies, thin bodies, brown, black, yellow, and pink bodies; happy men, sad men, weak and strong, confused, brilliant, angry, and certain. See them all as equally beautiful, all of them, without a criticizing eye, without making one better than the other. What diversity! And all of it men.

And continuing, look at what men have created: art, architecture, literature, science, poetry, and religion — all of it altogether new to the universe. Utterly unexpected, incredible products of male curiosity, courage, and imagination. If men could know the joy that lives in their hearts and the gifts they have already given the world, and if men could know what they might mean to each other, to their community, to the beauty, splendor, and completeness of the universe; if men could know that each is an irreproducible new miracle of the Creator, a work of art and brilliance, a new and necessary creation, then we would begin to know the beauty of men. The universe spent billions of years organizing energy into matter and then matter into life and the life into consciousness and form — and we are that! The universe did the unimaginable; it developed a part of itself capable of consciousness and thought, of even thinking about itself, and we are that part! How can a man be anything less than an infinite wonder? A man is already all he needs to be — and all he really needs to do is learn to see and realize this wonder. How the world would change if we fully understood what we are.

As discussed in Part I, this kind of appreciation of beauty often occurs in a boy around the dawning of his consciousness in the Spring of life. In my own case, I must have been about six. All I remember is being outside on the sunlit summer lawn. Nothing in particular happened. It didn't need to. It was just something about the light and the lawn and the warm velvet air, and a free, unencumbered joyous feeling. It was the comprehension of something wonderful, amazing, full. It was as if I had momentarily re-entered the dimension of being that precedes mind's conceptual categorizing, labeling, distancing, and discriminating. The light was so soft, the scene so gently but vividly alive and colorful. The world permeated with the presence of BEING. Everything was a soft seamless whole, beyond thought. This was original being. And I was part of this beauty.

This early appreciation of beauty extended to the early family as well. I recall my father in childhood. He seemed solid, intelligent, important, strong, practical, and wise. I can smell his suits, cigarette, hair creme. And I was awestruck by the perceptual realness of his life. Words fail to communicate this essentially preverbal nature of seeing. All that can be said is that he impressed me greatly and that I was so proud to be a part of this man's world. I gave him a brown and black abstract tie for Christmas. I wanted to be just like him. He was pure being, beautiful in all dimensions. He was my father. This is what I saw before judgment and disappointment could distance me from the pureness of perception.

My older brother, too, was beautiful and forever interesting because he could do so many advanced and grown-up things. He could go to the library by himself, he raised rabbits in a pen, he was always starting something new, creating adventures. He was constantly interesting. So were the house, the fish pond, the

willow tree, the summer rains, the humid heat, the sound of the car on the grav-
el driveway, learning to ride my bike, trips into town, neighbor boys, Easter egg
hunts next door, snow in the winter, hurricanes and electrical outages, birthdays
and birthday cakes, Dad coming home from work, Thanksgiving dinners, my
three little brothers that seemed to come into existence magically as time passed
in the wonder of those first years. Each of these events was new, fresh, clean,
bright, wondrous. God it was amazing!

New or first experiences often have this kind of wonder. I remember my first
ride on my father's shoulders, my first swim with my mother in the lake, trips to
a nearby stream to play, being bitten by a horsefly on Cape Cod where my grandmother lived, my first plane ride, how my little brother carried a rescued baby
squirrel in his shirt pocket and another little brother put on his Superman costume under the piano, my baby brother's joyous "famous dance," hitting a baseball hard, my first kiss, learning to drive, milking a cow, sleeping outside
overnight, the pleasure of nakedness and sexual feeling, my first real best friend,
my first girlfriend. On and on. Each happening was beyond comparison. Each
one expanded me, giving me more of my own wholeness. To experience something in this way is to take it in fully, to love it, to have it inside and outside all at
the same time. All these kinds of experiences have in common that they make us
more marvelously alive, more of what we are. We become conscious of all this
newness — nothing is excluded. Like a curious puppy, everything is interesting,
nothing off limits. All is taken in. Reality is constantly fresh and scintillating. The
more we experience, the more alive and joyously expanded we become. And it all
takes place in the presumptive context of a supportive parental ground. This
ground makes the world feel essentially safe — safe enough to explore and love.

What happened to this kind of original beauty, the infinite beauty men have
a right to know and feel? What a world it would be if men could see it again! How
is it possible that we can forget its wonder and, worse still, come to question its
worth; our worth, the worth of life itself? The change comes when our energy,
exuberance, and complete self-centeredness run afoul of parental tolerances; that
is, when a parent gets angry, impatient, and stern, sets abrupt limits that express
displeasure at us; when we are struck or yelled at in disapproval. Then something
horrible happens, something changes. We are expelled from the Garden of Eden.
The subjective wholeness of being feels shattered, spoiled, invaded, threatened,
or corrupted. A punitive trauma we do not understand is imposed on that wholeness. A different kind of pain is introduced into our experience. Not just the pain
of a scraped knee or bruised elbow, but the pain of being not wanted, valued, or
loved. The pain of rejection, unworthiness, and fear.

Suddenly, freedom and expansion are replaced by recoil, as if a hot stove had
been touched — and this stove is our parent, and the safe ground of love on
which we were growing ourselves itself becomes dangerous. There is nothing

more painful than a parent's anger and its emotional sting. The experience of self and world changes. Suddenly it feels as if there is something wrong with me. I am bad, ugly, unlovable. I am afraid. I am not good enough. Because I cannot bear this invaded or devalued feeling, I learn to split off from awareness whatever it was that just happened. I cannot let it threaten my attachment to the people who provide the safety and love I need because I know that I could not survive without them. And so we learn to suppress and disown whatever thoughts, needs, impulses, perceptions, or emotions that seemed to risk it all. We learn to disown parts of ourself. The result is not only the storing of repressed emotional conflicts and trauma which psychology has studied since Freud. It is more than that. The additional cost is that the original beauty we knew and lived in is also diminished, for we learn increasingly to close the pupil of our seeing in a careful and inhibiting vigilance, alert to the always potential danger.

In this anxiety, we sense that the atmosphere itself has changed, and we quickly withdraw our exuberant vitality. It is too great a risk. And when the pupil of the eye is narrowed, the world's brightness is dimmed. Angry, hurt, or frightened feelings cause us to contract ourselves in self-protection for they make us uncomfortable, uncertain, unsafe. Sometimes anger spills out beyond our limited control and we keep getting in more trouble. Shame builds. Still we try to conceal the feelings evoked by this fundamental betrayal. Worse, the world of open wonder has been replaced by a world of cautious distance, anxious vigilance, smoldering anger, and self-control. Then, as if this weren't bad enough, we unwittingly take the final step. We reduce our feeling of vulnerability by shutting down our openness of wonder. Feeling less than beautiful, less than perfect, at risk of losing more, we begin to try to grasp this distinction between good and bad. How did we become bad? What do they view as good? We learn to examine and judge our previously uncorrupted self. What's wrong with me? What must I do to be good enough? Are others better? In this highly critical questioning, we turn against ourselves, finding blame, badness, and shame. The split in our subjective wholeness and beauty widens. We begin to be three: who I really am, much of which must now be concealed; who I fear they think I am, which feels ugly and unwantable; and who I should be to preserve their approval.

Pure awareness, the inclusive and accepting consciousness that allows everything to enter and be experienced, inner and outer, is the basis of wholeness. A split consciousness, one that restricts parts of internal or external reality from being known and experienced, makes us feel less than whole, because we are. We have discarded part of that subjective wholeness. We know something is missing. We know we are not complete. The comparisons that become necessary for survival now establish a hierarchy of value. When some things are more acceptable or better than others, then we can no longer be intrinsically beautiful or whole.

Comparisons, as Krishnamurti used to say, are always a form of violence. And we do such violence to ourselves and to each other by comparing one against another. Sibling and peer comparisons — about grades, looks, sports, popularity, race, profession, income. It goes on and on, until the grid of comparisons virtually strangles us. Each time we believe we are lacking, we devalue ourselves. Wonder begins to wither or withdraw in anxiety or sorrow, as if we have viewed or condemned our very soul as ugly. By the end of Spring, we have learned the rules of good and bad and neither ourselves nor the world is unconditionally beautiful any more. So it is we who pull back from ourselves in sorrow and perceived unworthiness. Withholding our love from ourself and each other in judgmental comparisons becomes the greatest form of violence there is. When we stop seeing our beauty, our hearts break and our souls begin to die. We stop seeing it when others stop seeing it in us. This is the cause of so much sorrow, shame, violence, and insanity. This is the mechanism of the Great Wound. The beauty is not gone, but our ability to see it is.

Boys lose this beauty by the end of elementary school, often sooner. Self-consciousness and collective "objective" standards take its place. In middle school, escalating peer pressure creates even greater distrust for our true selves, and we unquestionably do whatever necessary for the approval of the social norm. What a tragedy. In addition, parents also worry about their children's social and academic standing, and reconfirm their child's core anxiety: Do I measure up? Thereafter, a culture of achievement, pressure, and competition takes over as worried parents live out their own unfinished insecurities through their children, and their children learn to worry about being good enough, too. Often, briefly, the beauty returns for moments during adolescent years. Warrior masculinity is inherently beautiful in its pure form: healthy, energetic, bold, youthful, idealistic and exciting, full of possibilities. Adolescent boys primp and preen; they love to display their beauty to young women and each other in athletics, romance, and dance. This is an enlivening and magical narcissism, when a boy, temporarily, falls in love with himself and the wonderful opportunities of his expanding horizons. Finding the princess in Summer years awakens the beauty again — wonderfully but briefly.

The crush of comparisons and expectations returns all too soon, and the beauty is lost again to the worry, performance anxiety, and pressure of adulthood. No one is beautiful then except the romanticized fictions created by movies, magazines, soap operas, and sports. Even men who reach those highest rungs do not truly feel beautiful — intrinsically and unconditionally beautiful — for if they lost their "looks," popularity, competitive ability, or money, they would no longer be beautiful to the world or to themselves.

This progressive destruction of the real magnificence of men, and its replacement with artificial standards, does tremendous damage. It is abuse of the soul and the world. And the severity of the childhood abuse, verbal, emotional, and physical, establishes the degree of damage to a man's psyche. When it involves physical violence, outright rejection, abandonment, or shaming, then men learn to hate themselves, to distrust, to experience the world as cold and devaluing, and their souls become cold and unfeeling in turn. They fail to develop the capacity for love and empathy for they have received none. Instead, they carry the rage of this terrible betrayal. Many turn against each other and against society. Harry Stack Sullivan called this a "Malevolent Transformation," and it surely is. ❦

CHAPTER 19

The Compulsive Warrior
Model of Masculinity

≫ "Atrial what?"

One evening in December, at the end of a particularly long day, sitting in therapy with one of my most stressful clients, I began to notice my heart pounding. My heartbeat felt hard and irregular, my chest felt tight. It was difficult to concentrate. I dismissed it, got through the session, and thought maybe I was just tired. Perhaps I was sitting in a funny position and developed a muscle cramp. I went home, talked to my wife about how I felt, ignored her pleas that we go to the emergency room right away, and went to bed thinking a good night's rest was all I needed. I woke up feeling the same and finally called my doctor for an appointment later in the day — and then went back to work again! This time, the beating was so distracting I couldn't concentrate. I canceled the rest of my day and went into the emergency room with my wife. I was seen immediately. The E.R. nurse announced routinely to her crew, "forty-six-year-old-man with first episode of atrial fib," and set me up in bed with blood pressure, EKG, oxygen, and pulse monitors. She drew blood for lab work and put in an I.V. of digoxyn. It took nearly six hours and two more doses of medication to get my heart to "convert" to its proper rhythm. At one point they were discussing electroconversion paddles.

When it was all over, I was told I had experienced atrial fibrillation, not a serious condition for a man of my age. I was placed on oral medication for three months, referred to a cardiologist, and discharged. I felt relieved, but not much better physically. Drained and weak for most of that weekend, I went back to work on Monday still feeling tired and tight in my chest, and finally called the cardiologist's office to complain again. The nurse had me come in for another EKG and blood work and reassured me everything was fine. I saw the cardiologist the next week who thoughtfully reviewed my story and lab work, reassured me again, and simply concluded, "These things just happen." I repeated my concern about the sensation of chest tightness and, astoundingly, he finally admitted in exasperation that he too experiences such sensations when he's tired. He said it was "normal!" So my wife and I went home feeling more relieved.

But the whole thing didn't add up. It wasn't over for me, not psychologically anyway. This event just seemed too dramatic and powerful to be dismissed as something that "just happens." There had to be more to learn about this experience.

For a week or so, I couldn't even ask the right questions. I was just too numb and rattled. Then, slowly, as if from out of a mental fog, numerous realizations began to emerge. To begin with, I saw how much my family really cared about me. My children and wife showed me through their anxious and helpful behavior just how frightened they were. I still get teary thinking about this. I realized then how much they love me, not because I make the money, pay the bills, or help with homework, but because I deeply matter to each of them.

A second and rather peculiar realization had initially come to me in the E.R., but I had put it aside. I was surprised to find that I was not as afraid to die as I had previously thought, and I felt a peculiar acceptance and comfort with this possibility. And this lead to another realization: I realized that a part of me wanted to die, to just let go and disappear. I was shocked. Gradually I began to understand why. I work too hard. I feel such a responsibility to support and take care of everyone around me, financially and emotionally, that I have always pushed myself to keep producing no matter how I feel. I've done this for years, first as the young professional wanting to be good at everything in his trade, then as the family breadwinner wanting to give everyone the best. I did it from a secret fear that I would end up letting my family down the way I felt my father had let us down.

In sum, I think my heart was telling me that it was weary. I recalled the cardiologist saying that these episodes sometimes come when a man is especially tired or stressed. My heart was saying "I am scared, I cannot keep up this pace. You are pushing me too hard." I wondered then how many other men feel like this, and how many of us secretly or unconsciously wish for a health crisis so we can get off the treadmill, perhaps to get some rest or quiet, or some of the TLC once associated with being sick when we were children. Men don't ask for what they need after they grow up. We are not supposed to. We do what we have to do and we die for it if we have to — that's the "manly" way. I think that was true for me. I think I would have welcomed a more serious crisis, a heart attack, or even death, to get off this treadmill.

The issue of death then became even more real to me. In this episode of atrial fibrillation, I felt I had come close to death. Maybe not literally, but close enough. I felt my heart racing out of control, at the edge. I was vulnerable. I could die. It was no longer an abstraction, but an immediate possibility, a direct kind of knowing. If death could be this near, I asked myself, what did I want to do about it? How did I feel? What welled up in me then, without anticipation, was a desire to get on with my love — not ego, not responsibility, not success, not money, but love — and to express it in as many ways as I could. I felt deeply that I was born to love and that this loving nature had been calling me all my life, especially since my midlife transition began six years earlier. My heart arrhythmia was a wake-up call to open my heart, get on that path, or die pulling a neurotic load.

Weeks later, I had this related realization: as you age, you have to give up, step by step, everything you think you are: health, career, identity, security, friends, family, and finally, body and life. There is no escape from this progression. This is an emptying of identity and persona, of all you think you are. But it is, at the same time and as so many spiritual writers attest, a necessary, natural, and developmentally programmed shift from ego to that "something more" that lives in us, to that other larger consciousness we know to be the sacred. This is the universal spiritual path, the path everyone must eventually take. My episode, my brush with death, was also a teaching, a signpost pointing to the necessary relinquishing of ego and control in life's later years.

Late in his own life, Jung said, "To this day, God is the name by which I designate all things which cross my path violently and recklessly, all things which upset my subjective views, plans, and intentions and change the course of my life for better or worse." (Edinger, *Transformation of the God Image*, p. 14). Certainly this medical crisis was such an epiphany. And certainly this defeat of the heroic was a teaching of vast significance to me.

So what does a health crisis like this mean? Any crisis is a metaphor about one's life. It is not that these things just happen. What's important is that we listen to their message.

Clearly our culture has lost its vision of men as beloved and beautiful, precious and divine. Men have become fallen angels, corrupt and evil. In the place of beauty, male society develops a compensatory standard emphasizing warrior invincibility and perfection. Why? Because we have forgotten how to see and love our beauty, and the resulting loveless void hurts deeply. From this great pain we fashion something else, something that we hope will help make us invincible to the pain and good enough to be loved again. Toughness, strength, power, and superiority will defend us from this sorrow and vulnerability. In this way, we stereotype healthy male rough-and-tumble toughness into a brutal standard of comparative personal worth. It is a standard based first on emptiness, sorrow, and deprivation, and then deified in a cultural demand that men be strong, competitive, and fearless. Against this unforgiving standard, we see only shortcomings and inadequacies. Unable to measure up to this compensatory model of superiority, secret feelings of ugliness and badness multiply. If only we were rich or famous, hard as nails, stronger than other men, then we would be good enough.

This is the Compulsive Warrior model of manhood, the traditional model of masculinity inbred so pervasively in Western civilization and American culture. Passed on insidiously from generation to generation, it has bullied and straitjacketed men for years into a destructively narrow and limiting expression of manhood. As the term "Compulsive Warrior" suggests, this is an involuntary model that says to a man that he must be tough, physical, athletic, fearless, powerful, competitive, aggressive, superior, ruthless, logical, shrewd, conquering, financially successful, unemotional, uncomplaining, and correct. Winning is the name of the game in work, sex, and life. A man is measured by his income and profession, the cost of his car, size of his house, and the attractiveness of his woman. As he gets older, tireless responsibility and material symbols of wealth become the important standards. How you make your fortune is not nearly as important as having it. Status, control, and invulnerability are the final measures of his personal worth and social value. Cultural heroes exemplifying this model are seen everywhere in movies and novels that glorify male violence, heroism, and invincibility. Rambo, the Terminator, Robocop, Dirty Harry. All this because we can no longer see the fresh, always new, timeless and original beauty of masculinity and being.

The Compulsive Warrior model further says to men that however life looks on the surface, it is a kind of undisclosed warfare. A man must be impenetrable. He must secretly plot to surpass other men. Constant readiness for invisible battle and competition must be maintained. Because you measure yourself against the victories and successes of the men around you, wounds and failures are kept to yourself. Neither cry nor tenderly console others. You'll just embarrass them. Naturally this model produces enormous numbness and isolation among men. Men do not ask for help, men tough it out silently. This model also says that our national manhood should be equally competitive, tough, and superior, and that violent solutions to world problems are acceptable if the other side is "asking for it." It is a stern, punitive, unforgiving masculinity.

Finally, this model also teaches men to override their needs and limitations, and learn instead to "crank themselves up," use adrenaline like amphetamines, and push onward relentlessly in spite of fatigue, hardship, illness, or desire. In this cultural classroom, a man learns to further violate the deep emotional self with all its beauty and giftedness. He learns that machines are to be emulated for their steady, tireless, uncomplaining productivity. As he ages, he learns that he can be replaced just like a machine if he fails to stay ahead. Finally, a man learns that sexuality is something to be performed, to succeed at, and that erections are anatomical tools that should never fail. The term "impotence" says it all.

It is hard for men to take risks with this comparative model because risks make failures and failure is the one unforgivable sin of manhood. If you failed, it means you were not strong enough, tough enough, smart enough, or disciplined enough. You get judged and analyzed, as if it were your batting stance that needed correction and that's why you failed. You should have worked harder. Failure is defined financially, sexually, athletically, and occupationally, and if you fail, you are indeed worthless and pitiable. It puts you on the street or on the dole.

"When the going gets tough, the tough get going" and "no pain, no gain" are slogans of this masculine ideal. Breaking down, giving up, being needy, being sad are all reasons for shame in this model. We believe there is no beauty in failure.

This is a model we have all felt. It is repeatedly described throughout the growing literature of men's studies. It is no new discovery or mystery. What is a mystery is that we still have so much difficulty confronting it. It is a very powerful and still largely invisible model.

Costs of the Compulsive Warrior Model of Manhood

The costs of this model to men and to society are grave. As men, we are dying inside emotionally and spiritually because of these soul-crushing rules. But these same rules forbid men to admit their injuries even to themselves. So men put on their business suits every morning and symbolically tie their pain in a tight knot around their neck.

Numerous writers from the men's movement have described the costs of this model in detail, including Robert Bly, Warren Farrel, Douglas Gillette, James Hillman, Sam Keen, Andrew Kimbrell, Aaron Kipness, John Lee, Michael Meade, Robert Moore, and Sam Osherson. Their combined work is a chorus of voices challenging men to face this injurious paradigm of manhood. Any review of such costs must include:

✔ **Health:** Men routinely and without complaint give up their health for the masculine model. Men still die sooner than women and have traditionally suffered more from the "wear-and-tear" diseases arising from the chronic stress of achievement pressure and Type A competition (e.g., heart disease, high blood pressure). Young men are expendable in wartime. They are not trusted or respected enough to ask for their voluntary involvement; rather they are "inducted" and, as we saw in Vietnam, sometimes compelled to commit atrocities that damage their psyches forever. Men are expected to sacrifice their bodies for the team, and to succeed like machines in endless productivity, at any cost. Some literally die in the workplace because of the careers and the rules they must follow. Finally, men have higher rates of drug and alcohol abuse, murder, suicide, and assault. It costs too much to live up to the impossible ideal of the compulsive warrior. Kimbrell aptly labels this cumulative damage "the holocaust of men." (Kimbrell, 1991, p. 73)

✔ **Violations of Conscience:** The demand for ruthless competition has caused men over and over to violate their own conscience, that is, to shame and defeat other men, to glory in being superior in sports and work, to treat women as objects, and to exploit the underprivileged here and abroad in the service of acquiring wealth and power. Like gladiators, men are turned against each other in work, sex, and sports. As Sam Keen notes astutely, "Business is just warfare in slow motion" and "Even sex in our culture tends to be centered around competition and conquest." (Keen, 1991, p. 57). With this warfare mindset, men are taught to override their inborn emotional aversion to producing serious injury or death. Later they pay for it in the discovery of deep guilt and shame.

ƒ Estrangement from Families: The long hours and emotional toughening required by this model cause men to lose touch with their own families. Men work nights, weekends, and long, long days. They are often too tired and too numbed to relate deeply and intimately with their families when they do get home. Men can also become addicted to the adrenaline rush of risk and competition, the ego inflation of productivity and success, and even take pride in the exhaustion of responsibility. But in doing so, they lose contact with real husbanding and fathering, and resent that the time and struggles of family life interfere with work. Everyone loses. Some men, enlightened about the importance of home and fathering, try to do it all. They rush from work to watch or coach their kids' teams, come home to chores and correcting homework, paying bills, and watching television. Everything is hurried, accelerated, tense. There never seems to be enough time. But much of it is not real contact. Real contact comes in unhurried and unscheduled time together — spontaneous meetings that allow who we really are to come through.

ƒ False Manhood: Unable to support their own emotional needs and longings against the tyranny of this culturally sanctioned model, men learn to assume a false facade of manhood. As Robert Moore describes, this is not mature life-giving masculinity, but instead the rigid, hard, deadened, and judgmental patriarchal stance women have properly railed against for years. False manhood simply reflects this pervasive defense of hardening — of tensing, bracing, and contracting ourselves and our bodies into a fist to control the confusion, helplessness, shame, and woundedness we really feel. The hardened arteries supplying our hearts are more than a metaphor. This is a model, as Kipnes has written, for "Making hardened men out of sensitive boys." (Kipnes, p. 20) It is from this righteous posture that we so easily justify war and exploitation. Men without personal knowledge of poetry and dance, love and sorrow, spirit and soul, empathy and compassion, cannot properly be trusted with the reins of government, much less the weapons of destruction.

ƒ Reckless Overuse of the Masculine Attitude: In their driven quest to control and conquer nature, men have created factories, chemicals, and war machines that have been taken far beyond their original purposes, to pollute and deface the earth. Capitalism and the consumption patterns of the "First World" leave hundreds of millions of "Third World" people in absolute poverty, and the class struggle within our own "First World" country leaves one out of two African-American children born into poverty. The feminine consciousness, that emotional makeup that embraces the welfare of everyone and honors the earth as our mother, has been overridden for centuries. It is not that technology and progress are themselves wrong; but when operated by an extreme masculine attitude of control and conquest, they can become driven, destructive, and empty.

✗ **Loss of Soul:** If we use soul as a metaphor for that which is deepest within us, that inner core of values and being which must be found and honored for our lives to feel authentic, meaningful, truly purposeful, and even sacred, then it can be seen that one of the greatest personal costs of the Compulsive Warrior model of manhood is the loss of one's soul. Men have sold their souls in the market place of ambition, success, and superiority. Ask men what is more important, the intangible soul or a new BMW or Mercedes. If there is no room for soul, for the opportunity to feel and know one's own nature and being, then there can be no personal or masculine depth, and hence nothing to give.

Assessing the Costs of the Compulsive Warrior Model of Manhood

Here are some of the common areas of self-betrayal demanded by the Compulsive Warrior model of manhood, and their associated costs. I invite you to go over these questions slowly, thoughtfully. Ask yourself inwardly, which ones still pervade and dominate your life and whether competitive manhood is really worth the price you pay?

Areas of Betrayal:

I. *The Workplace:*
- A. Do you still feel driven to be successful in the workplace?
- B. Do you compare yourself with other men?
  How does it make you feel?
- C. Do you fear other men (or women) getting ahead of you?
- D. Are you motivated by a secret fear of failure?
  What do you fear would happen if you failed?
- E. Do you sometimes feel you are barely holding together

at work? Do you ever feel close to burning out or
crashing under the demands or schedule you keep?
Do you keep it a secret?

F. Do you wonder if people really knew how you feel that
you'd still be respected and trusted to do your job?
Do you feel you are faking it sometimes at work?
Are you afraid of being discovered?

G. Do you push yourself even when tired, depressed,
or unmotivated?

H. How many hours do you work each week?

I. Do you use the language of warfare to describe your
work (e.g., making a killing, taking no hostages,
winning the battle, beating the enemy, striking
first, etc.)?

J. Do you feel you have to be "on" all the time,
in other words, always ready, sharp, perfect, together?

K. Is there anybody you could trust to share feelings
like these in your workplace?

L. Do you feel discouraged about your work?
Does it seem meaningless at times?

M. Do you ever give yourself unscheduled time to
relax, meditate, get in touch with yourself,
or just waste time?

Costs: Work stress and pressure, workaholism,
endless competition, burnout, and lack of
"vocation" as a higher calling.

II. Friends:

A. Do you have any really close and open male
friendships? How many?

B. Do you share with male friends your real fears
and feelings about yourself?

C. When was the last time you poured your heart out
to another man?

D. Have you ever cried with another man?

E. How do you reach out to other men who may
be in trouble?

F. Who would you turn to if you collapsed?

G. Can you feel love for another man without
worrying about your sexual orientation?

Costs: Male isolation and loneliness, lack of deep and

nurturing male bonds, lack of genuine support and community.

III. Family:

A. Are you an equal partner in child-rearing and discipline? Do you leave most of the details up to your wife (e.g., homework, medical and dental appointments, teacher conferences)?

B. Do you still spend more time away from home and family than you'd like to? How often do you work nights and weekends? Does your family complain about your work hours?

C. Do you feel close to your children?
   Is it hard for you to feel close to them?

D. Do you tell your wife how you really feel about yourself as a man, father, or worker?

E. Are you close to your own parents and siblings?

F. Do you secretly look toward other women for admiration, validation, and understanding?

G. Do you over-react to your children, under-react, or fail to react at all?

H. Do you feel your children really know you?
   Do you feel your parents really know you?

I. Do you find yourself rushing constantly to keep up with your work and family commitments, and fail in the process to really relate at all?

J. Do you wear yourself out or become resentful about trying to do everything and be everything for everyone in the family?

Costs: Family estrangement, missed relationships, superficial relationships, lack of family support, failure to give your children who you really are, more exhaustion.

IV. Your Father:

A. Were you close to your father growing up?
   Did he talk to you?

B. What kind of fathering did you receive from him?
   What did you do together?

C. What kind of warrior was your father?
   What was his attitude toward work, productivity,

and family?
D. Do you feel you have to prove anything to him or to
   live up to his standards in your work?
E. What did your father teach you about manhood?
F. Was your father competitive with you?
   What did he teach you about failure?
G. What virtues did your father instill in your work ethic?
H. Do you give your family what he never gave you?
   What is that?
I. What is the nature of your father wound?
   Have you really grieved it?

Costs: Repeating the "sins of the father," living up to standards
that are not your own, seeking "father approval" from an
older man, competitive and harsh self-judgments,
failing to grieve.

V. *Your Dream:*

A. Did you ever have a personal dream for your life?
   What happened to it? When did you lose it?
B. Do you have a dream that genuinely inspires you now?
   If not, what keeps you going? If so, are you realizing it?
   Have you told anyone your personal dream?
C. Do you put money, success, career, responsibility, or
   recognition ahead of other inner longings?
D. Do you feel like you have a purpose in life beyond
   providing for your family?

Costs: "Loss of soul," and lack of meaning, vitality, and
vision in life.

VI. *Health:*

A. Do you ignore or suppress unpleasant physical
   sensations?
B. Do you view colds or illness as wasted time or
   signs of weakness, and try to override them
   when you can?
C. Are you aware of stress-related physical problems
   (e.g, headaches, back or stomach pain, frequent colds,
   bowel disturbances, fatigue)? What do you think your body is
   trying to say to you?
D. Are you aware of stress-related emotional problems
   (e.g., depression, burnout, marital and family conflict)?

How do you respond to them?

E. Do you push yourself excessively to excel in exercise or athletics?

F. What are your negative health habits (e.g., smoking, drinking, too little or too much exercise, insufficient sleep, etc.)?

Costs: Abuse of your body, recurring health problems, self-induced illness, loss of contact with physical and instinctual energies.

VII. Deadening Behaviors:

Do you deaden your feelings or your pain with addictive, compulsive, or emotionally numbing agents or activities such as:

A. alcohol, drugs, or cigarettes

B. over-work

C. over-eating

D. workaholism

E. power, success, or wealth

F. obsessive sex

G. over-playing or over-exercising

H. television

I. gambling

Costs: Loss of self-contact, loss of feeling contact with others, lack of passionate intensity in life.

VIII. Personal Fears:

A. Do you ever fear you'll end up broke, homeless, on the street, etc.?

B. Can you admit to being or feeling lost, confused, flawed, imperfect, ordinary, etc.?

C. Do you typically see the world in terms of opposite extremes (good/bad, success/failure, strong/weak, rich/poor, all/nothing, etc.)?

D. Do you feel that you measure up to other men? Where do you think you fall short?

E. Would you feel ashamed if others knew how you really answered these questions?

Costs: Hidden depression, unspoken fears, self-rejection, self-depreciation.

IX. Beauty, Wholeness, and the Sacred:

A. Can you see the incredible beauty of the world around you and of your own life?

B. Do you devalue your relationship by judging your lover as imperfect or ugly?

C. Do you worry about being ugly yourself?

D. Do you feel incomplete and imperfect?

E. Are you searching for what's missing "out there," believing you can find it somewhere else or in someone else?

F. Can you feel sacredness in the world?

G. Can you feel the joy inherent in life itself?

H. How often do you feel wonder, reverence, and awe toward the world?

Costs: The pain of lost beauty, negative judgments of self and others, spirituality, and unconditioned joy. ❋

CHAPTER 20

Origins of the
Compulsive Warrior

≫ When Western civilization lost its perception of intrinsic male beauty and value, and replaced it with the Compulsive Warrior model of masculinity, is anyone's guess. There are, of course, always extraordinary individuals from every era, often artists, who carry the aesthetic, moral, and transcendent vision of beauty. And, as suggested earlier, most men glimpse such wonder in their lives several times in the course of their development, but then lose it. If we look around us, however, we can see how our blindness is culturally perpetrated, and identify some of the more recent (and continuing) causes.

Writers in the field of men's studies have cited numerous etiologies for the devaluation of men. The three most pertinent and commonly noted are the mechanization and exploitation of men, the deterioration of relationships between fathers and sons, boys and men, and the fragmentation of positive male community.

Rather than merely repeat what has been said better by others, I wish here to selectively re-emphasize, with prose and poetry, what is most important about these changes. I would like these words to call forth more than understanding; I wish them to resonate with your own real experience. Most importantly, I hope to begin dismantling the cultural blinders we all carry that damage our perception of beauty everywhere.

The Industrial Revolution and the Mechanization of Men: A significant degree of the degradation of male value and beauty can be associated with the enormous social, economic, and psychological changes introduced by the Industrial Revolution. Before the Industrial Revolution, ninety percent of people worked at home. Life was still essentially rural and people spent their working lives farming. Though many products were sold, purchased, or exchanged, the majority of manufacturing took place in the home with the whole family working together to grow and prepare food, make clothing, build homes, and care for animals. But the pace of life was tied closely and naturally to the agricultural seasons and changed little from one generation to another.

It is an ancient and curious propensity of man's psyche to imitate whatever is most important in the world around him. Early hunting man imitated his prey, and sought a kind of inner spiritual connection and communication with it in order to survive.

Thus, the recognition of absolute dependence evokes imitation as a survival response, and imitation takes in the characteristics of what is imitated. Agricultural man did the same, mythologizing his gods with the characteristics of crops, weather, and seasons. Our absolute dependence now is on technology. Machines fill our psyches. When men begin to imitate machines, they begin to emulate their characteristics. They want to be "on" any time or all the time, always reliable, perhaps in need of servicing but not rest, impervious to pain, shiny, coldly efficient, fast, and endlessly productive. In this new culture, to be a man is to be like a machine. And like a machine, he is also replaceable, expendable, and discardable — in war and industry.

And there were other costs. Technological advances allowed productivity to increase steadily, creating the illusion of unlimited progress and abundance. Egos were inflated by the enormous wealth generated in this early capitalism. Machines and productivity were further idealized. Faster and faster went the pace of work until men were not too different from the machines that ran them, and the seasons no longer regulated the nature or pace of a man's work. The overall goal of life, then, became ever increasing speed and unlimited productivity. This cultural grandiosity has become insatiable and addictive. Whether it is your income, your golf score, or your kid's grades, everybody wants it to get better, higher, more. The longer and harder you work, the more you crowd out those activities and experiences that nourish the deep and original self: solitude, quiet, feeling, beauty, creativity, clockless time, contemplation, and love. These essentials feed the soul. The more they are crowded to the margins of life, the more one achieves the machine ideal, the more emotional deprivation is actually generated.

A man can work sixteen hours a day and acquire all sorts of things. Despite his possessions, he will be emotionally and spiritually starved, and not know it. This seemingly invisible betrayal of the deep self creates tremendous emotional pain and, in the absence of insight or alternatives, the need to defend against it. The more successful, the more empty; the more empty, the more driven to fill the emptiness; the more driven, the more empty. The cycle of deprivation and compensatory drivenness is the psychic equivalent of the machine.

The Industrial Revolution, with its enormous capacity for productivity, invention, and control, inflated man's belief in his own machine-like ascendency over nature. We believe that everything should be used for some productive purpose. Simply put, we have lost respect for the natural order of life, for the beauty of things just as they are, and for the inherent value of man apart from his machine-like usefulness.

D.H. Lawrence grew up during the industrialization of England. He saw its effects with a prophetic accuracy. The mechanical life, the life that glorifies production as synonymous with male prowess and worth, is well described in his poem *Two Ways Of Living And Dying*.

Two Ways of Living and Dying
D.H. Lawrence

While people live the life
they are open to the restless skies, and streams flow in and out
darkly from the fecund cosmos, from the angry red sun, from the
*   moon*
up from the bounding earth, strange pregnant streams, in and out
*   of the flesh,*
and man is an iridescent fountain, rising up to flower
for a moment godly, like Baal or Krishna, or Adonis or Balder, or
*   Lucifer.*

But when people are only self-conscious and self-willed
they cannot die, their corpus still runs on,
while nothing comes from the open heaven, from earth, from the
*   sun and moon*
to them, nothing, nothing;
only the mechanical power of self-directed energy
drives them on and on, like machines,
on and on, with the triumphant sense of power, like machines,
on and on, and their triumph in mere motion
full of friction, full of grinding, full of danger to the gentle passengers
*   of growing life,*
but on and on, on and on, till the friction wears them out
and the machine begins to wobble
and with hideous shrieks of steely rage and frustration
the worn-out machine at last breaks down:
It is finished, its race is over.

So self-willed, self-centered, self-conscious people die
the death of nothingness, worn-out machines, Kaput!

Life is infinitely more than ambition and invention. In *The Sonnets To Orpheus*, Rilke compares our idealization of technological progress with vast, timeless, pristine, and awesome power of eternity. It is this experience that man longs for most ardently. And it is already here. Racing in search of progress will not bring it any closer.

The Sonnets to Orpheus
Rainer Maria Rilke

The New, my friends, is not a matter of
letting machines force out our handiwork.
Don't be confused by change; soon those who have
praised the "New" will realize their mistake.

For look, the Whole is infinitely newer
than a cable or a high apartment house.
The stars keep blazing with an ancient fire,
and still more recent fires will fade out.

Not even the longest, strongest of transmissions
can turn the wheels of what will be.
Across the moment, aeons speak with aeons.

More than we experienced has gone by.
And the future holds the most remote event
in union with what we most deeply want.

As these poems suggest, life is not solely or even primarily a business or industrial enterprise. It is first and foremost a matter of wonder and beauty. In this, it is sacred. We have lost this vision of beauty. Part of this broken vision is our own fault. Men no longer discuss a sacred vision of reality with each other or with their boys. If they don't have it, how can they share it? There is no initiation into the sacred. This brings us to the missing connections between fathers and sons, and boys and men.

Sons Without Fathers, Boys Without Men: The Missing Lineage of Male Beauty: Robert Bly, in his book *Iron John*, argues that another primary consequence of the Industrial Revolution was the breakdown of the bonds between fathers and sons, and between boys and men. With the industrialization of production, men in ever larger numbers began working away from home, in cities, for strangers, doing work the family never saw, often exploited, and coming home at night numb and exhausted. The family lost its intimate daytime contact with the father and the father lost his contact with the family. In the 1940s and '50s, he was often little known by the family, nor did he know them. He did his duty, and duty was the silent expression of the only way he knew how to show love. This loss of a real and human father, an emotional and energetic father, robbed something precious from the family. The sorrow has been there for generations.

Pamela Brown, in a poem called *Apology*, describes the awkward midlife moment of facing one's father when the distance has grown too great for words.

Apology
Pamela Brown

"Sorry" seems inadequate.
"I never meant it," fatuous.
And it's too late for tears.
How then to tell you all I've learned these twenty
*   years?*

I stand here in the cold December day
and thrust a gift-wrapped parcel at your chest
and say
"Best love from all of us.
A happy birthday, Dad."

A box of time remembered.

The same late gift you gave your father once
...and he to his.

Our fathers, as men, potentially carry the great beauty and the vitality of manhood. It is a gift always available, but in recent times, rarely given or even known. It would come from his smell, sweat, laughter, humor, side-by-side chores, instruction, advice, or the way he got mad, or what he stood for, or the things he knew. Perfect was not the issue. But he was someone to look up to, or at the very least, to learn about healthy or normal maleness. At the most wonderful end of the spectrum, a father can validate his son's natural perception of beauty, the intrinsic value of life, and the spiritual dimension of the world just by discussing the stars with him on a clear night, or talking about his mother as a woman of beauty, or sharing the story of his own life. But sadly, most of us didn't even know our fathers like this, not really, not from his inside.

These same gifts multiply when a boy is in the community of men. When working or playing together with other men, a boy can observe the larger range of masculinity and fatherhood. His own father does not have to carry all of manhood on his own individual shoulders, and a boy can find in other men some of the things his father may simply lack. This cumulative male experience awakens so much in a boy, stimulating more of what he is than he yet knows, and validating his masculinity in ways that mothers and women cannot.

Nowadays, it looks like things are getting better between fathers and sons. Younger fathers, recognizing their own father hunger, are spending more time with their children in child-rearing and recreational activities. But some of this change may be illusory. As noted earlier, many fathers are now trying to please too many masters, being the child's coach, teacher, chauffeur, and mentor. Does the stressed and hurried father really make good contact with his children? Do hurried and over-committed sons really connect with their fathers?

Drawing from the work of countless professionals, from the innumerable stories told in men's groups and gatherings, and from the individual reflections of almost every man I have seen in psychotherapy, the kinds of problems lingering from the loss of meaningful connection between fathers and sons, boys and men in industrial society still include:

Absent Fathers: With the industrialization reorganization of the workplace, boys no longer see much of their fathers or their father's work because they are gone all day. The father a son sees at night is too often the empty, tired, and used-up father.

Emotionally Wounded Fathers: With the industrial revolution, fathers were placed in roles they were never prepared for, roles in which they were subservient to bosses, management, and cold economics. They were no longer independent, no longer their own men, but instead often humiliated and diminished in laboring solely for others. In addition to being enslaved by an impersonal marketplace, recent generations of men also lost their place in the family and became secretly sad, isolated, and needy. This unconscious, unacknowledged, and certainly unacceptable loneliness and sorrow can twist a man's psyche.

Absent Men: Not only are fathers missing from the daily lives of their sons, but so too is the world of men. Boys see men doing jobs, but they are generally not invited to join. In elementary school years, a boy's primary contact is with mothers and female teachers, and even after that, a boy's primary contact with male groups is in gym and sports. Here contact is limited to one or two men who teach that competition and constant self-improvement are the standards of male success. The only other substitute is the land of television and movies with its brand of super-heroes.

Culturally Distorted Male Images: Men in the television set or on the big screen cannot replace fathers and the real world of men. Men portrayed in the media tend to be either hard, indestructible, and fearless heroes (e.g., Rambo, the Terminator, Superman, GI Joe, professional athletes) or inadequate, incompetent and bumbling boy-men with critical or domineering wives (e.g., Fred Flintstone, characters played by Bob Newhart, Bill Cosby). Frequently, men appear especially foolish and inferior where children, housework, and emotions are concerned. This is a tragic devaluation and humiliation of men.

ſ *Gender Imbalances in Child-Rearing:* Despite the recent possibilities of change, it is still common for boys to be raised by mothers or in female supervised daycare centers. This is not wrong, but it is unbalanced. Boys begin to incorporate women's views of men, fathers, and gender behavior. A boy is also silently hurt by listening to his mother's anger and disappointment with his father, and he is hurt even more when he colludes in this criticism to earn her approval or attention. He internalizes uncertainty and shame about being male, or being like his father. Another problem of gender imbalance is the matriarchal family. When the father is absent or ineffectual, and the mother is the primary authority figure, boys will grow up unable to defend themselves appropriately in their adult relationships with women, particularly in times of conflict. There will be an exaggeration of the power of women in a boy's psyche. The result can be another generation of passive men on one hand, or of over-controlled men who erupt violently toward women when they feel frustrated or criticized.

ſ *Loss of Male Initiatory Practices into a Community of Men:* In tribal society, men initiate boys at prescribed times into the activities, responsibilities, sacred myths, and rituals of manhood. These rites of passage give boys clear and community-based values and roles. Each youth learns that he is needed for the physical and spiritual survival of the tribe. The aboriginal world of men, instead of seeing boys as potential economic competitors to be defeated for as long as possible, values them as assets for the future and desires their participation. In an impersonal industrial society, a young man has to find his own way, and there are fewer and fewer clearly prescribed ladders, and little support.

It is often argued that initiatory rites of tribal societies are brutal or cruel. Many certainly seem so from the outside (e.g., circumcision). But it is sometimes specious logic to isolate a specific initiatory practice from the culture it serves. If life is brutal for a tribe, brutal practices may be the way they prepare their children for this reality. We have to realize that rituals have deep significance to each culture and cannot be understood without fully entering the life of that people.

ſ *Father Abandonment:* With the explosive divorce rates of the last several decades, the wound of the emotionally distant father has become the wound of the literally absent father. Father-child contact drops off rapidly after divorce, with the majority of boys having minimal real or daily contact with their fathers. When this occurs, a boy is deprived of a million father-son opportunities, a million chances to experience the masculinity of his father. In those rare instances where other men can become successful father figures, a boy's maleness can again be nourished. Sadly, this does not usually happen.

ƒ **Emotionally Wounded Sons:** It follows naturally from the above that boys often experience their manhood and their maleness as shallow or defective. The wounded gender image a boy incorporates then distorts his view of himself as a man, husband, and father. There is tremendous grief hidden in this wound. And emotionally wounded sons become emotionally limited men, husbands, and fathers, set up to repeat the wounds for another round.

ƒ **Father Hunger:** Growing from the hole in the man's psyche left by the absent father is often a secret yet profound wish for father approval and for an idealized father figure who would finally reach out to them to provide the love, teaching, and guidance they never had. Bly and others call this longing "father hunger." (Berry, 1990, p. 2) It is real. Men without their father's blessing, as we have seen, search for approval from older men. This search for the father, Hillman reminds us, is really the search for a mentor who can provide the unavailable blessing. In later life, men try again to connect with their fathers one more time, hoping for some kind of real acknowledgment or contact. Often the distance is insurmountable.

The "Father Wound": The Story of Everyman taught us that each son is wounded in some way by his father, and this wound is central to our journey of manhood. It is simply the case that our fathers are limited. They have their own problems. Late in life, fathers face the melancholy of regret, knowing too late the errors they made amidst conflicts of work, love, self, and family. Each man, even those who are certain they will not repeat the "sins of the father," will face this regret, for the story is universal. Perhaps you can identify with the interchange poetically captured by Michael Rosen.

> **Father Says**
> Michael Rosen
>
> *Father says*
> *Never*
> *let*
> *me*
> *see*
> *you*
> *doing*

that
again

father
says
tell you once
tell you a thousand times
come hell or high water
never let me see you doing that again

My brother knows all his phrases by heart
so we practice them in bed at night.

Like the man above, fathers in recent generations often seemed remote, impatient, preoccupied, nondisclosing, nonverbal, and unapproachable to their sons. These men were not born in the current psychological era that talks so incessantly about feelings, emotional dysfunction, or recovery. In fact, they didn't talk much to us at all except to give orders or lectures, or administer rules and discipline.

Osherson, in his sensitive book *Finding Our Fathers*, eloquently points out that whatever his father was like, a man will internalize a composite image of him based on innumerable specific interactions, fantasies that grow from these interactions, and things we are told about him from others. The image is not necessarily accurate, but it is a boy's internal reality that mediates how he experiences his father, men in general, and himself as a man, husband, worker, and father. When this image is wounded, he, too, is wounded.

A Father's Blessing: How does a father bless his son? What should a father tell his son as manhood nears? In *The People, Yes*, Carl Sandburg answers with what I wish my father could have told me.

The People, Yes
Carl Sandburg

A father sees a son nearing manhood.
What shall he tell that son?
"Life is hard; be steel; be a rock."
And this might stand him for the storms
and serve him for humdrum and monotony
and guide him amid sudden betrayals
and tighten him for slack moments.
"Life is a soft loam; be gentle; go easy."
And this too might serve him.

Brutes have been gentled where lashes failed.
The growth of a frail flower in a path up
has sometimes shattered and split a rock.
A tough will counts. So does desire.
So does a rich soft wanting.
Without rich wanting nothing arrives.
Tell him too much money has killed men
and left them dead years before burial:
the quest of lucre beyond a few easy needs
has twisted good enough men
sometimes into dry thwarted worms.
Tell him time as a stuff can be wasted.
Tell him to be a fool every so often
and to have no shame over having been a fool
yet learning something out of every folly
hoping to repeat none of the cheap follies
thus arriving at intimate understanding
of a world numbering many fools.
Tell him to be alone often and get at himself
and above all tell himself no lies about himself
whatever the white lies and protective fronts
he may use amongst other people.
Tell him solitude is creative if he is strong
and final decisions are made in silent rooms.
Tell him to be different from other people
if it comes natural and easy being different.
Let him have lazy days seeking his deeper motives.
Let him seek deep for where his is a born natural.
Then he may understand Shakespeare
and the Wright brothers, Pasteur, Pavlov,
Michael Faraday and free imaginations
bringing changes into a world resenting change.
He will be lonely enough
to have time for the work
he knows as his own.

The Fragmentation of Community: The Industrial Revolution also tore the social fabric of society. Rapid cultural and technological change, geographic movement and migration, global market places, job transfers, educational pursuits and ambitions, now take us all over the country and the world. American families no longer live together in multi-generational homes or even in the same town or state. The prize we have been taught to seek, the American Dream, is the single family dwelling — with each nuclear family enclosed in a space fenced off from each other family. Those less fortunate find themselves densely concentrated in apartment cities filled with strangers. Still, the boundaries of apartment walls serve to isolate inhabitants. We do not know our own neighbors intimately, and we know far less about those down the street and around the corner, and least of all those in poverty on the other side of town.

Thus, the pace of life, the ambitions of individual progress, and the separation by walls continually prevents community from taking place.

The Compulsive Warrior has gone too far: Every man is trying to conquer and build his own kingdom. Every man secretly, implicitly, desperately warring with every other man for the prize of well-to-do superiority, advantage, and isolation. We are off track. Violence, gangs, drugs, crime, prison populations, unwanted children, fatherless families, school drop-outs, unemployment, homelessness — all this and more scream about our errant ways. The Compulsive Warrior has also lost contact with the shared problems, tasks, and goals of community. In a small tribe, everyone matters. Survival depends on it and survival is a group process. Similarly, in real community, everyone matters. Everyone brings into the world something priceless to share, teach, show, or give. Along with conquering, mastering, or fixing problems, men also need to learn the generous art of supporting and facilitating community.

Community is our home, not the single family dwelling or apartment. Community is where we live and what literally supports us. It is itself a living organism with complex, dynamic, and differentiated but still interdependent parts. We could not live without the work we all do for each other. It is the "for each other" that makes community. The Compulsive Warrior ethic threatens community to its core, and the core is breaking open and flowing with pain and blood. The center will not hold unless we go beyond warrior strivings into community.

Finally, we have no real community when a shared involvement in the transcendent is missing. This is not about specific religions or institutions, or about which creed is the most correct, it is about humility, awe, nakedness, gratitude, and joy in the presence of the Great Mystery. Community comes together when there is a deep reverence for life. It heals itself in sacred rituals. Community becomes whole when individuality is transcended and all are included in a single experience of the sacred. We will be talking more about this in Part 4.

CHAPTER 21

Behind the
Compulsive Warrior

≫ What shape are men in these days? Michael Farrell and Stanley Rosenberg, in a profoundly important, but largely unrecognized book, *Men At Midlife*, document just how wounded men in American society really are. They studied two groups of men in the 1970s. The first group consisted of two hundred men between the ages of twenty-five and thirty, and the second group was comprised of three hundred men between the ages of thirty-eight and forty-eight. These two samples were carefully selected to be demographically representative of East Coast American society. Each man was interviewed in depth and administered selected psychological tests. The goal was to compare these two age samples and learn what was happening to men as they came into the middle years.

Four types of middle-aged men were identified. The first type, comprising 32 percent of the men, seemed to have the potential to at least be aware of, and open to, the tasks of the middle years. These men were typically professionals and middle class executives in urban areas. They were well educated, privileged, and relatively affluent.

The second group, making up 26 percent of the sample, were characterized as the "Pseudo-Developed Men," that is, men with a posture of mature masculinity held together with denial, distorted self-presentations, and authoritarianism. Primarily from the lower middle class, these were unhappy men who were pretending to have everything under control.

The third group, comprising 12 percent of the sample, appeared to be experiencing significant crises at midlife. Overwhelmed, bitter, and frightened, their problems were multiplying and they were losing ground.

The last 30 percent of the middle aged men were openly and seriously depressed. Psychopathology in this group was obvious and unhidden. These men had the least socioeconomic and familial resources and advantages growing up. They report deprivation, neglect, and brutality in their homes during childhood. These men are the most deeply wounded and their suffering is most obvious.

Of the entire group studied, only 32 percent (the advantaged group) appeared to have the tools or the awareness to deal with midlife changes. The remaining 68 percent were either going under, already defeated, or locked into denial.

This study, by Farrell and Rosenberg, also argues that the developmental tasks of the midlife passage are not really the cause of this vast suffering. The causes are seen to be primarily in the American culture which fails, in the majority of cases, to support men's real emotional growth and development.

Tragically, most men in the study were found to be emotionally distant from their families, isolated from real friendships, and disappointed with their careers. The researchers concluded, "Only a fraction of the men — perhaps a quarter to a third — avoid falling into the traps of material failure, lost self-esteem, or extreme self-estrangement."

The Panther
Rainer Maria Rilke

His vision, from the constantly passing bars,
has grown so weary that it cannot hold
anything else. It seems to him there are
a thousand bars; and behind the bars, no world.

As he paces in cramped circles, over and over,
the movement of his powerful soft strides
is like a ritual dance around a center
in which a mighty will stands paralyzed.

Only at times, the curtain of the pupils
lifts, quietly – An image enters in,
rushes down through the tensed, arrested muscles,
plunges into the heart and is gone.

Whether he is a laborer, accountant, lawyer, or truck driver, the kind of man we are describing is, in secret essence, like the panther in Rilke's poem. He is imprisoned behind the bars of a compulsive and conforming existence, the beauty of his masculine soul locked in tense, mechanical, and repetitive motion, and his powerful will now paralyzed.

Lawrence, too, makes an assessment of what is missing for twentieth century men. He argues that they have lost touch with primal passions — not just sex or lust — but the passion for life itself. Men secretly wish to drink directly from life's divine source, not from the rigid and brittle bottles of conformity. Soul and the deep masculine are too often "bottled" for us in formula movies, television stars, alcohol, drugs, glamour magazines, excitement, wealth, fixed religious doctrine, cultural prescriptions, and invidious comparisons.

The Primal Passions
D. H. Lawrence

If you will go down into yourself, under your surface
*   personality*
you will find you have a great desire to drink life direct
from the source, not out of bottles and bottled personal
*   vessels.*

What the old people call immediate contact with God.
That strange essential communication of life
not bottled in human bottles.

What ever the wild witchcraft of the past was seeking
before it degenerated.

Life from the source, unadulterated
with the human taint.

Contact with the sun of suns
that shines somewhere in the atom, somewhere pivots the
*   curved space,*
and cares not a straw for the put-up human figments.

Communion with the Godhead, they used to say in the
*   past.*
But even that is human-tainted now,
tainted with the ego and the personality.

To feel a fine, fine breeze blowing through the navel
*   and the knees*
and have a cool sense of truth, inhuman truth at last
softly fluttering the senses, in the exquisite orgasm of
*   coition*
with the Godhead of energy that cannot tell lies.

The cool, cool truth of pure vitality
pouring into the veins from the direct contact with the
*   source.*
Uncontaminated by even the beginnings of a lie.

The Masks of Injured Men

It would seem that most men come into midlife secretly wounded and cut off from the awareness of beauty, the energy of instinct, and the great reservoirs of deep masculinity and soul. They have lost too much of this leavening, transformational energy of male being. The result is a distorted, unfinished, or crippled masculinity. Even within Farrell and Rosenberg's four categories, this dysfunctional masculinity takes many forms. Let's look more closely at what these forms are and who we may have become.

"Boys Pretending to be Men:" Robert Moore uses this phrase to describe a manhood that is mostly pretense. He argues, "The devastating fact is that most men are fixated at an immature level of development. These early developmental levels are governed by the inner blueprints appropriate to boyhood." (Moore, 1990, p. 13) This identity crisis, he argues, has been masked by the patriarchal compensation, that is, the use of male dominance and oppression to cover the hidden weakness, inferiority, and insecurity of the undeveloped male. Describing the forms this compensation takes, Moore writes:

> "The drug dealer, the ducking and diving political leader, the wife beater, the chronically 'crabby' boss, the 'hot shot' junior executive, the unfaithful husband, the company 'yes man,' the indifferent graduate school adviser, the 'holier than thou' minister, the gang member, the father who can never find the time to attend his daughter's school programs, the coach who ridicules his star athletes, the therapist who unconsciously attacks his clients' 'shinning' and seeks a kind of gray normalcy for them, the yuppie — all these men have something in common. They are boys pretending to men. They got that way honestly, because nobody showed them what a mature man is like. Their kind of 'manhood' is a pretense to manhood that goes largely undetected as such by most of us. We are continually mistaking this man's controlling , threatening, and hostile behaviors for strength. In reality, he is showing an underlying extreme vulnerability and weakness, the vulnerability of the wounded boy." He concludes that what is missing is "an adequate connection to the deep and instinctual energies, the potentials of mature masculinity." (Moore, 1990, p. 13)

"Soft Males:" Robert Bly describes one particularly common face of the distorted masculine, the "Soft Male." He writes, "The male in the past twenty years has become more thoughtful, more gentle. But by this process he has not become more free. He's a nice boy who pleases not only his mother but also the young woman he is living with." (Bly, 1990, p. 2) Bly recalls, "In the seventies I began to see all over

the country a phenomenon that we might call the 'soft male.' Sometimes even today when I look out at an audience, perhaps half the young males are what I'd call soft. They're lovely, valuable people, I like them, they're not interested in harming the earth or starting wars. There's a gentle attitude toward life in their whole being and style of living." (Bly, 1990, pp. 2-3) But these men are not able to be fierce, to set limits, or be firm with those around them. These are men, he argues, who sought to escape the dark side of masculinity by "flying" above it in a quest for "higher consciousness," "spiritual transcendence," and other New Age beliefs."

Soft males, Bly describes, have the following common problems:

Passivity: These men are "tamed" and "domesticated." They have lost the "Wild Man" inside, the one in touch with instinct, desire, and the fullness of masculinity. The passive man is not really able to say what he wants. He also leaves much of the parenting to his wife, who handles the details of transportation, clothes shopping, homework, medical appointments. (Bly, 1990, pp. 61-62)

Naivete: Bly calls the Soft Male "naive." (Bly, 1990, pp. 63-67) What he is referring to is a crippling lack of boundaries. The "Soft Male" is too sensitive and too quick to be responsible for another's pain. He is often more in touch with his woman's pain than his own, and he will automatically discount his suffering to take care of hers. This man tends to accept all the blame for relationship problems and condemn himself in the process. Finally, this man fails to be a good container for his own soul. Because he is unaware of his boundaries, he cannot maintain them. He shares too much, revealing his inner life to the point of excessive vulnerability, and giving away his autonomy and personhood in the process.

Numbness: These men often do not know how they really feel. Emotionally numb, they cannot differentiate the full spectrum of emotions within. Accordingly, they cannot know or express their feelings as they arise. Because experiencing emotion is necessary for self development and interpersonal understanding, these men lack basic relationship tools. (Bly, 1990, pp. 67-68)

Having seen the "Soft Male" in myself, in my friends and clients, I would elaborate on Bly's observations to add the following qualities:

Fathering Problems: These men also have boundary problems with their children. Overcompensating for their own father wounds, they give too much and give in too much. Their children, as a consequence, often become overly demanding, arrogant, and self-centered. Because of their own inner deprivation, these fathers have difficulty setting limits. They mistakenly view such limits as creating their own experience of deprivation in their children, but it is not the same. Crippled by this misperception, they tolerate grossly inappropriate behavior until their anger finally explodes — inappropriately. Having over-reacted, they then fall pray to their own guilty self-recrimination.

Male Isolation: Though clearly sensitive, these men have few if any close male friends. Their best friends are women, either because it is easier to talk with them or because this has been a lifelong pattern. Having shared more with their mothers all these years, women seem more approachable. Having never healed their father wound or confronted the taboos of the compulsive warrior (especially those forbidden expressions of intimacy or weakness between men), "soft males" are afraid of speaking candidly to other men, particularly about their anger and powerlessness. Male isolation, of course, is a generic feature of an individualistic and heroic culture.

Excessive Guilt: Sensitive men, men who have listened to their mothers criticize their fathers or feminists criticize men in general, often feel tremendous shame and guilt for the historical atrocities of men through the ages, and, as a result, for their own maleness. Masculinity is almost synonymous with cruelty, violence, brutality, and exploitation. These men then make the mistake of discarding the very aggressiveness they might use in the service of real autonomy, appropriate boundaries, and positive social causes.

The "Soft Male" is an overcompensation to the compulsive warrior. These are the men who put down the John Wayne and Rambo persona, but found themselves left with only a young, immature, and underdeveloped sense of masculinity. Because they were often disciplined by strong women, they still unconsciously experience women as more powerful. This unconscious perception prevents them from making adult relationship boundaries or defending themselves appropriately in times of conflict.

Other Masks

In addition to the masks described by Moore and by Bly, there are others. As I look around me, I see many other faces of false manhood, frozen compromises that belie the heart of masculine wonder. The descriptions that follow are not meant to be either mutually exclusive or scientific. They are subjective impressions of masculinity gone awry. I'm sure you see them too. These faces include:

Hurried Men: All around me, I see men rushing frantically. Feeling that there is so much to do and never enough time to keep up, they are always trying to balance too many tasks, activities, and responsibilities at once. In this hurry, these men don't stop long enough to feel themselves, to reflect soulfully on their lives, or to really be with another person. Although they complain, hurried men seem pleased with all they get done. Look at what the compulsive warrior is accomplishing! They are going too fast to see what they are missing. Caught up in the culture's quest for speed, they have become accelerated machines themselves.

Grandiose Men: Wealth, fame, and power — grandiose men want it all. Sometimes they populate mansions, live in gated communities, and have private associations — all intended to reflect this wealth, fame, and power, and to keep the others out. Sometimes they may be drug dealers, crime families, or commercial entrepreneurs who are grabbing the same American Dream. For grandiose men, the ends justify the means and ruthlessness is a tool, not a matter of conscience. Caught up in the culture's glamorization of narcissism and power, they have become possessed by the power they acquire.

Competitive Men: These are men who are constantly in competition: at work, in sports, in the gym, on the road, with themselves, with their friends, even with their wives and children. They are addicted to television sports and are intense about their favorite teams. Winning and superiority are equivalent to manhood itself. They measure their competitive value in terms of income, possessions, sexual exploits, clothes, athletic skill, knowledge, and whatever other forms competition can take. Caught up in the culture's over-valuation of winning, they desperately need to prevail.

Lost Men: The silent majority seem to me to be comprised of lost men. These are men doing what they are supposed to do — conforming — without knowing who they really are, what they really want, or what else is possible. They are men who do not know how to ask hard questions, either because they fear criticism for challenging social assumptions, or because they fear the answers. Instead, they imitate the cultural norm and grow empty inside.

Dangerous Men: Around me, also, I see men dangerously near the edge of control. Wired on drugs, addicted to alcohol, explosive with the buried rage of childhood abuse and neglect, these men drive too fast, break laws, seek thrills, batter women, and are always capable of assault when challenged. Pushed to the edge of survival, these are often the under-controlled, easily ignited, and frightening men who populate our prisons.

Men Without Calling: These are men who have no moral conviction, no higher values than those in the collective marketplace, and no sense of ultimate purpose to their lives. For them, moral development has not been an individual and personal priority. Without real initiation into self, soul, or larger purposes, these men equate morality with the loose and convenient aphorisms of the culture. Integrity is relative and largely irrelevant, until injustice affects them directly, and then their outrage can be righteous. Their outrage does not extend to the hardships of others. These are men without vision, men without the knowledge of soul, men without calling. ❦

CHAPTER 22

Men at Midlife:
The Hero's Death

For Jung, as for no other writer, the essence of genuine psychological develop-ment involves a giving up of the hero. When heroic consciousness dominates, one thinks one knows better than the unconscious who one is and feels one should therefore be in control of one's life...Jung knew that the full psychological poten-tial of being a man is possible only when the hero finally bows his own head and submits to initiation, not at the hands of an outer man or woman, but at the dic-tates of his own anima. (Beebe, in Jung, 1989, p. xii)

Every new phase of development throughout an individual's life is accompa-nied by a repetition of the original conflict between the claims of Self and the claims of the ego. In fact, this conflict may be expressed more powerfully at the period of transition from early maturity to middle age (between 35 and 40 in our society) than at any other time in life. (Henderson, in Jung, 1964, p. 131)

We see the theme of sacrifice or death of the hero as a necessary cure for hubris, the pride that has over-reached itself. (Henderson, in Jung, 1964, p. 114)

The 'death' of the Hero is the 'death' of boyhood, of Boy psychology. And it is the birth of manhood and Man psychology. The 'death' of the Hero in the life of a boy (or a man) really means that he has finally encountered his limita-tions...The 'death' of the Hero signals a boy's or man's encounter with true humility. It is the end of his heroic consciousness. (Moore and Gillette, 1990, p. 41)

≫ The hero dies at midlife.

The questing, conquering, ever-invincible, and ever-progressing warrior dies. He dies because he can't achieve forever, because he is not a machine, and because there is a longing in his soul for something else. This pretense of man-hood runs out of steam.

The hero archetype is an invaluable resource early in The Story of Everyman. Filled with the energy of adolescence, and inspired by magic images of power and success released from within his own psychological core, it gives a young man the strength and the courage to do really heroic things: leave his mother, stand up to his father, and enter the frightening world of men, women, career, babies, and survival. Without this heroic energy and noble vision, a boy might never leave home.

For the majority of young men, this heroic vision carries them into their adult lives. Once activated, they build lives and careers. They become somebody in a world that finally belongs at least in part to them. Their myopic, absolutely singular striving, sometimes leaves wives and families feeling neglected, and this is one of the tensions intrinsic to the complementary developmental processes of men and women. But the fact that most men succeed in the fundamental task of acquiring a trade and supporting a household and family is no small matter. It is one of the great achievements of the heroic quest. Then men reach midlife.

We have seen in the previous section that the forces of midlife must defeat us. For men, what is defeated most centrally is the hero. By midlife, this glamorous image of the self has degraded into the compulsive warrior because the man inside this suit of armor is now tired and soul-hungry. More achievement is not what he really desires. Like the Woodcutter, he longs now for rest and renewal. More deeply and unconsciously, he longs for a submission to something truly greater than his own egoic grandiosity and the empty envy of other men. He wants desperately to stop serving the gods of success, capitalism, and income, to serve something higher.

Even for the fortunate man who began with an abundance of life's resources, found the blessing of a mentor, and identified the calling of his own soul, still all this is not enough. He must surrender his ambition and heroic dream. Neither the individual ego nor the culturally-sanctioned warrior can offer a man what he needs most at midlife: baptism by defeat. Midlife supplies the Compulsive Warrior with this preconfigured defeat so that the weary hero can sink deeply into his dark interior baptismal waters to die and be reborn.

The inevitable defeat of the hero is a man's initiation into the life of the spirit. He must allow the storm of midlife to break through the bulwark of his heroic persona and expose his very soul. Like Job, there is no hiding. The storm rages over and through him until something new and sacred is revealed from his deep psychic core. It will become the next equation of his life, a new organizing principle that reshapes his entire landscape. If he is not strong enough, and if he has no vision or grasp of the purpose of this violent time, a man may surrender instead to confusion, despair, flight, or collapse.

During such a cataclysm, therefore, a man needs friends to see him through, particularly other men who have survived this same defeat and found, on the other side, the gift of male friendship. This is the gentle, comfortable, and compassionate kind of friendship we see in older men's groups where comparison and competition are left far behind. Men see that the Compulsive Warrior mentality now has no more value to the soul and, in fact, must be discarded for the soul to be born. They see that each man must be challenged, broken, and defeated by the divine sculptor who knows things about his destiny that he, egoic man, can neither anticipate nor fathom.

The following poem grasps the necessary power, dynamic, and infinite value of this defeat. It is a poem about the dark, ominous, and timeless storm of impending change. For most men, this storm arrives at midlife. In our defeat, however, we are touched by an angel.

The Man Watching
Rainer Maria Rilke

I can tell by the way the trees beat, after
so many dull days, on my worried window panes
that a storm is coming,
and I hear the far-off fields say things
I can't bear without a friend,
I can't love without a sister.

The storm, the shifter of shapes, drives on
across the woods and across time,
and the world looks as if it had no age:
the landscape, like a line in the psalm book,
is seriousness and weight and eternity.

What we choose to fight is so tiny!
What fights with us is so great!
If only we could let ourselves be dominated
as things do by some immense storm,
we would become strong too, and not need names.

When we win it's with small things,
and the triumph itself makes us small.
What is extraordinary and eternal
does not want to be bent by us.
I mean the Angel who appeared
to the wrestlers of the Old Testament:
when the wrestlers' sinews
grew long like metal strings,
he felt them under his fingers
like chords of deep music.

Whoever was beaten by this Angel
(who often simply declined to fight)
went away proud and strengthened

and great from that harsh hand,
that kneaded him as if to change his shape.
Winning does not tempt that man.
This is how he grows: by being defeated, decisively,
by constantly greater beings.

And my own grandmother, so wise, wrote this poem when she was nearly eighty. She, too, understood the defeat of the hero and the victory of the soul.

Ride a Cock Horse
Agnes Claflin Adams

Ride a cock horse to Banbury Cross
To see a fine lady upon a white horse.
With rings on her fingers and bells on her toes,
She shall have music wherever she goes.
— Mother Goose

I

O watch how she rides, with balance and grace,
with youth and with vigor, with beauty of face,
With pride and with hope that her gallant will win.
Without apprehension, are those who begin.

The trumpets are blowing; the knights on the plain
Have no way of knowing the failure or pain,
Until they have fallen, in pride, and in vain:
When vanquished or victor, they wind home again.

The burden is heavy, the progress is slow,
A horse, overladen, knows not how to go;
But knights must ride on, they cannot turn back:
The world claims success; and scorns when they lack.

O how can we tell her upon her white horse
That sorrow is waiting at Banbury Cross;
And all of life's victory may turn to loss;
For clanking of armor can end in a Cross.

Shall we warn youth it's futile? Ah no, and ah no!
No gain without learning; and learning is slow.
Youth must suffer and suffer, and suffer to know.

II

Who was the fine lady upon the white horse?
The gallant in armor at Banbury Cross?
Was it you? Was it he? Was it I? Was it she?
My memory grows dim; my old eyes can't see.

It as all, everyone, the great and the small;
For horses will stumble, and riders will fall.
It was all, everyone, for gain or for loss,
We all rode together to Banbury Cross.

We rode our cock horses to Banbury Crosses
We were the fine ladies upon our white horses.
We were the knights charging along the vast plain;
We tilted and fought, for the pride and the gain;

We were the knights winning in gallant refrain;
We were the knights errant, who struggled
    through the pain:
We held all the praise, and we took all the loss:
And now we no longer seek Banbury Cross.

We can't try anew; we are old, we have learnt:
Ambitions have withered and fires have burnt.
We are the spent warriors, who slowly returned;
The gallants who fought, and the ladies who yearned.
No more shall we try; to try would be vain,
We left broken lances on Banbury Plain.

And we say to our children in honest refrain –
Truth will come, truth will come – but the ride
    will be slow.
We beg you, our loved ones, whever you go
To seek for the world by high road or low
With endeavor, success, and all of life's show,
Be sure to return to the Word, not the sword;
The contrition of hope, and the mercy of God.

III

O ride a cock horse from Banbury Cross
The challenge is over, the victory vain;
But the ride has been worth all the pride and the pain.
We went out to win, and we won through our loss.
The soul can stand upright, that mounted a Cross.

The hero's defeat is not the problem at midlife, it is the solution. As we saw in Fortune and the Woodcutter, giving up the Compulsive Warrior mode allows magic to return to life and the gold of self comes home. In *The Three Languages* and *The Crystal Ball*, we saw that the truly courageous thing to do is to go down into the depths of grief and sorrow to heal old wounds. And from *The Man Who Didn't Believe* we learned that self-centered exploitation of the world so common to the Compulsive Warrior offends both its natural and sacred order.

The hero dies at midlife. It was a complex that did its work and must now give way for the healing of soul and community. ❈

CHAPTER 23

Men's Work at Midlife: Healing Soul and Community

❧ Healing male soul and male community is the collective work of midlife men. In one form or another, it is what each man needs to do as his heroic quest begins to crumble. This chapter takes us into the nature of this work in more detail.

Healing Male Soul. As we have seen, D.H. Lawrence was way ahead of his time. He understood the real costs of the industrialization of men long before society could. In a poem entitled *Healing*, Lawrence captures the deep and painful emotional work men do at midlife when the machinery of false manhood breaks down.

Healing
D.H. Lawrence

I am not a mechanism, an assembly of various sections.
And it is not because the mechanism is working wrongly,
    that I am ill.
I am ill because of wounds to the soul, to the deep emotional
    self
and the wounds to the soul take a long, long time, only
    time can help
and patience, and a certain difficult repentance
long, difficult repentance, realization of life's mistake, and
    the freeing oneself
from the endless repetition of the mistake
which mankind at large has chosen to sanctify.

This poem suggests that the machinery of the Compulsive Warrior cannot and should not be fixed. Rather, men must drop down into their souls and confront the great "mistake" that "mankind at large has chosen to sanctify." What is that mistake? It is the masculine glorification of the machine as a model for manhood. Endlessly repeating this mistake will destroy a man and the world he inhabits.

It is at midlife that a man begins to reckon with the insolvency of the warrior mode. An internal bankruptcy shows up on his inner ledger when he confronts the costs of continued consumption, competition, aging, and death, and sees that

DEATH OF A HERO

more warrioring will incur an even more staggering and tragic debt. Men must account for this same default at societal and global levels, for ever-expanding industrialization of "First World" countries will not solve humanity's problems. Starvation, poverty, pollution, over-population, ethnic warfare, weapons' proliferation, and depletion of our worlds resources are the harsh accounts that man must soon settle at the midlife of world civilization.

But how does healing take place? How do midlife men heal the soul wounds we have been discussing? The most common forms of healing occur through men's friendships, individual psychotherapy, men's groups, men's gatherings, men's organizations, and male community. We will look briefly at each.

Male Friendships: Today, men begin to have more authentic male friendships after midlife. It is not uncommon for a man in summer of his life to say that his last "best friend" was in high school or college, or in the service, and that most of his closest friends are women. Though he may have many male acquaintances in sports and work, real male intimacy has been absent and generally continues to be. The standard of competition simply divides and isolates men, until the cost of isolation and loneliness becomes too painful. Then men feel the longing to reach out to other men.

Individual Psychotherapy: Not too many years ago, no real man would have been caught dead in psychotherapy. He would expect to be stereotyped as a mental case, someone who had failed the tests of manhood. Disclosure of psychiatric treatment has ruined politicians, for it supposedly meant that they were unstable, unpredictable, potentially bizarre, or unable to stand pressure. Thankfully, times are beginning to change. In my practice, I see men from all walks of life, men who have put their personal and psychological growth ahead of these shaming stereotypes.

The work we do together in psychotherapy can be life-changing. As we have seen, the majority of men carry significant childhood wounds hidden under the armor of denial. Most have neither the tools nor the map for identifying and healing these wounds. Men will often begin therapy by saying they had a "normal" childhood. They assert that nothing really bad ever happened. Without training in the art of feeling, how can this be otherwise? Others know it was painful, but don't know what to do with the pain that eats at them like open sores. Psychotherapy teaches men how to explore the developmental years of childhood and to locate the wounds that really did happen, wounds that were often deeply painful and sometimes crippling. In therapy, they receive the support and guidance to experience such feelings again, perhaps for the first time since childhood. And one of the key healing principles is: anything that a man can feel, especially with the empathic support of another, will change and move toward healing.

Finally psychotherapy with a male therapist is also a kind of masculine initiation, mentoring, and blessing. More than identifying and healing wounds, it adds the dimension of authentic male relationship. When a man finds a therapist with whom he can identify, and from whom he can experience masculine understanding and acceptance, then his own manhood can begin to be seen, valued, and validated. This experience becomes, in effect, a ritual of initiation into manhood. It is often the blessing a man needs to begin his own journey. The guidance provided from an older male therapist can also take on the gift of mentoring, teaching the ways of the male world and the male soul.

Men's Groups: I have found men's groups to be wonderful experiences. They come in many shapes and flavors. Some have leaders trained as therapists, some don't. Some are leaderless. Some groups include formal presentations or agenda, others let the learning and teaching come solely from the participants. Some are run like therapy groups and others like discussion groups. While the variations are almost endless, what tends to happen in a men's group transcends its format. Men come to realize that something deep and important has been missing in the lives: friendship and openness with other men. Most members are in their thirties, forties, fifties and even sixties. They may have plenty of "friends," guys with whom to make jokes, play ball, talk sports or do business, but none to tell the truth about confusion, loneliness, failure, rage, depression, addiction, sex; or, about joy, hope, yearning, and excitement.

Initially, men come together in fear because of the ingrained masculine taboo against exposing emotional vulnerability to another man. What men find when they do open up is not ridicule, criticism, or comparison, but a deep and truly remarkable wellspring of male compassion and universality. There is virtually no problem that one man carries that others have not in some way felt, experienced, or needed to admit. And the relief, even joy, men feel when they finally talk about all these forbidden topics is gratifying and healing.

What happens most powerfully in a men's group is often the least visible. It is simply the experience of men coming together and being with each other through births, marriages, divorces, deaths, breakdowns, retirements, life changes, problems with kids, illness, and aging. In this ongoing sharing of the male experience and life cycle, members sometimes form the deepest friendships they have ever known. They come to love each other. It is simply being with each other, with men in all their pain and diversity, that allows each man to find his own voice, his own energy, his own value and style. This is the initiation for which men have always searched, the affirmation unavailable in the world of competition and machine-like uniformity. Then, with the blessing of his brothers, a man finally knows what it means to be a man.

Men change in this process. Their marriages improve or end, their commitment to their children grows deeper. They often look for different or more meaningful work. And, most importantly, men find the courage to face their own core issues and to live their lives with integrity. As they mature, some men find their journey taking them out of the group to something new — and their departures are celebrated. Some, valuing the ongoing friendship, support and sharing they have found, continue indefinitely.

Men's Gatherings: What is a men's gathering? It is an event organized by men and for men only. The gathering may be as small as ten or fifteen men, or as large as one hundred or more. It may last a day, a weekend, or a week, or sometimes longer. It may take place in conference halls, churches, campgrounds or wilderness. Typically it is planned around a theme personally relevant to all men. Its structure often includes didactic presentations, community discussion, and opportunities for small group and one-on-one sharing. Equally important are experiences that awaken male energy, instinct, and soul — including poetry, myth, story telling, drumming, ritual, song, dance, exercise, and skits. Although men are almost universally skeptical and uncomfortable at first with the idea of such experiences, the majority end up loving them.

One of the most powerful stabilizers in a men's gathering is the recognition of elders. The older men, who are usually in their late fifties to seventies, are asked to sit in the front with the leaders. Often, for the first time in their lives, these men are welcomed and appreciated as elders. It is a profound and beautiful experience. In telling their stories, they are recognized for all they have learned and experienced, and all they have to teach. Moreover, younger men finally get a chance to be with older men, to seek their council and blessing, to learn more about their own parents, and to grasp the great achievement of simply making it through all they have experienced. When elders speak in this context, even when diffident and unsure, they are deepened and so is the community.

As the event unfolds, as night follows day, and the grime of civilization washes clean, something palpable happens in the small groups and in the gathering as a whole. A kind of village forms, a community of men, that becomes comfortable and familiar. And beyond that, something changes in the individual and collective consciousness — a slowing down, deepening, and opening occurs, especially in wilderness retreats. Men become more like men. They get more comfortable with male energy, humor, and beauty. As the soup thickens, a powerful and timeless experience of individual, collective, and archetypal masculinity emerges, and along with it a kind of mythic consciousness. This consciousness begins to feel the earth, woods, and streams in the ancient ways.

Finally, there is an experience of oneness that gels in a men's gathering. Singing, dancing, or moving to the rhythm of drums and self-made music, music that emanates from their own cellular beat, men feel joined as one. Likewise, a single man's poignant sharing of emotion or a riveting confict between two or more men can galvanize the whole community into a common experience of masculinity. In this moment of oneness, individuality and isolation are transcended, and every man is an irreplaceable part of the whole.

Men's Organizations: Numerous men's organizations have formed in the last decade. Some are dedicated to social and community issues, some to putting on conferences and gatherings, some to putting out newspapers and newsletters, and some meeting to share common interests or activities. Problems common to men frequently arise, such as competition, excessive task orientation, and exploitation of the organization for personal purposes. In general, the more men have grown together in friendship and community, the more they have done their own soul work, the more these organizations can mature as well.

Male Community: As more men are initiated together into candor, deep masculinity, and friendship, they can come together in a larger male community with a new spirit of cooperation and interdependence. But this kind of community is still in its infancy. It is easily lost amidst the pressures of work and family life, and the old habits of ego and competition. Authentic male community, however, is an enormous step of faith, trust, honesty, and cooperation.

The Men's Movement: Although it is still hard to define, and cannot yet be easily seen, there is, among the men I know, evidence of a men's movement. And if we look at men's writing in the last decade, we see a common male voice has sprung up all over the country. It is a hunger for honesty and a release from the tyranny of the compulsive warrior. Where this movement will go is unknowable. Embodying it is the work and challenge of every man.

Finding One's Own Masculinity: Much of what has been said about healing men's wounds involves recovering the experience of masculinity. But what is masculinity and how does a man find it? In men's friendships, groups, gatherings, organizations, and community, men find their own manhood in countless ways. Here, in no particular order, are some of the ways I experienced it:

Hearing my own voice amidst the voices of other men's; telling my own story; dancing and drumming to ecstasy and exhaustion; yelling, chanting, singing, crying as a single community, holding a man in sorrow, or being held: hearing poetry recited proudly and powerfully by men not afraid to look foolish; standing my ground in conflict without shaming or defeat; admiring, celebrating, and displaying male beauty; creating and then being transported by ritual; watching men move from isolation and defensiveness at the day's beginning to friendship and trust by evening; honoring other men for their remarkable accomplish-

ments; feeling awed by so many men's voices and stories woven into a tapestry of sharing and song; accepting my own male body amidst the wonderful diversity of male forms; vibrating in a room of six hundred dancing men and feeling the fullness of the male gender; loving men without fearing the old issue of homosexuality; being irreverent and ridiculous; standing in the moonlight in the woods or swimming naked in a pond; painting my body like a warrior; watching brilliant and ridiculous skits and men laughing themselves silly; talking about things I've never thought of before; taking the risk of speaking up in group and community and finding out I said something from the heart without planning it; overcoming male bashing and finding a male psychology that is worthwhile and honorable; learning we all have incredibly common problems and no longer need to hide them; ceasing self-devaluing comparisons with other men around money, strength, power, success, status, sex, and women; being pissed off and saying it without getting trashed or destroyed; reading poetry to a group of men for the first time; identifying with an animal in dance and then becoming that animal; watching men have the courage to face and admit past atrocities, petty motivations, guilt, and seemingly unforgivable actions, and then being profoundly valued by the group for doing so; feeling small and humbled by the vastness of space and millennial time and grieving my own insignificance; praying together and experiencing the sacred as a communion without feeling distanced, diminished, or confused by theology; knowing in my gut that no other man is better than me and no worse, and seeing that even famous leaders can make mistakes, have feet of clay, be prideful and foolish, and loving them all the more for it; seeing old men, physically broken men, ill men who can still dance and speak with soul, perhaps more deeply than any of the others; meeting men I will never forget whose courage still brings tears to my eyes; seeing older men transformed in dignity, wisdom, and value by simply being asked to serve as elders in a community of men who have needed elders all their lives; hearing eloquent men speak with wisdom and knowledge about the problems and tasks common to all men; having my own childish fantasies dashed by men speaking truths I was not ready to hear; laughing until I almost peed in my pants, and then laughing some more...

This is the magnificent side of masculinity rarely known or seen in the civilized world. This is the birth and experience of deep, full, rich, varied, wild, serious, loving, humble, and sacred masculinity.

From this wellspring of deep manhood comes the next poem. It calls out, "If you are a man..."

If You Are a Man
D.H. Lawrence

*If you are a man, and believe in the destiny of mankind
then say to yourself: we will cease to care
about property and money and mechanical devices
and open our consciousness to the deep, mysterious life
that we are now cut off from.*

The machine shall be abolished from the earth again;
it is a mistake that mankind has made;
money shall cease to be, and the property shall cease to perplex
and we will find the way to immediate contact with life
and with one another.

To know the moon as we have never known
yet she is knowable.
To know a man as we have never known
a man, as never yet a man was knowable, yet still shall be.

Lawrence is not literally arguing for the eradication of money, property, and machinery. He is asking us to put them in their proper places.

Healing Community: Our sense of community, both small and large, of being one people with common origin, identity, struggle, and fate has been seriously injured in the past century. Massive social and economic changes have weakened the very glue of community, which customarily includes:

✔ Relationships: everyday associations between people where social bonds are stable, open, honest, respectful, caring, and committed.

✔ Family: the unit of community that holds its emotional intimacy and off-spring.

✔ Neighborhood: the place where we find security and interdependence among families at the local level.

✔ Workplace: where economic security, pride, ownership, honest work, and fair wage provide the means and products of human survival.

✔ Community Organization: its ways of making decisions and regulating itself, uncompromised by false or exploiting leadership, disenfranchised peoples, or the scarcity of positive roles for all citizens.

✔ Morality: the recognition of our dependence on and obligation to the family of man, other species, and the earth.

✔ Identity: an integrated sense of who we are that makes us alike and understandable.

✔ The Sacred: where community is held together by meaningful ritual, shared cosmology, and communal awe and emotion.

One of the important paths for healing and rebuilding community is restoring the network of healthy and positive male relationships. This requires the genuine maturation of male community. The developmental tasks of this maturation are, of course, the same tasks critical to the accomplishment of mature masculinity in general, and include developing the capacity to:

⚡ Honor each individual's intrinsic, indisputable, unique, and equal value.

⚡ Hear and experience the story of each person, each ethnic group, and every other division of society, and be open to the emotional wounds of that story.

⚡ Support or challenge each individual and group to find their own individual character and their gift to the whole.

⚡ Foster communication skills and procedures that ensure everyone a chance to be heard, to raise issues, and provide direction to the community.

⚡ Develop egalitarian methods of decision-making, problem-solving, and conflict management that openly acknowledge both personal and community agendas.

⚡ Assume non-competitive and facilitating leadership roles.

⚡ Recognize the value of age and of the elders all around us who carry far more wisdom than even they know; learn from them, and celebrate them.

⚡ Develop a living relationship to the sacred and to sacred purposes, which includes understanding ritual, asking for spiritual guidance, and supporting individual and group forms of spiritual communion.

⚡ Renew rituals that give life and community larger meaning.

⚡ Renew a creation story and shared cosmology that gives life its meaning, value, and purpose.

Ultimately, it all goes together, and wounds to one part of community affect all parts. We cannot heal our personal wounds without also healing community wounds. In the end, healing the soul and healing the community turn out to be the same thing. ⚜

CHAPTER 24

Healing Our Love Relationships

≫ Because of the tremendous power and importance of love relationships in the maturation of men, healing in this realm deserves a separate discussion.

Love is not always what it seems. In the first place, "falling in love" is a complex alchemy, mixing unconscious images and fantasies of self, soul, sex, good parent, healed wounds, and eternal protection. It is a powerful brew. The first phase of attraction, infatuation, and attachment sets the bond and a new boundary around the couple. Then the inner chemistry of relationship begins. Just when things seem like they should be settling down, the love experience becomes increasingly murky. Frustrations, disappointment, differences, conflicts, and resentment tarnish the ideal. We understand the real nature of love only later (if at all), when all these hidden relationship problems have finally surfaced and challenged us to the core. To understand love, then, we need to understand all the problems that accompany it.

In our culture, nearly all intense and bonded romantic relationships consist of enmeshment in one form or another. An enmeshed relationship is one in which either or both partners feel unable to be or express what they really feel and want for fear of criticism, shaming, rejection, abandonment, or violence from the other. This desire to control the partner is typically rationalized with romantic notions of what love should be.

Once in a bonded relationship, a man reworks the stages of his individual emotional growth by repeating them: attachment (the basic, preverbal maternal bond); symbiosis (I can't survive without you, we are the same, I'll be whatever you want to get your love); differentiation (It turns out that I am different from you in important ways, I can and want to survive without you, I need to develop in my own way); autonomy (I can stand on my own and become my own self); and love (I can be who I really am, stand on my own, and love you from my own wholeness). Every man reworks these stages of separation and individuation with his woman over the years they are together. But there are snags, and the snags secretly tangle each partner into a more and more confining enmeshment, until pain and frustration force them to grapple with the truth.

It will come as no surprise by now that one of the most common snags are hidden childhood wounds. Wherever he was wounded as a child, a man will open up the same wounds in this love relationship, and there he will have to work them out. Another snag is that the original self he reclaims may be different than the self his spouse wants or fell in love with. Then, to complete the circle, this emerging conflict sooner or later threatens each partner's childhood wounds of abandonment, rejection, or control. These fears and vulnerabilities engage like gears to lock a relationship into enmeshment. Because exposing this process is so threatening and uncomfortable, there is a tremendous taboo against even questioning or examining these kinds of merged and enmeshed relationship bonds. We like to call it love, but it is much more complex.

For men in America, one of the origins of enmeshment over the last several generations has been the absence of strong and present fathers, uncles, and mentors and other older males. Such relationships teach men how to tolerate conflict without giving up the personal self. Passive, remote, absent, or violent fathers fail to provide a healthy model of male assertion, autonomy, and self-expression.

Strong mothers and weak, distant, or explosive fathers leave their sons emotionally handicapped in their own marriages. Enmeshed relationships are the result, relationships in which men seek approval, progressively give up their power, use passivity or intimidation as defenses, and wind up feeling stuck, trapped, addicted, dependent, inferior, powerless, resentful, or explosive. For a man to recover his real self and move increasingly into the energies of archetypal and mature masculinity, these relationship bonds need to be understood, challenged, and reworked. Without a real self, there can be no full and healthy relationship.

Because so many of the men I encounter still struggle with this kind of enmeshment, I suggest the following guidelines for the development of a healthy and autonomous self in relationship:

> *ƒ Don't try to "fix" the emotional conflicts in your relationship:* Trying to change yourself to fit your mate's demands, on the one hand, or seeking to fix her pain or her unhappiness on the other hand, only makes it appear that you are somehow responsible for these problems, which produces more feelings of blame, guilt, and failure. Try not to assume or accept blame, shame, guilt, or responsibility just because there is conflict, or because you are blamed and fear abandonment. Instead of capitulating, continue to express your feelings and explore the conflict. Understand that it's really okay for a woman to be angry or hurt with you. It may be painful, but it won't kill you.

> *ƒ You have a right to protect yourself against shaming and verbal devaluation:* Sam Keen counsels men, "We have to stop buying women's blame. There's a very negative faction within feminism that wants to blame men for everything bad since Western history began...We created the (patriarchal) system together." (Keen, 1991, pp. 99-100). You as a man are not responsible for the crimes, atrocities, or traits of other men now or in the past. You are responsible only for your own behavior.

Secondly, don't give yourself up just to keep peace or avoid criticism. Keen argues cogently, "Men don't know how to defend themselves against women. Psychologically, nine out of ten women will defeat nine out of ten men in a fight to the finish, not with direct, head-on aggression, but with guilt, shame, and blame." (Keen, 1991, p. 98) Finally, being open to attack does not make you a better person. Robert Bly explains, "The naive man feels a pride in being attacked. If his wife or girlfriend, furious, shouts that he is a 'chauvinist,' a 'sexist,' a 'man,' he doesn't fight back, but takes it. He opens his shirt so that she can see more clearly where to put the lances...He feels, as he absorbs the attack, that he is doing the brave and advanced thing...A woman, so mysterious and superior, has given him some attention. To be attacked by someone you love — what could be more wonderful?" (Bly, 1990, pp. 63-64).

✓ *Take responsibility for your own problems:* Don't get caught in the blaming game. By definition, you are responsible for half the problems in your relationship. Work on your half. Examine your assumptions, woundings, communication style, emotional avoidance, and abuse patterns. Get into therapy if you need to. Get feedback from other men and women. A remarkable process begins to happen when you change yourself. The whole dance of conflict changes for it is choreographed as a partnership. Most importantly, find and heal your old wounds. When they are finished, the whole fight deflates. Relationship conflict was the symptom, not the cause.

✓ *Loving relationships do not mean constant intimacy, harmony, and sensitivity:* Genuine and loving relationships do not require constant closeness, communication, vulnerability, merging or "oneness." Such constant symbiosis is unrealistic and unhealthy. Conflict, separateness, autonomy, distance, boundaries, and differentness are equally necessary and valid in a relationship. And you are not required to explain, confess, or reveal everything you think or feel just because you are in a bonded relationship. We lose the dignity, mystery, freedom, and sanctity of our souls when we feel compelled to expose everything.

Rainer Maria Rilke, writing on *Love and Other Difficulties*, teaches:

"I hold this to be the highest task of a bond between two people: that each should stand guard over the solitude of the other..." He adds, "But once the realization is accepted that even between the closest human beings infinite distances continue to exist, a wonderful living side by side can grow up, if they succeed in loving the distance between them which makes it possible for each to see the other whole and against a wide sky!

All companionship can consist only in the strengthening of two neighboring solitudes, whereas everything that is wont to call giving oneself is by nature harmful to companionship: for when a person abandons himself, he is no longer anything, and when two people both give themselves up in order to come close to each other, there is no longer any ground beneath them and their being together is a continual falling. There are such relationships which must be a very great, almost unbearable happiness, but they can occur only between very rich natures and between those who, each for himself, are richly ordered and composed; they can unite only two wide, deep, individual worlds." (Mood, 1975, pp. 27-30)

Healthy sensitivity means being equally sensitive and respectful to your own feelings and to those of your mate. Unable to see the cost of ignoring their own woundedness, and afraid to risk the conflict that might arise in voicing unhappiness, men tend to bear their pain silently. Unless it can get out in the open, this silent burden will only gain weight as the years pass. Caring and knowing more about your mate's needs, feelings, and wounds than your own inevitably diminishes self-awareness, self-activation, and, as a direct consequence, selfhood.

You have a right to take time for yourself. Make sacred some personal time to feel and cultivate your own self-experience and self-development. Rather than becoming selfish, such self-nurturing will actually grow a greater capacity for unconflicted love, intimacy, and generosity.

ƒ *Loving relationships do not mean accepting or excusing behavior that repeatedly or chronically betrays you or the relationship.* Neither spouse should justify, explain, or write off destructive behavior just because the other is having problems. These behaviors include lying, having affairs, chemical dependency, suicidal or self-injurious behavior, compulsive gambling, and spending too much time at work.

Confronting destructive behavior is not equivalent to making the other person change, "face reality," or become responsible. You can't change someone else. Confronting destructive behavior means knowing your own needs, saying them clearly, and, if necessary, being strong enough to walk away and bear the pain of loss if no other choice exists.

ƒ *Look at your own enmeshing tendencies.* How do you subtly look for approval, avoid telling the truth, or otherwise hide your feelings in order to maintain harmony and dependency. How is it easier to feel shamed or controlled than stand your ground? Look carefully at your underlying fears. Until you work through the childhood trauma underlying such avoidance, you will be unable to find another, healthier response.

ſ *Anger and the expression of it are okay and valuable.* Don't confuse anger with aggression or violence. It is not the same thing. Often, it is your anger that tells you when you are being wounded and need to set limits to protect yourself, or to protect others against the risk of violence. Anger is also necessary for individuation to take place because it establishes, maintains, and protects the individual space necessary to grow the inner self as a true and living expression of your inborn nature. Third, anger is an honest expression of self, a deeply revealing communication to the other about your inner world and emotions. To withhold this communication is to avoid intimacy. Anger also helps clarify issues by sharpening distinctions and differences thereby allowing a couple to see what issue they are really working on. Finally, conflict and anger draw attention to the enmeshed or suppressed self, because anger is felt when the self is being threatened, hurt, or controlled. In this way, anger creates opportunities for insight and change.

ſ *Work on your communication skills.* Changing topics, repeating old grievances, making threats, all-or-nothing generalizations, or resorting to violence — these kinds of communication patterns are useless and damaging. Learn to identify and interrupt them. Take workshops on communication skills and practice them, especially during your calmer moments.

ſ *Let yourself be imperfect, confused, frustrated, distant, angry, sad, or whatever else you feel.* Only by accepting your feelings will you find out what they mean and ask of you. Accepting your needs and feelings does not mean that you should act them out or force them on someone else. Sharing them is simply an acknowledgment of what you find in your interior experience.

ſ *Working through enmeshment requires you to examine the underlying wounds hidden or repeated in it.* We cannot heal our wounds by finding or making "perfect" adult relationships. Instead, it is necessary to access and feel the original hurt until it is completed. This is the deep work of midlife.

ſ *Men and women are different in biology, psychology, and socialization.* Learn to understand, accept, and celebrate these differences. Neither gender is superior. Each carries the mystery and wonder of the universe.

ſ *Sometimes men need to be with other men.* By the age of thirty, few men have really close male friendships. Men need to reverse this sad trend. Being close to other men in permissive and open relationships helps each man grow his own manhood. It allows him to express personal doubts and feel his own natural masculinity without fear of criticism. Male tenderness and acceptance are critical for genuine self-acceptance. Men also need the company of older men for validation, mentoring, teaching, and camaraderie. So when a man needs to leave his woman to be with other men for a while, it is not a personal rejection. It is part of his ancient masculine makeup.

Working on his relationships is one of the most important things a man will ever do. Instead of being a distraction from career or life dream, they are the very forum in which his soul is worked out. ❦

CHAPTER 25

Aging Men:
The Tasks of Winter

≫ As we reach the end of this section on masculinity, it seems only fitting to explore the final season of a man's life — Winter. What is the essential psychological and spiritual nature of Winter? What challenges does it ask of men? And most importantly, what does it really mean to be old?

In pursuing these questions we come to a fascinating paradox: the poets and the elderly view Winter in very different ways. This chapter examines these contradictory views, searching again for insights.

We begin with the poets' view. As we have seen, poets delve deeply into the symbolic and archetypal ground of their experience. What can they tell us about aging? For Winter especially, their search for timeless images and themes may help us understand this season's ultimate meaning.

At first, the Winter of life is painted by the poet to be a lonely, stark, barren, and purposeless time of waning physical and mental competencies. Isn't Winter like that? A time of desolation, darkness, coldness, and death; a time of endings? Robert Frost paints such a picture in *An Old Man's Winter Night*.

An Old Man's Winter Night
Robert Frost

All out-of-doors looked darkly in at him
Through the thin frost, almost in separate stars,
That gathers on the pane in empty rooms.
What kept his eye from giving back the gaze
Was the lamp tilted near them in his hand.
What kept him from remembering what it was
That brought him to that creaking room was age.
He stood with barrels round him — at a loss.

And having scared the cellar under him
In clomping here, he scared it once again
In clomping off; — and scared the outer night,
Which has its sounds, familiar, like the roar

Of trees and crack of branches, common things,
But nothing so like beating on a box.
A light he was to no one but himself
Where now he sat, concerned with he knew what,
A quiet light, and then not even that.
He consigned to the moon, such as she was,
So late-arising, to the broken moon
As better than the sun in any case
For such a charge, his snow upon the roof,
His icicles along the wall to keep;
And slept. The log that shifted with a jolt
Once in the stove, disturbed him and he shifted,
And eased his heavy breathing, but still slept.
One aged man — one man — can't keep a house,
A farm, a countryside, or if he can,
It's thus he does it of a winter night.

Theodore Roethke faces the starkness of Winter, but then introduces the sacred. In his poem, *The Lost Son*, he suggests that the spirit, symbolized by a special kind of light, returns in old age, bringing with it the promise of something holy coming. Be still and wait.

Lost Son
Theodore Roethke

It was beginning winter,
An in-between time,
The landscape still partly brown:
The bones of weeds kept swinging in the wind,
Above the blue snow.

It was beginning winter,
The light moved slowly over the frozen field,
Over the dry seed-crowns,
The beautiful surviving bones
Swinging in the wind.

Light traveled over the wide field;
Stayed.
The weeds stopped swinging.
The mind moved, not alone,
Through the clear air, in the silence.

Was it light?
Was it light within?
Was it light within light?
Stillness becoming alive,
Yet still?

A lively understandable spirit
Once entertained you.
It will come again.
Be still.
Wait.

Taking this theme further, Yeats, in the *Four Ages of Man*, addresses what he views as the ultimate task of Winter: yielding to God.

The Four Ages of Man
William Butler Yeats

He with body waged a fight,
But body won; it walks upright.

Then he struggled with the heart;
Innocence and peace depart.

Then he struggled with the mind;
His proud heart he left behind.

Now his wars on God begin;
At stroke of midnight God shall win.

But what kind of a meeting will this be, this meeting with God? As we saw in Rilke's poem, *The Man Watching*, a man grows spiritually "by being defeated, decisively, be constantly greater things." But will death be a terrible defeat? As so many poets do, T. S. Eliot also puts this meeting with death as the central destiny of Winter. In *East Coker*, he first points out that no matter who you are or what you accomplished, death awaits all.

Oh dark, dark, dark. They all go into dark,
The vacant interstellar spaces, the vacant into the vacant,
The captains, merchant bankers, eminent men of letters,
The generous patrons of art, the statesmen and the rulers,
Distinguished civil servants, chairmen of so many committees,
Industrial lords and petty contractors, all go into the dark,
And dark the Sun and Moon, and the Almanach de Gotha

And the Stock Exchange Gazette, the Directory of Directors,
And cold the sense and lost the motive of action,
And we all go with them, into the silent funeral,
Nobody's funeral, for there is no one to bury.

Yet the process of death, he intuits, may not be what we think. It may be a little like the changing of a scene in a play, the darkness of a tunnel, the nothing of anesthesia. Eliot tells us:

I said to my soul, be still, and let the dark come upon you
Which shall be the darkness of God. As, in a theatre,
The lights are extinguished for the scene to be changed
With a hollow rumble of wings, with a movement of
*   darkness on darkness,*
And we know that the hills and the trees, the distant
*   panorama*
And the bold imposing facade are all being rolled away —
Or as, when an underground train, in the tube, stops too
*   long between stations*
And the conversation rises and slowly fades into silence
And you see behind every face the mental emptiness deepen
Leaving only the growing terror of nothing to think about;
Or when, under ether, the mind is conscious but
conscious of nothing —

And yet, where are we going? Eliot answers:

Home is where one starts from. As we grow older
The world becomes stranger, the pattern more complicated
Of dead and living. Not the intense moment
Isolated, with no before and after,
But a lifetime burning in every moment
And not the lifetime of one man only
But of old stones that cannot be deciphered.
There is a time for the evening under starlight,
A time for the evening under lamplight
(The evening with the photograph album).
Love is most nearly itself
When here and now cease to matter.
Old men ought to be explorers

Here and there does not matter
We must be still and still moving
Into another intensity
For a further union, a deeper communion
Through the dark cold and the empty desolation,
The wave cry, the wind cry, the vast waters
Of the petrel and the porpoise. In my end is my beginning.

Eliot seems to be saying that with aging, this mystery of life becomes more keen and intense, present in every moment. And that the mystery of death is universal and cannot be deciphered. In our winter of preparation, however, there is time for the wonder of evening under lamplight and for reminiscing. Then we move into the timeless and sacred intensity of love and communion. There, life returns to where it began. We are going home.

Finally, Josephine Johnson challenges us not to turn away from the terrible ways we have wounded life as we grow old, not to hide in creature comforts from the carnage of the undisciplined heart, but to face our own responsibility. In her poem she tells us we must still stand for conscience and social justice.

From Year's End
Josephine Johnson

Now as the year closes and turns,
And the earth hard and naked and ringing
Under the night and the clean wind and the frost,
There is a salty lesson still to be learned,
And a page to be turned, and an answer given;
And there is one answer only.
> *Old and paunchy, or strong as animals,*
> *Or wise in the parlor clown game of finance,*
> *Or young and full of the knowledge of love and battles and customs,*
Yet must we sit down again as the year turns,
As the year closes and turns, sit down like children,
Restive and uncomfortable, longing for recess and the consolation of a
> *cream puff,*
With the hard lesson, the old lesson, still to be learned:
> War is of poverty, and poverty of greed, and greed is of
> the undisciplined heart....
Write this on all the pencil-tablets of the mind.
Write this on all the blackboards of the heart:
> There shall be no Kingdom and no Commonwealth.

There shall be no classless state, and no abundant life,
And there shall be no peace —
Until each of us, each of us — squirming here in the
too-small desk,
In the too-hot room,
— Until each of us shall have said,
"It is I, Lord, It is I!"

We have seen now some of the ultimate themes poets uncover in the Winter of life. Curiously, most people in Winter do not think as deeply as the poets about such archetypal themes. In fact, most elderly people say they do not feel old on the inside and are surprised that others treat them so. As Eric Johnson explains in his lovely work, *Older and Wiser*, elderly people may lament whatever loss of physical health, stamina, memory, and well-being that has come with aging (and, of course, the passing of loved ones), but most do not think a lot about death. Though they fear the prospect of illness and worry that dying may be painful, incapacitating, or undignifying, the majority say they do not fear death itself. In fact the percentage of people acknowledging fear of death drops steadily from midlife on!

The cultural misconception that aging invariably brings retreat, illness, and inactivity is also contradicted by the majority of healthy and active seniors. Older people are still curious about life. They are often creative, perhaps more so than ever before, and they have numerous interests, hobbies, and friendships. For most, life is more fascinating than ever and appreciated for the miracle that it is.

What do we make of these curious contradictions between the poets' keen interest in death in Winter on the one hand, and the elderly's interest in life on the other? While poets may have unearthed the deepest meanings of this transitional time, men in general are far more interested in life and living. They feel that death, itself, will answer the question of death.

This apparent disinterest in death is due to a mixture of factors. One could initially argue that it conceals a denial of fear and despair. However, I think the elderly would disagree. More important, they would say, are the following factors. The first is the recognition that one cannot ever really be prepared or fully know what lies ahead. It is not in our hands so why obsess about it? And having witnessed many deaths, elderly people also begin to realize that for most, death is actually a quiet, peaceful, and painless moment. Second, the fact that there is little or no future left now brings one's focus and interest into the present. I am here now. This is what is real for me. Things that are really important to me can't wait until next year. As a result, there is an even greater interest in living in the now. Everyday is important and the quality of life, love, and learning is what matters most. Third, it is likely that most of our poets wrote their works on death in the midlife or Fall of their lives. As we saw in Part 2, this is exactly the time when the issue of death stalks us most profoundly and calls for profound answers. Once this deep work is done, however, something quiets down. Then, by Winter, most people have formed their final beliefs, expectations, defenses, and coping attitudes. They are as prepared as they can be. Now, instead of delving into these ultimate (and ultimately unanswerable) questions, they often want to learn more about life.

As we've seen, each season of life has within it a cycle of mini-seasons. Although it sounds paradoxical, Winter begins with a Spring of new freedom and new possibilities, which extends into a mini-Summer that can last a long time. Then, something causes a man to reach the midlife of this season, and recognize its waning and the impossibility of finishing all he would like to do. The mini-Fall arrives as a time of reflection about life and preparation for death. This is a time of life review, putting affairs in order, giving what one still can to children and grandchildren, and saying one's good-byes — for these become the final tasks of the season. Reviewing one's life becomes especially meaningful in Winter because this whole experience, almost done as it is, still asks for meaning and perspective. What, after all, was it all about? To die in peace is to have put one's life in both practical and emotional order, so that there is as little unfinished as possible, so that one can let go when the time comes.

Winter usually ends quietly. In one moment our life is just gone, the story complete. When the time comes, it is okay. Winter itself moves from emptiness to fullness and back to emptiness. There will be fullness again. ❧

PART 4

Return to Sacred Ground:
The Mystical Experience in the Transformation of Men

Sometimes a man stands up during supper
and walks outdoors, and keeps on walking,
because of a church that stands somewhere in the East.

And his children say blessings on him as if he were dead.

And another man, who remains inside his own house,
stays there, inside the dishes and in the glasses,
so that his children have to go far out into the world
toward that same church, which he forgot.
(Bly, 1981, p. 49)

And those who live the mystery falsely and badly (and they are very
many) lose it only for themselves and nevertheless pass it on like a sealed
letter, without knowing it. (Rilke, 1986, p. 40)

One of our problems today is that we are not well acquainted with the litera-
ture of the spirit. We're interested in the news of the day and the problems of
the hour...When you get to be older, and the concerns of the day have all
been attended to, and you turn to the inner life — well, if you don't know
where it is or what it is, you'll be sorry. (Campbell, 1988, p. 3)

We're so engaged in doing things to achieve purposes of outer value that
we forget the inner value, the rapture that is associated with being alive is
what it's all about. (Campbell, 1988, p. 6).

Out of my experience with those thousands of patients, I have become con-
vinced that the psychological problem of today is a spiritual problem, a
religious problem. Man today hungers and thirsts for a safe relationship to
the psychic forces within himself. His consciousness, recoiling from the dif-
ficulties of the modern world, lacks a relationship to safe spiritual condi-
tions. This makes him neurotic, ill, frightened. Science has told him that
there is no God, and that matter is all there is. This has deprived human-
ity of its blossom, its feeling of well-being and safety in a safe world.
(McGuire & Hull, 1977, p. 68)

CHAPTER 26

An Overview

≫ In the Hindu religion, there is a time after one has completed career and family obligations that is specifically devoted to seeking God. Our society, in contrast, has forgotten this ancient tradition.

Rilke's words suggest that a man needs to go beyond himself in the twilight of his life to seek the sacred hidden somewhere in life's dawning. If he fails to take this journey, he may end his years brittle and rigid like glass, for the male soul has an inborn longing to touch the great mystery directly. Today we receive the sacred mystery like a sealed letter and have to find a way to open it ourselves. The way we strive to open it becomes our spiritual search or practice.

Campbell, too, warns that when we live our lives concerned only with the "news of the day" and the "problems of the hour," we will not know how to open our inner spiritual life when we get old. Having long ago forgotten the rapture of simply "being alive, sacred ground will also elude us at the end." Then, Jung adds his weighty conclusions: materialism and rationality will not solve our problem. They will not answer the spiritual questions of life. Our psychological problems arise because we seek the "wrong answers to the questions of life," betraying not only our deeper spiritual questions and longings, but also our long-awaited human blossoming. In the end, our feeling of safety and security in the world depends directly on our relationship to the divine.

In the middle years of adulthood, the questing and invincible hero of youth evolves naturally and imperceptibly into the devoted father and tireless breadwinner of family life, but neither role adequately prepares a man to confront the ultimate questions and awe-inspiring mysteries of life. As the years go by, he discovers that both his traditional roles eventually erode, giving way sooner or later to the descent into the grief and ashes of midlife. Faced with declining energy, the collapse of his grandiose dreams, and the departure of his children, and intuiting the deep despair of unconquerable realities — of time, death, and suffering — a man's journey finally reaches an all-important crossroads. He either begins searching for a more profound and sacred grasp of life's meaning and purpose, or he heads down a road of superficial comfort, illusory security, and smug materialism; or worse, a road of cynicism, melancholy, or frightened rigidity. Putting off the grief of lost dreams or a life unlived is no solution either. The emotional and spiritual debt simply grows.

The second half of life, Jung observed, is that time when the inborn religious outlook emerges most prominently (Jung, 1933). Less able to serve the culturally sanctioned gods of capitalism and materialism, men in the middle and later years begin to seek more transcendent values. Often they struggle to find some form of spiritual practice or heart-felt service to community or humanity that can embody these values. But this metamorphosis is not an easy one, for our culture lacks the wisdom and the rites of passage that could support an older man's spiritual awakening. And many men, armored by years of tough, compulsive conditioning, fail to hear the quiet voice of their own spiritual longing. Complicating matters further, of course, is the disdain, distrust or defiance some men feel toward organized religion in any form. This attitude often dates to smoldering resentments associated with hypocritically or dogmatically presented religious prescriptions, rules, and orthodoxy in childhood.

Yet there is a profound, immediate, and irrefutable spiritual experience that is always available. It is a remarkable awakening of individual consciousness beyond the ordinary and confining boundaries of empiricism and rationality. In this experience, man suddenly sees and understands the spiritual nature of the universe and his place in it. And from this extraordinary moment, he develops his sacred cosmology with all its attendant ritual, spirituality, theology, and mature stewardship for life. It is mankind's highest blossoming. In its pristine clarity, it is the mystic's vision of the world.

Part 4, "Return to Sacred Ground," explores the universal mystical experience. It seeks to understand and revalue this forgotten core of mankind, and to emphasize its role in restoring meaning to life. But prepare yourself. This is going to be an unusual, unorthodox, and rather surprising section for several reasons. First of all, it's about spirituality, something we psychologists have avoided talking about for decades. Second, it's about the unmediated mystical experience still happening in the world today. That is, what ordinary people actually report about their sought or unsought confrontations with the divine. Third, "Return to Sacred Ground" examines what these profound and transformative experiences can teach us about our lives and the world. What you learn will surprise and amaze you.

In the following chapters, I quote extensively from mystics, poets, and writers with first-hand spiritual experiences. I do so because I want you to see that this vision of spirituality is not some strange and eccentric religion of my own, nor is it an agenda I secretly wish to impose on you, but in fact a timeless view of spiritual reality available to all peoples in all times. The mystic vision does not belong to any religion but is the source and core of every religion. It not only bears the seeds of healing and renewal, it is the healing and the renewal. This vision illuminates the sacred ground of man's very existence. It is the wellspring of his most profound experience and knowledge of the universe. Perceiving in this new way, even for a moment, can shift an individual's perspective, mood, attitude, and motives — sometimes forever.

The mystical experience, as we will see, has direct relevance to this exploration of a man's development in the second half of life. It answers the deepest questions posed by the midlife passage and by the search for authentic masculinity. It answered my father's questions — for him and for me — for it speaks directly to the nature and meaning of life itself and man's place in the world. ❊

CHAPTER 27

What is the
Mystical Experience?

≫ Rather than intellectualize about religion or what the religious experience is, I want to start with some examples — examples drawn not from the mystics, saints, or saviors two or three thousand years ago, whose language and culture are so foreign to us that we can easily misunderstand their descriptions, but taken instead from twentieth century people who recorded their mystical experiences to share with us. Most are ordinary individuals who were not seeking any mystical experience at the time, some are more well known, and a few are religious seekers in the truest sense of the word. As you read these people's words, put yourself for a moment in their place and try to imagine the experience they are describing. Then we'll look at the commonalities to see what we can learn about the essential mystical experience.

"I saw things as they really were..."
Our first account gives this description of his mystical experience:
"The room in which I was standing looked out onto the backyards of a tenement. The buildings were decrepit and ugly, the ground covered with boards, rags, and debris. Suddenly every object in my field of vision took on a curious and intense kind of existence of its own; that is everything appeared to have an inside — to exist as I existed, having inwardness, a kind of individual life. And every object, seen under this aspect, appeared exceedingly beautiful. There was a cat out there with its head lifted, effortlessly watching a wasp that moved without moving just above its head. Everything was urgent with life...which was the same in the cat, the wasp, and the broken bottles, and merely manifested itself differently in these individuals...All things seemed to glow with a light that came from within them.

"I experienced a complete certainty that at that moment I saw things as they really were, and I was filled with grief at the realization of the real situation of human beings, living continuously in the midst of all this without being aware of it. This thought filled my mind, and I wept. But I also wept over the things, themselves, which we never saw and which we made ugly in our ignorance. And I saw that all ugliness was a wounding of life...I became aware that whatever it was that had been happening had now ceased to happen. I began to be aware of time again, and the impression of entering into time was as though I had stepped from air into water, from a rarer into a thicker element.

"My immediate reflections on the experience at the window were as follows: I saw how absurd had been my expectations of a vision of God — my notions of what such a vision would consist in. For I had no doubt that I had seen God; that is, had seen all there is to see. Yet it turned out to be the world that I looked at every day... I should say that though I should regard my experience as a 'religious' one, I have no patience whatever with organized religion and do not regard my experience as lending support to any of its dogmas. On the contrary, I regard organized religion by its very nature hostile to the spirit of mysticism.

"I think I said to you that once my life was meaningless and that now it had meaning. That was misleading if it suggested that human life has a purpose and that I now know what that purpose is...On the contrary I do not believe that it has any purpose at all. As Blake put it, 'all life is holy' and that is enough; even the desire for more seems to me mere spiritual greed. It is enough that things are; a man who is not content with what is simply does not know what is. That is all that pantheism really means when it is not tricked out as a philosophical theory. It would be best not to talk of meaning at all, but to say that there is a feeling of emptiness, and then one sees, and then there is fullness." (Stace, 1960, pp. 71-75)

"...everything was literally alive"

This woman, with whom I have corresponded, described her experience in the following words: "It was a morning late in July...I awakened on that morning to a world altogether different from the one I had closed my eyes upon the night before...I was aware of an unusual feeling of joy...Even before my eyes were really open I was aware of much light in the room and I recall a moment's wonder at how there could be so much light when the heavy drapes were closed...Everything around me had come to life in some wondrous way and was lit from within with a moving, living radiance...I saw objects in the ordinary way as well as with some extraordinary extension of the visual faculty. I saw into them with an inner vision and it was this inner sight which revealed the commonplace objects around me to be of the most breathtaking beauty...I was literally transfixed as my gaze rested upon first one thing and then another...The one thing that was, above all, significant was that everything was literally alive; the light was living, pulsating, and in some way I could not grasp, intelligent. The true substance of all I could see was this living light, beautiful beyond words.

"As I gazed about the room on that first morning, one of the things which particularly fascinated me was that there was no essential difference between that which was animate and that which was inanimate — only in form and function, not in basic substance, for there was only the one Substance, that living, knowing, Light which breathed out from everything...Ever since I could remember, I had accepted the fact of oneness in all life and manifestation, but it was purely theoretical, an intellectually accepted condition. But here I was literally beholding the fact itself so very far beyond any concept I had ever held...I was near-bursting with a tremendous, non-conceptual, understanding of life...I gasped at the beauty of a neighbor's cat which ambled slowly across the lawn, and at the lawn itself which was a sea of shimmering jewels, an ocean of iridescent light in both sun and shade...I became intensely aware of the underlying rhythmic tide which made of it all a cohesive, living organism...The presence of this great flowing symphony of form and light and color, and the indestructible harmony of it flooded my consciousness...I thought, 'We dwell in a fairyland of unimaginable beauty and sublimity and know nothing of it.'...My new found world was an immense cathedral in which I moved, flooded with wonder, joy, and reverence." (Starr, 1961, pp. 6-13)

"I knew now that eternity is here always..."

Sitting at her desk as a college student, a woman recalls, "The small, pale green desk at which I'd been so thoughtlessly gazing had totally and radically changed. It appeared now with a clarity, a depth of three-dimensionality, a freshness I had never imagined possible. At the same time, in a way that is utterly indescribable, all my questions and doubts were gone as effortlessly as chaff in the wind. I knew everything and all at once, yet not in the sense that I had ever known anything before...

"...Over a period of many months there took place a ripening, a deepening and unfolding of this experience which filled me with wonder and gratitude at every moment...I had plunged into a numinous openness which had obliterated all fixed distinctions including that of within and without. A Presence had absorbed the universe including myself, and to this I surrendered in absolute confidence...Activity flowed effortlessly. This new kind of knowing was so pure and unadorned so delicate,...I knew with absolute certainty the changeless unity and harmony...of the universe and the inseparability of all seeming opposites...Feeling myself centered as never before, at the same time I knew the whole universe to be centered at every point...All was meaningful, complete as it was. Each bird, bud, midge, mole, atom, crystal, was of total importance in itself. As in the notes of a symphony, nothing was large or small, nothing of more or less importance to the whole. I now saw that wholeness and holiness are one.

"Passing the campus chapel, I remembered how I had been taught in church to think of myself as here on earth and of God as above and out there, to aspire to heaven as in some future time and place...I knew now that eternity is here always, that there is no higher, no deeper, no separate past or future time or place...I felt that I was done forever with all seeking, all philosophic and religious doctrines, all fear of dying or concern with the future, all need for authority other than this...As for my relations with others, another person now filled my shoes. Laughter and delight seemed to fill my life. Somehow I had become more human, more ordinary, more friendly and at ease with all kinds of people.../

"Walking along the street I was aware of the street flowing past and beneath me, the trees or buildings moving past all around and the sky moving above as if I were immersed in one flowing whole. A child-like unknowing pervaded perception. The immediate word had acquired a new depth and clarity of color and form, an alloyed freshness and unexpectedness. Rooted in the present, every moment opened to eternity...(This experience) awakened appreciation for the inexhaustible delights of everyday living, the smell of smoking damp leaves, the taste of fresh Michigan apple, the sounds of the thrush in the early morning. It had also made me more aware of the sufferings of others, so much of it self-inflicted...Knowing that it was perhaps impossible, I still longed to tell others something that would help open their vision as mine had been...How inadequate words were to even suggest this experience to anyone else. What seemed to me the most marvelous and significant experiences seemed hardly of passing interest to others." (Courtois, 1986, pp. 47-61)

"There is something perfect"

This man, walking home from a train station, described, "It was now that I found myself looking at a certain house, one with which I am very familiar, as if I had never seen it before. There was a cloudy moon, and the house, some of its windows lighted, was outlined against the night sky. According to one's ordinary perceptions, it is rather an ugly little suburban villa; but now it appeared to be quite otherwise. In fact the proper way of putting it is to say that it did not merely appear to be anything: it simply was. And the 'is-ness' of it was all I knew and all I needed to know. I stood and stared at it, and the mere sight of it filled me with an indescribable joy...It was another house, and yet I knew that it was the ugly little villa I pass nearly every day. I realized that, could one always live on the different psychological level on which I was living at this moment, then the whole world would be changed; it would be another world in which there could be nothing which we habitually call ugly or evil, and nothing which we habitually call beautiful or good either, since the truth of things is beyond these contradictions, and somehow takes them up into itself.

"...Time had very little significance, but I must have been in this different state, sometimes more, sometimes less, for rather over half an hour. Not only did the realization of the truth, the astonishing new reality, of everything that saw persist, everything I saw was mysterious and wonderful...My ability to see, my actual and physical eyesight, was greatly sharpened. Even distant things, the cloud-formations, the moon, were miraculously clear.

"The sheer joy I experienced in all this is beyond expression. I felt that the world of nature was utterly right and literally an act of God's, and that to know this, and to be permitted to appreciate so much of the wonderful and the adorable, was nothing less than bliss. And this was reality. That is the whole point. The feelings and the thoughts we usually have are not real by comparison with this new condition of being into which I had moved. My knowledge of this reality which lies beyond where we normally are was undeniable and irrefutable...

"At one point in this walk, it flashed upon me with the same effect of irrefutable conviction: of course there is God...God was here; he was in everything that I looked at and in me who looked...I was in God's presence...

"On one of the crests of these waves of renewed intensity, when the aperture of consciousness was at its widest, I heard, vividly, shockingly, and as instantaneously as one might see a flash of lightning, what I can only call an inward voice which said, 'There is something perfect.' The phrase conveys nothing of the meaning it bore at that moment, for it had unbelievable depths of significance. The voice seemed to be telling me in those four words everything that is important and necessary to know. 'There is something perfect' was a summary of what it is to be in the presence of God who is perfection's self...

"I stood on the road, filled to the brim with this wonderful and joyous realization, that whatever we may have to endure of pain, sickness, grief and man's inhumanity to man, there is still something perfect within all created things; that, ultimately, they live by it, and that nothing else matters. Tears fell from my eyes. I had an impulse to go on my knees, there in the road beneath the stars... (Laski, 1961, pp. 419-421)

"I caught a glimpse of the ecstatic beauty of reality."

Next is an example from a woman convalescing in a hospital after surgery, who had for the first time been wheeled out onto the porch to look at a dingy winter scene. She recalled, "Entirely unexpectedly (for I had never dreamed of such a thing) my eyes were opened and for the first time in my life I caught a glimpse of the ecstatic beauty of reality...its unspeakable joy, beauty, and importance...I saw no new thing but I saw all the usual things in a miraculous new light — in what I believe is their true light...I saw...how wildly beautiful and joyous, beyond any words of mine to describe, is the whole of life. Every human being moving across the porch, every sparrow that flew, every branch tossing in the wind was caught in and was part of the whole mad ecstasy of loveliness, of joy, of importance, of intoxication of life...I saw the actual loveliness which was always there...My heart melted out of me in a rapture of love and delight...Once out of all the gray days of my life I have looked into the heart of reality; I have witnessed the truth." (Stace, 1960, pp. 83-84)

"I became acutely aware of a presence..."

Bill Wilson, once a "hopeless alcoholic" who later founded Alcoholics Anonymous, had this now famous conversion experience, which is described in *Pass It On: The Story of Bill Wilson and How the A.A. Message Reached the World*. "He had reached a point of total, utter deflation — a state of complete, absolute surrender. With neither faith nor hope, he cried, 'If there be a God, let Him show Himself.'"

"What happened next was electric. 'Suddenly, my room blazed with an indescribably white light. I was seized with an ecstasy beyond description. Every joy I had known was pale by comparison. The light, the ecstasy — I was conscious of nothing else for time.

"Then, seen in the mind's eye, there was a mountain. I stood upon its summit, where a great wind blew. A wind, not of air, but of spirit. In great, clean strength, it blew right through me. Then came the blazing thought, You are a free man. I know not at all how long I remained in this state, but finally the light and the ecstasy subsided. I again saw the wall of my room. As I became more quiet, a great peace stole over me, and this was accompanied by a sensation difficult to describe. I became acutely conscious of a Presence which seemed like a veritable sea of living spirit. I lay on the shores of a new world. This, I thought, must be the great reality. The God of the preachers.

"Savoring my new world, I remained in this state for a long time. I seemed to be possessed by the absolute, and the curious conviction deepened that no matter how wrong things seemed to be, there could be no question of the ultimate rightness of God's universe. For the first time, I felt that I really belonged. I knew that I was loved and could love in return. I thanked my God, who had given me a glimpse of His absolute self. Even though a pilgrim upon an uncertain highway, I needed to be concerned no more, for I had glimpsed the great beyond." (Wilson, 1884, p. 121)

"I saw that everything, just as it is now, is IT — is the whole point..."
Describing his own mystical experience, Zen author Alan Watts recalls:

"At the same time, the present seemed to become a kind of moving stillness, an eternal stream from which neither I nor anything could deviate. I saw that everything, just as it is now, is IT — is the whole point of there being life and a universe...Each thing, each event, each experience in its inescapable nowness and in all its own particular individuality was precisely what it should be, and so much so that it acquired a divine authority and originality. It struck me with the fullest clarity that none of this depended on my seeing it to be so; that was the way things were, whether I understood it or not, and if I did not understand, that was IT too. Furthermore, I felt that I now understood what Christianity might mean by the love of God — namely, that despite the commonsensical imperfection of things, they were nonetheless loved by God just as they are..." He concluded, "These experiences, reinforced by others that have followed, have been the enlivening force of all my work in writing and in philosophy since that time..." (Watts, 1958, pp. 30-31)

"I just rang!"
A humorous example of the same experience of oneness from the Zen tradition:

"It was very early in the morning at a Zen monastery near the town of Takeda, northwest across the mountains from Edo (Tokyo). The monks were close to the end of a strict retreat. The man who was to become one of the greatest of all Japanese Zen masters, Hakuin, was seated in profound meditation in a small temple some distance from the main hall. The deep sound of the temple bell calling all to the chanting of the sutras broke the morning stillness. Upon hearing the sound Hakuin was enlightened and shouted out with joy, 'I just rang!'" (Lee & Hand, 1990, pp. 31-32)

"I found everything in the room soaked as it were in bliss..."
Capturing the same experience, Stace relates this rather humorous example of the 19th century Hindu mystic Sri Ramakrishna, "He was at one time priest in charge of a temple of Kali, the Divine Mother. His extraordinary doings caused much embarrassment to the temple authori-

ties. On one occasion, he fed to a cat certain food which had been reserved as an offering to the image of the goddess. He defended himself by saying that 'the Divine Mother revealed to me that...it was she who had become everything...that everything was full of consciousness. The image was consciousness, the altar was consciousness...the door-sills were consciousness...I found everything in the room soaked as it were in bliss — the bliss of God...That was why I fed a cat with the food that was to be offered to the Divine Mother. I clearly perceived that all this was the Divine Mother — even the cat." (Stace, 1960, pp. 76-77)

"God is all. He is not far away in the heaven; He is here...The grass under your feet is He."

This woman recalled, "On the afternoon of Wednesday I went to see a friend, a farmer's wife, and we drove over the harvest fields to take some refreshment to her husband who was working with his men. When I was going away she gave me two very beautiful Marechal Niel roses. I had always had a passionate love of flowers, but the scent of these and their exquisite form and color appealed to me with quite exceptional force and vividness. I left my friend and was walking slowly homeward, enjoying the calm beauty of the evening, when I became aware of an unutterable stillness, and simultaneously every object about me became bathed in a soft light, clearer and more ethereal than I had ever before seen. Then a voice whispered in my soul: 'God is all. He is not far away in the heaven; He is here. This grass under your feet is He; this bountiful harvest, that blue sky, those roses in your hand — you yourself are all one with Him. All is well for ever and ever, for there is no place or time where God is not.'" (Bucke, 1923, p. 358)

"I had awakened to a consciousness that spanned centuries..."

Jean Houston, a psychologist who has researched and written widely on religion and mysticism, had her own mystical experience at the age of six. She recalls wishing for a vision of the Virgin Mary after seeing a movie about her. When no vision came, she gave up. Then, "Spent and unthinking, I sat down by the windowsill and looked out at the fig tree in the backyard. Sitting there drowsy and unfocused, I must in my innocence have done something right, for suddenly the key turned and the door to the universe opened. I didn't see or hear anything unusual. There were no visions, no bursts of light. The world remained the same. And yet everything around me, including myself, moved into meaning. Everything — the fig tree in the yard, the dogs in the closet, the wall safe, the airplane in the sky, the sky itself, and even my idea of the Virgin Mary — became part of a single Unity, a glorious symphonic resonance in which every part of the universe was a part and illuminated every other part, and I knew that in some way it all worked together and was very, very good.

"My mind dropped all shutters. I was no longer just the little local 'I,' Jean Houston, age six, sitting on a windowsill in Brooklyn in the 1940s. I had awakened to a consciousness that spanned centuries and was on intimate terms with the universe. Everything mattered. Nothing was alien or irrelevant or distant. The farthest star was right next door and the deepest mystery was clearly seen. It seemed to me as if I knew everything. It seemed to me as if I was everything. Everything — the fig tree, the pups in the closet, the planets, Joey Mangiabella's ribs, the mind of God, Linda Darnell, the chipped paint on the ceiling, the Virgin Mary, my Mary Jane shoes, galaxies, pencil stubs, the Amazon rain forest, my Dick and Jane reader, and all the music that ever was — were in a state of resonance and of the most immense and ecstatic kinship. I was in a universe of friendship and fellow feeling, a companionable universe filled with interwoven Presence and the Dance of Life.

"Somewhere downstairs my father laughed and instantly the whole universe joined in. Great roars of hilarity sounded from sun to sun. Field mice tittered and so did the gods and so did the rainbows. Laughter leavened every atom and every star until I saw a universe spiraled by joy, not unlike the one described by Dante in his great vision of the Paradiso...d'el riso del universe (the joy that spins the universe).

"Childhood kept these memories fresh. Adolescence electrified them and gave them passion, while first maturity dulled and even occasionally lost them. But even so, my life, both personal and professional, has been imbued ever since with the search for the unshuttered mind, the evocation and application of this mind in daily life and experience, and the conviction that human beings have within them the birthright of capacities for knowing and participating in a much larger and deeper Reality." (Houston, 1982, pp. 186-187)

"All men were shining and glorious beings who would in the end enter incredible joy."

"Vauxhall Station on a murky November Saturday evening is not the setting one would choose for a revelation of God...The third-class compartment was full. I cannot remember any particular thought processes which may have led up to the great moment...For a few seconds only (I suppose) the whole compartment was filled with light...I felt caught up into some tremendous sense of being within a loving, triumphant, and shining purpose. I never felt more humble. I never felt more exalted. A most curious, but overwhelming sense possessed me and filled me with ecstasy. I felt that all was well for mankind...All men were shining and glorious beings who in the end would enter incredible joy. Beauty, music, joy, love immeasurable and a glory unspeakable, all this they would inherit...In a few moments the glory had departed — all but one curious, lingering feeling. I loved everybody in that compartment. It sounds silly now, and indeed I blush to write it, but at that moment I think I would have died for any one of the people in that compartment. I seemed to sense the golden worth in them all." (Cohen & Phipps, 1992, p.3)

"...my 'self' was melting away into something infinitely larger..."
This person remembered:

"One afternoon, as I was looking out of the window into the crown of an ancient tree, my thoughts, with great intensity, spiraled from reflections upon my own life ever deeper in the Nature of Dharma (a Buddhist term meaning in this case simply Reality). And as my 'self' was melting away into something infinitely larger than myself, there was just one huge wave of warmth, Love, and Delight. At last, there was only One, not two. There is nothing but the Dharma. Nothing else. I am myself: just this.

"Later the question of my identity arose and I realized with great clarity and joy that as a person I am the Dharma as it manifests itself in the way of L (her name). This is my true nature. It does not belong to me. It is the ever-changing right-here-now. L's way can never be separate from the actuality of this moment. It has no form. It cannot be pinned down, for it has no substance. But it is...Then later on, during a walk outside: Everything shone forth with incredible simplicity of Being, of which I was an integral part. It was really impossible to describe, for actually there was no 'I' who was experiencing or thinking this. Just utter, utter, utter peaceful thusness. Nothing special!" (Lee & Hand, 1990, p.27-28)

"...it was such a miracle that someone or something could be alive..."
Another man described this event to me which occurred at the age of nine. He described:

"The experience itself was just...normally I have like a dialogue in my head — what I'm thinking about, a conversation with myself. This had no words and no conversation. It was a flooding of a feeling of joy. I was in the backyard in the springtime. It was warm but not hot. I just felt so alive and full of life that I just started dancing and prancing around the yard. It couldn't have lasted more than a minute but I don't have a sense of time. I've remembered it all my life just as clear as if it happened yesterday.

"There was a mystery of consciousness. I felt the import of the fact that I was conscious and it really was important to me that I could see and breathe and think.

"Everything was really green and fresh, colorful — the flowers, the overall smell. The light was a medium glow, but everything was very well illuminated. And it felt warm.

"I really liked it. It was extremely joyful. I felt that there was a reason for being, that the fact that I was conscious was right and extremely important. It differentiated me from the inanimate objects around. It seemed as though it was such a miracle that someone or something could be alive and that I was alive. At the time I didn't think about God. Maybe I didn't put two and two together.

"I look at it as a vividly memorable experience from childhood that I have no explanation for. And there was some kind of feeling attached to it that I have almost felt at other times." (Anonymous, 1994)

"A few feet in front of me...stood a numinous figure..."
This woman recalls:

"I lay down for a nap on the living room sofa...I had a dream of levitation...There was a further fragment of a dream, something about the beating of wings above and around me. Then I woke up....I saw nothing unusual with my outward eye, but I nevertheless knew that there was someone else in the room with me. A few feet in front of me and a little to the left stood a numinous figure, and between us was an interchange, a flood, flowing both ways, of love. There were no words, no sound. There was light everywhere...the world was flooded with the supernal light that so many of the mystics describe, and a few of the poets. The vision lasted five days...There was no one around to whom I could tell it...I knew that I was in a precarious situation...Yet the experience was so overwhelming good that I couldn't mistrust it..." She concluded, "Even though such a vision has faded...it altered my life permanently... Any work that I did thereafter was done not as a personal achievement, but as an offering to the Other whom I now recognized. There is no longer so much of the feeling that I do this and this...as that life lives itself through me...I have had ever since an intuitive awareness of being 'companioned.' That numinous figure is still there." (Foster, 1985, pp. 42-49)

"I passed from hell to heaven..."
This person's experience followed years of psychological darkness and suffering. He remembered:

"Often during my late twenties and early thirties I had a good deal of depression, not caused by any outward circumstances...at the age of thirty-

three I felt I must be going mad. I felt shut up in a cocoon in complete isolation and could not get in touch with anyone...things came to such a pass
and I was so tired of fighting that I said one day 'I can do no more. Let
nature, or whatever is behind the universe, look after me now.'

"Within a few days I passed from hell to a heaven. It was as if the
cocoon had burst and my eyes were opened and I saw.

"The world was infinitely beautiful, full of light as if from an inner
radiance. Everything was alive and God was present in all things; in fact,
the earth, all plants and animals and people seemed to be made of God. All
things were one, and I was one with all creation and held safe within a
deep love. I was filled with peace and joy and with deep humility, and
could only bow down in the holiness of the presence of God...if anyone
had brought news that any member of my family had died, I should have
laughed and said, 'There is no death'. It was as if scales had fallen from my
eyes and I saw the world as it truly was. How had I lived for thirty-three
years and been so blind? This was the secret of the world, yet it all seemed
so obvious and natural that I had no idea that I should not always see it so.
I felt like going ground and telling everyone that all things were one and
that knowledge of this would cure all ills...Psychologically, and for my
own peace of mind, the effect (of the experience) has been of the greatest
importance." (Cohen & Phipps, 1992, pp. 20-21)

"...direct contact with an intensely conscious universe..."

Gopi Krishna described a twenty-five year progression of psychic
development, beginning in his early midlife at thirty-five, which carried
him through times of profoundly blissful psychophysical transformations,
and times of illness, immense suffering, and near death. On one occasion,
he recalled:

"Near me, in a blaze of brilliant light, I suddenly felt what seemed to
be a mighty conscious presence, sprung from nowhere, encompassing me
and overshadowing all the objects around me...I expanded in an indescribable manner into a titantic personality, conscious from within of an immediate and direct contact with an intensely conscious universe, a wonderful
inexpressible immanence all around me...this real, interpenetrating and
all-pervasive ocean of existence...stretching out immeasurably in all directions...I was intensely aware of a marvelous being so concentratedly and
massively conscious as to outlustre and outstature infinitely the cosmic
image present before me..." (Krishna, 1970, pp. 201, 207)

"...individuality itself seemed to dissolve and fade away in bound-less being..."

Alfred Lord Tennyson, the poet, described this recurring mystical awareness:

"I have never had any revelations through anaesthetics, but a kind of waking trance — this for lack of a better word — I have frequently had, quite up from boyhood, when I have been quite alone. This has come upon me through repeating my own name to myself silently, till all at once, as it were out of the intensity of the consciousness of individuality, individuality itself seemed to dissolve and fade away in boundless being, and this was not a confused state but the clearest, the surest of the sure, utterly beyond words — where death was an almost laughable impossibility — the loss of personality seeming no extinction but the only true life." (James, 1936, pp. 374-375)

"The city seemed to stand in Eden, or to be built in Heaven"

Childhood is often a time when mystical awareness is still acutely present. Few remember this early realm of sacred experience as well as Thomas Traherne, a seventeenth century English shoemaker turned priest. He vividly recalls:

"Certainly Adam in Paradise had not more sweet and curious apprehensions of the world, than I when I was a child. All appeared new, and strange at first, inexpressibly rare and delightful and beautiful...All things were spotless and pure and glorious: yea, and infinitely mine, and joyful and precious. I knew not that here were any sin, or complaints or laws...I was entertained like an Angel in the works of God in their splendour and glory, I saw all in the peace of Eden...All Time was eternity...Is it not strange, that an infant should be heir of the whole World, and see those mysteries which the books of the learned never unfold?

"The dust and stones of the street were as precious as gold...The green trees when I saw them first through one of the gates transported and ravished me, their sweetness and unusual beauty made my heart to leap, and almost mad with ecstasy, they were such strange and wonderful things...And young men glittering and sparkling Angels, and maids strange seraphic pieces of life and beauty! Boys and girls tumbling in the street, and playing, were moving jewels. I knew not that they were born or should die, but all things abided eternally as they were in their proper places. Eternity was manifest in the Light of the Day, and something infinite behind everything appeared...The city seemed to stand in Eden, or to be built in Heaven." (Happold, 1990, pp. 368-370)

He concludes, "Your enjoyment of the world is never right, till every morning you awake in Heaven; see yourself in your Father's Palace; and look upon the skies, the earth, and the air as Celestial Joys...The world is a mirror of infinite beauty, yet no man sees it. It is a Temple of Majesty, yet no man regards it. It is a region of Light and Peace, did not men disquiet it. It is the Paradise of God...It is the place of Angels and the Gate of Heaven." (Happold, 1990, p. 371-372) ❈

CHAPTER 28

The Core Mystical Experience: Summary and Dimensions

➢ Many of those who have had profound mystical moments like the ones just cited went on to study them. Their goals were generally twofold: first, to provide a summary of the actual subjective experience, and second, to describe and conceptualize its core nature and dimensions. Clearly speaking of the same mystical consciousness, these writers repeatedly reinforce and eloquently extend the first hand descriptions just reviewed. As you read the following summaries and dimensions, continue to develop your "feel" for this remarkable state of consciousness, for it is a threshold to the opportunities of life's second half.

Summaries:

Richard Bucke, a ninteenth century physician, coined the term "Cosmic Consciousness" to describe this universal mystical experience. Recalling his own personal experience and those of others, he summarized,

"The person suddenly, without warning, has a sense of being immersed in a flame, cloud, or haze..." He feels "...bathed in an emotion of joy, assurance, triumph,...that no special 'salvation' is needed, the scheme upon which the world is built is itself sufficient..." It is, he explained, an "ecstasy, far beyond any that belongs to the merely self conscious life..." And, "Simultaneously or instantly following the above sense and emotional experiences there comes to the person an intellectual illumination quite impossible to describe. Like a flash there is presented to his consciousness a clear conception (a vision) in outline of the meaning and drift of the universe. He does not come to believe merely; but he sees and knows that the cosmos, which to the self conscious mind seems made up of dead matter, is in fact far otherwise — is in very truth a living presence. He sees that instead of men being, as it were, patches of life scattered through an infinite sea of non-living substance, they are in reality specks of relative death in an infinite ocean of life. He sees that the life which is in man is eternal, as all life is eternal; that the soul of man is as immortal as God is; that...all things work together for the good of each and all; that the foundation principle of the world is what we call love, and that the happiness of every individual is in the long run absolutely certain." "Especially does he obtain such a conception of...an immense WHOLE as dwarfs all conception, imagination, or speculation...as makes the old attempts to mentally grasp the universe and its meaning petty and even ridiculous." The individual feels as if he "...saw into the being of God; whence the birth or going forth of the divine manifestation. Nature lay unveiled to him — he was at home in the heart of things." In this revelation, Bucke adds, there is also "An absolute conviction of immortality, not just an intellectual belief...(and) "With illumination, the fear of death which haunts so many men and women at times all their lives falls off like an old cloak." Sin is gone: "It is not that the person escapes from sin; but he no longer sees that there is any sin in the world from which to escape." Finally, a "Great joy follows: An ocean of deep, deep joy, unending, infinite...(and)...Beyond words, beyond the power of speech to capture." (Bucke, 1923, pp. 72-74)

Alan Watts expands on this with:

"The most impressive fact in man's spiritual, intellectual, and poetic experience has always been, for me, the universal prevalence of those astonishing moments of insight which Rich Bucke called 'Cosmic Consciousness.'...To the individual thus enlightened, it appears as a vivid and overwhelming certainty that the universe, precisely as it is at this moment, as a whole and in every one of its parts, is so completely right as to need no explanation or justification beyond what it simply is. Existence not only ceases to be a problem; the mind is so wonder-struck at the self-evident and self-sufficient fitness of things as they are, including what would ordinarily be thought the very worst, that it cannot find any word strong enough to express the perfection and beauty of the experience. Its clarity sometimes gives the sensation that the world has become transparent or luminous, and its simplicity the sensation that it is pervaded and ordered by a supreme intelligence." (Watts, 1958, pp. 17-18)

He continues, "The central core of the experience seems to be the conviction, or insight, that the immediate now, whatever its nature, is the goal and fulfillment of all living. Surrounding and flowing from this insight is an emotional ecstasy, a sense of intense relief, freedom, and lightness, and often of almost unbearable love for the world, which is, however, secondary. Often the pleasure of the experience is confused with the experience and the insight lost in the ecstasy, so that in trying to retain the secondary effects of the experience the individual misses its point — that the immediate now is complete even when it is not ecstatic." (Watts, 1958, pp. 18-19)

Drawing from his extensive experience with states of enlightenment, Gopi Krishna explains,

"During the ecstasy or trance, consciousness is transformed and the yogi, sufi, or mystic finds himself in direct rapport with an overwhelming Presence. This warm, living, conscious Presence spreads everywhere and occupies the whole mind and thought of the devotee; he becomes lost in contemplation and entirely oblivious to the world. The mystical experience may center around a deified personality such as that of a savior or prophet...or it may be centered on an oceanic feeling of infinite extension in a world of being that has no end. It is not merely the appearance of the vision that is of importance in mystical experience. Visions also float before the eye in half-awake conditions and in hysteria, hypnosis, insanity, and under the influence of drugs and intoxicants. It is the nature of the vision — the feelings of awe and wonder excited by the spectacle that transcends everything known on earth. The enlargement of one's being, the sense of infinitude associated with the figure or the Presence, and the emotions of overwhelming love, dependence, and utter surrender mark the experience and make it of paramount importance as a living contact with a state of being which does not belong to this earth." (White, 1984, pp. 155-156)

He continues, "Even a momentary contact with the divine is a stupendous experience. Some of the most famous men on earth — the greatest thinkers and the ablest writers — such as Plato, Plotinus, Parmenides, Dante, Wordsworth, and Tennyson had the experience. Emerson and many, many other renowned men and women had this singular experience thrust upon them, often to their grateful amazement. Most of them had undergone no spiritual discipline, and there were even some who had no firm belief in God. For even when unexpected, the experience leaves a permanent mark on life which uplifts the individual and grants him insights into the nature of things that are not possible for those who never see beyond the veil...

"For a short time we are invincible, eternal — immune to decay, disease, failure, and sorrow. We are but drops in an ocean of consciousness in which the stormy universe of colossal suns and planets looks like a reflection that has absolutely no effect on the unutterable calm, peace, and bliss that fills this unbounded expanse of being. We are a wonder, an enigma, a riddle; even those who have access to it some time in their lives cannot describe mystical experience in a way others can understand. For the soul belongs to another realm, another state of existence, another plane of being where our senses, mind, and intellect flounder in the dark." (White, 1984, pp. 155-156)

Describing the same mystical phenomena, Wilson Van Dusen writes,

"Experiences at this level can range from a peaceful unity of all things to the appearance of the Lord Himself. The Lord appears as a tremendously intense love, knowing all there is. If there is any trace of awareness of self the Lord may appear in the zenith of the individual and unites with the individual in the *unio mystica*. All personal values are suddenly shattered. There is only God. The One and Only then shows Itself through all the levels of creation. With painful love the One chooses to create Itself into the individual who gradually awakens again as a person. There are secret understandings exchanged between the One and the individual. The stunned individual gradually returns again to personal awareness. It is not uncommon for the individual to be dreadfully disappointed at finding himself alive again in the ordinary world. The whole inner values of the person have been turned around.

"This the big satori, the ultimate, highest experience possible to the individual. Obviously the loss of selfhood cannot be made by the individual. It and satori are given by grace. The knowledge gained in satori is noetic; that is, it is given as fully true. There is no possibility of even questioning it until the little self appears. At the same time it is given there is no individual around to doubt it. The general understanding given is that there is only One. The One is pleased to experience itself through all possible orders of creation. Being all that is, It cannot but create all that is. It experiences Itself on all levels. Out of love it creates Itself as creation and suffers Itself through all possible orders and limitations of creation. The individual is the One in limited form, seeking its way back to Itself. The individual, all creation, and the One are the same. The purpose of creation is that the One playfully experience all its possibilities, so to speak, just to pass the time. Each individual is a possibility that leads back to the One." (Van Dusen, 1981, pp. 164-165)

Dimensions of the Core Mystical Experience

Numerous writers and mystics have attempted to conceptualize this basic mystical experience into its core and universal dimensions. They include Thomas Agosin, Roberto Assagioli, William Bucke, Joseph Campbell, Matthew Fox, Stanislov and Christina Grof, Aldous Huxley, Gopi Krishna, William James, Marghanita Laski, Lawrence LeShan, David Lukoff, Abraham Maslow, Sogyal Rinpoche, Marsha Sinetar, W.T. Stace, Evelyn Underhill, Wilson Van Dusen, and Alan Watts, to name just a few. It goes far beyond the scope of this book to give a detailed review of all this material and the reader is encouraged to explore it further.

What I do wish to present, however, is a dimensional summary of the pure mystical experience. I do so for two reasons: first, to differentiate it from theology, popular spiritual writings (e.g., New Age), Near Death Experiences, parapsychology, and abnormal psychological states, and second, to assist the reader in more closely examining his own experiences, for we shall begin to see that mystical moments may be more available then previously realized.

What follows are the essential experiential features of the mystical experience. In brief, it is:

ʃ **Direct, Unmediated Contact with the Divine:** Mystical experience is a direct, intense, subjectively undeniable, and profound religious experience. A deeply personal moment unique to each individual, it is invariably and unquestionably felt to be an immediate contact with the sacred and divine source of the universe. In its original and immediate form, it is not a philosophy, code of morals, or branch of theological or occult knowledge, though any of these may be formulated as secondary attempts to grasp and communicate its meaning and value.

ʃ **Beyond the Scope of Language to Describe:** Mystical experience is invariably described with words like "ineffable" because it involves experiences and illuminations that defy conventional language. Over and over people struggle to find everyday descriptions that can give even a hint of this larger-than-language consciousness. Metaphor, simile, and hyperbole strain to connote its power and majesty, which are infinitely beyond the communicative capacity of our paltry words.

ʃ **Beyond the Grasp of Personal Will:** The ego cannot intentionally evoke or control this experience; spiritual practices and contact with spiritual teachers may prepare the psyche or create the conditions necessary for its breakthrough, but the encounter with the divine cannot be voluntarily controlled. This is one experience that will not be dominated, manipulated, or exploited by man. Although one can develop an intuitive sense for the mystical, intuition is not equivalent to the experience itself. This moment of expanded consciousness is also generally viewed as a gift of grace, totally unpredictable in its timing and content.

ʃ **Luminous:** The mystic vision is universally associated with a heightened quality of light that feels transcendent in origin. It is described as luminous, numinous, and celestial. The light is often felt to be itself alive — to embody the actual presence of the divine, enveloping the experiencer in absolute love and acceptance.

⨍ **Timeless:** In the mystic experience, the divisions of past, present, and future are felt to be irrelevant, or to coexist or overlap. Opening into eternity, the present moment is all that exists. More than that, the consciousness of this moment is described as the very essence of life. Time is then seen to be an invention of mind. Some liken time to a roll of movie film. All the events of one's life already exist, right now, but have not yet been played. The light shining through the film is likened to divine consciousness itself, beyond time altogether.

⨍ **Ecstatic and Joyous:** The mystical experience involves an experience of unbounded joy, rapture, and bliss that transcends any known in our daily lives. It is, itself, absolute happiness, serenity, contentment, security, harmony, acceptance, and peace. There is a temporary loss of fear, anxiety, and worry and in its place a total relaxation into an all consuming feeling of being unconditionally loved and eternal. Joy, in all its variations, is felt to permeate the universe, or more, to be its very substance.

⨍ **A Radically New and Transfiguring Perception of the World:** Everything seems new, alive, crystal clear, fresh, radiant, sacred, holy, and gloriously bathed in divine love. The world is seen anew with what Fox calls "Radical Amazement." (Fox, 1958, p. 51) Rather than seeming like a "vision," the world is seen more clearly. Vision itself seems much sharper and there is typically a richness and heightening of sensory perception. As Maslow describes, everything is seen in loving ecstasy like a mother looking at her newborn baby. (Maslow, in White, 1972, p. 358) No part is more important than any other part and there is "…an awakened appreciation for the inexhaustible delights of everyday living." (Courtois, 1986, p. 57). This is mystical awe, an awareness that everything is literally saturated with holiness.

⨍ **A Sense of Presence:** A loving and conscious presence is felt to absorb the universe and the experiencer, and to this presence one surrenders completely and gratefully. This presence radiates unconditional love, understanding, and acceptance. The universe is known to be alive and sentient, animating all things and filling all spaces. In fact, one senses that there is really only the one consciousness, portions of which individual minds take to be their own. God has not left creation, God is creation. As White summarizes, "For, in truth, God is not outside His world. He has not 'created' the world — He has become the world." (White, 1985, p. 112) Afterwards, the belief that God is separate, out there, or someplace else, is replaced by a feeling of God as always here, pervading creation, eternally present. This experience is the real origin of Pantheism.

Absorption in Unity and Loss of the Individual Self: The personal, separate, familiar self is sometimes joyously and gratefully lost to this union with the divine, becoming an experience of total self-forgetting and egolessness. Without a separate observing self, the experiencer discovers that he is everything, he is the same as the All. Duality of subject and object are replaced by unity. There is felt to be only one, seamless whole, one living Being that permeates all existence. Multiplicity and separation are seen then as illusions. All things are, in fact, only the one Being. Like a raindrop falling into the ocean, the ego is merged into the One. The discriminating, categorizing, conceptual modes of thinking responsible for the experience of separation are transcended.

Loss of Awareness of Surroundings: Although rare, the individual may lose his awareness of his surroundings altogether, melting or being drawn into the Oneness in a blissful swoon and rapture. Occasionally profound supernal visions accompany this otherworldly rapture, leaving the experiencer later to believe he was taken into another divine world.

Without Goal or Effort: In the mystic experience, there is no feeling of problem, effort, goal, or struggle. Immersed in the loving fascination of this wondrous wholeness of being, behavior seems to flow naturally, no longer motivated by intention, worry, survival anxiety, or feelings of deficiency. One's own behavior seems to become an effortless contribution to the living waltz of life.

Authoritative Revelation of Ultimate Knowledge and Reality: The ultimate nature of the universe and God are temporarily opened to the individual in the mystical experience. Some feel they have, for a moment, entered the mind of God. This kind of direct knowledge has been called noetic. The experience and its meaning are also felt to be authoritative and absolutely beyond question to the individual. It is not a matter of speculation, analysis, or proof. It is instead felt to be direct and subjectively known truth, entirely self-justifying and intrinsically worthwhile.

Life and World Affirming: The mystical experience seems to be totally life and world affirming. One comes to know that existence is not random or meaningless, accidental, or futile, but instead rich in inherent purpose, validity, holiness, and love. Wholeness and holiness are felt to be two aspects of the same oneness. Huxley describes, "There is...a sense of what may be called the ultimate alrightness of the universe, the fact that in spite of pain, in spite of death, in spite of all the horrors which go on all around us, this universe somehow is all right." (Huxley in White, 1972, pp. 47-48) Much more than that, the world itself is, for a moment, paradise. Maslow describes the mystical experience as like "...a visit to a personally defined heaven...and the conception of heaven that emerges...is one which exists all the time all around us, always available to step into for a little while at least." It is, he says, a sense of "standing in Eden." (Maslow, quoted in White, 1972, p. 363)

ƒ **Transcendence of Polarities, Especially the Morality of Good and Evil:** If everything is seen as sacred and beautiful, how can it be evil? Critical, moralistic, and judgmental attitudes toward others and the world evaporate immediately amidst all the revealed splendor. The world is seen as beautiful, precious, desirable, and intrinsically worthwhile. It is never felt to be evil or undesirable, even though man's everyday perceptions make it seem so. One realizes, sadly, how much humanity lives in the viewpoints that arise from the conceptual, categorizing mind rather than from reality itself. It is man who misperceives the true nature of the world and in so doing creates evil and ugliness.

ƒ **Not Ego-Centered:** Feelings of spiritual superiority, inflation, pride, power, or personal gain are totally missing in the mystical experience. Neither is it about acquiring pleasure, visions, or knowledge as one does material possessions or academic credentials. Some people, however, may be temporarily overwhelmed or disoriented by the power of the experience, and become grandiose. They may feel they have achieved some sort of personal superiority for having had the experience, or confuse the personal self and the divine and believe they are God. Such inflation, however, is not inherent in the experience itself. It is, instead, a pathological disturbance of normal ego and identity.

ƒ **Full of Gratitude:** Within and after a mystical experience, the individual often feels an immense sense of gratefulness and thankfulness for the enormous gift they have received, and for this vast miracle of life itself.

ƒ **Full of Humility:** In this experience of unimaginable power and grace, one senses how little and insignificant is the individual ego. Profound humility, natural and without resentment, becomes the only spontaneously appropriate response to such divine revelation and generosity.

ƒ Transient: Unfortunately, the mystical moment cannot be sustained indefinitely, and the individual returns to "normal" reality. The customary ego orientation returns, and with it the subject-object duality as the film of intellect covers reality again. Assagioli writes, "Such an exalted state lasts for varying periods, but it is bound to cease. The personal self was only temporarily overpowered, but not permanently transformed. The inflow of light and love is rhythmical as is everything in the universe. After a while it diminishes or ceases and the flood is followed by the ebb." (Assagioli, 1977, p. 46)

ƒ Remarkably Ordinary: Ironically, following this remarkable experience of sacred reality, the individual returns to the everyday world feeling more ordinary. He is comfortable now simply being human, real, and natural. There is no need to be more or better. In the wonder of each and every moment, invidious comparisons become irrelevant and unimportant, and efforts to improve on this beauty seem ridiculous.

ƒ Impact: Not surprisingly, the mystic experience is usually profoundly impactful. It is never forgotten and often retains its original power and immediacy for years. The experiencer knows that this was one of the most important experiences in his life. As we will see later, however, how one's life is changed depends on the capacity to integrate and continue learning from the experience.

Understanding the dimensions described above is important. Though imperfect and incomplete (for there is no way to fully delineate the mystical), they provide a rough standard for discriminating between authentic and bogus teachings and teachers, and for evaluating your own mystical experiences. We will be elaborating such distinctions later. But for now, I want to move more deeply and subjectively into the mystical vision itself, and to give you an experiential glimpse of the world seen by the mystics. ❊

CHAPTER 29

Exercise: Experiencing
the Mystical

≫ What do the mystics see? To further our intuitive grasp of this experience, I borrowed from the first-person descriptions and general dimensions reviewed earlier to create the following exercise. Its goal is to move you toward a more subjective, first-hand, and personal awareness of the mystical; that is, to momentarily clean the lens of perception just enough to give you a glimpse of the extraordinary world they see. Though this exercise is not equivalent to the full mystical experience, it can give us a hint of what is there.

Instructions:

1. Put aside some time so you won't feel hurried. Find a peaceful place where you will not be interrupted. Unplug the telephone. Begin reading this exercise slowly, or better, tape record it or have someone else read it to you. Be sure to pause frequently as you proceed, so that the reality and implications of each idea or section can really sink in. Take all the time you need and go only as far as you like or is productive for you in each practice session.

2. This is not a guided imagery exercise. You don't need to fantasize or imagine anything. Instead, try to see and experience the world as clearly as you can and begin to discover in it dimensions you may have missed with your ordinary consciousness.

3. This is an experience, not a test or a race. Don't worry about whether you are doing it right or how far you get, because then your frustration may become distracting. If you find it difficult or troubling, stop and try again another day. Don't do the exercise if you are tired, irritable, or upset. Wait until you are in a frame of mind that is calm and focused, and try to be gentle and supportive of yourself. Spiritually advanced people have worked on developing this kind of awareness for their whole lives, so be patient and willing to let it happen gradually, over time, rather than trying to force it.

4. When you are experimenting with this exercise you can practice a part of it or all of it as many times as you like. Focus on the positive; that is, what is working, not what isn't. Simply observe the ways in which your perception actually does change. For example, you might notice a subtle change in the light, in colors, or in the clarity of your perception. Or perhaps your appreciation of beauty around you might begin to increase at first.

5. Trust what you experience. Don't talk yourself out of anything just because it doesn't fit your conventional or skeptical view of the world. Remember that it is the critical mind that separates us from the mystical in the first place.

6. Try not be put off by the word "God" in this exercise. It is meant simply to be a reference word for the sacred. If you are uncomfortable with it, use whatever name you like, preferably one that evokes a feeling of reverence or holiness.

7. Some of the ideas I introduce later in the exercise may seem a bit far out at first. Don't get stuck on something you don't like. Just start over or skip it and move on. Later you can return to any snags you found and explore them. For now, the critical and criticizing mind needs to be disarmed, so you can learn to see again. Get ready. Here goes…

Be still for a moment. This moment. Gradually quiet your thoughts and bring your attention to a clear and sharply focused awareness. Let your conceptual mind cease its activity. For the next few moments, there is nothing you have to do, no place to go, nothing to figure out, no one to be, no role to play, no goals to pursue, no problems to solve or understand. Let go of all that and focus carefully on these directions.

Breathe quietly, naturally, slowly, deeply and feel each breath as a totally new and complete experience. Don't let yourself get sleepy or dreamy. Don't drift off. Stay alert and examine everything carefully, slowly, deliberately. Try to avoid letting thoughts interfere with your direct awareness. You may at times want to figure this out, defeat or analyze the exercise, or even ridicule it. Whatever your skeptical mind tempts you to do, don't. Just be present, alert, absolutely aware, and completely here.

Consider this very moment. What if time could cease? What if now is the timeless eternal present? Let that awareness in. The immediate now is all that exists. No future, no past, no thoughts, no worry. Put memories, imaginings, and troubles aside for this moment and let go of your customary self consciousness. Right now, this awakened moment is all that exists, all that matters. It is the whole of existence, and the goal.

Come ever more fully into the present, into pure, sensory awareness. Just sit, and be radically aware of sitting as an immediate and remarkable physical expe-

rience: here, now, just as you are, nothing to change. Try to sharpen and intensify all sensation: sound, temperature, color, light. Stay alert! Let your perception
become ever more open and precise, keenly observant but without thought,
analysis or categorization. Perception now is all there is — rich, colorful, distinct,
vibrant — and if you are amazed by its crystal clearness and the incredible beauty of anything you really look at, or listen to, or touch, or smell, you are beginning to glimpse the mystic's reality. Keep looking, for it will happen when you
can see the world without the screen of thought.

Try this: Bring your vision from far to near. Really look at your hands, closely. Move them very slowly and intentionally in front of you. Examine your skin,
its wrinkles, color, shape. Now investigate something else close to you, inspect it,
see it just exactly as it is, not as an example of a class of objects that you know all
about, but simply and totally as it is right now in front of you, as a pure, fresh,
and unique sensory perception. Notice as you do this how the world may become
brighter, more colorful, more amazing in detail as you examine it, slowly, mind-
lessly, thoroughly. Everything is just what it is and should be. Each "thing" has
its own perceptual fullness, an intrinsic inner reality or life that is its own yet also
seemingly a variation of that single substance of which everything is made.

Now I want you to see this world in an even more radical way. This reality,
here, now, is always new, fresh, pristine, and radiant. It is a shimmering, dazzling,
wondrous, almost fairyland world of light, color, shadow, and sensation. Can you
see even just a little of this sparkling splendor? Complete and beautiful, just as it
is. Every object is perfect in color and texture; the arrangement of people,
objects, sights, and sounds is amazing. No single piece needs to be changed or
removed. No part is more or less important, more or less necessary, more or less
beautiful than any other part. A living miracle! In this way of perceiving, perhaps
you will also see that all things exist and operate for the good of each of us and
for the good of the whole. It is an amazing world!

Realize now that you, too, are part of this incredible beauty. Look at yourself
again. You are made of the same amazing stuff. And you are exactly right as you
are, just what you should be. You belong here, for you are an irreplaceable part
of the wholeness and perfection, and absolutely necessary to it. You too are the
miracle. Vision, hearing, touch, feel, smell, and taste are all miraculous, and even
more miraculous is your capacity for thought, consciousness, love and the perception of beauty. Think of it! You are part of this amazing wholeness, and the
beauty of this moment is beyond comprehension. All this: one wondrous, seamless, indescribable whole. It is all that it needs to be. Can you begin, just begin,
to know the world in this way?

Amidst this incredible beauty and perfect "all rightness," perhaps you can let
go a little more of your everyday pattern of worry and insecurity, and instead, just
for this moment, permit yourself to feel happy. Understand, there is nothing you

really must do or earn to be happy. You already know how. Happiness is inborn and natural to your nature. For example, if you won the lottery, you'd know just how to feel ecstatic, immediately. You would dance with joy! It would come bounding up from who you really are. In this garden of beauty, in this remarkable banquet of vibrant, abundant reality, you have won: you already have all you will really need or want, much more than you can imagine. So, at least for this moment, be happy, joyous, enraptured, peacefully content, or effortlessly serene.

Now consider this possibility. This immediate and wondrous reality you are in is itself filled with the divine. What if this were the scriptural Garden? What if you never left, but just forgot how to see it? How would you feel if this, all around you, were "Heaven on earth," the "Kingdom of God" people think is somewhere else? If you can see the world in this way, you are beginning to sense Eternity. It is already here, you just couldn't see it. The filtering lens of your thinking mind with its habitual reality assumptions and beliefs caused you to overlook it. For this moment, if you can open to this radical possibility, you are back in the Garden. Don't let your skeptical mind interfere because of the extraordinary nature of this idea — just open to it as much as you can. Earth is the garden! It's the jewel of the solar system, the galaxy, possibly the whole cosmos. There is nothing else like it anywhere we know — nothing so rich, verdant, beautiful and full of life. What a gift. See the gift!

Now, the mystics also know, immediately and undeniably, that reality is itself alive. It is a Presence: a living, eternal, infinite, loving, and joyous consciousness. This Presence pervades the manifest and unmanifest world. It envelopes us right now. It makes up everything, animate and inanimate. All of life is alive in its blessing and you are personally known and loved by this Being.

Whether or not you think you can really feel this Presence, simply reflect on it for a moment. What would it be like to feel it? What would it be like to sense that God is here, in this very place, present and alive in all forms. If this were true, then this place is itself sacred. In the light of this revolutionary consciousness, this all pervasive sacred reality, there would be no good or bad, no sin, evil, or ugliness, no problem. These judgments would be seen as incredible misunderstandings created by our reactive, conceptualizing, separative mind, a mind unable to see the immediately present, always existent, infinite beauty of being. Poverty, sickness, death, pain, and suffering — we have created the negativity in these experiences with our fear-driven recoil and distorted vision. They are not what we make them out to be! We make the world ugly. In this profoundly transformed perception, wherever you are, whatever you have, is enough if you can truly see it. Everything is a part of the same sacred creation. And, as mystics all over the world repeatedly emphasize, such enlightened perception is always available. It is our negative and fearful beliefs and the ambitious ego that block the way.

If you are ready and willing, let's take one more step into this extraordinary vision. Realize this: God is what everything is made of, including you. This body, these hands, this movement, this moment, this light, this thought, this place, this breath, it is all God. Each of us is a living and potentially conscious embodiment or incarnation of the divine. God has not left creation; God is creation, and you are made of that same sacred being. God looks through your eyes, hears through your ears, feels through your body. God can be felt as the very energy, presence, and consciousness of your being. What you customarily take to be "your" consciousness is alive, it is a Presence, a living Being breathing our breath, animating our movements, and pervading our body. What this means, say the mystics, is that our becoming one with God requires only that we undo the perceptual errors that make us seem separate and different. In fact, knowing God directly and becoming one with this cosmic consciousness is the very purpose of creation. The mystics are simply those individuals who realized this first, and who show the way for the rest of us.

Now let's step into this radiant consciousness. See if you can begin to feel some of its inherent joy. This all-pervasive, single, radiant consciousness of which we are all made is, in its essential reality, a living ocean of love and bliss. Feeling this body of yours to be made of the living God simply evokes ecstasy! The mystics have been telling us this since time immemorial. And from this joy one begins to realizes that all existence is itself conscious and ecstatic, one joyous infinite being. In time we realize that we have mistakenly externalized this being, as if it were someone separate from us, then give it some name (like God or Yahweh or Shiva or Christ or Allah or the Great Spirit or...), and thus create a God figure outside ourselves, separate and far away. But all this is the cognitive structuring of reality, not reality itself, which is instead the one living presence. Artificially separated from this divine reality by our conceptualizing mind, we also create the idea of an autonomous self and believe we are alone, at risk, destructible, mortal, separate. What a tragic misperception. You are not the idea of self you have manufactured. Actually, the mystics say, there is really no one to be, no separate self, and nothing one has to do to become one with God except to remove the original mistaken perception of self and separation. See if you can be the Oneness you are sensing now.

This is the great mystical realization that melts self into blissful unity with the All. In whatever ways you can, be they little or big, see if you can see, touch and feel this truth. You are already divine. This place is the sacred. This is your true nature. This is it.

Debriefing

What did you see? What did you learn? How did you feel? Let your reactions seep into consciousness. How do they change the way you look at yourself or the world? Take whatever time you need to digest this experience. Remember that the perceptual changes described above will probably come slowly, often imperceptibly at first, and sometimes only later in the hours or days after a practice session. What is important, however, is simply to notice these changes, no matter how subtle, and to open yourself to their effects and implications.

You can repeat this exercise whenever you wish. Let it increasingly alter your perception and consciousness over time. Try to bring some of the feelings you had doing this exercise into your daily routine. Stop what you are doing occasionally during the day, stand still, and really open your eyes to glimpse this mystical world more often. It is a remarkable experience. You might also take some time to reflect on how your life would change if you lived in this consciousness more often. We'll talk more about that later.

Finally, it is important to understand that we all move at our own pace. Some persons have profound experiences very quickly while others must be patient. If we feel dissatisfied and anxious about our ability to have mystical experiences, then we are merely adding another layer of negativity to our psyche. This holds us back and prevents us from experiencing more. The trick is to cultivate an attitude of openness toward these experiences and concepts, and to be thankful for what we receive, whether it is a lot or a little. ❧

CHAPTER 30

The Poet's Vision

❧ Mystical poets from all times have had this transcendent vision of reality in mind when they composed their work, and their poetry incorporates many of the themes and dimensions enumerated above. If we can get inside their words and images, they can take us to the same mystical moment. Read these words slowly, try to feel or intuit what they really mean.

The son of an eminent theologian, Jelaluddin Rumi (1207-1273) was born in Afghanistan and by midlife had established himself as a rather orthodox and conventional religion professor. Houston recounts, "He was somewhere between the ages of thirty-nine and forty-three when a wild-looking dervish climbed over the wall in the court where Rumi was teaching, took his valuable books and threw them in a pool of water saying, 'Now you must live what you know.'" (Houston, 1987, p. 192) As the story goes, Rumi saw in this man the face of the divine, instantly fell into blissful devotion, and gave up his formal teaching. Thereafter, Rumi established the religious order and practice that came to be known as the "Whirling Dervishes" and wrote some 50,000 verses of spontaneous mystical poetry. What an example of the midlife's spiritual eruption!

These poems speak of Rumi's ecstatic identification and union with God. He cannot separate himself from God, for he sees, feels, and knows God to be alive in and as everything, including himself.

> Lo, I am with you always, *means when you look for God,*
> *God is in the look of your eyes,*
> *in the thought of looking, nearer to you than your self,*
> *or things that have happened to you.*
> *There's no need to go outside.*
> *Be melting snow.*
> *Wash yourself of yourself.*
> (Moyne & Barks, 1984)

> *I am rid of everything*
> *but your Essence. You know how I am with You,*
> *as the orchard is with the rain, and twenty times*
> *that! Living in You, rejoicing in You,*
> *like a beggar receiving all he needs directly*
> *from Wealth itself, with no one's hand in between.*

Not united, not separated. Perfection. No!
No qualities, no description, no cause.
(Barks & Moyne, 1988)

Hand me, says the mystic poet
to the One he can't see, Your Cup.
You are my face. No wonder I can't see You.
You are the intricate workings of my mind.
You are the big artery in my neck.
When I call out in the desert, O God,
I'm only pretending, to distract the others,
so they won't notice Who sits beside me.
(Barks & Moyne, 1988)

Mad with thirst, he can't drink from the stream
running so close by his face. He's like a pearl
on the deep bottom, wondering, inside his shell, "Where's the Ocean?"
    His mental questionings
form the barrier. His physical eyesight
bandages his knowing. Self-consciousness
plugs his ears.
    Stay bewildered in God,
and only that.
(Barks & Moyne, 1988)

Born in 1398 of a low Muslim caste, Kabir was a poor Indian weaver who lived near the holy city of Benares. He had no formal education yet by the end of his life, Kabir had became one of the most popular and renowned saints of all India. As a young man, he fervently wished to be accepted as a disciple of the Ramanand. Determined to meet him, Kabir secretly lay on the steps in the Ganges river where Ramanand bathed early each morning and was struck in the head by the great saint's foot. Ramanand exclaimed, "Ram, Ram!" As Sethi describes, Kabir later told Ramanand, "'Sir, I was initiated by you on the steps of the Ghat. You touched my forehead with your foot and gave me the mantra 'Ram Ram'. Ramanand, a noble and truthful soul, could not deny it and accepted Kabir as his disciple.'" (Sethi, 1984, p. 11) Kabir far outdistanced his teacher in his spiritual teaching and was said to have attained the highest form of mystical experience: God realization. His vast outpouring of poems and Sufi teachings are still alive in India and the world. In the following pieces, Kabir emphasizes the importance of experiencing the divine here and now, wherever you are, for all creation is felt to be pervaded joyously by the sacred.

In this first piece, Kabir argues that man must find the eternal and divine here and now, in this world, and not miss it waiting for some other world.

> Friend, hope for the Guest while you are alive.
> Jump into experience while you are alive!
> think...and think...while you are alive.
> What you call "salvation" belongs to the time before
>   death.
>
> If you don't break your ropes while you're alive,
>   do you think ghosts will do it after?
>
> The idea that the soul will join with the ecstatic
>   just because the body is rotten —
>   that is all fantasy.
> What is found now is found then.
> If you find nothing now,
> you will simply end up with an apartment in the City
>   of Death.
> If you make love with the divine now, in the next life,
>   you will have the face of satisfied desire.
>
> So plunge into the truth, find out who the Teacher is,
> Believe in the Great Sound!
>
> Kabir says this: When the Guest is being searched for,
>   it is the intensity of the longing for the Guest that
>   does all the work.
> Look at me, and you will see a slave of that intensity.
> (Bly, 1977)

Like Rumi, Kabir knows that he will find God everywhere, but most immediately, in himself. These three poems describe the grateful and rapturous experience of that union.

> Are you looking for me? I am in the next seat.
> My shoulder is against yours.
> You will not fine me in stupas, not in Indian shrine
>   rooms, nor in synagogues, nor in cathedrals:
> not in masses, nor kirtans, not in legs winding around your own neck,
> nor in eating nothing but vegetables.

When you really look for me, you will see me
    instantly —
you will find me in the tiniest house of time.
Kabir says: Student, tell me, what is God?
He is the breath inside the breath.
(Bly, 1977)

Next we see Kabir's expression of natural humility and ecstatic joy he finds in experiencing the divine. Releasing the burden of effort and narcissistic perfection, he finds a universe of love.

The Guest is inside you, and also inside me;
you know the sprout is hidden inside the seed.
We are all struggling; none of us has gone far.
Let your arrogance go, and look around inside.

The blue sky opens out farther and farther,
the daily sense of failure goes away,
the damage I have done to myself fades,
a million suns come forward with light,
when I sit firmly in that world.

I hear bells ringing that no one has shaken,
inside "love" there is more joy than we know of,
rain pours down, although the sky is clear of clouds,
there are whole rivers of light.
The universe is shot through in all parts by a single
    sort of love.
How hard it is to feel that joy in all our four bodies!

Those who hope to be reasonable about it fail.
The arrogance of reason has separated us from that
    love.
With the word "reason" you already feel miles away.

How lucky Kabir is, that surrounded by all this joy
he sings inside his own little boat.
His poems amount to one soul meeting another.
These songs are about forgetting dying and loss.
They rise above both coming and going out.
(Bly, 1977)

William Bucke, who coined the term "Cosmic Consciousness," and Walt Whitman, our next poet, were nineteenth century contemporaries and became great friends. After reading *Leaves of Grass*, Bucke became convinced that Whitman was a mystically realized man. Meeting Whitman was "the turning point in his life." (May, 1991, p. 7) He later wrote, "I have never seen any man to compare with him...He is an average man magnified to the dimensions of a god..." (May, 1991, p. 8) These selections, taken from *Song of Myself*, celebrate a divinity in body, self, and world, and admit an empathic oneness with all men whatever their condition.

We begin with Whitman's joyous proclamation of the miracle of simply being human and living in this wondrous and divinely perfect world.

I believe in the flesh and the appetites,
Seeing, hearing, feeling, are miracles, and each part and
*   tag of me is a miracle*

Divine am I inside and out, and I make holy whatever I
*   touch or am touched from,*
The scent of these arm-pits aroma finer than prayer,
This head more than churches bibles, and all the creeds

I believe a leaf of grass is no less than the journey-work of
*   the stars,*
And the pismire (ant) is equally perfect, and a grain of sand,
*   and the egg of the wren,*

And the tree-toad is a chef-d'oeuvre for the highest,
And the running blackberry would adorn the parlors of
*   heaven,*
And the narrowest hinge in my hand puts to scorn all
*   machinery,*
And the cow crunching with depress'd head surpasses any
*   statue,*
And a mouse is miracle enough to stagger sextillions of
*   infidels.*

Whitman reveals next his identity with all life.

Not a youngster is taken for larceny but I go up too, and
*   am tried and sentenced.*

Not a cholera patient lies a the last gasp but I also lie at
*   the last gasp,*

*My face is ash-color'd, my sinews gnarl, away from me
people retreat.*

*Askers embody themselves in me and I am embodied in
    them,
I project my hat and sit shame-faced, and beg.*

Akin to all the mystic poets, Whitman too views himself (and all men) as
divine, unmeasurable, already perfect. Yet this perfection is found in the all ordinary moments of human life.

*I heard what was said of the universe.
Heard it and heard it of several thousand years;
It is middling well as far as it goes — but is that all?*

*Magnifying and applying come I,
Outbidding at the start the old cautious hucksters,
Taking myself the exact dimensions of Jehovah,
Lithographing Kronos, Zeus his son, and Hercules his
    grandson,
Buying drafts of Osiris, Isis, Belus, Brahma, Buddha,
In my portfolio placing Manito loose, Allah on a leaf, the
    crucifix engraved,
With Odin and the hideous-faced Mexitli and every idol
    and image,
Taking them all for what they are worth and not a cent
more,
Admitting they were alive and did the work of their days...
Accepting the rough deific sketches to fill out better in
    myself, bestowing them freely on each man and woman
    I see,*

*Discovering as much or more in a framer framing a house,
Putting higher claims for him there with his roll'd-up sleeves
    driving the mallet and chisel,
Not objecting to special revelations, considering a curl of
    smoke or a hair on the back of my hand just as curious
    as any revelation.*

Whitman has this to say about his own journey and philosophy of life.

*I tramp a perpetual journey, (come listen all!)
My signs are a rain-proof coat, good shoes, and a staff cut*

from the woods,
No friend of mine takes his ease in my chair,
I have no chair, no church, no philosophy,
I lead no man to a dinner-table, library, exchange,
But each man and each woman of you I lead upon a knoll,
My left hand hooking you round the waist,
My right hand pointing to landscapes of continents and
the public road.

Finally, Whitman talks directly to the reader. He wants the reader to recognize his own mystical journey and awaken his own mystical realizations. The reader and Whitman are one on the same journey of awakening.

Not I, not any one else can travel that road for you,
You must travel it for yourself.

It is not far, it is within reach,
Perhaps you have been on it since you were born and did
not know,
Perhaps it is everywhere on water and on land.

My words itch at your ears till you understand them.

I do not say these things for a dollar or to fill up the time
while I wait for a boat,
(It is you talking just as much as myself, I act as the tongue
of you,
Tied in your mouth, in mine it begins to be loosen'd.)

And this is what Whitman has to say about seeing God.

Why should I wish to see God better than this day?
I see something of God each hour of the twenty-four, and
each moment then,
In the face of men and women I see God, and in my own
face in the glass,
I find letters from God dropt in the street, and every one
is sign'd by God's name,
And I leave them where they are, for I know that where-
soe'er I go
Others will punctually come for ever and ever.
(Whitman, 1969)

William Wordsworth (1770-1850) was an English poet of the romantic school. The poem that follows is one of the most famous in English literature and, interestingly, was completed at the age of thirty-seven. In it, he recalls vestiges of the mystical experience in early childhood and the inevitable loss of this vision on reaching adulthood.

Ode: Intimations of Immortality
from Recollections of Early Childhood

There was a time when meadow, grove, and stream,
The earth, and every common sight,
   To me did seem
   Appareled in celestial light,
The glory and the freshness of a dream,
It is not now as it hath been of yore; —
   Turn wheresoe'er I may,
   By night or day,
The things which I have seen I now can see no more.
Our birth is but a sleep and a forgetting;
The soul that rises with us, our life's star,
   Hath had elsewhere its setting,
   And commeth from afar:
   Not in entire forgetfulness,
   And not in utter nakedness,
But trailing clouds of glory do we come
   From God, who is our home:
Heaven lies about us in our infancy!
Shades of the prison-house begin to close
   Upon the growing boy,
But he beholds the light, and whence it flows,
   He sees it in his joy;
The youth, who daily farther from the east
   Must travel, still is Nature's priest,
   And by the vision splendid
   Is on his way attended;
At length the man perceives it die away,
And fade into the light of common day.

(Wordsworth, in Warren, 1955)

Born in 604 B.C., Lao-Tzu refused to write down his philosophy of life until the very end. He has, therefore, only one work, the Tao Teh Ching, which translates to

The Way of Life. It is said that the great Chinese philosopher Confucius once visited Lao-Tzu, after which he told his disciples, "Of birds I know that they have wings to fly with, of fish that they have fins to swim with, of wild beasts that they have feet to run with. For feet there are traps, for fins nets, for wings arrows. But who knows how dragons surmount wind and cloud into heaven? This day I have seen Lao-Tzu and he is a dragon." (Bynner, 1944, p. 13)

> *Those who would take over the earth*
> *And shape it to their will*
> *Never, I notice, succeed.*
> *The earth is like a vessel so sacred*
> *That at the mere approach of the profane*
> *It is marred.* (p. 58)

> *Existence is beyond the power of words*
> *To define...*
> *The core and the surface*
> *Are essentially the same,*
> *Words making them seem different*
> *Only to express appearance.*
> *If name be needed, wonder names them both:*
> *From wonder into wonder*
> *Existence opens.* (Brynner, 1944)

Rainer Maria Rilke (1875-1926) is not only one of Germany's most famous poets, he is recognized as one of the greatest poets of the twentieth century. His poetry flowed from a tormented yet brilliant soul. Some of his greatest works were said to have poured forth between the ages of thirty-seven and forty-six almost fully formed from a voice neither "within nor outside" him. (Mitchell, 1985, p. 7) Here again is the eruptive power of midlife! The power Rilke refers to is the very energy of Being, and his experience of a simple apple reveals an openness to mystic reality described earlier.

The Spanish Trilogy

> *Why must a man keep standing like a shepherd,*
> *exposed, in such an overflow of power,*
> *so much a part of this event-filled landscape,*
> *that if he were to lean back against a tree trunk*
> *he would complete his destiny, forever.*
> (Mitchell, 1989)

The Sonnets to Orpheus

Dare to say what "apple" truly is.
This sweetness that feels thick, dark, dense at first;
then, exquisitely lifted in your taste,

grows clarified, awake and luminous,
double-meaninged, sunny, earthy, real:
Oh knowledge, pleasure — inexhaustible.
(Mitchell, 1985)

John Robinson Jeffers (1887-1962), the son of a theology professor, was an American poet who lived a non-conforming life on the rugged and isolated coast of northern California. He is quoted to have said that most great men produce their major works by thirty, but at that age, he had not yet been "born." The following piece was published at the age of fifty-four. Though described as pessimistic and critical of humanity, he loved the wilderness and this poem seems to speak with that loving voice.

The Excesses of God

Is it not by his high superfluousness we know
Our God? For to equal a need
Is natural, animal, mineral: but to fling
Rainbows over the rain
And beauty above the moon, and secret rainbows
On the domes of deep sea-shells,
And make the necessary embrace of breeding
Beautiful also as fire,
Not even the weeds to multiply without blossom
Nor the birds without music:
There is extravagant kindness, the fountain
Humanity can understand, and would flow likewise
If power and desire were perch-mates.

William Butler Yeats (1865-1939) was an Irish poet who won the Nobel prize for literature in 1923. He is said by many to be one of the greatest poets of his time. The following poem would appear to speak directly to the mystic vision. As can be seen, it occurred at what would probably have been the close of the midlife transition.

Vacillation IV

My fiftieth year had come and gone,
I sat, a solitary man,
In a crowded London shop,
An open book and empty cup
On the marble table-top.

While on the shop and street I gazed
My body of a sudden blazed;
And twenty minutes more or less
It seemed, so great my happiness,
That I was blessed and could bless.
(Finneran, 1983)

This last piece was written by a friend. Its very existence argues that mystical poetry is not limited to the great and famous. Its inspiration is available to everyone.

The Mystical Sun

Deep in the heart of space,
In the center of that dark and infinite interior,
Burns a mystical sun:
I can hear its rumbling fission,
I can sense its slow revolution,
It is alive.

The mystical sun is awakening.
As it slowly turns inside my core,
Flooded by a new consciousness,
I hear and see in a wondrous way:
Everything is alive.
A new dawning as old as time:
He is here.

In the heart of the mystical sun,
In its whitelight fusion,

Burns the originating mind of existence:
It is the mind that lights the world,
From which my mind is drawn:
I am the seer, the seen and the act of seeing,
and the one in whom it all arises.

In His mind, such a marvelous dream is born:
Living, acting, being, goaling, having, losing, dying.
In rapt wonder, I am drawn into this bold adventure as
If it were what it appears. I want it all so badly,
Until I realize it is merely His wonder —
Dazzling fireworks of imagery, magic and miracle
That seem to hide the interior sun, until I see into it again.

In this timeless moment: A consciousness not my own,
A living awareness that permeates my limbs, nerves and mind.
The universe is alive with Presence!
Let go. Forget yourself! I fall into this spacious One, until
Who I am disappears into a joyous funeral pyre,
And the world is dancing light —
I am who He is, I welcome this consciousness.
Flooded with joy, infinitely in love, eternally alive —
I live in His effortless grace — a mirage.

D.H. Lawrence (1885-1930) struggled with the nature and purposes of religion his whole life. The spirituality he was drawn to was an ancient one that intimately knew the living nature of the whole wondrous cosmos. In his very last book, aptly entitled *Apocalypse*, Lawrence challenges us to be in this sacred embodied experience here, now, before we die. Though not explicitly poetry, we have seen that Lawrence is a poet and what follows is most certainly the poet's mystical vision.

"To the ancient consciousness, Matter, Materia, or Substantial things are God. A pool of water is god. And why not? The longer we live the more we return to the oldest of visions. A great rock is god. I can touch it. It is undeniable." (Lawrence, 1931, p. 85).

"What man most passionately wants is his living wholeness and his living unison, not his own isolate salvation of his "soul." Man wants his physical fulfillment first and foremost, since now, once and once only, he is in the flesh and potent. For man, the vast marvel is to be alive. For man, as for flower and beast and bird, the supreme triumph is to be most vividly, most perfectly alive...We ought to dance with rapture that we should be alive and in the flesh, and part of the living, incarnate cosmos." (Lawrence, 1931, pp. 199-200) ❦

CHAPTER 31

Putting the Mystic Consciousness
Into Perspective

≫ So far, we have only addressed the mystical vision itself, what it is and what it illuminates. The reader has patiently and graciously postponed an understandably growing list of questions, reactions, and opinions. Although they cannot all be anticipated, the points that follow below will hopefully respond to most. See if these additional ideas help put the mystic consciousness in better perspective for you.

ſ *All mystical experience is, in its essence, the same awareness:* Profound mystical experiences, because they all involve contact with the same ultimate source, are essentially the same all over the world. The apparent differences are created by the cultural, linguistic, political, and religious contexts surrounding it.

Maslow, a psychologist, studied such mystical moments which he named "peak experiences." In describing the "core-religious" nature of peak experiences, he hypothesizes, "...to the extent that all mystical or peak-experiences are the same in their essence and have always been the same, all religions are the same in their essence and always have been the same." (Maslow, in White, 1972, p. 353). He goes on, "This something common, this something which is left over after we peel away all the localisms, all the accidents of particular languages or particular philosophies, all the ethnocentric phrasings, all those elements which are common, we may call the 'core-religious experience' or the 'transcendent experience.'" (Maslow, in White, 1972, p. 353).

Sogyal Rinpoche, a Tibetan Buddhist, continues the same theme, stating, "Saints and mystics throughout history have adorned their realizations with different names and given them different faces and interpretations, but what they are all fundamentally experiencing is the essential nature of mind. Christians and Jews call it 'God,' Hindus call it 'the Self,' 'Shiva,' 'Brahman,' and 'Vishnu'; Sufi mystics name it 'the Hidden Essence,' and Buddhists call it 'Buddha nature.' At the heart of all religions is the certainty that there is a fundamental truth, and that this life is a sacred opportunity to evolve and realize it." (Rinpoche, 1992, p. 47)

✔ *Mystical experience is available to everyone:* Rather than being a rare or abnormal state of mind, the mystic consciousness is available to everyone, say the mystics. This true and uncontaminated consciousness is obscured by consensual beliefs, egocentric anxiety, and the habitual dullness of mind. Mystic awareness occurs in little ways off and on all day, in bigger but usually unrecognized ways many times in our lives, and in big ways only rarely.

Regarding the prevalence of mystical experiences, Maslow observed that as he became a more skillful interviewer, he discovered that almost everyone could remember such moments to some degree. They had simply ignored their significance. In the end, he described being surprised only when he found an individual who could not report any. (Maslow, in White, 1972) Van Dusen concurs, "Judging from contact with a wide variety of people under psychedelic drugs, in anesthesia, in madness and normality, satori (enlightenment) in some degree is relatively common. It has been given and probably will be given to many. If the lesser levels of mystical experience are included, then probably no one has been fully excluded. The big satori, in which personal identity is totally lost for a while and only God exists, seems uncommon, but not rare. Satori does not seem to be limited to individuals of any particular station of life, culture, religion, or time. It has occurred to prisoners in solitary confinement, to isolated explorers, to madmen, and to ordinary housewives." (Van Dusen, 1981, p. 165)

Matthew Fox concludes unequivocally, "A basic teaching of all in the creation mystical tradition is this: everyone is a mystic." (Fox, 1988, p. 48)

✔ *Mystical events are not abnormal.* The incidence of mystical events has also been scientifically surveyed. Lukoff, Lu, and Turner reviewed six studies between 1970 and 1985 supporting the conclusion that "30 percent to 40 percent of the population have had mystical experiences..." (Lukoff et al, 1992, p. 678). Greeley and McCready asked 1,500 people whether they had ever "felt as though they had become completely one with God or the universe." Over 20 percent said yes. Furthermore, these everyday mystics were not people disadvantaged socially, economically, educationally, or psychologically. Rather, "All of the respondents were creative, happy, dynamic individuals." Fearing reproach or disapproval, however, virtually all their respondents kept their experience a secret even from family and clergy. (Greeley and McCready in Goleman and Davidson, 1979)

Near death experiences, clearly a related kind of mystical event, are also far more frequent than realized. Now well described by numerous authors, these experiences occur to roughly a third of persons at the point of bodily death. The individual involved leaves his body and journeys to a heavenly world, where deceased relatives and sacred figures are encountered. It is nearly always felt to be a profoundly religious experience. A survey by Gallup in 1982 estimates that 8 million American adults report such an experience. (Gallup, Adventures in Immortality, 1982)

⨍ **Mystical experiences are of varying intensities.** Mystical experiences vary from little moments of awakening we may have each day that we forget or dismiss, to the extraordinary experiences described above by our mystics — and include many intermediate levels. At the small end, Wilson Van Dusen explains, "The lowest level of mystical experience lies in finding some degree of awe at the mere presence of existence...it lies in a childlike capacity to be impressed by things, be they flax seed, man, cities, clouds, or remote stars. The root of the experience is to be impressed with things just as they are. Some find this bit of awe easiest in the presence of nature." (Van Dusen, 1981, pp. 156-157)

⨍ **There is a difference between religion, spirituality, and mysticism.** It is useful and important to distinguish between *religion* (a formal and institutional system of faith, belief, and worship addressing the supernatural realm or higher power, with associated code of conduct, practice, and morality), *spirituality* (the personal experience of relating to that realm or power), and *mysticism* (the actual first-hand experience of that power).

It is easy to confuse religion, spirituality, and mysticism. One can be spiritual or mystical with or without an organized religion and a mystical event may occur to anyone, whether or not they consider themselves to be religious or spiritual. Formal religious training guarantees neither real spirituality nor true mystical knowledge, though we often assume trained people have such knowledge. Conversely, mystical experience guarantees neither spirituality nor any specific religious knowledge, for many individuals never understand or integrate into their spirituality. Finally, religion may provide many invaluable non-spiritual and non-mystical social and educational experiences, including a fellowship, community, emotional support, ongoing teaching, and volunteer work. We will be further elaborating some of these distinctions later on.

⨍ **Despite its frequency and normalcy, the mystical experience has routinely been suppressed and mistrusted by the religious and mental health establishments.** Despite its profound importance to mankind, the mystical experience has been suppressed and distrusted by authorities in orthodox religion and by experts in the mental health since the dawn of formal religion and civilization.

Van Dusen, a psychologist himself, observes, "It is very curious to me that the religious have as much difficulty with mystical experiences as psychologists do, if not more. Most religions imply that the great vision has been given to their prophet in the remote past and that no really great vision is to be expected until the judgment day. This makes the experience remote, other-worldly, and mostly unattainable. Most religious leaders have had no profound mystical experience. They are disturbed by reports of it in others and often give it little or no credence whether or not the one reporting it is within their own faith." (Van Dusen, 1981, p. 166)

Maslow has a unique explanation of orthodoxy's distrust of mystical experience. He began to study "non-peakers," who he described as "...not the person who is unable to have peak-experiences, but rather the person who is afraid of them, who suppresses them, who denies them, who turns away from them, or who 'forgets' them." (White, 1972, p. 354) These were said to be very obsessive-compulsive people who organized their lives around denying and controlling emotion for fear of being overwhelmed by it. Maslow hypothesized that these were the very people who "organized" the mystical experiences of "peakers" into prescribed formulae, ceremonies, and rules. Having repressed or never had such peak mystical experience themselves, they were more interested in controlling others' behavior or allegiances than in learning from their experiences. One might easily extrapolate from Maslow's remarks that these were also the people who sought to suppress whatever violated their orthodoxy, leading to religious oppression, inquisitions, and witch hunts.

Regarding mental health professionals, Lukoff et. al explain, "Surveys conducted in the United States consistently show a 'religiosity gap.' Both the general public and psychiatric patients report themselves to be more highly religious and to attend church more frequently than mental health professionals. In a 1975 survey conducted by the American Psychiatric Association Task Force on Religion and Psychiatry, about half of the psychiatrists surveyed described themselves as agnostics or atheists. A study of psychologists found that only 43 percent stated a belief in a transcendent deity. These figures contrast with between 1 percent and 5 percent of the general population who consider themselves atheists or agnostics." (Lukoff et. al., 1992, p. 675) Mental health professionals are also far less likely to take part in organized religion and their training very rarely includes discussions of spirituality or mysticism.

Psychiatry and psychology have historically been very skeptical of mysticism, typically pathologizing it as errant brain chemistry or mental illness. For example, the Group for the Advancement of Psychiatry, a medical committee that addresses specific topics in the field of mental health, met to study reported cases of mystical experience in 1977, but acknowledged that they had been unable to confirm a distinction between mystical and psychopathological states (*Journal of Nervous and Mental Diseases*, in Goleman and Davidson, 1979). They were, in effect, unable to affirm the validity of one of the oldest and most significant experiences known to man.

Until only very recently, psychotherapists in general have been very uncomfortable discussing religion, spirituality or mystical experiences with their clients or even with each other. Believing spiritual issues and mystical states were either symptoms of an underlying disorder or matters that should be referred to the clergy, mental health professionals inadvertently colluded in suppressing their mention, discouraging clients from revealing their mystical experiences.

ʃ *Despite the professional distrust of mystical experience, it is of tremendous interest to people in general.* There is a general revival of religious interest in the world today. Overall, U.S. church membership has grown 37 percent since 1960 (from 114 to 156 million) with the most dramatic growth occurring in churches that emphasize personal religion and charismatic, evangelical, emotional forms of worship (i.e., Pentecostals and Jehovah's Witnesses). A recent Gallup poll found that 94 percent of Americans say they believe in God. Mainstream denominations with more abstract theology and impersonal spirituality, however, have experienced dramatic declines since 1970 (e.g., the Episcopal church has lost one-third of its membership in the past three decades, with mainline Protestant churches down by up to one-third of their membership). Public interest in nontraditional forms of spirituality (psychics, channelers, astrologers, faith healers, angels and past-lives hypnotists) as well as non-Western religions (Eastern and Native American) has also grown enormously.

It is likely that the present generation of "baby boomers" are returning to religion and spirituality searching for answers to the big questions that commonly arrive at midlife.

ʃ *Our perception of the world is heavily influenced by our collective beliefs about it:* The view we have heard from the mystics would suggest that the world we perceive is not necessarily as real as we think. Watts, for example, writes, "Such experiences imply, then, that our normal perception and valuation of the world is a subjective but collective nightmare." (Watts, 1958, p. 24)

The world we think we see everyday is indeed created by what we think, not by what we see. Anyone who has practiced meditation quickly learns how much our consciousness is absorbed with dreamy thoughts and preoccupations, and how little it is simply open, aware, and non-thinking. In fact, we spend more time in thoughts about the world then in the world itself, thoughts concerning emotional and financial security, what others think, recent upsets, and fretful imaginings on future problems. These thoughts blind us to the world seen by the mystics; worse, our thoughts of the world become our world. They entrap us in another "reality" where anxiety about survival, competition, success, popularity, finances creates a self-perpetuating worry system, and we rarely stop long enough to see the miracle of the world itself.

✗ *The mystic vision need not contradict science:* Like psychotherapists, scientists, until very recently, have been very reluctant to discuss mysticism and spirituality. Albert Einstein was a notable exception. He said, "I want to know the mind of God. The rest is all details." (Einstein, in Fox, 1988) He also expressed, "The most beautiful emotion we can experience is the mystical. It is the sower of all truth and science...To know that what is impenetrable to us really exists, manifesting itself as the highest wisdom and the most radiant beauty, which our dull faculties can comprehend only in their most primitive forms — this knowledge, this feeling, is at the centre of true religiousness. In this sense, and in this only, I belong to the ranks of devoutly religious men." (Einstein, in Laski, 1961, p. 201).

In recent years, the tide has begun to shift, as high-energy physicists, molecular biologists, and others, their progress impeded by the limitations of traditional science, have been forced to seek answers within the realm of spirituality. Modern science is beginning to open up.

Mystical experience is not primarily religious excitement, emotional fervor, visions, healing, or solving personal problems (though any or all of these can occur).

White explains, "[The mystical experience] is not an altered state of consciousness, whether induced through meditation, drugs, sex, or any other mid-altering psychotechnology...Neither is enlightenment a dazzling display of psychic phenomena or paranormal powers. Nor is it a vision that transports you to some celestial realm...Enlightenment can include all that but it also infinitely transcends all that." (White, 1984, p. xiv)

He further states, "...the critical point to understand is this: the value of mystical and transformative states is not in producing some new experience but in getting rid of the experiencer." (White, 1984, p. xiv)

Most of us have been led to believe that such experiences should consist of dramatic visions, directives from on high, and other supernatural events. While unusual phenomena may occur, they are not the norm nor are they what validate the experience. The mystic experiences and dimensions described in previous chapters are far more typically the case and characteristically leave the individual with an unshakable sense of intrinsic validity.

ƒ Keep in mind developmental and evolutionary perspectives: James Fowler explored the development of religious experience and belief across the individual life span. Several progressive stages were defined in his book *Stages of Faith*, moving from: (1) the imaginative and literal beliefs of the young child, to (2) a conformity to traditional religious authority of the older child, and then (3) the young adult's need to re-examine his faith in light of his own experience and mental capacity. Fowler reported that the majority of people do not go much beyond this point. He observed that around midlife, some people are capable of a "radical openness" to the common truths in all religions. They recognize that divine reality "overspills" all religions' attempts to define it. (Fowler, 1981, pp. 186-187) In this stage, there is a "…new reclaiming and reworking of one's past…," an "…opening to the voices of one's 'deeper self,'" and "…new depths of experience in spirituality and religious revelation." (Fowler, 1981, pp. 197-198) Individuals in the subsequent stages increasingly trust and develop their own spiritual intuitions, and see the expression of these across religious boundaries.

Movement into Stage 6 involves not only more "universalizing apprehensions" of spirituality, but also "…a disciplined activist incarnation — a making real and tangible — of the imperatives of absolute love and justice of which Stage 5 has partial apprehensions." (Fowler, 1981, p. 200) The hallmarks of this last stage are "…the criteria of inclusiveness of community, of radical commitment to justice and love and of selfless passion for a transformed world, a world made over not in their images, but in accordance with an intentionality both divine and transcendent." (Fowler, 1981, p. 201)

Fowler's work suggests that the radical revisions of self that can occur in the midlife passage represent a doorway to this highest stage of authentic religious development. Moreover, the realized mystic is usually not the passive, withdrawn or detached stereotype portrayed by society. He is actively involved in confronting the world with the great discrepancy between the divine reality he knows and the tragic way men live.

How does the profound mystical experience relate to these stages? The mystical experience is frequently said to be part of a developing capacity for consciousness in the human race. Gopi Krishna, for example, viewed his twenty-five year experience of mystical transformation as merely one instance of a general evolutionary development moving inexorably toward the raising of consciousness for all mankind. (Krishna, 1970) On an individual level, this capacity most often manifests as one ages, for with age, many people achieve a greater openness to the transcendent. Or as White put it, "We are manifestations of Being, but like the cosmos itself, we are also in the process of Becoming — always growing, changing, developing, evolving to higher and higher states that ever more beautifully express the perfection of the source of existence." (White, 1984, pp. xv-xvi) "This world is not finished, it is becoming, it is a progressive conquest of the divine, by the divine, for the divine…" (White, 1984, p. 115)

ƒ *Mystical triggers are wide ranging:* Several writers have studied the circumstances and events that seem to trigger mystical feelings and experiences. These typically include, nature (e.g., water, sunsets, bird calls, mountains, streams, sounds, weather, sky), art, light, religious conversation, sexual love, childbirth, rhythmical or swift movement, scientific knowledge, creative work, silence and stillness, poetry, recollection of a previous ecstasy, meditation, introspection on religious ideas, death, suffering and desolation, and contact with an enlightened master. (e.g., Laski, 1961) Many people can identify which triggers tend to awaken mystical feelings or apprehensions for them and find they are drawn to such experiences. While circumstances like these can rather predictably evoke mystical feelings, they do not reliably trigger the full blown mystical experience. Major revelations, like those described above, arise unpredictably.

ƒ *There are many paths, practices, and stages of mystical realization:* Spiritual and mystic writers describe numerous paths, practices, and stages of mystical realization. The sheer number of methods and conceptualizations described in eastern, western, and shamanic traditions is humbling to any writer seeking simple syntheses. Coming from different cultures, traditions, and eras, it is also extremely difficult to compare the processes, methods, and sequences described by the various experts. In addition, most writers build their disciplines and conceptualizations around their own personal experiences of enlightenment, or around those of their teachers or tradition. Given all this diversity, it is probably a mistake to believe that there is only one correct way to proceed and only one accurate model of enlightenment.

A spiritual seeker can spend a lifetime studying the world's religions and experimenting with different practices. Eventually, however, most people evolve into a personally unique form of practice, belief or worship shaped by temperament, indoctrination, and experience. Their practice continues to evolve with age, becoming increasingly fluid and natural, eventually representing a living expression of their own spiritual energy, intuition, perception, and authority.

In general, most mystics emphasize that one cannot achieve spiritual maturity without struggling. The journey is often marked by times of hardship and long barren spells. While there is no guarantee of success, the final achievement described by the great mystics and saints serves as a beacon and encouragement to anyone on the path. Moreover, when an individual has reached a certain level, when he has, so to speak, tasted of the mystical, he understands that there is only one way to go.

ʃ The importance of the guru varies: There is debate about whether the presence of an enlightened teacher is absolutely necessary. Most of the Eastern Mystics emphasize the necessity of sitting with an enlightened one. They report dramatic mystical experiences arising simply in the presence of a spiritually realized adept and this is said to be one of the more frequent triggering conditions. The majority of the spontaneous mystical experiences described above, however, arose in the absence of a teacher. There are others who say the teacher is within or that the mystical awakening is a matter of grace and an answer to prayer. Some of the greatest mystics became fully awakened without such teachers. In sum, it would appear that contact with an enlightened master has been known to facilitate one's awakening, but such contact does not work for everyone, nor is it the only way. In addition, the role of the guru, as we will see later, is further complicated by the number of false but convincing teachers that exist and the damage they do to their disciples' lives is a serious problem. (Feuerstein, 1991)

ʃ Mysticism is inherently paradoxical: How can the world be perfect and beautiful when there is so much injustice and suffering? Where is that infinite love when we are in pain? Why do people have this great mystical experience and then continue to struggle with everyday problems of personality and existence? If God is everywhere conscious, if paradise is here, why can't we experience it?

The world seen in our everyday mode of consciousness and the one seen by the mystic cannot really be compared. The mystic consciousness sees everything differently. Even pain can be an exquisite experience. Even loss and death can be understood as ultimately perfect processes. Yet we cannot use these insights to avoid our everyday pain or live as pollyannas. It doesn't work that way. So it is that we may know about the mystical experience, even know it first hand, and at the same time experience a world of suffering. The biggest mistake we can make, however, is to reject this profoundly transformative experience because it isn't logical, "doesn't make sense" or violates some culturally held belief system.

Assessing Your Experience

The genuineness of any mystical experience can roughly be appraised by how much it reflects the dimensions listed above, and the reader is encouraged to use these dimensions as an evaluative tool. We can also assess our experiences by examining how they have affected us. In particular, it is important to focus on the degree of narcissistic self-importance that occurs. Mystical experience does not inflate the ego, it dissolves it. Specifically, we might ask,

- ✔ How much importance, judgmentalness, and presumed superiority of knowledge do I observe in myself? How much do others observe?
- ✔ Am I certain my way is best for everyone? How much do I still try to control, coerce, and convince others to accept my views?
- ✔ How much rigidity and conceptual complexity remain in my thinking? Are my spiritual beliefs based primarily on intellectual concepts? Is my thinking intrusive, distracting, accelerated, or overly intellectual?
- ✔ How deeply have I been touched by my mystical experience? How much joy, gratitude, love, reverence, acceptance, kindness, selflessness, and humility is present in my consciousness? Has my social compassion and conscience evolved meaningfully?

Other Forms of Spiritual Experience

It should be pointed out that the mystical vision is not the only valid form of spiritual experience. The range of spiritual experiences is wide and can include everything from a normal daily routine to:

✔ **Near Death Experiences:** This turns out to be a profoundly religious experience. It is a mystical experience associated with those acute health crises that bring one close to actual death, or to an experience of actual, temporary, clinical death. For those who move through its stages (e.g., leaving the body, feeling peace and serenity, going through the tunnel, life review, meeting deceased loved ones, and the being of light, etc.), it is both unforgettable and life-changing. This is usually not a pathological experience and should not be treated as one, though emotional distress may follow if the experience is invalidated by others.

✒ *Religious Dreams:* Not infrequently, and often at times of very significant life crisis or deep oncoming personality change, people have dreams
that they feel are religious. Such dreams often have archetypal religious
symbols, figures, or messages. These dreams are qualitatively different
from the normal nightly fare. They are more authoritative, powerful, and
riveting. One simply knows that something spiritual has been conveyed.
The task of the dreamer is to understand the import of the message.

✒ *Spiritual Crises:* Impending, ongoing, or recent mystical experiences can
be intense and disturbing, and create an emotional crisis for the unprepared who fear they are "going crazy." Mystical experiences have been
mistakenly viewed as psychopathology for years and psychotic breakdowns
sometimes manifest religious themes. The discrimination between spiritual and psychiatric crises, then, is not always simple or easy. Later we will
discuss this interface and its dangers.

✒ *Religious Conversions:* Under the stimulation of religious messages,
group pressure, excitement, or emotional breakdown, people can have various degrees of mystical breakthroughs. The pressure to package their
experience in the group's belief system, however, can distort the experience and exploit it for the collective purpose. On the other hand, conversions that occur spontaneously often can and do meet all the criteria of
mystical experience. In this case, the term conversion is simply one used
frequently by traditional religion. It might just as easily be called enlightenment, satori, self-realization, or cosmic consciousness.

✒ *"Other People's Far-Out Religions:"* I use this phrase facetiously to refer to
anything different from your own comfortable beliefs. Depending on what
your beliefs are, "other people's far-out religions" might include Eastern religions, meditation, the Twelve-Step Program, the use of psychedelic drugs for
religious purposes, channeling, New Age rituals and courses, or unusual or
secretive groups. Genuine religious experience can occur in any context and
be wrapped in endlessly varied secondary beliefs. Any belief or practice, on
the other hand, can lead to false experiences and self-deception.

✒ *Spiritual Healing:* The powers of the human body to heal itself through
suggestion, prayer, imagery, and the will to believe have been known for
centuries. Each of these activities can meaningfully contribute at different
times to bringing about actual healing. The new medical field of
psychoneuroimmunology is, as the name implies, investigating these critical
mind-body connections and their relationship to illness. On the other hand,

healing practices can all be used in the service of exploitation or manipulation when financial, egoic, or other hidden agendas affect the healer's motivation. Most indigenous healers, for example, do not take personal credit for the healing energy they mediate nor do they charge money, require large donations, or favor the wealthy. Shaman, medicine men and other healers believe it is the spiritual dimension that heals and that the healer's role is to serve in whatever way he can to carry or channel this healing.

ƒ **Guilt, Shame, Secrecy, Money, Control, Ascetic, or Risky Practices:** Unfortunately, religious and spiritual practices can also include the negative. This catch-all category refers to all the common problems that arise in the name of religion or spirituality, but actually impede the spiritual quest. Punishing or manipulating people with guilt and shame is not compatible with the authentic religious experience. Neither is secrecy and exclusivity; that is, the attitude that religious experience is something only certain people can have, know about, teach, or authenticate. Authentic religious experience is not about money (e.g., coerced donations, required self-sacrifice, etc.) or controlling others (e.g., coercive cult beliefs and behavior). Asceticism can be truly religious when it evolves naturally from giving up the attitude of greed, materialism, and scarcity. When it emanates from rigid self-restraint, it becomes abusive and reflective of masochism or self-hatred. Similarly, it is unwise to equate ultimate truth with ultimate risks or ultimate sacrifices.

Conclusions

There are as many points of view on the spiritual process as there are religious "experts." The psyche and the spiritual realm are as vast as the cosmos and cannot be easily reduced to a single system of thought or practice. A single teacher cannot know the divine entirely, cannot know all paths to God and cannot know which paths are right for everyone.

Spiritual beliefs are heavily influenced by the culture in which they arise, and it is not easy to change, adopt, or blend cultural forms without significant confusion and misunderstanding. In all this complexity, the bottom line is to trust your own feelings about any given teacher or teaching; never cease critical reflection, and never turn your thinking entirely over to someone else. As mystics have pointed out for ages, the great majority of what passes for religion is not grounded in the authentic religious experience. It involves, instead, secondary belief systems, institutional dynamics, personal agendas, personality, and social needs. It is not that these extras are always wrong, for religion as an institution meets other deeply valid human needs. And it is not that any particular religious institution and tradition is not also spiritual or mystical. It is just that there are so many ways to become confused or controlled, ways that do not, in the last analysis, represent truly sacred communion. Authentic spiritual growth and progress will always remain the seeker's responsibility. ❧

CHAPTER 32

Outcomes of the Mystical Experience

≫ Tom is a forty-six year old carpenter, now disabled four years by a back injury at work. As a result of this accident, he lost his occupation, identity, income and retirement savings, and his pride as the family provider and man-around-the-house. He cannot find sedentary employment and his wife has gone to work. Once driven by a ferocious work ethic, Tom sits home alone with nothing to do, feeling helpless, humiliated, and bitter.

Not surprisingly, Tom has been very depressed and numerous times has prayed to die. He has also thought seriously about ending his life. One time, while feeling extremely bleak about his finances, Tom sat alone at the kitchen table looking at his gun. Just as he was preparing to end it all, the telephone rang. It was his insurance claims examiner calling to say she was very worried about him. She had never called before. One month later, sitting again in the kitchen with his gun, Tom's son called from school just to see how he was doing. His son had never called home before either. Then, feeling more hopeless than ever, Tom overdosed enough medication to knock him unconscious or worse. Nothing happened. The next day, he put his loaded gun to his head and pulled the trigger. Again nothing happened. He pointed it at the ground, pulled the trigger again, and it fired.

Tom desperately wants to believe these events mean that God intervened on his behalf to keep him alive. And he wonders why. Why am I still alive? Is there a purpose to my life? Why would God even care about me? One day, while teaching himself to play the guitar, Tom had a profoundly religious feeling that his purpose in life was to write and perform music to make people happy. Overflowing with happiness and joy, Tom believed his prayers had been answered. But now he thinks that he has to do something great, like become a recording artist, to find his purpose. Tom cannot see what is right in front of him; that when he is happy, he is experiencing the sacred inside, and this is the source of his ecstasy. Sharing this happiness makes his family and friends happy, and gives life beauty. Connecting with this source will release more meaning, joy, and love than anything he may outwardly accomplish.

Is there a God? Has God kept Tom alive? Does his life have any purpose? Tom will need to answer these questions for himself. The answers are in him somewhere,

and in his way of seeing the world. How he goes about searching for answers, however, may determine what he finds. He needs to see that searching involves a choice
and an attitude: Will he choose love, faith, and happiness, or cynicism, resentment,
and despair? If he chooses the former, his life can fill with meaning and wonder. If
he chooses the latter, it will seem to remain empty and bitter. Ironically, this choice
itself may determine whether Tom will find God and the purpose for his life. But
until he knows this, he is like "The Man Who Didn't Believe," who could not see
the beauty and purpose of life everywhere around him. In a way, it's up to Tom.

Stan is a medical professional, the second of four sons, who grew up in a
painfully dysfunctional family. His older brother had a psychotic breakdown at
seventeen and never fully recovered. His mother was a prescription drug abuser
and self-centered manipulator; his father was passive and uninvolved. Stan had
no real relationship with his parents, who subsequently divorced when he was
fourteen. Thereafter, he felt increasingly responsible to become a parent-figure
to his brothers, looking after his older brother and putting the younger ones
through college.

Stan's childhood, as you can imagine, was deeply depressing. A shy, lonely
boy, he turned to other families for the closeness, guidance, and attention he
needed from his own. He also tried to be a good and religiously "evolved" person, reading about the great religions and trying to purify his own thoughts and
behavior. But the emptiness grew too heavy and through the ten or so years of
college and medical training, Stan began using drugs to numb his pain and emptiness — marijuana, morphine, cocaine, steroids, sleeping pills, and tranquilizers.
He also thought frequently of suicide.

After he was in medical practice for five years, after numerous lost weekends of
drug abuse, after years of uncommunicated emptiness and depression, Stan overdosed on 750 tabs of Phenobarbital. It should have killed him. His best friend, alert-
ed indirectly by something in a phone call, found him barely alive. Stan was rushed
to the hospital where his stomach was pumped. He was extremely lucky to survive.

Afterwards, Stan admitted that he had overdosed to see if there really was a
God. While unconscious to the outer world, he had a profound and extended near-
death experience during which he left his body, traveled to a place he knew to be
heaven, met various people from his past, and reviewed his life. He recalled that the
people there were not happy about his suicide attempt but were preparing him to
stay. Then, somebody said he couldn't stay in this in-between place and would have
to make a choice. The next thing Stan knew, he woke up in the hospital.

Stan's near-death experience was very important to him. He would reflect on
the feeling of peace it gave him every day through his slow recovery from the toxic
effects of the medication on his brain. When he meditated on the experience, it
would seem to come alive again and even move forward in time. As a result, Stan
was really happy and peaceful for the quiet month-and-a-half he was home fol-

lowing his hospital discharge. But as we talked about his real life, the old feelings of sadness returned and he expressed fears of becoming depressed again.

Stan experienced a profound and undeniable religious experience, one that unequivocally answered his original questions. But this experience was not enough to erase the depressive core of his character. Mystical experience does not automatically fix the past or the painful scars childhood wounds leave inside. Stan's challenge is to face and heal his old pain so that he can take in and use this new spiritual knowledge. If he returns to his defensive pattern of numbing himself, he will numb his spirituality as well. You can't cut off bad feeling without affecting your whole feeling capacity, which of course includes the spirit.

What impact does the mystical experience really have on the individual? Is the experiencer changed forever or is the vision eventually forgotten, without leaving a trace? The answer includes the full range of possibilities.

The outcome of the mystical experience appears to vary widely. Its impact depends on the individual's maturity, prior spiritual development, religious sophistication, social support, and mental health. Many writers, focusing on the higher range of human possibilities, idealize the personality changes said to follow the mystical experience. In particular, they describe the spiritual attainments of the founders of the great religions and later by their saints. Others see less profound though still "therapeutic" after-effects said to occur in more average people. Finally, many writers caution against idealizing any outcomes, noting that people with mystic experiences must still face and struggle with all the personality and life problems they had before. We will briefly review outcomes associated with each category.

Idealized or Extraordinary Changes

The final and highest achievement of the mystical way has been described by Evelyn Underhill as the "Unitive Life." She explains, "The Unitive State is essentially a state of free and filial participation in eternal Life. The capital marks of the state itself are 1. A complete absorption in the interests of the infinite, under whatever mode It is apprehended by the self; 2. A consciousness of sharing Its strength, acting by Its authority, which results in a complete sense of freedom, an invulnerable serenity, and usually urges the self to some form of heroic effort or creative activity; 3. The establishment of the self as a 'power for life,' a centre of energy, an actual parent of spiritual vitality in other men." (Underhill, 1974, p. 416)

William James also explores an idealized version of mystical transformation. "The saintly character," James writes, "is the character for which spiritual emotions are the habitual centre of the personal energy; and there is a certain composite photograph of universal saintliness, the same in all religions, of which the features can easily be traced." (James, 1936, p. 266) These "spiritual emotions" include: "1. A feeling of being in a wider life than that of this world's selfish little interests; and a conviction, not merely intellectual, but as it were sensible, of the existence of an Ideal Power... personified as God. (James, 1936, p. 266)... 2. A sense of the friendly continuity of the ideal power with our own life, and a willing self-surrender to its control. (James, 1936, p. 266) 3. An immense elation and freedom, as the outlines of the confining selfhood melt down. (James, 1936, p. 267) (and) 4. A shifting of the emotional centre towards loving and harmonious affections..." (James, 1936, p. 267)

James argues that these fundamental inner shifts have the following practical consequences: "a. Asceticism: Following from self-surrender, the individual may take pleasure in sacrifice and asceticism, "...measuring and expressing as they do the degree of his loyalty to the higher power." (James, 1936, p. 268) b. Strength of Soul: "...personal motives and inhibitions, commonly omnipotent, become too insignificant for notice, and new reaches of patience and fortitude open out. Fears and anxieties go, and blissful equanimity takes their place. Come heaven, come hell, it makes not difference now! (James, 1936, p. 268) c. Purity: The sensitiveness to spiritual discords is enhanced, and the cleansing of existence from brutal and sensual elements becomes imperative...In some temperaments this need of purity of spirit takes an ascetic turn, and weaknesses of the flesh are treated with relentless severity. (James, 1936, pp. 268-9) d. Charity: "The shifting of the emotional centre brings, secondly, increase of charity, tenderness for fellow-creatures." (James, 1936, p. 269)

James continues, "Religious rapture, moral enthusiasm, ontological wonder, cosmic emotion, are all unifying states of mind, in which the sand and grit of the selfhood incline to disappear, and tenderness to rule...Like love or fear, the faith-state is a natural psychic complex, and carries charity with it by organic consequence." (James, 1936, p. 274) Finally, James describes such equanimity as, "A paradise of inward tranquillity," an "unaccountable feeling of safety," and "...the abandonment of self to this power is passionate." (James, 1936, pp. 279-280). There is similarly a "contempt of danger" and "religious imperturbability" contributing to the capacity for martyrdom. (James, 1936, pp. 282-283) He finishes, "The transition from tenseness, self-responsibility, and worry, to equanimity, receptivity, and peace is the most wonderful of all those shiftings of inner equilibrium...This abandonment of self-responsibility seems to be the fundamental act..."(James, 1936, p. 284)

Such idealizations are wonderful. Their language captures the real or imagined essence of the mystic's final realization. Few reach this exalted state and it clearly represents more an ideal than a likely possibility. If we hold it up as the requirement for spiritual progress or the validity any particular experience, then we run the risk of devaluing the experiences reported by our everyday mystics, and ourselves. What happens to more normal people?

"Therapeutic" Aftereffects

"Therapeutic" aftereffects consist of less dramatic changes in personality, behavior, and value system that can be awakened by the profound realizations in the mystic vision. Maslow lists the following "therapeutic" changes he has noticed among people reporting "Peak Experiences." The individual becomes more of a real person, more of who he really is, and the creative center of his own life. Increasingly in tune with the laws of the "higher life," he is more loving, accepting, spontaneous, and honest. Grateful for all he has received, he is motivated to contribute positively to the world. Lastly, the "unitive conscious" develops; that is, a perception and ongoing awareness of the sacred operating in everyday life.

Assagioli also describes a range of positive effects, stating that this "harmonious inner awakening is characterized by a sense of joy and mental illumination that brings with it insight into the meaning and purpose of life; it dispels many doubts, offers the solution of many problems, and gives a sense of security. At the same time, there wells up a realization that life is one, and an outpouring of love flows through the awakening individual towards his fellow beings and the whole of creation. The former personality, with its sharp angles and disagreeable traits, seems to have receded into the background and a new loving and lovable individual smiles at us and the whole world, full of eagerness to please, to serve, and to share his newly acquired spiritual riches, the abundance of which seems almost too much for him to contain." (Assagioli, 1977, p. 46)

Jung emphasizes another interesting outcome: "As far as I have been able to understand it, the (mystical) phenomenon seems to have to do with an acute state of consciousness, as intensive as it is abstract, a 'detached' consciousness which...brings up to consciousness regions of psychic events ordinarily covered with darkness...As a rule, the phenomenon is spontaneous, coming and going on its own initiative. Its effect is astonishing in that it almost always brings about a solution of psychic complications, and thereby frees the inner personality from emotional and intellectual entanglements, creating thus a unity of being which is universally felt as 'liberation.'" (Wilhelm, 1962, pp. 106-107)

Breaking such positive outcomes down into more specific categories yields the following list of frequently reported personality changes:

✦ *Loss of the Fear of Death:* Nearly every writer and mystic reports that the fear of death is dissolved following a profound mystical experience. There is a certainty that consciousness cannot be killed and that death is merely a doorway into the next reality. Moreover, this spiritual threshold is known to be a safe and loving one, where one will be warmly greeted by those who have gone before.

✗ **Feelings of Relief, Safety, Joy, and Gratitude:** This world, here and now, is experienced as safe, loving, joyous, abundant, and sufficient. It is no longer a question of scarcity and survival. This world is increasingly felt to be a garden filled with bliss and wonder, to which one responds with joy and heart-felt gratefulness. Though the rules of the material world must still be obeyed, and suffering still occurs, there is all the while a sense that whatever the conditions, it is okay, that loving and timeless spiritual laws are in operation, and that what is happening is for our benefit, to teach us how to live and how to love.

✗ **An all-Embracing Love for the World:** One is in love with everything, everywhere, always. This world is all a manifestation of the living divine and hence absolutely love-worthy. A reverence for all life is an integral part of this new view. Love flows and loving becomes much more important and satisfying than being loved.

✗ **Loss or Relativization of Self and Identity:** The individual self often becomes less important after a mystical experience. In fact, who you are is no longer of much importance at all. Love and its expression, learning of spiritual laws, and helping others become much more important than identity or self-importance. Thomas Merton explains, "The only true joy on earth is to escape from the prison of our own false self, and enter by love into union with the Life Who Dwells and sings within the essence of every creature and in the core of our own souls." (Merton, 1961, p. 25).

After a mystical experience, the ego may become less important as an orienting reference. The "I" now is increasingly experienced as a computer cursor, a focus of consciousness, not as a thing itself. In fact, opened into the mystical dimension, the "I" often becomes, temporarily, the whole cosmos, big and small. Seeing the sun, one feels somehow that "I shine" or am part of the shining. In a storm, one feels, "I, too, am part of this blowing, swirling, crashing energy — I am it."

Aurobindo describes, "One begins to feel others, too, as part of oneself, or varied repetitions of oneself, the same self modified by nature in other bodies. " (White, 1994, p. 119)

In this new consciousness, the ego, with its penchant for narcissism and hoarding, is felt to be irrelevant and ridiculous, for there is no one to be and nothing to hoard that isn't everywhere. Worldly interests, as ends in themselves, now become unpleasant distractions and painful separations from unitive consciousness.

ƒ Mystical Consciousness as the Center of Behavior and Perception:
Aurobindo explains, "There is no longer an ego, a person definite and
definable, but only consciousness, only existence, only peace and bliss; one
becomes immortality, eternity, infinity. All that is left of the personal soul
is a hymn of peace and freedom and bliss vibrating somewhere in the eternal." (White, 1984, p. 117)

ƒ A Direct Kind of Knowing: Aurobindo states, "One begins to know things
by a different kind of experience, more direct, not depending on the external mind and the senses. It is not that the possibility of error disappears, for
that cannot be so long as mind of any kind is one's instrument for transcrib-
ing knowledge; but there is a new, vast, and deep way of experiencing, seeing, knowing, contacting things; and the confines of knowledge can be
rolled back to an almost unmeasurable degree." (White, 1984, p. 119)

ƒ Increased Interest in the Spirit and the Laws of the Spiritual Life:
What captivates the interest of the newly anointed mystic? Sogyal
Rinpoche replies, "All the spiritual teachers of humanity have told us the
same thing, that the purpose of life on earth is to achieve union with our
fundamental, enlightened nature. The 'task' for which the 'king' has sent
us into this strange, dark country is to realize and embody our true being.
There is only one way to do this, and that is to undertake the spiritual
journey, with all the ardor and intelligence, courage and resolve for transformation that we can muster." (Rinpoche, 1992, p. 127) Jung chimes in,
"...one may look upon sages like...Sri Ramana...as modern prophets...
Their life and teachings form an impressive warning not to forget the
demand of the soul in all new things of Western civilization and their
materialistic-technical and commercial concerns of the world...It is
undoubtedly more comfortable to dwell in a well-ordered and hygienical-
ly furnished house, but that does not answer the question as to who is the
dweller in this house..." (Maharshi, 1972, p. ix)

ƒ Challenging of Hypocrisy and Convention: Matthew Fox explains that
the mystic is "...invariably dangerous and always in trouble." (Fox, 1988,
p. 63) Recalling some of the greatest mystics in history, he describes,
"Hildegard of Bingen at the age of eighty-one was excommunicated along
with her entire convent of nuns for burying a young revolutionary on their
property; Francis of Assisi had his order snatched from him while he was
still alive...Thomas Aquinas' death was precipitated by his constant battles
with secularists on the one hand and anthropocentric religious spiritualists
on the other... Mechtild of Magdeburg was literally driven from town to

town because she was a Beguine (a member of the women's movement of the thirteenth century) and dared to criticize those in power for their greed and indifference to the plight of the poor, the young, and the sick. Meister Eckhart was condemned a week after he died and though in reality he is the greatest Christian mystic of the West, he remains on the condemned list to this day." (Fox, 1988, p. 63) Jesus, of course, is the mystic we are most familiar with and he was certainly a revolutionary.

ℐ *World Impact:* The impact of such mystical personality changes on the world also varies tremendously. Some mystics become saints due to their inspired work (e.g., Mother Theresa) while a few in the course of history become "world class mystics" (e.g., Jesus, Buddha, Muhammad) who alter the course of human history forever with their ultimate vision and life work. Some people simply return to their lives personally affected but not outwardly changed. It is said in much of the mystic literature of the East that these unassuming persons help to change the world by the simple agency of their presence.

ℐ *Psychospiritual Effects:* Numerous psychic consequences have been described by individuals following intense mystical experience. The Grofs describe the "Awakening of Extrasensory Perception" and other paranormal abilities during and following intense mystic experiences. (Grof & Grof, 1990, p. 91) These can include phenomena such as remote viewing, precognition, telepathy, out-of-body experiences, past life memories, expanded consciousness, and contact with spirits." (Grof, 1990)

Everyday Outcomes

What happens to the average mystic experiencer? Van Dusen comments, "Is the fully enlightened one someone special? Hardly, since even bums and psychotics may have a glimpse of the big picture. The person is special only insofar as his fruits are special. Enlightenment doesn't even mean that the person should go out and save the world. The fully enlightened janitor may just do his job very well and be a nice person to be around. In a cosmic sense this may really be the fruit sent from heaven." (Van Dusen, 1981, p. 169)

In fact, most people do not become superhuman and world-saving, but still gain and carry a sense of the sacred within. For example, most important in Gopi Krishna's final experience was his normalcy, frailty, and humility. He was totally dependent on his wife during and after profound spiritual experiences when she literally nursed him back to health. He felt in no way superior to other men and normal in all ways save the alterations of consciousness he now carried within.

Actually, his bodily system was in some ways more delicate and vulnerable. He wrote, "But when I look outside, I am what I was, an ordinary mortal in no way different from the millions who inhabit earth, a common man, pressed by necessity and driven by circumstance, a little chastened and humbled — that is all." (Krishna, 1970, p. 232)

Most of the people I have met who had the mystic vision feel that it was and remains a profound and important teaching. It often does change their views on death, spirituality, and the value of life. Sadly, however, everyday struggles and everyday personality problems return and life goes on largely as it had before. It takes a very unusual person to experience the saintly stature idealized above. The real work of spiritual growth occurs after the mystical experience, when the individual must learn to re-access its power, vision, and import, and repeatedly apply it in his life in practical ways. ❧

CHAPTER 33

True Self as Spiritual Reality

» In Part 2, we discussed the true self in psychological terms. We can also discuss the true self in spiritual terms, for across mystical traditions there is an understanding, first, that the true self is really an experience of the divine; and, second, that even this spiritual self will eventually have to give way in order to reveal the living mystery of man's divine nature. The man who comes this far finally recognizes that any self is, in the end, a barrier separating him from the all-pervading sacred reality described by the mystics. Recognizing these unfolding spiritual realities, however, adds wondrous new freedom and opportunity to life, and affirms the teachings of the mystic vision.

Speaking first of the false psychological self, Thomas Merton argues that whoever we think we are, whatever self we construct in the world will, in the end, turn out to be an obstacle to experiencing the sacred. He writes, "Our external, superficial self is not eternal, not spiritual. Far from it. This self is doomed to disappear as completely as smoke from a chimney. It is utterly frail and evanescent." (Merton, 1961, p. 7) He clarifies, "We do not detach ourselves from things in order to attach ourselves to God, but rather we become detached from ourselves in order to see and use all things in and for God...The obstacle is in our 'self,' that is to say, in the tenacious need to maintain our separate, external, egotistic will. It is when we refer all things to this outward and false 'self' that we alienate ourselves from reality and from God." (Merton, 1961, p. 21) He firmly asserts, "The only true joy on earth is to escape from the prison of our own false self, and enter by love into union with the Life who dwells and sings within the essence of every creature and in the core of our own souls." (Merton, 1961, p. 25).

Merton then uses the concept of the false self to explain the nature of sin. He states, "My false and private self is the one who wants to exist outside the reach of God's will and God's love...For most of the people in the world, there is no greater subjective reality than this false self of theirs,...All sin starts from the assumption of my false self, the self that exists only in my egocentric desires, it is the fundamental reality of life to which everything else in the universe is ordered. Thus I use up my life in the desire for pleasures and the thirst for experiences, for power, honor, knowledge, and love, to clothe this false self and construct its nothingness into something objectively real. And I wind experiences around myself and cover myself with pleasures and glory like bandages in order to make myself perceptible to myself and to the world, as if I were an invisible body that could only become visible when something visible covered its surface. But there is no substance under the things with which I am clothed. I am hollow, and my structure of pleasures and ambitions has no foundation. I am objectified in them. But they are all destined by their very contingency to be destroyed. And when they are gone there will be nothing left of me but my own nakedness and emptiness and hollowness, to tell me that I am my own mistake." (Merton, 1961, pp. 34-35) Powerful words!

Merton continues, "When humility delivers a man from attachment to his own works and his own reputation, he discovers that perfect joy is possible only when we have completely forgotten ourselves. And it is only when we pay no more attention to our own deeds and our own reputation and our own excellence that we are at last completely free to serve God in perfection for His sake alone." (Merton, 1961, p. 58) Merton then affirms, "Love is my true identity. Selflessness is my true self. Love is my true character. Love is my name." (Merton, 1961, p. 60) More than this, Merton speaks to our essential identity and origin in God. He explains, "His presence is present in my own presence. If I am, then He is…my knowledge of myself in silence (not by reflection on my self, but by penetration to the mystery of my true self which is beyond words and concepts because it is utterly particular) opens out into the silence and the 'subjectivity' of God's own self." (Merton, 1956, p. 70)

Commenting on Merton's work, James Finley writes, "Merton leads us along the journey to God in which the self that begins the journey is not the self that arrives. The self that begins is the self that we thought ourselves to be. It is this self that dies along the way until in the end 'no one' is left. This 'no one' is our true self. It is the self that stands prior to all that is this or that." (Finley, 1988, p. 17) Describing the empty self further, Merton writes, "The true inner self, the true indestructible and immortal person, the true 'I' who answers to a new and secret name known only to himself and to God, does not 'have' anything, even 'contemplation.' This 'I' is not the kind of subject that can amass experiences, reflect on them, reflect on himself, for this 'I' is not the superficial and empirical self that we know in our everyday life." (Merton, 1961, p. 279) Discussing contemplation, Merton adds, "So it is with one who has vanished into God by pure contemplation. God alone is left. He is the 'I' who acts there. He is the one Who loves and knows and rejoices." (Merton, p. 286-287)

The true self, then, is a mystical self, an experience of God's self. Matthew Fox explains further, "The mystic in us, by ever exploring the depths of one's experiences — whether of light or of darkness, of joy or of suffering — is unleashing and creating what Paul calls the 'inner person,' the true self. Co-creation happens here, for the birth of the mystic is a birth with God of what is divine and truly oneself. It is the outward birth of the image of God from within. Each self is a unique mirror of divinity and therefore each person births a unique creation when he or she lets the true self be born." (Fox, 1988, p. 64) And he punctuates,

"Alice Miller writes that 'soul murder' occurs when an individual is denied access to his or her true self. In a culture that denies the mystic, i.e., the development of the true self, soul murder is a regular event." (Fox, 1988, p. 65) The true self is that unique experience of God we are capable of being after the false self has died. It is born from our capacity to directly experience union with the divine.

Let me try to express these same ideas with some of the concepts used earlier in this book. The true self is that person we were born to be. Our most natural, loving, joyous, and spontaneous self, it is the part that got lost amidst our early woundings and replaced by a false self constructed to please those people upon whom our survival depended. But there is more. The true self carries the gift we were given to bring into the world. In fact, who we really are is the gift, and it is a gift made of the divine being. Recovering the true self activates this divine potential which further develops to the extent that we are able to know and experience this center of mystical union.

We come into the world carrying that form of God that we were meant to be and contribute. This is the true self, and experiencing it represents an opening of one's soul. At its core is an unconditional feeling of joy and love, which arises naturally in the experience of communion. Though we cannot know it in the beginning, finding and contacting this spiritual self is the reason we take the hero's journey in the first place. First we seek the lost psychological self, then the spiritual essence hidden within it. This is also the reason we have to rework our adult relationships, no matter how painful this process may be or how long it takes, for if the true self remains lost or imprisoned in enmeshing bonds, the gift and spirituality it bears will never be known.

Now the final, most miraculous realization can again be voiced. The true self, ultimately, becomes the whole miraculous world. Finley describes, "We suddenly see the true self in an old woman pulling weeds, in a rose bush heavy with blossoms sagging in a summer storm. We hear the true self in a squeaky gate swinging in the wind. We hear it in our next breath. We touch it in our reaching out to our brother and sister. And we see, hear, and touch the true self not by mystifying everything but by simply letting each thing be. Each thing is only what it is, and in that alone each thing is a manifesting of the ALL from whom all came, in whom all is sustained, and to whom all return." (Finley, 1988, p. 133-134) Here again, the mystic vision has been affirmed, for the whole world is seen to be sacred. The more one knows oneself as divine, the more the world becomes so also. It is all one indivisible whole.

For many men, the relief felt when the effort at self can finally be released comes a surprise. They suddenly see how hard it has been all along trying to "be somebody," and how wonderful it feels to let that self go, even the true self they worked so hard to find and express. It is finally understood that the true self was like a seed with each man its gardener. If the gardener can be conscious and thoughtful about his sacred task, the seed-self will germinate, flower, manifest its gifts beautifully in the world, pass on its seeds, and then gradually die. What is left when the flower of self dies, however, is what has been here all along: the divine background which is now everything. As we will see later, this sacred homecoming is our greatest joy.

The realization that the true self can die during a man's lifetime does not mean that one operates without a self-reference or identity in the world. However the self is now more of a convenience than a reality. A self is necessary for social and legal interaction, but it need not be taken so seriously. In the end, it becomes merely an idea and a practical reference point rather than something to defend, protect, strengthen, or inflate. Once a man opens to the world as sacred experience, why would he ever want to cling to any kind of self, especially if it separates him from the joyous communion he sought all along? Like the flower, the self has done its work. ❆

CHAPTER 34

Dangers On The Path

❧ The spiritual journey is not all wonder and light. There is a dark side. There are dangers on this path of mystical experience, numerous ones in fact. Anyone serious about understanding spirituality needs to understand these all too common pitfalls, which include:

ƒ *Passivity and Fatalism:* Rapt with wonder and no longer discriminating good and evil, the risk of inaction and over-tolerance is said by some to be a danger. For example, some people after intense near-death experiences have been described as so fascinated by the living spiritual wonder of the world around them that they care little for the mundane and practical demands of everyday life. Others, stunned by the power of the Divine Presence, may give up their responsibility for maintaining the order of their lives, and become passive and fatalistic. These behaviors reflect a failure to successfully integrate the mystical experience back into one's life.

ƒ *Confusing the Sacred World with the Profane:* It is possible to get lost in sacred revelations. Jung, aptly describing an example, wrote,
"I am reminded of another mental case who was neither a poet nor anything outstanding, just a naturally quiet and rather sentimental youth. He had fallen love with a girl and, as so often happens, had failed to ascertain whether his love was requited. His primitive participation mystique took it for granted that his agitations were plainly the agitations of the other, which of the lower levels of human psychology is naturally very often the case. Thus he built up a sentimental love-fantasy which precipitately collapsed when he discovered she would have none of him. He was so desperate that he went straight to the river to drown himself. It was late at night and the stars gleamed up at him from the dark water. It seemed to him that the stars were swimming two by two down the river, and a wonderful feeling came over him. He forgot his suicidal intentions and gazed fascinated at the strange sweet drama. And gradually he became aware that every star was a face, and that all these pairs were lovers, who were carried along locked in a dream embrace. An entirely new understanding came to him: all had changed — his fate, his disappointment, even his love receded and fell away. The memory of the girl grew distant, blurred; but instead he felt with complete certainty that untold riches were promised him. He

knew that an immense treasure lay hidden for him in the neighbouring observatory. The result was that he was arrested by the police at four o'clock in the morning, attempting to break into the observatory.

"What had happened? His poor head had glimpsed a Dantesque vision, whose loveliness he could never have grasped had he read it in a poem. But he saw it, and it transformed him. What had hurt him most was now far away; a new and undreamed of world of stars tracing their silent courses far beyond this grievous earth, had opened out to him the moment he crossed 'Proserpine's threshold.' The intuition of untold wealth — and could any fail to be touched by this thought? — came to him like a revelation. For this poor turnip-head it was too much. He did not drown in the river, but in an eternal image, and its beauty perished with him." (Jung, 1966, p. 146)

ƒ *Ego Inflation:* The inflated ego is always listed as a danger along the path. Assagioli explains, "An incapacity of the mind to stand the illumination, or a tendency to egotism or conceit, may cause the experience to be wrongly interpreted and there results, so to speak, a 'confusion of levels.' The distinction between absolute and relative truths, between the Self and the 'I', is blurred and the inflowing spiritual energies may have the unfortunate effect of feeding and inflating the personal ego." (Assagioli, 1977, p. 44)

At the extreme, this confusion can be most readily seen in psychiatric patients who declare that they are God and surround the delusion with various fantastic beliefs. Assagioli states, "The inner experience of the spiritual Self, and its intimate association with and penetration of the personal self, gives to those who have it a sense of greatness and internal expansion, the conviction of participating in some way in the divine nature." (Assagioli, 1977, p. 44) However, the inability to distinguish between the little self and the transpersonal Self "...leads to absurd and dangerous consequences" such as "self-exaltation and self-glorification" (Assagioli, 1977, p. 45) This inflation can also lead to cults and fanaticism.

ƒ *Spiritual "Crises":* Spiritual crises occur when intense spiritual experiences break into the awareness of people unprepared for them. Assagioli explains that one such difficulty involves conflict within the personality arising from "...the awakening of religious aspirations and new spiritual interests, particularly in middle age." (Assagioli, 1977, p. 37). Regarding the most profound breakthroughs, he writes"...so great a change, so fundamental a transformation, is marked by several critical stages, which are not infrequently accompanied by various nervous, emotional, and mental troubles. These may present to the objective clinical observation of the therapist the same symptoms as those due to more usual causes, but they have in reality quite another significance and function, and need very different treatment." (Assagioli, 1977, p. 39) Though the nature, diagnosis, and management of spiritual crises goes beyond the purpose of this book, it is important to keep in mind that spiritual crises can mimic psychiatric ones. Mental health practitioners therefore need to differentiate between them, for misdiagnosis and mismanagement can be extremely painful, confusing, and injurious for the individual involved. Agosin, Assagioli, and the Grofs have described these issues extensively, and the reader is encouraged to learn more from their experience.

⌁ *Fascination with Psychic Power or Visions:* "One can become so fascinated by the wonders of the superconscious realm," Assagioli writes, "so absorbed in it, so identified with some of its special aspects or manifestations as to lose or paralyze the urge to reach the summit of Self-realization." (Assagioli, 1977, p. 39) Similarly, Gopi Krishna explains, "The difference between the genuine quest of the soul, or God, and the hunger for psychic phenomena and miracles, has been clearly recognized by the illuminated from immemorial times. The practices of fortune-telling, astral projection, mental healing, witchcraft, etc., were in existence from the very beginning of culture in Sumer and Egypt, more than five thousand years ago. Since then, countless men and women in all parts of the earth have tried to benefit from them in some way. Millions have tried to become proficient in these activities in order to win power, gain fortunes, communicate with spirits, destroy enemies, work miracles, or prolong life and conquer death." (Gopi Krishna, in White, 1984, p.162) But he cautions, "Almost all great spiritual teachers have pointed out the dangers of succumbing to the lure of psychic powers or visionary experiences on the astral or mental plane, for these constitute entanglements for the soul as confusing and as hard to shake off as the entanglements of the earth." He concludes, "The desire for visionary flights, psychic gifts, and miraculous powers implies a wish to continue under the domination of the ego, mind, and senses in order to experience on subtler planes what one experiences on earth. To perform surprising feats with invisible psychic or other cosmic forces is descending again to the plane of earth." (Gopi Krishna, in White, 1984, p. 165) Such fascination has always been described as a distraction on the path, a subtle pull of an ego again interested in control and self-aggrandizement.

⌁ *Spiritual Misconceptions:* Misconceptions about spirituality and spiritual experience may cause additional problems and suffering. Secret teachings, guru-chasing, seeking spiritual power, "highs" or visions," over-interpretation of signs, believing one is above concrete reality (e.g., bills, food, relationships, illness, aging, etc.) are all indications that one has lost his balance. This confusion affects therapists, spiritual teachers, and clients alike. Reality is real, and when we ignore it, we become like Icarus who ignored the warning of his father, Daedalus, that wings made of feathers and glue would melt if he flew too high, too close to the sun. Kornfield states, "I think our earlier vision was naive. We thought spiritual highs would take care of everything else in life. That turned out to be completely untrue...The second misconception we had was a sense that the goal of spirituality was to attain a particular state where you then stayed...One cannot retire in enlightenment; there is, rather, a process... It can't be found any more in an ashram than in a day-care center." And, he notes that just as enlightenment can be attained, it can be forgotten as well. (Kornfield, 1993, p. 40).

ƒ *Seeking a "Spiritual Bypass" of Emotional Problems:* Many people try to bypass the tough work of personal growth with an adherence to rigid black-and-white religious beliefs on one hand, or with a rush to attain the higher states of consciousness on the other. Jack Kornfield, who is both a psychologist and Buddhist monk explains, "People often think that they can do a spiritual bypass, that they can go for the rapture, visions, and cosmic experiences and never have to deal with the pain of their personal existence. What I discovered in myself, and over and over with students, is that you can't do that for more than a little while. After that, what has to be healed will resurface." (Kornfield, 1993, p. 37) Contrasting Western and Eastern approaches to emotional problems, Kornfield adds, "Half of the people in any group of 100 or 200 that come to a meditation retreat are grieving or dealing with the trauma of abuse. They are dealing with divorce, co-dependency, conflict in their current life. Western psychology describes these problems and provides tools designed to help deal with them." (Kornfield, 1993, p. 37) He concludes, "I want people to understand that while spiritual practice can offer a profound awakening of every dimension of life, it doesn't happen automatically and you can't skip steps." (Kornfield, 1993, p. 38)

ƒ *Confusion About Spiritual Teachers:* Who are spiritual teachers? How do we know if they are, themselves, truly realized or masquerading as gurus? There are countless stories of teachers with hidden sexual and chemical addictions here and abroad. Charismatic and convincing, these teachers were nonetheless guilty of abusing their students or parishioners. The arguments that some teachers are "wild" and teach with "crazy wisdom," or that some students elicit what they need for their awakening, seem more to rationalize than confront this problem.

The personal problems of therapists, clergy, and spiritual teachers or leaders are real. Clients and parishioners, however, are prone to idealizing them. In doing so, they are vulnerable to the personal problems of these authority figures. When teachers and professionals have not addressed their own shadow issues such as sexuality, money, power, and narcissism, then they can and do injure their students and clients. For example, Kornfield describes, "The training of meditation masters — whether they're Zen masters or swamis or lamas, or even Catholic priests, for that matter — rarely includes any self-knowledge about sexuality, power, intimate human relations, or transference." (Kornfield, 1993, p. 40) Without training in these areas, deception, tragedy, and foolishness abound.

Daniel Goleman, who has studied numerous groups led astray or injured by harmful or pathologic leaders, concludes, "When you find a teacher you idealize, who gathers a group of students around him or her, there's a high likelihood that the teacher is very narcissistic and that the part of the students that's being appealed to is also their sense of being special and elect. That becomes a blind spot of the entire group." (Goleman, 1990, p. 27) Also, the Dalai Lama has noted the difference between Western and Eastern views of the teacher. To be a teacher in the East, all you need are students. He warned that students should be careful not to see all of a teacher's actions as noble or divine, and added that it is appropriate for students to criticize a teacher for unsuitable behavior. It is hard, he admitted, for students to judge whether a teacher is qualified or not. (Dalai Lama, 1990, p. 38)

As we have seen recently, cults can also be seductive and extremely dangerous. Daniel Goleman warns that one should be wary of any leader or group characterized by taboo topics, secrets, spiritual clones, "group think," belief in being the "elect," no graduates, assembly line mentality, loyalty tests, duplicity, a singular "unifocal" world view, and lack of humor and irreverence. (Fields, et. al, 1984, pp. 282-283). James Gordon, who has also studied spiritual groups in America that went awry, notes these common characteristics: nearly all the groups are apocalyptically oriented; their leaders tend to be narcissistic and charismatic and encourage their disciples adoration; the leader's awakening shapes the group's structure and ideology; the leaders' weaknesses tend to be made into virtues and enshrined, the leaders tend to be loners and their isolation is mirrored in the group's isolation from the world; and they have an enormous and overriding sense of mission. (Gordon, 1990, p. 25) It is equally clear that cults and guru worship frequently represent an unconscious repetition of deep-seated disfunctionality in the member's own family of origin. It is this very disfunctionality that blinds the aspirant from seeing the same kind of disfunctionality in the leader.

Psychologically, the relationship with the guru can be likened to the relationship with a teacher, mentor, or psychotherapist. All such relationships incorporate the basic processes and stages of what psychologists call *transference*. In this process, an individual unconsciously ascribes the characteristics of emotionally important childhood figures, usually parents, to the current important figure. Positive characteristics are usually experienced first, followed by negative ones. Thus, in the early stages, the figure is idealized and can do no wrong. This idealization is eventually followed by disappointment as the individual's wishful fantasies finally meet the reality of the other. With insight, the individual can learn to recognize the operation of such unconscious projection and then to withdraw it. In understanding this pattern, one is freed from its unconscious repetition with others in the future. In fact, psychotherapists intentionally focus on the transference relationship as a central source of insight.

As we have seen, idealization also occurs with the mentor, usually followed by disappointment, but the experience as a whole helps a man to become his own person. People often describe their experience with a spiritual teacher or guru in exactly the same terms, idealizing them in the beginning only to discover later on that they were human like the rest of us. Despite the disappointment, important learning still takes place. We learn that no one is perfect, that the real teacher is within or life itself, and that the absolute and decisive responsibility for learning always rests with the seeker.

Finally, about finding a genuine teacher, Sogyal Rinpoche suggests that "...true teachers are kind, compassionate, tireless in their desire to share whatever wisdom they have acquired from their masters, never abuse or manipulate their students under any circumstance, never under any circumstances abandon them, serve not their own ends but the greatness of the teachings, and always remain humble." (Sogyal Rinpoche, 1992, p. 130) Assagioli adds the therapeutic dimension, stating, "...it is apparent that, in order to deal in a satisfactory way with the psychological troubles incident to Self-actualization, a twofold competence is required — that of the professionally trained psychotherapist and that of the serious student, or better still, the experienced traveler along the way to Self-Realization. This twofold endowment is at present only rarely found." (Assagioli, 1977, p. 57) Taking Assagioli's argument further, the Grofs emphasize specialized training in the recognition and management of spiritual crises. (Grof & Grof, 1989)

ƒ The Difficulty of Spiritual Work: Despite its idealization, the spiritual path is rarely easy or simple. It can be difficult, exhilarating, disappointing, awe inspiring, frustrating, renewing, and long. It is not an easy path nor does it end during our lifetime. Exploring this path is an invitation to all the problems listed above. It should not be over-sold. It is not a panacea. Teachers and therapists too can fall into the wishful fantasy that spirituality would solve their clients' problems. The psyche and cosmos are too large of this kind of self-deception. So we need to guard against the defensive avoidance of the basic pain and hard work of the spiritual journey. Opening to spirituality does yield more opportunities and richness in the journey of life, but it does not necessarily make it easier. ❈

CHAPTER 35

Indigenous Spirituality: Coming Full Circle

Richard Heinberg:

"...the world view of the ancients, in which rocks, trees, rivers, and clouds were living parts of a living whole; in which the Cosmos was alive and conscious, partaking of the same intelligent force by which we ourselves are animated; and in which human beings were the link between Heaven and Earth — between the inner dimension of spirit and the outer world or form...(held that) every event was meaningful and every individual knew that his or her life was the embodiment of principle and purpose. In the archaic vision of reality, even the most mundane activities had an overarching significance and were performed not as personal, private acts but as part of a cosmic drama...To the sanctified consciousness, time and space were themselves sacred, and every atom of creation was part of one joyful chorus...To the ancients all was sacred, because everything had significance in both a mundane and a cosmic context; matter itself was sacred substance. The role of humankind...was to realize that sacredness by coordinating traffic between Heaven and Earth...For tribal peoples, the sacred dimension was not just an object of speculation; it was experienced reality." (Heinberg, *Memories and Visions of Paradise*, pp. 11-12)

Mercea Eliade:

"For religious man, nature is never only 'natural,' it is always fraught with a religious value. This is easy to understand, for the cosmos is a divine creation; coming from the hands of the gods, the world is impregnated with sacredness...The cosmos as a whole is an organism at once real, living, and sacred; it simultaneously reveals the modalities of being and sacrality." (Eliade, 1961, pp. 116-117)

"...the religious man of primitive and archaic societies...courageously assumes immense responsibilities — for example, that of collaborating in the creation of the cosmos, or of creating his own world, or of ensuring the life of plants and animals, and so on...It is a responsibility on the cosmic plane, in contradistinction to the moral, social, or historical responsibilities that are alone regarded as valid in modern civilizations." (Eliade, 1961, p. 93)

"It is his familiar everyday life that is transfigured in the experience of religious man; he finds a cipher everywhere. Even the most habitual gesture can signify a spiritual act." (Eliade, 1961, p. 183)

"...nonreligion is equivalent to a new 'fall' of man — in other words, that nonreligious man has lost the capacity to live religion consciously, and hence to understand and assume it; but that, in his deepest being, he still retains memory." (Eliade, 1961, p. 213)

Malidoma Some:

"Indigenous people are indigenous because there are no machines between them and their gods. There are no machines barring the door to the spirit world where one can enter in and listen to what is going on within at a deep level...Thus the two worlds of the traditional and the industrial are diametrically opposed. The indigenous world, in trying to emulate Nature, espouses a walk with life, a slow, quiet day-to-day kind of existence. The modern world, on the other hand, steams through life like a locomotive...Such life eats at the psyche and moves its victims faster and faster along, as they are progressively emptied out of their spiritual and psychic fuel...Any person in modern culture who is aware of this destruction from the machine world upon the spiritual world of the individual realizes that there is a starvation of the soul." (Some, 1993, pp. 33-34)

Holger Kalweit:

"The shaman's view of the world leaps across our conventional ideas about time and causality, contracts space telepathically, and subscribes to communicating with all that is. It considers the individual as being harnessed to a universal energy field of magic, in which ever the most fleeting thought causes the whole universe to tremble, the outspoken word kills your neighbor, and common sense is annihilated by ecstatic communion with the environment...all tribal societies as well as our ancestors — and cultures of both the Old World and our present world — did at one time subscribe to the idea of such a universe. Our modern Western culture forms the only exception to this general rule...The shaman, on the other hand, speaks of the vitality of all that exists and of a global relatedness to all beings and phenomena at every level. To him the universe is pervaded by a creative essence which not only transcends normal existence but lends to it an inner cohesion." (Kalweit, 1988, pp. xi-xii)

» Indigenous spirituality is really spirituality experienced everyday. Ideally, it is the essence, the basis, and context of the day, and of all life. As a personal connection to the sacred, this kind of spirituality is also part of a larger tribal cosmology that gives meaning, place, and purpose to all phases and activities of life. It is not a new spirituality, it is instead the original one, ancient and timeless. Its particular garment of words and ideas may vary among peoples, but its essentials do not.

The life of pre-industrial man is one in which spirituality comes first, not last. It is a constant recognition that he is as dependent on the spiritual world as on the material one, perhaps more so, and that he is responsible to it. All life is linked by a spiritual power and invisible structure that runs through everything. There is, in other words, a cosmic order: violate it too often and you and the material world will suffer. Violate it chronically, and the world you know will progressively deteriorate until the spirit can, once again, break through.

Indigenous man embraces a highly symbolic spirituality — a spirituality where everything has spiritual meaning — in order to understand, maintain, and restore the harmony and balance of his life. Indigenous man seeks first to live in the spiritual realm and second in the material one, not the reverse, as Western man does. Problems are diagnosed and treated spiritually, and spiritual guidance is always available. In fact, such guidance is felt to be the source of all meaningful answers, discoveries, and solutions. The quest for spiritual understanding and development are thus present in every task and activity of life.

To indigenous man, the entire world is alive. Spirit is everywhere. The "other world" penetrates this world and man's sacred responsibility is to understand, honor, and serve this invisible realm. Aboriginal man organizes his whole life around his spiritual sight and understanding. Rituals are top priority. They are developed to evoke or honor the spirits, understand the spiritual purpose of manifestation, integrate the material and spiritual realms, responsibly participate in maintaining the order of being, support the growth of the soul, and deal with the great passages and individually unbearable events of life. Ritual, spiritual understanding, and mystical contact comprise the primary structure of life. Survival is based on it. Everything else comes second and serves to support the spiritual.

Indigenous man tends to view the world as meaningful. Everything exists for a reason and a teaching, and we are to learn about the sacred from each animal, plant, insect, rock, sunset, storm, and event. Everything is holy and is therefore to be honored for its participation in the single unity of life. And all comes from the sacred. Life is abundant but only to the degree that it is spiritually honored and valued. Everything flows freely, generously, and lovingly from the spiritual realm to manifest in reality, particularly if man has a right relationship to the sacred. Faith, prayer, and conscious communion with the divine provide all the "technology" and ingredients necessary for living. Living outdoors is especially important as it offers a continual contact with the living dynamic nature of reality. Temperature-controlled homes filled with electric energy disconnect man from such direct sacred contact.

For indigenous peoples, then, all events have spiritual significance and nothing happens randomly or without purpose. Whatever transpires does so because of the emotional and spiritual condition, intention, and degree of health of the individual or community. And whatever happens must be understood symbolically and in relation to the inherent spiritual laws and reality infusing the universe. Moreover, life unfolds as it is destined to with man growing or dying to the degree that he can understand and attune himself to the spiritual universe. We come into the world to learn lessons and it is here that a man must evolve himself.

Talk does not exist for its own sake. Indigenous peoples are often sparse in conversation, choosing not to talk unless communication is truly meaningful. Words and emotions are felt to be spiritually powerful and should not be used irresponsibly. They affect the spiritual and material worlds. One of man's most important tasks is to learn the positive and negative effect of emotions — on his health, the health of the community, and the health of the earth. It is believed that the intent of an action and its emotional energy determine the outcome of an act as much or more than the action itself. Everything can be communicated with in a kind of mental empathy that feels into the very nature and purpose of its object.

There is a kind of group consciousness in indigenous community. Part of it is social and part spiritual. Group consciousness has been criticized by western writers as limiting individual development, and that may be true. Individual development comes second to survival, and in indigenous life, survival is usually a group enterprise. It holds the community together. But it is also a consciousness that gives individual meaning and direction to life, for everyone must struggle with his own problems and their spiritual import. In group consciousness, all members participate in a way that affirms the interdependence and oneness of the tribe.

To many pre-industrial peoples, especially nomadic groups, land ownership seems meaningless and ridiculous. Who can own the sacred? It is here for every living thing to participate in interdependently. Controlling property is an affront to the spiritual order. This planet is a gift to all, a garden for all to share and honor. Individual control of it, excluding others from it, constitutes a profound violation of shared being. Excessive attachment to material things is similarly seen negatively as a source of spiritual pride and vanity which, because they violate the order of the universe, will only lead to misfortune. There is felt to be enough here for everyone and everything if the natural order of life is valued and preserved.

Time, too, is of little importance to indigenous peoples. When time and schedules become too important, people are driven away from the spiritual and natural rhythms of the universe. Life flows from these rhythms in a timeless way that is enough. Behavior is not driven by clock or calendar time which obstructs the original consciousness of being.

The Western world has devalued the indigenous way of life as superstitious and unscientific. Western medicine, for example, can cure illnesses that the shaman cannot. But as careful observers have seen, the shaman can cure many illnesses too. Moreover, he can find, within his tribal cosmology, a spiritual core and basis to illness that feeds his "patient's" need for meaning and soul. Western man's aversion to suffering is itself part of his loss of contact with the spirit. Viewed from the indigenous consciousness, illness is itself a cure, an experience of cleansing necessary for the work of the soul to be born, to come through the psychological barriers of everyday routine, familiar boredom, and the certainty of ego. A medicine that focuses only on cure robs modern man of this vital connection to ultimate purposes and reality.

Interestingly, indigenous man also knew about the calling of soul in the adult years of life. Deep in the redwoods of the Northern California coast at the 1992 Mendocino Men's Gathering, Malidoma Some explained that his people, the Dagara of West Africa, understand that each person's life is chosen for a purpose pre-agreed upon in the spirit world, and that this purpose, unrealized, agitates a man's soul in adulthood. He explained, that a man is "given permission to run a project here." He adds, "At maturity, the part of that person where that process hides, starts to tick, and you need something to propel that project." At that time, a man "needs somebody who will help him articulate that thing as his vocation." One of the central tasks of initiation is remembrance, that is, learning to remember what that project from the other world was. He clarified, "When that part wakes up, we feel the energy. Vocation is permission given to the soul to begin its project and have alignment with the body." But, "If we don't respond to it, it drives us nuts. If you don't respond, eventually you develop a physical illness which is the project's way of telling them they are not responding to that project's call. We don't get to choose. The fact that we are born says that we were given permission for this project and if you don't do what you are going to do, you might as well return to where you have come from." (Some, 1992) Elsewhere Some summarizes, "Every person is sent to this outpost called earth to work on a project that is intended to keep this cosmic order healthy. Any person that fails to do what he or she must do — energetically stains the cosmic order." (Some, 1993, p. 30) This is a theme found repeatedly in the cosmologies of indigenous peoples.

The agitation of soul that comes to Western man typically arrives at midlife. It, too, may be seen as a calling to do what it is you have come here to do, to live out that gift or project carried in your soul. When a culture forgets the task of initiation at adolescence, that is, when its rituals no longer uncover a member's true calling and invite it into the world of men, then it becomes the developmental task of midlife to recognize and reclaim that calling — or it dies along with whatever the calling had to offer the individual, the community, and the cosmic order.

Indigenous spirituality has not left the industrial world, but it is in hiding, suppressed by man's preoccupation with science and materialism. In the time span of man's social evolution, however, the scientific paradigm represents only a very recent and thin layer. As Eliade points out, "It should be said at once that the completely profane world, the wholly desacralized cosmos, is a recent discovery in the history of the human spirit." (Eliade, 1961, p. 13) The antiseptically profane world view, he adds,"…is an experience accessible only to a minority in modern societies, especially to scientists. For others, nature still exhibits a charm, a mystery, a majesty in which it is possible to decipher traces of ancient religious values." (Eliade, 1961, p. 151) The sacred world of the aborigine and the mystic are, in other words, still around us everywhere.

Indigenous spirituality also reminds us that there is a certain uniformity to all levels of creation. The cosmic order is felt to be identical or isomorphic with the order of the individual psyche and of the community. Each realm affects the other and all realms carry this invisible order within and without. Violations in one realm reverberate through the others. The individual, community, and sacred worlds are not separate, they are interpenetrating. They form one underlying whole. This realization, of course, corresponds to the great mystic realization of the oneness and uniformity of creation. Put slightly differently, the ultimate structure of things is a psycho-spiritual one. It is an order that is deeply affected by consciousness, will, intention, desire, expectation, and emotion. Indigenous man tells us that it is our responsibility to understand and serve the laws of this sacred nature.

So we have come full circle — from the hero and Compulsive Warrior of the industrialized world to the original spirituality of our ancient ancestors. Midlife began this journey. Movement into male community deepened it. Mysticism opened it to us directly. Now it is time to put it all back together and go beyond The Story of Everyman. ❦

PART 5

Beyond the Story of Everyman

*It seemed to me then, and seems to me still, that if God speaks to us at all
in this world, it is into our personal lives that he speaks...life itself can be
thought of as an alphabet by which God graciously makes known his presence and purpose and power among us...*
(Buechner, 1982, pp. 1-6)

*We, if we are holy, are the paper;
our sufferings and our actions are the ink.
The workings of the Holy Spirit are his pen,
and with it he writes a living gospel.*
(deCaussade, 1975, p. 45)

*Thus every man, in the course of his life, must build...starting with
the most natural territory of his own self — a work, an opus, into
which something enters from all the elements of the earth. He makes
his own soul throughout all his earthly days; and at the same time
he collaborates in another work, in another opus...the completing
of the world...Beneath our efforts to put spiritual form into our own
lives, the world slowly accumulates...*
(de Chardin, 1960, pp. 50 & 61)

CHAPTER 36

Review, Reflections, Return

This chapter explores the relationships between the previous four sections: The Story of Everyman, the Male Midlife Passage, Masculinity 2000, and Return to Sacred Ground. Let's begin by reflecting briefly on where we have been.

Review and Reflections:

⋙ The Story of Everyman presents an overview of the remarkable and inspired journey hidden in each man's life. It symbolizes the potential movement of his psyche and soul through the seasons of life. Through living out this story, he has the opportunity to experience something authentic, wondrous, beautiful, and alive in himself and the world — if he can take the journey. The second half of man's life is that time when he can most truly and consciously participate in the story's completion, and learn where it has been leading all along.

The midlife passage, the experience of deep and authentic masculinity, and the mystic vision represent three profound and overlapping realms of transformation available in the second half of man's life. The transformation in each realm, however, is only potential because few men in our accelerated, materially focused, and machine driven age hear the call of this journey. As we have seen, it is often a lonely, courageous, and difficult journey.

To begin this journey, a man must enter the cataclysmic realm of midlife change. He begins this phase alone, and his task is to confront and dismantle all that has become dead and false in his life. Midlife is a deeply personal descent into grief and sorrow. If he has the courage, support, and perspective to continue, this phase of the journey may take him back in time in search of that most true, natural, and inborn self that was lost or damaged in the Springtime of childhood woundings and the Summer of warrior competition and questing. Only he can face the wounds of his injured soul. Unfortunately, no man is really prepared and maps of the territory are few.

It is often during the collapse and renewal of midlife that men, solitary and broken, can find one another and enter the healing realm of male friendship. Together, men can confront the unbearable costs of the "compulsive warrior" model of manhood and, in its place, discover a new yet ancient form of masculinity and male community.

The men's movement represents a naturally evolving cultural and community change process focusing on healing men's individual and collective wounds.

Participation in groups, gatherings, conferences, and colleague networking is the healing process in action. It deepens naturally in the presence of older, mature men, men who have come through these trials into a more conscious masculinity.

The reason so few men appear to be experiencing an actual and productive midlife passage is that they are uninitiated, overwhelmed, and unprepared for such a disruptive and ego-demanding life transition. There has been no support for them, no mature male community to receive, nourish, teach, and guide them; in effect, to love them. The men's movement attempts to remedy these limitations by providing structure, legitimacy, and support in this transition.

From deep in these waters of self, soul, and masculinity may come another longing. As men age, a need grows to know, surrender to, and serve something larger than status or economic motives. Understanding the meaning and purpose of life becomes a man's personal hunger and responsibility. Admitting this need, a man enters the realm of the sacred.

This mystic's realm need not be as complicated as formal religious traditions have taught. When his natural spiritual skills and basic self-trust are cultivated, a man finds himself increasingly capable of experiencing the divine in the ordinary. In this third transformational realm, he intuits a remarkable and entirely new life of wonder, purpose, and joy. This awakening of mystic consciousness amidst the restoration of self, masculinity, and community is not an ending, but a threshold of endless new beginnings. It is a world alive with possibilities — for loving, service, joy, gratitude, and spiritual learning.

On a larger scale it may be argued that our culture, itself, is in a kind of midlife transition, shifting uneasily from warrior modes of doing, conquering, controlling, directing, and exploiting the material and political world, to more integrative and generative modes emphasizing being, accepting, honoring. This large-scale transformation cannot be accomplished where there are individual egos to enlarge and defend, separateness and ownership to maintain, and winning and controlling as central motives. Ultimately, it is the mystic vision that can give us the faith and wisdom to proceed, even in times of fear, chaos, and danger.

Throughout time, men have given form to the sacred experience through religious ritual and tradition, including teaching ancient truths, evoking spirit in dance, drumming, and visions, speaking of his deepest experience, and accepting responsibility not for the world — the divine takes care of that — but for what man does to the world. There is a need, therefore, for renewed ritual awareness to move into the sacred in the twenty-first century. This, too, is one of the collective tasks of midlife. This experience is too big for one man to hold, or for individuals to hold individually. Somehow men must do this together and with a constant and reverent awareness of life's intrinsic holiness.

Examining these realms in retrospect, we see that the hero's death restores man to a vibrancy of being that has always been present. This is the radiant and sacred ground of the world, the shining energy seen by the mystic. Rather than being in control and certain of his goals, a man lives in this second half with something larger, a consciousness not his own, and a voice that seeks to overcome the small but strident insistence of ego. Men, coming together in this spirit of transcendence, caring for a brotherhood that is spiritual as well as communal, can find a divine synergy of love and purpose.

The second half of life breaks down a man's rigid personal and cultural barriers to the reality seen by the mystic. As we have seen, men's barriers take the form of false stories they tell themselves, individually and culturally, about who they are and what they should be doing. Midlife disorganizes the personal barriers and mature male community disorganizes the collective barriers. Both processes represent an unraveling of false beliefs and false self so that the true nature of reality can shine through and provide new modes of living.

Viewed from a sacred context, midlife itself is a mode of initiation. It is the initiation by the archetypal journey itself. The broken warrior, broken marriage, broken work life, broken dreams, and broken soul — these are piercing injuries, sacred wounds, that open a man to the Great Story and to the mystic vision. Spirituality for indigenous man was not an afterthought or part-time interest, it was almost more important than food itself. Western man is slowly realizing that he misses this profound level of participation in the sacred. Man's technology is part of his evolution, but it is empty and self-consuming without spirit.

Just as each man has some residual contact with the divine in very early childhood and then loses it while assuming the rules, roles, and identities of the dominant culture, he unconsciously searches everywhere for it in life pursuits, and eventually finds it only at the end when the rules, roles, and identities are shed like skin. So, too, must society shed its old story and its consensual beliefs about reality to find a new one that can open to the endless, immanent, and divine present. This living reality, here, now, is the final healing. It is about knowing that this reality is pervaded by the sacred and always present divine. The birth of the soul at midlife, the deep forests of masculinity, and the vast implications of mystic vision, together weave a texture of consciousness leading here, to where you are right now. This consciousness releases into a timeless, relaxed, unhurried, joyous celebration of sacred being and presence. This is the doorway men have always been searching for. It is hidden in The Story of Everyman. It is intuited by the soul born of the midlife passage. It is in the deep interior of authentic masculine community. And it is seen in its all its resplendent fullness in the mystic vision. The mystic is the modern day shaman who shows us the way. We must learn to follow, because touching the divine and bringing it into this world is one of the prime sacred tasks of manhood. When manhood moves from conquest to soul, this sacred task can begin. ❦

CHAPTER 37

Telling the
Sacred Story

➤➤ We have told the story of man several times in this book. First it was presented as a psychological journey through the four seasons of life. We told it again in fairy tale and myth. These stories were told as allegories of the developmental tasks men must address in their lifetimes in order to grow self and soul. Now it is time to tell the story of man one last time in its sacred form.

Given the profundity of life revealed in the mystic vision, one would almost have to search The Story of Everyman for its spiritual significance. What is it trying to teach us as a religious story? At the spiritual level, The Story of Everyman represents a great drama that stretches and deepens each of us through its chapters, crises, trials, and initiations. Every event, each twist and turn in the story, has meaning at this greater level. The story's ultimate purpose, we will see, is to grow the soul's capacity for spiritual knowledge, mystical consciousness, and unconditional love. Major tasks!

Presented below is The Story of Everyman in its spiritual form. As you read it, keep several thoughts in mind. First, this crowning version is an abstraction, a roughly distilled essence. It is admittedly incomplete and comes in many symbolic variations. Each man's personal version may include parts that are missing here or may leave out some of the parts I have emphasized. Second, each man's journey only goes so far. We never experience it all and we are never done. But search for the whole story. Sense its plot and outline. Remember, too, that much of this story is communicated in whispers, hints, colors, textures, scents, images, and intuitions. Its pattern emerges and forms like dew drops on a spider web on a spring morning — it just appears and then, for a moment, we see something of its order and beauty. But not all of it. Finally, this concluding rendition is not meant to be a literal prescription for what anyone should think, feel, or experience. It is a hunch and a parable. Its personal meaning will be found in the listener's ear.

The Spiritual Story of Everyman

In the early Spring of life, a boy discovers that he is awakening in a magic kingdom of consciousness in the brightness of divine light. Though he has no words for it and certainly no perspective of its meaning, still the boy experiences the world as a mystical garden of beauty and fascination, a living and divine world that evokes all his natural potentials for wonder, exploration, confidence, happiness, and love. This dimension is an endlessly remarkable place. It is a heavenly domain spread infinitely over the earth. It is the place glimpsed later, and only occasionally, by mystics, dreamers, lovers, and those in unhurried wonder, for this is original being before the organization of mind and socialization of perception fooled us into accepting the lens of consensual reality. This is the world of the child-mystic. This is the garden, and here a boy knows only the innocence of a young god.

Populated also with archetypal fairy tale characters: wizards, dragons, kings and queens, giants, and fairies, it is an experiential world alive with an imaginal magic that says anything can happen — anything. Adventures are everywhere: behind the tree, down the gopher hole, over the fence. Here, a boy is born to be a god in a world not yet reduced to inert matter, and he has some of that original divine consciousness from whence he came. Even feeling his own life energy is a magic beyond belief. He is part of the same divine energy that pervades creation. He, too, is part of the wonder. At times, the joy he feels is unbounded and he leaps like a fish from the sparkling water. But...

In time, a boy cuts off his contact with this pristine consciousness and its all-encompassing beauty and wonder. In one way or another, he is told it is untrue, that there are no fairies, but there are chores to be done. Time is important now, and the world is run by clocks. He may be gently dissuaded, more ominously threatened, or rudely shocked by the rules, expectations, and reality conceptions imposed by the titanic giants his parents seem to be. Their reality is too powerful to argue with. The young god is outmatched. He is easily frightened into quickly and decisively stepping out of Eden. His nervous system is simply too vulnerable to tolerate this trauma, this dual reality, so he forgets the first world. No longer a child god in a mystic realm, the curse has fallen, and he is deluded into believing that this world is material only, governed by rules of conduct and perception that become bars around his soul. A boy will not remember the enchanted garden, but its reality is secreted in his soul, and waits to be known again. He longs to know it again. If he can be still, it may call to him at midlife.

The memory of his divine self and sacred consciousness are thus split off from awareness and buried deep in a forgotten dungeon. They are not gone, but our child god forgets his true identity and mistakenly believes that his magic must be out there somewhere else. This is how the Great Wound produces a separation of awareness from its own radiant source. Yet, at the same time, hidden in the emerging story is the way back. The story holds the keys to the dungeon and the garden. But the way back is a long one. It may take a lifetime to come home.

So in the Spring of his life, the boy "grows up." He learns about so many things — the physical capacities of his body, the proliferating conceptions of his mind, how he is to think of himself, and what others think of him. Year by year, age by age, grade by grade, a story is given to him and he is its main character. The character he is given usually holds a lie — it is not really who he is, but who he is supposed to be. He may be told he is good, bad, strong, weak, mother's hero, a loser like his father, a great warrior, or invisible peon. None of these characterizations are true, but he must wear them like armor until the armor hurts.

Each boy's story, its purpose and plot, are also scripted by the rules of conduct and perception of his particular family, subculture, society, and historical era. Hence it is always a local story, a personal tale. But hidden beneath its local guise is a universal story, a parable gradually revealed in the adventures of his life. It is borne by his secret strivings to recover self, soul, and original wonder; that is, to return to the paradise first seen in earliest childhood. His life's personal drama, with all its stages, events, surprises and outcomes, is a vestige that keeps hinting at this transcendent goal. All who have come before leave ancestral footprints of this same journey.

Whatever the cultural story, glimpses of enchanted reality and the sacred nature of self occur often in Spring. The world can still shine with magic and possibility. Preschool imagination, heroes, and bold and ennobling adolescent visions light up his life, bringing moments of ebullient energy, far-reaching inspiration, and empowering confidence. The boy also learns more about the mind and personality he was born into, and discovers new abilities, interests, and desires which themselves seem magical, and are. Previously unknown talents may take him intensely into music, athletics, art, academics, adventure, or his first stirrings of romantic love. These unfolding powers thrill him with the energy of divine being; the enchanted mystery still sparkles, and sometimes he almost remembers he is born of gods.

Then, without warning, love is born. No one knows how this happens but it, too, is a miracle. Love itself is a sorcerer's mirror, for the one he loves is a reflection of something deep in his own mystical psyche, his very soul; and just as remarkable is his own capacity to love. A power greater than all others. And, unbeknownst to him, love shows a boy his divine nature. In looking for love, he is secretly searching for the joy of unbounded loving lost in mists of time.

A boy cannot know all these things, but he does know with all his heart that he must respond to life — as a calling, as an adventure, and as an epic search. Finding himself is much deeper than the social colloquialism suggests. It is an urgent mandate to retrace his steps and recover the sacred magic lost in childhood. In time the boy will understand that his goal and his destiny are to become who and what he already is and was born into. The magic is hidden in his soul. But he cannot know this yet. Spring ends when he leaves his childhood home to take on the great adventures and contests of the world.

Summer finds the boy, now a young man, questing after the external reflections of his own secret vision; that is, whatever outer goals reflect the inner fires of desire that have been building up steadily since he gave up his soul in the Great Wound. He strives to recover his soul, for in his soul is the divine world he has suppressed, and the capacity to see it again. Having replaced Edenic perception with the viewpoints of socialization, he thinks he has to search for the magic somewhere out there. Perhaps it can be found in the world of adventure, accomplishment, and conquest. Perhaps it is in the princess' eyes, in the major leagues, the lion hunt, or the MBA degree. Sometimes it is in all these things and more. Along the way, the young man's quests may change several times and his princess may get tired of his crusades. Sadly, by the end of Summer, the magic has gone from these strivings. Although the adult man may have indeed conquered many lands, made a family, and attained great responsibilities, he hasn't found the soul he was searching for. Though there is much to be proud of, something is still missing. The golden light is still somehow out of reach. Our hero grows weary, for he cannot find outside himself that which he suppressed so long ago.

Summer's end is the great divide in this journey. Rather than being a success, the hero's quest is bankrupt. He did not find what he was really after. Worse, he not only forgot what he was looking for, he failed to realize that this was actually a spiritual quest all along. Can this tired and disillusioned facade reverse directions, and can a search begin for what he needs most? Can he give up his local identity and imposed story, and respond instead to the grief of all he has lost in his successful climb to manhood? Can he follow the cries from deep in an interior dungeon full of tormented beasts in order to find the treasure he buried long ago? Time has run out. Whatever must happen, it must happen now. This is our hero's greatest challenge so far. If he enters this inner world, and fights its inner battles to find the inner way, then a man can recover the lost gold of his soul, the original perception of sacred reality, and the timeless consciousness of being he lost a lifetime ago. Only then can a truly new season begin.

In the Fall, with the passing of the heroic mission, a calmer, deeper man hears the call of a different world. The world of the past is dying. It is dying all around him. Slowly, like autumn leaves, it falls away; the monuments he constructed, the aspirations he pursued, and the identity that hides his soul. The fire is leaving his body and his sword. The warrior's ambitions have rusted. In this time, our journeyer comes home to the present, to other men, and to this world. A new world now calls him.

The poetry of his soul teaches him the wisdom of the seasons, of surrender, and of death and rebirth. He begins to reflect on such ultimate questions seeking to make sense of his life journey so far. He is trying to remember the world into which he was born.

An older man, he seeks the friendship and company of other older men who have been on the same road. They compare notes and the world seems to grow brighter. Free from the burden of ambition, a man in Fall tentatively tries on new roles. Sensing his original identity more and more, and the still voice of wisdom that emanates from his transcendent nature, he begins providing something of this hard-won sagacity of age to his family, tribe, village, or community. He has things to teach. They come directly from his experience of life.

Released at last from his old story, the man in Fall finally gives form to his soul's aspirations, and the work that comes through him now has tremendous satisfaction, along with increasingly universal themes and values. This work is a harvesting of his life, of all he has learned and experienced. The fruit of his life is ripe now and has so much to offer. It has become mature enough to be a teaching for any who wish to apprentice. A man is a true mentor now, for he has been initiated by life and has found the work of his soul. His hands belong to the divine sculptor and the world becomes his clay. He is almost god-like, for he is coming closer to his truth. Open to the flow of creation, he senses his identity with all men and with the world as his community.

Like stepping into a slow moving stream, life flows more easily now. As Fall moves toward Winter, as time and future run out, man is left in the infinity of the present. This is all that remains. But what a wondrous gift. This is the place he forgot! He begins to sense that same timeless now that he knew in early childhood, that consciousness that holds everything joyously and perfectly in the holiness of Being. This is the "ending of time" symbolized in myth and religion. It is the ending of time's controlling role in his life. Without a future, every breath of everyday is a miracle.

In his own limited and finite ways, the mature man returns now to the garden and he becomes its gardener. Everything is, once again, radiant, and each spring seems more beautiful than the last — the greenness, the incredible living brightness of color, the sharpness of detail and form, the light itself. It is almost too much beauty to bear. More and more, a man's sees his secret garden everywhere. And if he looks closely, he will also see that something else is beginning to shine through it all. It is a new kind of light that seems to come from within reality itself, and a new kind of joy, for the real work now is in his eyes and heart. Can he once again see this world as a living, divine reality as he did long ago, and feel the original and unborn ecstasy of being? When he can, the search for love has ended. Love is his very nature, and when he feels it, love includes everything, and the circle is complete.

If a man has ripened in such a Fall, if his bounty has been rich and he has become a "man of all seasons," then Winter, rather than being a time of terrible struggle and despair, fills instead with renewed appreciation and interest in life. The sacred is found everywhere and everything here is a miracle. Having finally found his way back to the garden, and knowing his real purpose was always to understand sacred reality and this mystic consciousness that forms it, our hero cannot get enough. It is all fascinating. Life, he senses, is a temporary classroom and graduation is near. Knowing he will leave soon enough, a man opens his heart to the incredible gift of life itself, and gives to it all he has left. What a great ride he has had! It has all been worth it. Knowing this last adventure will literally end, he drinks life in with a new passion.

The ending of Winter arrives as a man's material shell deteriorates, for that is its destiny. He retires from active involvements. With his core energies spent in the world, his consciousness nestled in the realm of love and acceptance, a man can slowly give himself over to his final task: releasing himself physically and psychologically back to the divine from where he came. More and more he intuits the transcendent reality that is present everywhere in his heart, and mind, and world. More and more he accepts that the fruit is so ripe, it must drop from the tree and ferment in its own sweetness. There is no one left to be and nothing left to do. The earth will reabsorb his body soon. All that matters is this subtle song he hears and how the notes of his own life have played in the symphony that holds the universe together. Oh, there are final problems — aging bodies, failing competencies, constricting life orbits, losses, and frustrations. But they, too, are part of the teaching and they have a sacred purpose: to loosen his attachment to what he thinks he is, so that he can let go.

The journey back for a man requires the one last crisis of bodily death. Again the maturational competencies he has developed in aging prepare him for this final passage. He can relax, for having known the imminent divine, he knows it will receive him unconditionally and that the paradigm of death and rebirth is more than metaphor. When death finally arrives, it is anti-climactic, for he is no longer afraid. It has all been a great story, a remarkable dream, a wisp of smoke. He knows this parting of the curtain will open to something else he intuited all along. He will awaken somewhere else; he will be coming home. Thus, the enlightened man dies with a smile. From there, so the story goes, his consciousness carries him across the threshold into the other world he has been sensing all along. There he will have new tasks, new experiences, and new transformations. But that story is for then, and we live now, so we too release Everyman to his becoming, and know our turn is waiting in the wings. As always, a man will only understand when he arrives. ❦

CHAPTER 38

Teachings of the Sacred Story

➤➤ The problems a man has in his work, his marriage, his friendships, and his body are very often indications that he is operating outside the sacred journey. It is especially easy to betray this journey in the second half of life because here our cultural stories fail us so completely. They fail us because there are no positive models to guide and validate the older man's passage from competitive hero to brother and mystic, and because the prevailing machine and warrior allegories that do exist view elders as used up parts, ready to discard, or as men who are no longer competitive, and hence invisible.

Men know all about the achievement demands of Summer, but our culture teaches them almost nothing of the great psychological and spiritual accomplishments of midlife, Fall, and Winter. Nor do our cultural stories validate the longing men have for male community. The presence of other men, so simple and yet profound, stirs something in a man that calls back to ancient times, times the "old mind" knows but which modern man has forgotten. A man cannot become mature through biology alone. His manhood must be evoked and experienced in the company of men who trust the male body and its rhythms, and who can help the uninitiated man trust his own. Masculine maturity is not a biological given, it is a work of initiation, consciousness, sweat, and art.

Contemporary stories that guide spiritual awakening are also missing for the average man. His hunger for the immanent sacred is rarely acknowledged. Devalued by the narcissistic stories of fame and fortune told by the warrior-machine culture he has produced, he feels ashamed of his longing. The stories of the great world religions that do exist, though still valid and profoundly informed with transcendent teaching, no longer seem to speak powerfully to many twentieth century men, or they no longer know how to listen to them. Actually, the great stories of Buddha, Jesus, Mohammed, Moses, and others are spiritually sharpened versions of the universal story. Though the variations may differ slightly, they reveal the journey of spiritual transformation secreted in all the myths, fairy tales, parables, and fables. These stories bear ultimate teachings and the essential architecture of death and rebirth — death of the false self and reality, and rebirth of the divine self into a sacred reality. But men have been deluded by their false stories, beleaguered by survival struggles, and uninitiated in the secret teaching of transformation. Western men have mostly become lost in the most profound way of all; practical, worldly vision has displaced mystical vision.

I had a dream several years ago. In it, my African-American mother was visiting, talking to me about God. Then the telephone rang and I answered it. It was God! I was stunned by a most powerful and authoritarian voice. He said many things I immediately forgot in my awe. But he made one statement I never forgot. He said, "Men listen to the word of man, not to the word of God." Yet sacred stories are everywhere. Dropped like envelopes on the street, as the mystic poet says, we fail to notice or open them. They manifest in the journey of our lives, in literature and media, and in religion, but we pay no attention. We ignore the sacred story that is everywhere.

Perhaps related to this failed vision is the lack of meaningful initiatory experiences that help men recover it. There are few forms of real spiritual initiation available to men at this time and ever fewer men who are aware of the yearning for such initiation. We need to relearn how to feel and see the immanent divine again, and let it sacralize our lives so that living, itself, can be a religious matter, reflecting a reality far more important than individual achievement. Though industrial man has forgotten this life, the ancient man inside us has not. The man of the West, therefore, needs the chemistry of living myth, mysticism, and ritual to recover this larger story, and he needs elder males to teach, inspire, and continue its tradition.

If a man knows himself only through the collective perceptions of body, income, and persona, then aging may be a bitter and empty time. For this man, there may be nothing new and no recovery of ecstasy through the Fall and Winter of his life. Only disappointment and clinging. But open to the vast wonder of sacred reality illuminated by the mystic, a man may instead become a "lover" who is in love with the whole world of manifest existence. From such mystic consciousness, he can mentor, guide, love, and care for the world around him in beautiful and generous ways, for there is so much to do and so much to love. Attending to the divine in the world, he returns to the garden. What a magnificent task! What a joy! What a reward for the hero's death at midlife! This new work then becomes celebration, love, and wonder. Doing becomes being, ego is infused with the light of soul, and the world increasingly returns to the mystics' enchanted garden. A man's work now is to help others overcome the tragic myopia of consensual reality and to bridge the separation responsible for the suffering — the separation between peoples, and between man and the sacred.

Interpretive Principles for Understanding the Sacred Story:

Our personal stories, examined psychologically, mythically, and spiritually, have taught us that something larger is happening through our lives; something meaningful, purposeful, and sacred. The mystic experience teaches us that the world is already perfect and infinitely precious, that it can show us far more than we know. When we explore this teleology of story and mysticism deeply enough, it is possible to discern some of the fundamental laws and patterns governing our lives. Over and over we have seen that there is an order, a pattern, a purpose. Understanding this underlying order can provide us with guiding and interpretive principles so we can appreciate our personal stories from a higher place, a vantage point of spiritual meanings and purposes. These principles can also move our individual stories along by giving them clearer direction, energy, and value. Finally, at this sacred level, we can pose the ultimate questions of our own lives: Why was I born? Who am I really? What is the meaning of my life? What am I here to learn? What is my true work? What is my role in creation?

Ask these kinds of ultimate questions of yourself. Then consider the following interpretive principles in listening for answers.

ʃ *The Universe is everywhere alive, intelligent, and loving.* Each thing, each person, each part of your life, each stage of your journey — the whole order and fabric of reality — is not random, accidental, or meaningless. It is not a matter of good or bad luck. A journey of awakening, when fully understood, is seen to be just what it should be. This sacred energy and consciousness creates, structures, and carries our lives. We are held lovingly and personally by this infinite consciousness until we can feel it directly, and then we increasingly become what we feel. This kind of immediate knowing brings the universe alive, and the whole story is about living in this universe.

ʃ *What has happened in your life to date was necessary and purposeful.* The structure of the story we live is preformed as a vehicle of awakening. Your particular family and circumstances, the particular wounds you had to bear, the problems of childhood, past mistakes — these are all parts of the story's plot. The events of your history did not just happen. They had to happen for you to be where you are now, and for you to wake up now to who you really are. This plot forms an invisible pattern of your life's unique purposes and ultimate learnings. It is part of the universal story and your own version of it. In trying to find out why these things happened and what the story is teaching you, learn to trust your story. Let go of blame, guilt, and self-recrimination, and seek to find meaning. The story has its purposes — but only you can find them.

ʃ *You are just where you should be.* It is not a mistake to be in this setting, this circumstance, this problem. It is the culmination of all your story and experience to date. There is nowhere else to be. Whatever is happening is not a problem blocking your journey, it is your journey. If everything is holy, then even your problems are part of that holiness. Your assignment is to experience your life with awareness of its sacred nature, and work on what is in front of you now, for its true nature can transform you. Love and want this exact situation, and your love will transform it. Even the pain. It is exactly the teaching you need right now to expand your consciousness and understanding. If your reject and devalue it, you will not learn its lessons. You will be thrust into the same situations again, repeating the same lessons over and over until you do learn them.

✓ *Personal emotional work cannot be skipped.* Much of the work necessary to understand the story involves identifying and healing old emotional wounds. Each of us has personal wounds that removed us from sacred reality and set us on a quest that could not ultimately work. Each wound, however, is also a sacred wound that can bring us back into the great story if we can understand its significance. In each wound are profound teachings about life. If you skip your negative autobiographical material hoping to avoid the pain, or attempt to stay only in positive emotions, the old pain will eventually pull you down. It repeats until we resolve it.

✓ *There are no coincidences or accidents.* Things that happen together in a time period may not seem directly or causally connected, but are reflective of something else, something larger. Jung and others have called this coincidental patterning of experience "synchronicity." In your life's past and present, unexpected and even unwanted happenings are a secret pattern critical to your story and the stories of those around you. You and the people and the happenings in your life are all interconnected and are happening just as they should. The oneness of life means that inner and outer, here and there, now and then, you and I, are all sides of the whole. We are like components of a dream. Only when we acknowledge this larger gestalt can we also see the symphony of meanings and purposes swirling in our lives.

✓ *Your individual story's plot encodes a specific project that you are working out here. Find it and live it.* There is something you have been trying to accomplish here. Every man is born with a gift, with his own particular genius. You keep coming back to it. You feel excited whenever you are close. You feel deflated and hopeless when it seems lost. Your story holds the key to finding it. It is your gift to the world and your unique way of feeling the divine. Pieces of this gift may be reflected in your parents' stories, hidden in your joys and sorrows, or carried in your ambitions and fantasies. It is so much in front of you that you miss it.

✓ *Thoughts, emotions, intentionality, and responsibility are far more causal than you realize.* Because we are a creating part of this cosmic creating whole, what happens around us is also partly our own doing. We automatically create far more of our lives than we understand, and we need to assume responsibility in this process. Script, ambition, longing, and decisions shape our lives — if we let them. Negative thoughts, emotions, and expectations evoke equally negative circumstances, while positive and loving intentions and emotions, expressed toward ourselves and others, create an entirely different kind of world. What kind of world have you created?

✓ *You can get just what you need at every point if you ask and are thankful.* Helpers and gifts come constantly when we let them. Opportunities for love, growth, insight, and joy are everywhere present and we are given infinitely more than we realize. But we must ask for what we want with all our hearts and gratefully accept what we get. Open your perception to see the helpers and gifts all around you, and be thankful. When we assume a grateful attitude toward all we have been given, joy and sacred vision are restored and the value of each circumstance becomes apparent.

✓ *Get out of the way.* Especially in the second half of life, we need to get out of our own way. Who we think we are and what we think we want, and our desire to control and run the show — such egocentrism becomes an increasing barrier to enlightenment and to the movement of our story. The ego is necessary as a carrier of consciousness and comprehension. It is the instrument critical to grasping the meanings and new directions, but it can no longer be the goal. The competencies of the ego must now be turned toward realizing the divine.

✓ *Love the world unconditionally.* We see the world most clearly when we love it unconditionally; that is, without concern for ourselves or for any particular outcomes. When we withhold love, or love only conditionally, our vision is narrow and self-centered, and our lives barren to the extant of this betrayal. To love the world is to love it inclusively, completely, and gratefully, and to see it as a constantly unfolding and miraculous gift. Loving like this, we can see our own shortcomings and those of others with humility and without judgment, and we see how happy life is meant to be. As the mystics know, love is itself the nature of the sacred. When we love, we are joined with that essence.

✓ *You are part of something larger.* Something larger is happening in the world. Culture and society are changing. Growing numbers of people are in the same wave of expanding consciousness, part of a profound paradigm shift. A new conception of reality is arising. Begin wondering about your life with this perspective in mind. What is changing in society and in the world, and what is your role in it? This is not about narcissism or more heroic achievement, but about living in the world in a spiritual way.

✦ *Our common task is the spiritualization of our lives, beginning with oneself.* The mystic experience suggests that we are here to know this "cosmic consciousness" and to be open to its always present flow of love, generosity, joy, wonder, and peace. Experiencing our own spiritual nature, we connect with the source of that same loving and joyous current. Then ego becomes servant in place of master, and we exchange it for the greater happiness of this awakened life.

✦ *Let your values and actions come from your spiritual connection.* There is an Eastern proverb that predates the Vedic scriptures of India, which are said to have originated as far back as 5000 B.C. It is: "Spontaneity knows its own morality." What this means is that when we let go of our conscious attempts to determine right and wrong, when we align ourselves with our innermost, spiritual knowing, we will sponta-neously and effortlessly choose what is right — for ourselves, for others, and for the entire creation.

✦ *The journey never ends.* We do not retire someplace in our story or in enlightenment. Each step is a growth of consciousness taking us into the next realm, and each realm has its own teachings. This process of learning is transformation. Keep opening to your own expansion.

Exercise: Raising Your Own Story Into The Sacred One

Can you apply the interpretive principles listed above to your own life story? Can you see why things had to happen as they did and begin to see the story's desire for your potential transformation? Here I use my own story as an example and a personal teaching.

Both my parents, in their "enlightened" and liberated twentieth century world view, rejected religion, leaving us children with no tradition for connect-ing to the universe or to our beginnings. As a result of this, I was ashamed of my own spiritual interests. In retrospect, I see that this lack of formal religious train-ing was a gift, for I was marvelously free to confront ultimate issues and to exam-ine the world without doctrinaire blinders.

I see now that my parents' views — my father's questions about the meaning of life and the authentic role of a man; my mother's boldness and social vision; both parents' keen intellectual questioning — in their own way spurred me onward in search of meaning. I now see that the sense of abandonment I felt gave me space for my own soul to find its place.

Like most men, I first had to leave home and heroically strive for achievements that the world would validate. By midlife I was both successful and successfully lost. In conquering the outer world, I had buried my soul, and so I had to find it to begin again. I found it by collapsing into the great wound. Fortunately, I found a mentor to help me do this work. Then, by coincidence, I stumbled into the men's movement and suddenly saw another piece of what had been missing from my life: a language of poetry and soul that could speak of ultimate things, and a recognition that men can be far more than successful egos.

Still unfinished, I continued searching for the last missing piece — the sacred. I had been reading spiritual literature all along, but never really had the clarity or personal conviction to apply what I learned. Yet books, people, and lessons appeared when I needed them. Finally, I arrived home to the consciousness I had forgotten in my early Spring; a revolutionary yet ancient perception of sacred reality. And with this I began to understand the real wonder of existence.

The point to relating this is this: as I look back I see that I was given whatever I needed along each step of the way. I see that the people in my life were so much more than I first perceived. As I look back over my life, I see how the whole fabric of experience seems to fit together. Midlife, masculinity, and mysticism — each part was a piece of my puzzle, and the pieces are still arriving because the mystic consciousness is a steadily transforming process.

I began this chapter by stating that it is easy to betray the sacred journey in the second half of life because our cultural stories fail us so completely, and because there are so few positive models to guide and validate man's passage from competitive hero to brother and mystic. Yet the sacred journey is an archetypal force field which underlies all aspects of a man's life. He may, at times, take two steps backward for every step forward, but the ultimate direction is inevitable. No matter how our individual lives play out, no matter how many detours we unintentionally take, no matter how fate seems to fling us through the vicissitudes of outrageous fortune, each of us is nevertheless being inexorably guided home — home to our common spiritual source. And so the conclusion to each individual story is, must be, and always will be the same. ❈

CHAPTER 39

Mystic Consciousness:
The Ending of Time and Story

I think what we are looking for is a way to experience the world that will open to us the transcendent that informs it, and at the same time forms ourselves within it. That is what people want. That is what the soul asks for...not only to find it, but to find it in our environment, in our world — to recognize it. To have some kind of instruction that will enable us to experience the divine presence. (Campbell, 1988, p. 53)

Eternity isn't some later time. Eternity isn't even a long time. Eternity has nothing to do with time. Eternity is that dimension of here and now that all thinking in temporal terms cuts off. And if you don't get it here, you won't get it anywhere...But the experience of eternity right here and now, in all things, whether thought of as good or evil, is the function of life. (Campbell, 1988, p. 67)

The illumination is the recognition of the radiance of one eternity through all things, whether in the vision of time these things are judged as good or as evil. To come to this, you must release yourself completely from desiring the goods of this world and fearing their loss..."If the doors of perception were cleansed," wrote Blake, "man would see everything as it is — infinite." (Campbell, 1988, p. 162)

≫ The Story of Everyman leads back to the mystic consciousness forgotten in childhood. This is where the story has been heading all along: to the transcendent that informs the world and our very being. When there is nowhere else to go, no one else to be, nothing left to achieve, and no more future, then we are very close to the "kingdom."

In Part 4 of this book, we shared the mystical experiences of others and, through some basic exercises, perhaps tasted a bit of it, ourselves. This chapter explores the spiritual world a man re-enters after the "end of time." We will see that the mystic vision evolves naturally in the second half of life, that it fulfills the mythological promise of a return to "paradise," and that a new story is forming in our world about this return.

A Brief Summary of the Mystic Vision

What is this world a man returns to that he forgot so long ago? How does he see it now? We begin with a summation.

This wondrous present moment, this moment that we are all in right now, is itself incredible; it is eternity opening to us. It is all there is or needs to be. There is no place to go, nothing has to be achieved or fixed or figured out. This is the garden of original being and original blessing.

This world, when it is seen afresh, is found to be already infinitely beautiful and infinitely precious. The world and everything in it is holy. It is a living, divine consciousness. Everything is filled and lived by the sacred presence. The Creator is in the creation. The Creator is creation. This immediate reality is everywhere you are. The Kingdom of Heaven is already here, spread out all over the earth. It always has been. We are in the garden. We just misperceive and misunderstand this place. Our eyes are covered with dark filters through which we lose eternity.

You and me, she and he, we are all made of this same living consciousness. What you really are is holy. Everyone is.

At the very heart of being, in everything that is felt in its pureness, is the unlimited happiness of existence. This unlimited happiness and love, this divine being, radiates and animates all things and can be felt as what you, too, are made of. The happiness you are looking for is what you are, where you are, and those around you. It is here now.

Religion is not about being good so you can get into heaven. It is not about finding God someplace else. Life is not about putting off love and joy until you retire, get rich enough, find the right person, or have enough power or fame. Life is now. It is complete and joyous now. We already living in an awesome, radiant, and joyous abundance of being. There is nothing missing. It is our artificial separation from this immediate experience of wonder, love, and joy that creates the feelings of scarcity, loss, deprivation, isolation, and emptiness that motivates our false story, and, at the same time, urges us to find the way back.

This world is enough. It is overflowing with the sacred. To know this is to concretely and intimately know and experience the nature of what is.

Finally, to experience this reality directly is to have access to ultimate knowledge; not necessarily facts, predictions, or scientific equations, but of the essence of all things, the knowledge which illuminates all things. Such knowledge flowers in you as you experience it. It teaches and guides. It's lessons are fundamental to living life in this world.

When a man realizes this vision, his quest has ended. He can know and enjoy the world as sacred. There is nowhere else to go. This is enough and he needs no more for himself. This reality is the true source of happiness. The mystic vision itself is the ending of the story and the ending of time. But this startling conclusion begs further explanation.

In its spiritual version, the Story of Everyman describes a search for whole-ness, which is really the search for that sacred self and reality abandoned in early childhood. How can we be whole without it? We suppress our capacity to see the spiritually alive world, and then forget we lost it, but still we know that something infinitely important is missing. This intuitive knowing propels a man's quest, much of which he lives in the outer world of consensual reality. His heroic vision, his life mission, the princess he pursues, his trials and initiations, his eventual defeat — all these elements are symbolic externalizations of this search for self, soul, and the garden. The story persists in its endless variations until this split is healed. Then it is no more.

This archetypal story is, we see now, a kind of cryptically encoded solution to the problem of separation. It is a kind of secret map telling us what we have to do, where we have to go, and what problems we have to solve to find our way back to the mystic's garden, and to the lost treasures of original self and divine perception buried in it. It is about coming home. Every fairy tale, every myth, and every religious story speaks to one or more parts of this journey of healing and return.

Each part of the story involves the real and symbolic working out of the Great Wound and the psychological conflicts built upon it. This early wounding is responsible for the problem of separation, for our leaving the garden of mystic consciousness, and only when it is healed will a man be home again. The ele-ments of the story — for example, the call of adventure, descent into the dun-geon, and search for the princess — represent a multifaceted working out of this wound. They symbolize the problem solving quest, the healing of old pain, and the recovery of soul. When a man finally solves all the story's riddles, when he is transformed by the journey itself, then there is no more need for the story.

The story's completion occurs at the same time a man reaches another startling and momentous discovery. He has reached the "ending of time." An older man no longer has the endless future of Spring and Summer. The present is everything and holds everything. Now is all there is. This realization can trans-form his consciousness, for he finds in the timeless present the eternity he lost years ago. Time and future were symptoms of his separation and barriers to its resolution. This place, where we have been all along, is the timeless realm. It is the completion of his journey. The search for meaning has ended. We see that questions of meaning, like my father's, were themselves symptoms of this deep unhappiness, this lost connection to the original divine self and the sacred world. When one arrives home again, as my own father did at the end of his life, there is nothing left to want, to figure out, or to solve.

Return to Paradise

In mythology and religion, arriving home symbolically means returning to paradise. But it is a mistake to believe that paradise will only arrive at some future time, for this belief inserts the temporal barrier again. Such literalizing of story and myth prevents us from finding the garden here and now. As the first hand descriptions of mystical experience taught us, enlightenment — that moment of intense, perception-enhancing wakefulness — transforms the world back into Eden. "Heaven on Earth" is the realization of the sacred world now.

Joseph Campbell's rich expositions on mythology and religion clearly support this idea. In *The Power of Myth*, he explains, "Getting back into that Garden is the aim of many religions...We're kept out of the Garden by our own fear and desire in relation to what we think to be the goods of our life...The difference between everyday living and living in those moments of ecstasy is the difference between being outside and inside the Garden. You go past fear and desire, past the pair of opposites...into transcendence. This is the essential experience of any mystical realization." (Campbell, 1988, p. 107). He goes on to quote the *Gnostic Gospel According to St. Thomas* in which a disciple asks, "When will the kingdom come?" Campbell notes that Christ answered, "The kingdom of the Father will not come by expectation. The kingdom of the Father is spread upon the earth and men do not see it." (Campbell, 1988, p. 213) Campbell then concludes, "...this is it, this is Eden. When you see the kingdom spread upon the earth, the old way of living in the world is annihilated. That is the end of the world. The end of the world is not an event to come, it is an event of psychological transformation, of visionary transformation. You see not the world of solid things but a world of radiance.' (Campbell, 1988, p. 230)

Richard Heinberg has written an entire book on this theme. Discussing the anthropological research of Mircea Eliade, he reviews, "One of the recurring themes in Eliade's books is that the religious experience is a window into a reality that is 'higher' than the physical, mental, and emotional world in which modern humanity spends its days. That higher reality is characterized by the subjective qualities of Paradise: peace, creativity, power, and ecstatic union with the divine. Eliade writes that every historical culture has regarded the human condition as being under a temporary spell of unnatural limitation and separateness, and that the primary purpose of all religions has been to help the individual and society to break free of that spell...It is not ancient but modern humanity that is asleep, unconscious, or infantile, according to Eliade." (Heinberg, 1989, pp. 197-198) Heinberg concludes, "Paradise — the immaculate condition of mind and emotion that is the objective of every spiritual technique — is immediately available to every human being." (Heinberg, 1989, p. 200).

The implication of this argument, and of the mystic vision itself, is that while the reality of such mystical union never changes, our ability to experience it does.

Heinberg argues, "Paradise myths seem to say that the experience of universal oneness is the natural, healthy condition of human consciousness, and that the customary state with which most of us are familiar — that of egocentric separateness, with all its ramifications — is unnatural and unhealthy. The idea that mystical or paradisal consciousness is innate and natural is also met with in the teachings of nearly every religious tradition." (Heinberg, 1989, p. 210).

Heinberg then raises one of the most critical questions of this work: "Edenic consciousness may be recoverable by individuals in rare moments of spiritual insight. Perhaps nearly everyone glimpses Paradise at some instant during his or her lifetime. But is it also possible for all of us together to live in the Garden once again — to return and stay?" (Heinberg, 1989, p. 239) He answers, "At any time, a sudden change of state may occur and Paradise will be present, if only for a moment...Suddenly, the hero realizes that Paradise has been there all along, unnoticed. Even after the hero has momentarily achieved paradisal awareness, he must still learn to sustain and communicate that state. From this point on, he is certain that he has known the true and natural condition of human consciousness...After having developed the ability to consistently maintain paradisal consciousness, the hero returns to the mundane world with a healing balm. Having found Heaven, he must share it — which means sharing himself, his state of being." (Heinberg, 1989, p. 252) This certainly sounds like the experience and challenge faced by our novice mystics. It is also the challenge faced by our aging "everyman" if he can step into the end of time, touch this mystical eternity, and then somehow share it with the tragically blinded, frenzied, and suffering world of man. His sacred function now is to guide others back.

It should be clarified that the "Kingdom of Heaven" we find ourselves in on earth need not be the whole Kingdom. The mystics have shown us that this paradisal world is just part of a vast divine wholeness that is the cosmos and beyond. The artificial division between this world and the next has always contributed to our erroneous belief that we are apart from the sacred. The Kingdom embraces the whole, is the whole, and perhaps includes more worlds than we can realize at this time. Another version of the Kingdom may be in the next world as well. But to speculate and obsess about the future, to create rules for its admission, is to create a lens of time and sin and deprivation once again. As the mystics ask us, if you don't find it here, what makes you think you will find it somewhere else?

The Collective Evolution of a New Story?

It has occasionally been argued that the stories of man, from the ancient Egyptian and Greek myths to the Bible, *Grimm's Fairy Tales*, the *Legends of King Arthur*, all the way up to *Star Wars*, suggest an evolution of consciousness that has been in the making across the millennia. Consciousness is evolving.

Joseph Campbell has said we are forming a new myth, for the old ones can no longer hold all that has changed within the last two thousand years (Campbell, 1988). But what are this new consciousness and new myth? What could this evolution be moving toward? And how do these ideas relate to the transformative realms of midlife, masculinity, and mysticism opening to individual men and to culture as a whole on the eve of the twenty-first century?

Western civilization seems to be entering a time of tremendous reorganization. We watch the collapse of one patriarchy after another and the failure of the rational-mechanistic model to really solve the emotional problems in our world. Crises of ecological adaptation are already occurring. The industrial machine and population bomb are reaching the inherent limits of our earthly domain. But does this mean the world is coming to an end? The end of a millennium is often a time for eschatological prophesy, for religious or hysterical "end of the world" speculation and proclamation. As Campbell asserted, however, "The end of the world is not an event to come, it is an event of psychological transformation." It symbolizes that the "...old way of living in the world is annihilated" not the world, itself. (Campbell, 1988, p. 230)

Metaphorically, we may envision the human species living a single life span. The Story of Everyman may also be the story of the species now at its midlife. Just as the individual midlife is rife with disappointment, disillusionment, disorientation, and despair, so is our cultural midlife. And just like that of an individual, this societal heroic quest is not working. It cannot solve all our problems. Civilization, too, has forgotten what it was after all along.

As a culture, we have forgotten that everything is sacred, including all people, places, and things. Unending conquest, industrial productivity, and domination over others, not to mention military machines and war, are all incompatible with the truly sacred. As required in the individual midlife, the time is coming for mankind to dismantle all that is false in our collective story, and return to something more authentic. Instead of worshipping the "Compulsive Warrior" paradigm, western culture may need to experience a "descent into grief and ashes." There will be pain, confusion, and disillusionment in the process. This is exactly why "everyman's" understanding and experiencing the midlife passage is so important to our world as a whole. It teaches us about the fundamental psychological and symbolic structure of this transformation so that we do not deny it or maladaptively act it out. It also teaches that, despite the darkness and dismay, the other side is waiting.

The Story of Everyman, then, is also the story of culture. Anthropologists and mythologists tell us that all cultures have creation myths, stories of a divine beginning, that symbolize how and why men came into being and the purpose of manifestation. As Heinberg chronicles, nearly all cultural traditions also have stories of the fall; that is, the separation of man from the original divine reality caused by some basic failure of his character, and the establishment of a false value system based on greed and selfishness instead (Heinberg, 1989). In one way or another, myths and religions say that man builds this false and secular kingdom through adulating and worshipping the wrong things, including ego, productivity, and wealth. The culture, just like the individual, must dismantle this false story.

In The Story of Everyman, the "fall" of the individual man occurs at the "beginning of time," that is, in early childhood. This is when the cognitive framework of time itself is imposed on the experience of eternity, creating an artificial temporal perspective of schedules and time urgency. Contact with the pristine moment of open timelessness is shattered by the adult demand that a boy must do something productive, and do it by a certain time. Increasingly thereafter, in school, work, and every other aspect of life, clocks, calendars, and deadlines run the whole show. Time becomes the drill sergeant driving production. Internalized, this insistent time orientation drives the "Compulsive Warrior." A man typically believes this clock-driven existence will dominate his life until retirement, when he secretly hopes to be freed from this unwanted burden. It is a tragic mistake to postpone sacred reality until some time in the future, for the future will always be the future, never now. Releasing this heroic task orientation with midlife, however, allows the man of insight to gradually restore his connection to the timeless sacred.

Just like individuals, groups, families, and cultures go through cycles of birth and death. The collective consciousness moves away from its magical beginnings into the world of time, goals, and problems, constellating a perilous adventure of growth and crystallization. Then the forms that are structured become rigid and constraining. At the midlife of this developmental course, when it is most suffocating and destructive, consciousness strives to move from the secular world of rules and institutions it created back to the original timeless sacred from which it arose. Daily and weekly worship are meant to be small versions of this kind of return. Shifting world priorities toward healthier values constitute larger versions.

Cultural disorganization is the extreme conclusion. Sometimes groups and cultures, like individuals, die. They disappear altogether. All cultures also "die" and are "reborn" continuously, as each new generation redefines its values and goals. Collective man is accelerating too quickly. Like the man at midlife, collective man needs to slow down and return to the silence and wonder of creation from where he came.

This is the mystic vision. In the universal story, man comes from unity into the world of differentiated consciousness and soon develops a separate ego with all its knowledge and capacities. He then mistakenly worships his own accomplishments, creating hubris, narcissism, and more recently, "Type A" machine man. He forgets his sacred origins. This falseness must collapse to find the sacred. Then, ego consciousness opens again to ultimate consciousness, and creation becomes conscious of itself as a single and undifferentiated whole, one divine consciousness opening to joy, wonder and love for no other purpose than to grow and know itself. This is the flowing and flowering of the sacred into creation. It is man's great and sacred task to open himself and the world to this divine and always present consciousness.

As we have seen, most of man's existing stories have to do with the understanding and healing the great personal wound and achieving psychological wholeness. Restoring the split between the secular and sacred worlds, however, is the part of the universal story we understand least. The ending of time and story potentially confronts us with the possibility of healing of this split. Eschatological warnings, symbolized in catastrophic accounts of the end of the world as we know it, reflect our collective fears of the collapse of the cultural warrior. Rather than desperately wait for a literal ending of the world to rescue the holy, perhaps we need new stories that can guide our passage through this cultural midlife.

If there are to be new stories of man, they will probably be ones that show us the way back, the way of returning in some form to the mystic vision. What would be some of the features of these new stories? If a man's individual midlife is any indication, and I think it is, then the passage to the maturity of mankind in the Fall season of our species may be marked by a set of characteristics similar to those found in the mature individual's Fall years, only on a broader scale. It will be born spontaneously in the images, dreams, creativity, and cultural experiments of all mankind.

Is the new story visible yet? My hunch is that its outlines are. I think it is emerging in the new social movements all around us. Some of the themes of this new story are:

ƒ *Turmoil and Struggle.* Just as in midlife, this will be a time of turmoil, struggle, pain, and reassessment. Mankind must work through these crises and resist acting them out. If we can hold this great passage in consciousness, understand its purpose, and give it guidance and ritual forms, then a new synthesis may be born.

ƒ *Emergent and Inductive Answers.* Instead of using logic, deduction, and pre-existing prescriptions, the new story will emerge through sharing, discovery, and surprises. It will happen spontaneously, in the context of decency, good will, and receptivity. Productive group problem solving always has this dynamism. Something new is born from the creative exchange, something more than any individual member came in with.

ƒ *Inclusion.* All peoples will be included in the new story. Just as the repressed parts of the psyche must be recovered and integrated at midlife, so too the oppressed parts of our world must be included. If any part is suffering, we are all suffering. And, if we look closely, we will see that we are all suffering, for what the "third world" lacks in material resources, the "first world" lacks in spiritual ones.

✦ *Return to the Sacred Mystery and the Garden.* The new story will be one of return. It will help us see and experience the world as a sacred living mystery. It will teach us to perceive the infinite beauty and preciousness of life around us and to know that this is the "kingdom." The ecological movement, with its focus on caring for the earth and all its creatures, certainly begins to embody this theme — as long as it resists the militancy and polarization tactics of the old masculine story.

✦ *Gardeners Not Conquerors.* We will learn more about honoring sacred reality in place of exploiting it. Man's role will change from conquering reality to living with it more naturally and interdependently. The metaphor of nature and its cycles reminds us to be more patient, to let things grow, to learn from the natural order of the world. Gardeners appreciate what they grow. They avoid waste. And they learn from observing the wisdom of life itself.

✦ *The Motivation of Love and Joy.* Rather than finding security and self-esteem in owning and controlling resources, man may begin to live from the intrinsic happiness of being and oneness. In the mystic consciousness, the self and others are seen as part of the same indivisible whole. From this place, generosity flows and all are truly secure, for we take care of each other as we would ourselves.

✦ *The Consciousness of Being over the Compulsivity of Doing.* Being means knowing subjective experience in a perceptually pure and feeling way. It occurs, for example, when you simply feel into what you are, into your capacity for love. From this kind of awareness streams the natural rhythms of activity and rest, openness and closedness, work and celebration, introversion and extroversion. Compulsive doing, like the machine it emulates, violates this natural energy.

✦ *Ongoing Contact with the Divine.* In this final story, life is first and foremost predicated on contact with the sacred. Man would spend much more time in spiritual practices such as remembrance, prayer, ritual, teaching, generosity, and grateful celebration. Living in sacred reality would be his primary concern and all else would follow naturally.

✦ Healing Individual Vision First. The founders of the world's great religious traditions restored their own sight first. They took individual journeys first to open their hearts and eyes. Then and only then did they have anything truly wonderful to share. This new story will probably have the same theme, for it is part of the timeless story. Healing will not be about trying to convince others to accept our beliefs, but in living from direct communion with the sacred, from which love (the greatest teaching of all) flows naturally and selflessly. We really cannot impose change on others. We can, however, change ourselves, and relate to others differently. In this way, perhaps, they may see what is possible for them.

✦ Realistic and Tolerant. Hopefully, our new story will also be more realistic and tolerant. Utopian ambitions or religions, no matter how well conceived, will never eliminate the foibles and limitations of our still-evolving human nature. Mankind will continue to have difficulty dealing with the myriad problems created by its limitations. Knowing that the world is already infinitely perfect, precious, and beautiful, the story will teach that kindness and patience are the natural way to help others heal from the terrible nightmare of separation and suffering.

The emerging story is one that seeks to invite mystical consciousness back into the world, to make it once again a spiritual reality. The story will be a bridge to guide our homecoming. The story is still taking shape. ❧

CHAPTER 40

Sacred Story and the Mythology of Personality

≫ Presented here are some further reflections on the sacred and its relationship to personality. The vocabulary of this chapter organizes words we have used before — like self, soul, gift, sacred essence, original perception, ego, and false self — into a mythology of personality. Like poetry, it may be hard to follow, for ultimately the phenomenology of being, too, is ineffable, intangible, and ephemeral, and proposing a mythology of personality is no less ambiguous. These reflections, however, are not really new, for myths in every age and time have described the real man in such terms. This is simply a look at the universal character of man. Let the words work on you even if you don't understand them. Because it represents more of what is becoming than what has become, it is cannot be perfectly clear. But it can speak to you and encourage your story to reveal more of its hidden spiritual facets.

Let's look again at the mythology that informs each life. First and most generally, it is a story about coming from the sacred dimension before time and identity, and bringing its essence into the realm of matter and form. This essence, which includes a kind of vestigial knowledge, communion, and perception of sacred reality, is hidden deep in the forming self. The self is like a seed that holds this essence. The self and its divine core also embody the unique and particular gift or mission one comes to actualize. Actually, the gift is the self, for when we become this core potential, what we are is the gift. The self, then, is akin to one's genetic inheritance; absolutely unique, full of potential, but invisible and unpredictable, knowable only to the extent that it can blossom. It is also equivalent to what we call soul. As such, it is both who we really are and our connection to the divine.

As the individual awakens in this world, he gradually becomes aware of the forming self and its mystical center. All too soon, however, the socially conditioned persona, all we are supposed to be, closes like a the pod around this seed of self. As this pod closes, we forget the gift of self and its sacred essence, and manufacture a false and socially acceptable self instead. Then we develop our ego abilities in preparation to take the great journey of life. Ideally, what cracks the pod is the weariness of the journeyer and the urgency of the true self to enter the world, for this is, after all, one of our primary purposes in this realm. Thus, the journey of life requires the construction of a strong ego and identity to protect and carry the self and its transformative core, and a life structure capable of moving us through the seasons of life until we are broken open again. Then, as we relocate the true self and its mystical center, we and the world increasingly resume our original spiritual nature and the work of creation flowers in ways ultimately incomprehensible and unpredictable to our limited minds.

Movement through the many doorways of understanding, illumination, and transformation sequenced in our lives is propelled by our personal story, which is secretly the story of how we lost touch with our sacred core and what we must do to find it again. We understand this story only by telling it — first to oneself and then to others. When we tell our story over and over and in increasingly public forums, we begin to learn what the story is really about and what it has been trying to tell us. We also discover that whatever self-consciousness existed about it disappears and we are freed from any emotional attachment to it. What was at first personal and private gradually becomes impersonal and collective. We gradually learn that our story is, at its most profound level, a universal one; the mythic Story of Everyman through the seasons of life.

Separation from the divine is a universal problem, so the story must be, in essence, a holy story; that is, a divine archetypal structure with its own energy, purpose, direction, and destiny. It works silently in the darkness of the psyche, giving meaning and form to the events of our lives. In its unfolding process, we move from our personal psychology to a collective psychology and ultimately to what Jean Houston has beautifully described as a Sacred Psychology.

Only by asking ultimate questions about this process can we listen within for ultimate answers. So what is this story of life, this parable? Why is a man called into life and changed so many times through its seasons? Each stage seems to happen to him, and each is like a sculptor and he is the clay. A man is pulled, stretched, compressed, compacted, opened, widened, strengthened, and then broken and stretched again for yet another stage. Over and over, season by season, we are broken and stretched, stretched and broken, until we are eventually stretched into an opening consciousness, until we are what that sacred process is making us; again and again, until we become that process, individuals moving by a single loving consciousness, separated like cells yet always part of an indivisible whole and always evolving. For this is the nature of sacred reality; this is it wants from us, and we, in turn, dive deeper and deeper into this ocean of spirit to be bathed by the intentions and operations of its consciousness.

Put another way, it is the divine story being told in our lives. It is this Great Being's story of me, and you, and each of us, which is the story of His own creation, for they are the same. This is what is meant by the proposition found repeatedly across religions that man was created in the image of God. Humans were created as the divine itself was created. Why? This Great Being is full of love and all life manifests this love. This Being wants to know and be known, to love and be loved. This is the ultimate teaching of the mystic experience itself: like ourselves, the universe is alive and conscious, and the purpose of life is the manifestation of love. Life is a secret invitation from the sacred to man, the beloved, to learn the sweet mystery of love. And the fulfillment of a single life arrives in the awareness and unlimited expression of this love and joy. We are made of it and it flows through our reins. Becoming conscious means becoming conscious of that ground of being.

Midlife is one of these tremendous storms that opens our soul. It swirls like a whirlpool until the hardened form of the first phase breaks and falls away to reveal the germinal seed of the true self. It is potentially a new man who comes into being at midlife, a man who can share himself authentically with other men and who can finally do the work of his soul, whatever that is to be. As he interacts with the images and promptings of his now-opened center, a man develops his own authority and begins to step forward. He stands now for his own experience and finds at last his own voice. This is men's work at midlife: to arrive now in the world as a mature man, one's own man, finally, to do the work of his own soul, and at the same time to become a man full of consciousness, wonder, and joy. The deep archetypal energies of the masculine and the soul restoring friendships of male community facilitate this evolution further and provide a context that welcomes the changing man. The heart and culmination of this work is a search for a sacred and life-authenticating religious perspective, a sacred understanding and cosmology that tells men why they are here.

And as we experience the progression of this journey and of this work, as we see how the divine has stretched, called, and received us into this open moment, we may finally grasp how the entire story is sacred. This is Creation, and the mystic consciousness is itself the source and the next chapter. Our life struggles ideally grow our capacity to hold and then open to this ultimate consciousness. The goal is to find ways of experiencing and expressing the divine in all the countless ways of which the imaginative mind is capable so that it may flow into the world. This is myth, religion, creativity, compassion, and love. For this to happen, a man must get out of his own way.

The "I" identity, that was so important in the first half of life, was a necessary fiction, a temporary container or structure of consciousness required for the world to take on form. But this "I" mistakenly becomes too important; it even becomes the goal. So it is broken apart for an ever purer light to shine through. Living in this light, a man may be called wise, foolish, or mad. But he is most centrally a man who can give form to the constantly emerging energies of the divine in his own consciousness. This is the mythic purpose of personality in the sacred story.

Aging is the final movement from what a man thinks he is to what the living divine consciousness already is. As he ages and the competencies of body and mind gradually fade or recede, something else leaks in. A man's mystical sense grows and increasingly one may sense the larger mind, the vast and open consciousness, the sacredness we live in and the sacredness that lives in each of us. Now, gratefully, it is no longer his life — it is a larger one. As if opening an inner window into eternity, all personality boundaries within and without become permeable and the divine being is his center and his life is everywhere. ❦

CHAPTER 41

Implications
of the Mystic Vision

Embrace the present moment as an ever-flowing source of holiness. The activity of God is everywhere and always present, but it is visible only to the eye of faith. If we could lift the veil and if we watched with vigilant attention, God would endlessly reveal himself to us and we should see and rejoice in his active presence in all that befalls us. At every event we should exclaim: 'It is the Lord' (John 21:7.) Nothing could happen to us without our accepting it as a gift from God. (deCaussade, 1975, p. 36)

Listen to me: let your hearts demand the infinite, for I can tell you how to fulfill them. There is never one moment in which I cannot show you how to find whatever you can desire. The present moment is always overflowing with immeasurable riches, far more than you are able to hold. Your faith will measure it out to you: As you believe, so will you receive. (deCaussade, 1975, p. 41)

It is the kingdom of heaven which penetrates the soul. It is the bread of angels which is eaten on earth as well as in heaven. There is nothing trivial about our passing moments, as they enclose the whole kingdom of holiness and the food on which angels feed. (deCaussade, 1975, p. 52)

This work in our souls cannot be accomplished by cleverness, intelligence, or any subtlety of mind, but only by completely abandoning ourselves to the divine action, becoming like metal poured into a mold, or a canvas waiting for the brush, or marble under the sculptor's hands. (deCaussade, 1975, pp. 56-57)

» What is sacred living? How do we find this spacious, pristine, wondrous, and loving experiential mode described by both ancient and present mystics? How do we learn to live in such mystic consciousness more often, more fully, and what would it mean to do so?

Implications of the Mystic Vision:
For the Individual

The mystic vision itself teaches us volumes about sacred living. Consider for a moment how this powerful and remarkable vision would change reality for yourself, for man and society. The possibilities are endless. Here are some that have occurred to me.

ƒ This vision, when truly known or experienced, would eradicate:

Greed and materialism: If all reality is sacred, if we live in an overflowing abundance of being, what is there to possess? It would be like hoarding sand in the desert.

Narcissism: Who can be more important than anyone or anything thing else? Any superiority at all would constitute painful separation from the joy of being. Who wants that?

Exploitation: What is there to exploit? It is all here and more than enough. Exploitation comes from the experience of greed, deprivation, and inadequacy. Such conditions don't exist to the mystic eye.

Competition and winning: If the prize is everywhere, if it is right in front of you, for what is there to compete?

Prejudice: All people are wondrous and infinitely precious beings. Who could choose between them? Why would you want to? Each has something so precious to offer. Diversity is a celebration.

Power: We do not have the power, the power has us. It lives us! Feeling the boundless joy inherent in this pervasive cosmic energy, who could want more? Power is sought by those who cannot feel it.

ƒ This vision opens us to love, joy, and happiness now. We don't have to continue to live in tension, deprivation, and misery. Happiness is inherent in sacred living. This conclusion is not "pollyannish" thinking. For the mystics, it is absolutely real. The vast majority of people distrust happiness. They believe they must put it off until they get rich, lose weight, get promoted, find the right partner, or retire. What a tragedy. With a little practice, one can almost always find that steady capacity for happiness that exists in this wondrous body of life right now. Why wait?

ƒ The mystic vision awakens a sense of transpersonal purpose. It is a vision we can serve and that can serve the world. It provides a constantly new and sacred reason for life: to be and to love without limitation or condition. Each day becomes something too vastly important and wonderful.

✓ Historically, the mystical experience gave men their sacred cosmologies and rituals. It can also renew and enliven our own, though we may have to relearn the art and architecture of communion.

✓ The mystical vision nourishes the older male. When a man gives up questing and conquering, and proceeds through the grief and ashes of his midlife descent, he can emerge to discover the sacred, living reality all round him. It is worthwhile for this reason alone. It is our nourishment as men.

✓ The mystical vision also allows men to be elders. It is a sacred understanding of the larger reality in which death, suffering, pain, and sorrow occur, not solely as terrible tragedies, but as part of the whole transformative story. As an elder, a man sees the whole picture and gently mediates the struggles of those caught in throes of suffering. Pain is real, but there is something larger holding it and something more inside it. In sum, this sacred perspective fosters a non-cynical acceptance of the aging process and of the cycles of life.

Implications of the Mystic Vision: For Community

The mystic vision also has remarkable implications for community. As we have seen, it teaches that we are all one, and this oneness is the core and most legitimate basis for authentic community. But how do we make this transition from the abstract idea of spiritual unity to a living appreciation of oneness as community?

The underlying oneness of community may be understood with the help of the following example. Consider a large, broad palm leaf, a living thing attached to a plant with roots in the earth. If we tore this leaf into twenty pieces, each would have the same color and texture, but each would also be different, having a unique shape, size, and location. Individuals are the pieces of the social leaf — everything is part of the cosmic leaf. We form one living whole. Moreover, each piece is absolutely necessary to the whole. Leave one piece out and the leaf is wounded, incomplete, disordered, troubled. So it is with life and consciousness. Each person seems to be different and unique, and indeed each is, but we are also profoundly interconnected, sustained by the same single pervasive life force, one unifying whole, everything connected to everything else.

Our interconnectedness is through feeling. We make feeling bonds to one another and when those bonds are broken or lost, we feel deep pain. Death is an obvious example of broken bonds, and the resulting pain is deep. From this perspective, we readily see that it is love that holds this whole thing together. Love is the nature and the force of our interconnection. And we connect not just to people but to everything — earth, sky, water, plant and animal life. When these bonds are injured, we also hurt. For example, living disconnected lives in run-down and polluted inner-cities fills us with this kind of pain, and the symptoms of the deep wound are hidden in violence, drug abuse, and despair that grow from these loveless places.

The body provides another example and metaphor of wholeness. Each hair, red blood cell, heartbeat, and neural impulse are individual and unique, yet vital to the whole. Each contributes to the whole and yet the whole is more than all its parts. When body parts begin competing for resources, the body itself has developed a kind of cancer or cannibalism that threatens its survival. Likewise, the whole of humanity is a cohesive, functioning being. Each of us is part of that living whole we call Mankind. Even more, we are part of the living organism we call the earth. Finally, as we have seen, the universe itself seems to be alive as a single conscious being, differentiating its wholeness in ever varied forms.

Here is a third analogy. Take a piece of paper. The white paper represents this single divine consciousness. Draw the outline of a person on the paper. Draw several. Draw the outlines of some plants and animals, landscape, whatever you like. What do you see? The separate forms exist, they appear to have boundaries, but they are made of the same thing! The outlines now appear as artificial divisions of one pure, indivisible, and uniform being. So it is with man, animals, plants, land, space, stars, temperature, song, praise, love, and wonder — all temporary forms that give diversity to life and consciousness, yet all composed of the same unity. Each of our mystics knew this absolutely.

Authentic community really comes from this same natural oneness. We experience it all the time, but overlook its importance. Hints of oneness occur when individual boundaries are temporarily lost in moments of love, song, dance, prayer, ecstasy, or sport. At such times, our separateness disappears. Suddenly all is one, all is held together in a single moment of experience. Then individuality is seen as a temporary state. If, on the other hand, we believe that we must separately compete for scarce resources, if we believe that our survival is in conflict or incompatible with the survival of other people or life forms, then we are violating the divine oneness. You cannot begin cutting parts of the leaf, body, or page without damaging the whole. It is equally absurd to think that a single part can own another part or own the infinite, indivisible, eternal consciousness. We must respect this ultimate archetype of order, which is, in effect, the living and radiant ground of being underlying all things and all processes. This is the sacred one.

This model of wholeness has tremendous implications for authentic community. Ultimately, it is the basis of community. To live in the sacred as community means that:

✗ We recognize that ultimately we are not in charge. We are, in fact, totally dependent on something larger that has its own order, purpose, and consciousness. Ultimately the value of what we do depends on how it relates to this consciousness and the whole.

✗ To participate in this larger life, we must make conscious and reverent connection with it. Technology is not enough. We must also learn how to listen and to find guidance, purpose, and values from this living mystery.

✗ Each individual part, each of us, each living and non-living thing, is filled with this divine consciousness. Each thing, living and non-living, is itself perfect, invaluable, and necessary to the whole. Thus, each person should be celebrated without judgment for what he or she uniquely brings to the survival, beauty, wonder, and completion of the whole.

✗ A community that recognizes these principles helps each person discover their part in holding and contributing to the holiness, beauty, and survival of the whole. Each person and each animal, plant and thing is a gift to the other and to the universe, and can only function at its highest level when its gift is actualized.

✗ Leadership in authentic community arises from service to the whole. It is not about power, control, domination, coercion, intimidation, status, or importance; but instead about service, contribution, and gratefulness. This kind of leadership recognizes no hierarchy or value. It knows that each person is a leader relative to the talents they bear, and that this matrix of leadership constitutes the whole. And it knows one more thing: that what each person offers is really that which flows through them from the conscious universe. Leadership is not one big person with huge powers and responsibilities, but countless individuals offering their simple gifts to one another, neighbor to neighbor, friend to friend, here, now, in grateful simplicity.

✗ It follows that the work of community begins in smallness — in the neighborhood, street, village, and workplace. We need again to feel our bonds in these small units of life that occur so naturally. When we each form such simple community, here, now, in this sacred place — then we will be changing the world, for we will be changing that part of the world we are here to love and tend. Take care of your own garden and the world will be cared for as a whole.

✕ Narcissism obviously has no place in community. It is a sign of disease and spiritual emptiness. So are aggression, hoarding, caste and class hierarchies, poverty, and starvation. These are not problems that can be solved by a president or government, but only by countless individuals responding to one another in bonds of felt connection. No one can carry the whole burden. Moreover, our real purpose here is to love and to serve lovingly. The secret is that hidden in the heart of loving service is joy — for love is its own reward, greater than anything that can be obtained, owned, or heroically accomplished.

✕ Community does not mean loss of individuality or autonomy. Men who have worked out their individuality find that they move back and forth between the oneness of community and the separateness of independence. Space for solitude and soul deepens a man, gives him more of himself to bring to community. Community, in turn, stimulates a man and gives him a social context for self-expression, communal work, and community identification. Each contributes to the other.

✕ Coming full circle, community needs to be based first and foremost on its relation to the sacred. We live not to achieve or succeed in personal or national terms. We are not here to make our kids more competitive than others, to make more money than our neighbor, or to have a gross national product that continuously expands or outperforms another country. We are here to live in and know the sacred. Authentic and meaningful community asks each person to experience, honor, and communicate with this sacred oneness — daily, weekly, yearly, and communally — through whatever means.

The Story of Everyman thus leads back to community and to the world. It is here that a man's journey must express the lessons he learned in his midlife, in the wondrous energy of his masculine form, and in his mystic intuitions. We are here to be conscious of this living divine presence that permeates everything, to be moved by the love and joy it awakens in our bodies and lives, to care for each other as we would a newborn fawn, and to know a universe that is one.

Implications of the Mystic Vision: For Religious Beliefs

Serious students of the world's religions recognize that mankind has developed numerous, almost endless, ways to experience and conceptualize the divine. For some, there is only one supreme being; for others a supreme being with intermediaries, spirits or angels; for others, a pantheon of gods in the other world; for some, God is the world itself or the divine self within each person; others find spirits everywhere in the animate or inanimate world; and for some, all this is a dream in the cosmic mind. Similarly we find multifarious differences in beliefs about heaven, hell, sin, good and evil, salvation, saviors, enlightenment, duality, and the proper form of religious life. This diversity may be disquieting or disorienting for anyone who already has a comfortable or certain way of worship. For example, in Western civilization, we often feel most comfortable with an "I-Thou" relationship, which often takes the form of a relationship to a personal God. Eastern religions not infrequently adopt an "I Am That" orientation, conceiving man's essential identity as the sacred itself. Indigenous religions frequently give rise to multiple relationships with the spirit world, which may include animals, nature, and ancestors. What do we make of all these differences?

Certainly one of the main causes of this variation of beliefs is the nature of the conceptualizing mind. Although the sacred is ultimately beyond form and finite knowledge, the mind of man keeps developing images and ideas for it. This is a rich and creative process. Because it is infinite and the human mind is not, no individual or culture can fully grasp this vast and sacred mystery. But we try, over and over, because it is our most important mystery and, as the mystics have said for eons, we hunger to know our true condition. As cultures vary in their languages, words, and life styles, so do their images and beliefs.

This explanation, of course, is neither new nor revolutionary. What I do find fascinating, however, is that the mystic experiences recounted in Part 4 seem to include most of these differences. Several examples come immediately to mind. First, there is an "I-Thou" relationship in the mystic experience, yet there is also, at times, the feeling of being so merged with the sacred that separate boundaries are lost and there is only the one — the "I Am That." Mystics have always seemed to move back and forth across this border even though organized religion has frowned on the idea of becoming God. In the second place, the mystic vision also sees everything as alive, as pulsing with consciousness and life, even inorganic nature and non-living things. It is not hard to see how peoples who live very close to the earth might "tune into" this consciousness in everything around them, sensing the unique form of the spiritual in animals, plants, elements, and natural forces. Third, mystics from virtually all traditions have written of spirit intermediaries: non-human beings who operate for good or evil on this plane and others. How can we presume that the material world is the only realm of life, especially once we realize that man himself is a spiritual being? Fourth, some mystics argue that this realm is but a dream. When we understand from the mystics that we miss the divine reality and see instead a collective nightmare of ugliness, warfare, and strife, perhaps the idea of unreality is not far off the mark. We may be seeing our own negative thought forms and dream images far more than the real world. And, finally, if God is everywhere, then in a way we are all forms in the one mind. It is not hard to see, therefore, how a culture or individual could abstract one or more these features of the mystical experience and limit the definition of spirituality to those features only. Then dogma follows definition, and soon the "experts" use this dogma to make proclamations about the "truth."

The implication of this analysis for the seriously religious individual is this: whatever form you feel most comfortable with is that facet of the divine that is alive and real for you. None are more true or real than the others. The divine includes all these facets. The deeper you go into your worship or communion experience, the more of these other facets may appear to you. The important thing is not the differences, but the depth.

Implications of the Mystic Vision:
For Spiritual Practice

What role does spiritual practice play in the development of mystical consciousness? Almost all teachers recommend some kind of practice, which really means some kind of consistency and perseverance in the spiritual quest. Jumping around too much between teachers or practices means one never goes very deeply into any. On the other hand, this advice doesn't mean slavishly following only one path or suffering at the hands of a teacher simply because he says it is necessary. There are so many ways to see and enter paradise. No teacher or discipline has the only key. Moreover, each seeker has within him certain inborn response possibilities, like a tuning fork with a special frequency all its own, and he must find these spiritual exercises or practices that resonate with this intrinsic nature. The message is: try as many paths as you need and trust your own response in choosing. Explore as many teachers and the teachings as you find necessary, but don't be naive. There have been fools, phonies, and true guides in every tradition. Ask discerning questions and then find your own way.

Practices come in so many shapes, sizes, flavors, and colors. As all searchers know, there is no dearth of resources in the spiritual path. Books, courses, and whole disciplines are available for each form of practice. The criteria for measuring progress is the depth or fullness of your communion, and the resulting feelings of unconditional happiness, serenity, trust, beauty, timelessness, goallessness, oneness, compassion, and love.

Here is a partial listing drawn from the vast spiritual literature. Again, see which practices naturally call to you. They will probably be the ones that seem easiest, for our gifts are often found in activities that seem ridiculously simple or easy. Check off the ones you find most naturally interesting and explore them. Add to the list.

1. Reading mystical or inspirational literature.
2. Meditating with any techniques or tradition that calls you.
3. Praying and learning about prayer.
4. Conscious movement, sight, hearing, and touch.
5. Learning to live more in the eternal present.
6. Ritual in any of its forms and purposes.
7. Taking time for religiously inspiring dance, song, drumming, or music.
8. Evoking and trusting your own deep insights.
9. Simple, honest, and generous living.
10. Learning emotional balance.
11. Staying in silence and solitude amidst worldly noise.
12. Making spirituality a priority.
13. Wishing or asking fervently for your heart's deepest desires.
14. Letting a practice go when it becomes compulsive or dry, and returning to it some later time when it feels alive again.
15. Practicing happiness and love; the core feelings of the mystical mode.
16. Volunteer work as spiritual practice.
17. Monitoring in your personal life what spirituality is not (e.g., fanaticism, proselytizing, coercion, pressure, grandiosity, etc.).
18. Seeing divinity, the sacred story, and the opportunity for spiritual growth in every life event, even if tragic.
19. Being in the company of men past midlife who have lived through hardship and come into their own manhood.
20. Being in the company of spiritual people and doing spiritual practice together.
21. Doing what you love (as Joseph Campbell taught: following your bliss opens doors never before possible or even conceived).
22. Writing letters to God and writing what you imagine would be the response.
23. Taking classes on spiritual subjects.
24. Talking to religious professionals about your concerns and questions.
25. Seeking spiritual guidance from a trained director or teacher.
26. Spending time alone in nature and sensing the mystical energy of the natural world.

The Final Implication: Is The Leap Too Big?

Before it was published, I showed this manuscript to my brother Jim, a Harvard trained Unitarian minister, and asked him for feedback. After saying many nice things, he grew more serious and asked me the following questions, "How does the average person, the ordinary 'everyman,' return to the 'garden' and attain such mystical consciousness? Your leap between recovering the true self at midlife and finding the mystic vision is too big. Is that what men are supposed to do? How is it really done? And what about the people who are happy with their personal relationship to the creator, whatever form it takes? Is their practice wrong and somehow less than what your mystics describe?" Jim's questions were right on target. The leap is too big.

As I reflected on my brother's questions, I realized that the full blown mystic experience is really not the ultimate prerequisite for a man's spiritual maturity — but knowing about it can point the way. This conclusion derives from our earlier observations that:

1. Very few people experience the full blown mystic realization.
2. Even people who have full blown mystical experiences do not necessarily become more psychologically mature or spiritually advanced.
3. Almost anyone can find smaller glimpses of sacred reality in their lives.
4. Most people fail to notice or appreciate moments of mystical consciousness when they do break through.

So, now does all this add up? If you can really appreciate the full mystical vision, then you can increasingly expand your little moments of mystic consciousness toward deeper and deeper communion with sacred reality. I believe the missing ingredient is the decision to practice seeing and feeling the mystic consciousness until it becomes an expanding part of your life.

Speaking personally, I know for myself that there is something in the mystic anecdotes that speaks to me profoundly, as if each one momentarily lifts the veil for me and I see what really is. These visions also call forth memories of a magic reality from early childhood and glimpses of Eden that now occur not infrequently in my everyday life, moments where the world is indeed bathed in celestial light, sparkling beauty, and I find my consciousness filling with wonder and appreciation. Perhaps most interesting to me is that exploring this vision has stimulated personal forms of meditation which seem to cultivate the same consciousness in me. As I practice seeing and feeling in this way, the world becomes brighter, loving and joyous feeling grows in me, and I become ever more confident of this entire argument.

Clearly, though, the answer to Jim's question is that there is no perfect and predictable method for entering the garden nor is it a prerequisite for maturity or spiritual growth. There are endless techniques, strategies, and teachers, but no certainty. Each man must follow his own mapless path, as all the greatest teachers have through history. Part of the problem is that we have been lead to desire an illusory and grandiose spiritual experience (e.g., extraordinary visions of god), and are not prepared to see the divine right in front of us (i.e., the miracle of this reality). The former leads to fruitless fantasy and searching; the latter leads to blindness and ignorance of all that really is. We can, on the other hand, let the mystic vision be a guide and a stimulus for our lives. You don't have to be a world class runner to enjoy running, and you don't have to be a God-realized saint to know and feel the mystical in everyday life.

These caveats notwithstanding, I think I have learned some important personal lessons. I list them below for your interest.

- ✗ Learn about the mystic experience in its pure form so that it can be intuited in everyday life activities. Read the mystical accounts over and over; get inside them, recite mystical poetry, and experience it. Then stop thinking and come into the timeless present: here, now, always. Shift from conception to perception. Stop and look. Opening into the mystic consciousness in this way, begin to see the world through mystical eyes.

- ✗ Cultivate the feelings of the mystic consciousness. Practice evoking an unconditionally loving feeling toward the world. Practice praising, trusting, knowing, pleasing, serving, feeling, thanking, and being God in whatever way comes to you. Practice wonder. Notice that in the center of this practice, in the core of your physical being, bubbles a boundless joy. When you feel this joy, you are on the path and your heart and eyes are opening. Unbounded happiness is one of the most wonderful signposts on the spiritual path.

- ✗ Just as importantly, confront the beliefs that deny, forbid, or kill this kind of consciousness. For example, some elements of traditional religion and certainly much of our culture tell us that this the mystical vision is a ridiculous idea; or worse, some form of denial, paganism, quackery, self-deception, or satanic trickery. We are told, "You can't know the sacred. You shouldn't try. Only those properly trained should tell us what to believe." Or we are told, "Becoming a mystic means you'll turn into a weird, wild-eyed, unkempt, selfish, or irresponsible stranger. No one will want to know you. You better not." Worse still is our own skepticism, for we fear, "This stuff is too crazy. Don't talk about it. People will think you're nuts. You're a fool to waste time like this when you should be doing something important." We discount the sacred reality right in front of us all the time.

ƒ Manage your emotions. Nothing takes you farther from the garden than anger, upsets, jealousy, or greed, because we stop seeing directly and dwell entirely on the upset in our imagination. We play and replay the incident, plan revenge, seek sympathy. An emotional dust storm, it obscures all vision of the sacred. ❦

CHAPTER 42

Coming Home:
My Father's Consciousness

⁕ We are reaching the end of our odyssey through the Story of Everyman, the midlife passage, deep masculinity, and the mystic vision. This last chapter is about homecoming, coming back to the start. In this sense, then, I return to the first subject of this book — my own father.

It was when he was dying. Smaller than I remembered, hair taken by the chemotherapy, his body was thin and wasted. He drifted in and out of consciousness. The smell of dying filled the room. I cried and held his bony shell. It was so hard to let him go. Yet he was already almost gone. He seemed far away, beyond knowing me.

But in those last hours, I also remember sensing that he was comfortable. His body seemed more and more like a lump of clay, and that seemed strangely all right. What was left of him was calm, peaceful, somehow even radiant. A few hours earlier, he said that he had "glimpsed the other side," and it still shone through him. He had seen the other world and was content. His essence was melting, dissolving dreamily back into eternity; he was leaving this world. There were no more questions. He was going home. Though deep in grief, I was so grateful to him for showing me this final transfiguring experience — the old shaman's last trick. But what was this penultimate illumination and how had he merged back into the sacred? Those questions have been waiting inside me, unanswered, for two decades.

As my work on this book was coming to a close, I began to wonder what was so different about his consciousness in those concluding hours, and my own consciousness now? Does one have to wait until the very end of life to experience the oneness he was flowing into? Once again, it was the mystics who resoundingly answered my question. "No! You don't have to wait to come home. You are home. Open your eyes and see it. Open your heart and feel it." For them, sacred reality is already here. The next world may be waiting, but our world is hallowed even now.

Before passing on, my father had dissolved completely into the larger Father. I sensed he somehow knew this, surrendering with relief and gratitude. But I wondered, as we all do, what this experience was like and what happens to those still living in this world who are able, to some extent, to merge with the same brightness of being? For me, these final answers have blossomed gradually from my own intensifying mystical experience. They are surprisingly consistent with what I sensed in my father, with what I have read of the world's mystical literature, and within themselves. They form a single, integrated spiritual vision, one that grows progressively deeper with age, time, and practice.

Coming Home: One Man's Vision

— Please pause here —

In the Preface to this book I cautioned that it would seem sometimes like I was mixing "psychobabble" with paradox and pirated Zen. Now that you have read much or all of the book, you may feel that some of the stories, poems, ideas, and personal experiences were a bit much — far out or unbelievable. Now, if you decide to read the rest of this chapter, your credulity will be stretched farther.

I hesitated to include this material in the book. It's not my wish to proselytize or to attempt to include myself among the illuminated. Yet if a single reader can be touched by my own revelations, that is justification for including them.

So with this disclaimer, here goes. What follows are intuitions and revelations that arise spontaneously from my own meditational practice. Once again, as you have done many times throughout this book, try to feel these words rather than analyze them. If comfortable for you, let them be a meditation. You will notice that my language changes in this mystic realm, for this field of consciousness evokes a looser, more subjective, paradoxical and inspired language. It is redundant, radical, and ecstatic because it can't find enough ways to say the miraculous. It is neither meant for everyday discussion nor for logical analysis.

In the following meditations, I use the word God in reference to the sacred. I don't believe God is reducible to male or female, human or animal, or any other form. Using the pronoun God is meant to be inclusive of all forms. Similarly, the use of the masculine pronoun "He," an unfortunate artifact of recent Western civilization, is not meant to connote gender. Please feel free to substitute names and terms that are most comfortable for you.

To find God is to find Him here, in the immediate perceptual stillness, in the timeless present just as it is now. His presence is in everything, is everything. Our hearts beat with it; He breathes us, it is His body we call our own. To be conscious is to be in His consciousness, for it is His consciousness that we mistakenly call our own. It is trying to act independently of this consciousness that is the great problem, the origin of "sin" and separation. We are God's substance, his differentiated self. He loves us. He is us. We are his happiness. The greatest happiness we feel is evoked from our contact with Him. We were made to know Him, to carry and be His consciousness, so that love could be multiplied, multifaceted, mutual, and experienced. It is from fear and imagination that we worry about pain, mortality, and control. It is His happiness, the happiness of being in God, that is the fount of all joy, generosity, and peace.

God is present now. There is nothing else that you have to know or do. All that is left is to release effort and worry, and feel into the incredible joy of knowing that you are already full of God, that you are all there is and all you need. Merge into the divine Being of your being. When consciousness enters Being and feels it, there is an indescribable experience of bliss, freedom, and unconditional, unqualified, unlimited love.

The earth is alive. The universe is alive. Reality is alive as one living consciousness. Pain, hurt, negativity, and fear are misexperienced sensation. They cause us to recoil from our oneness with this living Being, to contract and then to feel the additional pain of separation, aloneness, isolation, and doubt.

God:

...Is the living, conscious, intelligent divine energy and love that makes up everything. He is what we are. He is infinitely loving, supporting, happy, and free, and that is our intrinsic nature as well, for we are what He is.

...Feels us as we feel ourselves, knows us as we know ourselves and the world, and lives us as who we are before we overlay this consciousness of existence with ideas of self, inferiority, comparison, and mortality. He is the conscious energy of being, the Being which mind compartmentalizes into self, other, and world.

...Is the one that loves everything infinitely and, in fact, everything is made of His love and bliss. It is this that we feel when we love and when we are happy.

Happiness:

...Is releasing and forgetting oneself in this joyous, infinite, living sea of Being.

...Is what I am when I am free of individuated, boundaried contraction, when I am like helium gratefully released from its balloon prison back into the atmosphere.

...Is reveling in the wonder and joy of my own form of Him, the way He is as me. It is a temporary form for my pleasure and His, so that I may have consciousness of His Being.

...Is knowing that there is no goal and no problem to solve: we are already awesomely beautiful, wonder-filled, and happy.

The Body:

...Happiness is in the body. It is the body itself when felt as pure being. The body is our most direct way of feeling into the pure nature of being. The happiness in

the body is so great as to be almost unbearable, when it is realized to be God. And this awareness is so amazing, wondrous, exciting, and joyous, that merely to know and feel it is to be awakened and flooded with Him. To focus and merge consciousness in the body is to tap into this great, boundless joy.

To Love God:

...Is to love all beings and all things just as they are right now in their timelessness.

...Is to know that God is the love that we love with. When we love, it is God who is loving.

...Is to know that His love is everywhere — we are in a vast sea of love, and to love God is to love with that love, to float in it, to know that there is enough for everyone.

...Is to know there is an opening in your soul through which love pours, and that you are the love itself.

...Is to forget everything else and just love, blindly, indiscriminately, always, under all circumstances and all conditions.

...Is to know that life is in fact a miracle of wonder and grace — a gift of inestimable beauty and joy.

...Is to love the very fire from which we are made. God roars in us like a fire, and it is this fire of love that will consume all we are until there is nothing left but the fire of loving God.

To Praise God:

...Is to see everything as a miracle, from the smallest cell or grain of sand to the Grand Canyon, the ocean, the stars, and yourself.

...Is to be aware of the miracle of seeing, hearing, colors, forms, sounds, touch, smell; of consciousness, knowledge, empathy, emotion. All this, free, given without strings, without tricks, for us to know and to be.

To Trust God:

...Is to know that God is the trees, is He who moves the stars, is He that lives your body, sees through your eyes, hears with your ears; is He that walks and breathes and lives you, as you; and to trust this sacred reality just as it is, here, now.

...Is to know that I, as I, am not important. What a relief! He is already all of this. I am here as a wonderful incidental piece of this, to feel it, give testimony to it, love it, and be it.

...Is to know there is no death, just the dropping of one's identity and one's place for new ones.

To Know God:
...Is to understand that you are God being you in His creation.

...Is to know that it is God that is the knower and He is known. He is who we are and we are the reason for his manifestation.

...Is to realize that it is God's mind that we think is our own.

...Is to be filled with His joy at being known.

...Is to know that Reality is the dream of His happiness.

To Please God:
...Is to relax, lighten up, and love the ones you are with.

...Is to be happy, and know that happiness is the purpose of our existence.

To Serve God:
...Is to be His happiness and to share it with others, to share His joy and radiate it to the whole world.

...Is to remain in the fountain of love, in the arms of love, always and forever, loving all who are found in your life, for they are your responsibility to love. We are called upon to love all beings always. The reward is in the loving and is worth countless times what might have been exacted in punishment, victory, revenge, greed, power, possession, or fame. We are here to serve the Being of love by being that love ourselves.

To Feel God:
...Is to feel and love His mighty presence without fear.

...Is to feel the great power of happiness and joy and infinite love that wells up inside.

...Is to feel that He is here, the very energy of your being.

To See God:
...Is to see Him everywhere.

...Is to be seen by God.

...Is to know that it is God that sees, not us. He sees through our eyes and he sees us seeing.

...Is to know that the physical laws we see are in fact the mind of God manifesting.

To Hear God:
...Is to hear Him in every vibration, for he is the sound of voices, wind, machinery, music, and the cry of the newborn babe.

...Is to melt into the slience of His Infinite Being.

To Thank God:
...Is to be eternally grateful for this incredible opportunity of consciousness, of being able to love, to work, to play, to sing, and to partake of all aspects of the dance of life.

To Merge with God:
...To merge with everything is to lose the boundaries separating us from the one infinite loving Being of Light. And if everything is living God, if this body itself is God as is every other body, then the discrimination of opposites, of good and evil, of want and fear, rich and poor, also disappear. They are seen then as abstractions of the mind separating us from direct knowledge. For in mystic truth, all is the infinite love-bliss existence of God. From this ultimate apprehension, boundless joy, relief, and freedom explode from our very being and we dance in fountains of happiness.

...Is so simple. It is to forget being yourself, to get out of your own way, and to allow the energy of happiness and love to flow through you. To merge with God is simply...to be.

Heaven and Hell:
This material world seems to be a meeting ground between heaven and hell. In this world, as in all other realms of existence, our state of mind determines where we are. We can be in the heaven of love, joy and communion; or in the hell of separation, torment, rage, bitterness, and contraction. The material world is one of many playgrounds for this discovery.

Ultimate Purposes, Ultimate Knowledge:

Life is hard on the material level because we greatly misunderstand it. Matter rises and falls, comes and goes, and passes through all phases of being, becoming, and dissolving. We are here to learn that the world viewed through our "normal" perception is, in reality, a misperception. The radical man, the man of knowledge, sees existence from an entirely different perspective from the conventional man who takes things for what they appear. The man of knowledge is thus set apart from his peers who walk in ignorance of this great ocean of bliss and ultimate knowing. The radical man cannot explain what he knows to the conventional man — for only confusion, debate, ridicule, alienation, and disturbance will result. But for one who walks in this ocean of God consciousness, debate is of diminishing significance. Joy and love, and their manifestation in service, become the sole motives for behavior.

We are here to love and to liberate the world so that love can be the sole operating principle. Everywhere there is ignorance and the suffering that only love can heal. Pain is the strain of attachments and control. When events exceed our current ability to tolerate and respond, when our current form is too rigid to contain the intensity of what is happening, then we feel pain. Pain and hardship are always opportunities for practicing love — for ourselves, our problems, our enemies, our trials, our wounds, and our defeats.

What is in the way?

If what has been described above feels so true, why is it is so difficult to stay with and to expand? There is a ring in our bodies constricting the expansion of joy, and there is a tendency to avoid the pain of this ring's constriction by turning away from it. Instead, we try to numb or distract ourselves by buying objects, drinking, or filling our hours with meaningless activities.

Why do we have this ring? It is there because of all the admonitions from adults that we internalized growing up. We were told to sit down, be quiet, and behave. Such admonitions are painful. They cause us to contract and to hate and distrust ourselves. And so we learn to constrict ourselves, seeking instead to conform, and we lose the flow of joyous expansion. The contraction is the ring and the ring is pain.

To open this constricting ring is to be infinitely happy and alive and free. How is it opened? Not by endless exercises and practices, which only contract us with more seriousness, effort and worry, but by release — intentional joyous release into being. We must overcome the fear of ridicule, judgment, and rejection that tightens the ring. We must take the risk of being happy and free, to go with the flow of being, joy, and happiness rather than against it.

What would it mean right now to release yourself totally? To go with the flow of being, joy, happiness rather than against? To walk away from the rigid, limiting, and constricting rules, beliefs, social conventions and expectations, and do what moves you nat-

urally toward joy, love, happiness, and wonder? This is the doorway, the threshold, the hidden passage, the living ecstasy.

This is the leap of faith — to live in the bodily joy of God, and let go of our need to control and our concern about outcomes, for they are a major cause of the ring. The risk of not doing this is a life never moved or flooded with its feeling, never lived as it wants.

Always we are confronted with social boundaries — social norms that govern acceptable and unacceptable behavior. They are invisible, but nonetheless experienced. They are walls that turn us back. But again and again, if we are truly conscious, we can see that from the happiness evoked in knowing God-as-this-body-right-now comes innumerable impulses to go beyond, to say "I love you," to forget restrictive rules, to cease shrinking from this great joy, and to be infinitely more than what you think you are. What you are will then lead you. You are so much more than what you think. God pours Himself into and through each of us. He pours Himself! And all we have to do is allow ourselves to feel the joy and generosity we are made of, for that joy is God's essence.

This world does not need more rules and laws, it needs more ecstasy. It needs the union of this ecstasy with all beings, things, energies, wonders, spaces, places, and infinity itself, for love and happiness open us to the reality that there is only one, and we are that One, and He is us.

Can we live a kind of steadily expanding life, opening forever this heart energy of joy and love? Others may resent the changes they see in us, for they need us to fulfill their expectations. Whenever others feel abandoned by our growth, we must stay strong, supporting our own joy while they are working through the darkness within themselves. Can we embody God in this way? Can we risk going beyond man's rules to know God's infinite joy and presence? Will we face the threat of rejection, loss of love, devaluation, or ostracism? Each moment of awareness is the crossroads.

To Meditate:

...Is to close your eyes and feel into the essence of reality as God.

...Is to know that what you experience directly as being, as pure awareness, is God.

...Is to know that entering into our being is entering into His being — there is no difference.

A Different Psychology

The viewpoints offered in this book, especially those in this last section, derive from a different psychology. That psychology is not linear, or "objective" or externally scientific. It does not make sense in the logical, pragmatic world, but it is as old as mankind. It is the psychology of radical pantheism and infinite love. ❧

POST SCRIPT

❧ I finish this work with a few final reflections.

This work has been a gift to me every step of the way. Ideas, books, presentations, conversations all came to me just when I needed them. So many people helped. Serendipity everywhere. When I pushed too hard, when I was going beyond my connection to the work, my laptop computer failed, I lost a couple of disks to a virus, I made stupid mistakes. It could not be rushed.

Then, when it came time to finish this book, to sit down and put it all together, everything in my life suddenly became quiet. My telephone at work stopped ringing — hardly a message unless it was someone canceling their appointment. My schedule opened up and I would write for hours without noticing the passage of time. My publisher appeared quite by coincidence and we hit it off immediately. We both knew what this book was about. He found an editor who also knew. And the moment I understood the meaning of the ending of time and shared it with my wife, my watch stopped. Literally stopped.

Even the lowly fortune cookie helped. Talking to my wife in a Chinese restaurant, I wondered aloud how I might honor the Everyman team that I worked with on three wonderful men's gatherings and numerous presentations. In a cookie I got this fortune, "Behind an able man, there are always other able men." What a truth! Thank you Keith, Dan, Phil, Fred, Bob and Cai. The night before I began sending manuscripts out for review, I felt overwhelmed with self-doubt. Were these ideas just too "far out" to risk sharing? Putting on a shirt I hadn't worn in months, I found another fortune in the pocket. I have no recollection of reading it before. It said, "Sell your ideas — they are totally acceptable."

Then, most amazingly, I had this dream: I was working on the manuscript at my mother's dining room table, finishing it up. I looked up through the doorway into the hall by her stairs, and there he was — my father! I was so astonished. I hugged him and marveled awe-struck at his presence. He was really there and it was wonderful. I knew, too, that this was not a dream image to be interpreted psychologically: this was my father. He had come to show me how proud and happy he was with me.

In the end, the book all came together right as the last deadline was reached. Obviously, its season has come. I hope it has the kind of value for you that it did for me.

Last of all, I'd like to hear from you. Have the themes and ideas in this book made sense to you? Were they too far out? More importantly, has this work touched you? Please let me know by writing to me in care of Tzedakah Publications, P. O. Box 221097, Sacramento, CA 95822. ❦

ACKNOWLEDGEMENTS

Assagioli, Robert: From PSYCHOSYNTHESIS: A COLLECTION OF BASIC WRITINGS. Copyright (c) 1965 by Robert Assagioli. Reprinted by permission of Sterling Lord Literistic, Inc.

Bahti, Mark: From PUEBLO STORIES AND STO-RYTELLERS by Mark Bahti. Reprinted by permission of Treasure Chest Books.

Bly, Robert: From THE KABIR BOOK by Robert Bly. Copyright (c) 1971 by Robert Bly. Reprinted by permission of Beacon Press.

Bly, Robert: "Snowbanks North of the House", from THE MAN IN THE BLACK COAT TURNS by Robert Bly. Copyright (c) 1981 by Robert Bly. Used by permission of Doubleday, a division of Bantam Doubleday Dell Publishing Group, Inc.

Bly, Robert: IRON JOHN. (Excerpted from pp. 2-3), (c) 1990 by Robert Bly. Reprinted by permission of Addison-Wesley Publishing Company, Inc.

Brown, Pam: "Apology" by Pam Brown from FOR FATHER WITH LOVE, published by Exley Publications Ltd. Reprinted by permission of Exley Publications Ltd., Great Britain.

Bucke, Richard M.: From COSMIC CONSCIOUS-NESS: A STUDY IN THE EVOLUTION OF THE HUMAN MIND by Richard M. Bucke. Copyright (c) 1923. Reprinted by permission of E.P. Dutton: New York.

Buechner, Frederick: SELECTED QUOTES FROM PAGES 1 - 6 from THE SACRED JOURNEY by FREDERICK BUECHNER. Copyright (c) 1982 by Frederick Buechner. Reprinted by permission of HarperCollins Publishers, Inc.

Bynner, Witter: 9 LINES FROM PAGE 31 AND 6 LINES FROM PAGE 58 from THE WAY OF LIFE ACCORDING TO LAO TZU edited by WITTER BYNNER. Copyright 1944 by Witter Bynner. Copyright renewed (c) 1972 by Dorothy Chauvenet and Paul Horgan. Reprinted by permission of Harper Collins Publishers, Inc.

Campbell, Joseph: From HERO WITH A THOU-SAND FACES by Joseph Campbell. Copyright (c) 1968. Reprinted by permission of Princeton University Press: Princeton, N.J.

Campbell, Joseph: "Excerpts", from THE POWER OF MYTH by Joseph Campbell & Bill Moyers. Copyright (c) 1988 by Apostrophe S Productions, Inc. and Bill Moyers and Alfred Van der Marck Editions, Inc. for itself and the estate of Joseph Campbell. Used by permission of Doubleday, a division of Bantam Doubleday Dell Publishing Group, Inc.

Chinen, Allan B: Reprinted by permission of The Putnam Publishing Group/Jeremy P. Tarcher, Inc. from ONCE UPON A MIDLIFE by Allan B. Chinen. Copyright (c) 1992 by Allan B. Chinen.

Chinen: From IN THE EVER AFTER: FAIRY TALES AND THE SECOND HALF OF LIFE by Allan B. Chinen. Copyright (c) 1989. Reprinted by permission of Chiron Publications.

Cohen, J. M. and Phipps, J. F.: From THE COMMON EXPERIENCE: SIGNPOSTS ON THE PATH TO ENLIGHTENMENT by J. M. Cohen and J. F. Phipps. Copyright (c) 1992. Reprinted by permission of Stanley Paul/Cresset, Random House UK Limited: London.

Courtois, Flora: From AN EXPERIENCE OF ENLIGHTENMENT. Copyright (c) 1986. Reprinted by permission of The Theosophical Publishing House, Quest Books, Wheaton, Ill.

deCaussade, Jean-Pierre: From ABANDONMENT TO DIVINE PROVIDENCE by Jean-Pierre de Caussade. Copyright (c) 1975 by John Beevers. Used by permission of Doubleday, a division of Bantam Doubleday Dell Publishing Group, Inc.

de Chardin, Pierre Teilhard: SELECTED EXCERPTS FROM THE DIVINE MILIEU by PIERRE TEILHARD DE CHARDIN. Copyright (c) 1957 by Editions du Seuill, Paris. English translation copyright (c) 1960 by Wm. Collins Sons & Co., London, and Harper & Row, publishers, Inc., New York. Renewed (c) 1988 by Harper & Row Publishers, Inc. Reprinted by permission of Harper Collins Publishers, Inc.

Edinger, Edward F.: From TRANSFORMATION OF THE GOD-IMAGE: AN ELUCIDATION OF JUNG'S ANSWER TO JOB. Copyright (c) 1992. Reprinted by permission of Inner City Books.

Eliade, Mircea: Excerpts from THE SACRED AND THE PROFANE: THE NATURE OF RELI-GION by Mircea Eliade, copyright (c) 1957 by Rowohlt Taschenbuch Verlag BmgH, English translation by Willard Trask copyright (c) 1959 and renewed 1987 by Harcourt Brace & Company, reprinted by permission of Harcourt Brace & Company.

Eliot, T. S.: Excerpts from "East Coker" in FOUR QUARTERS, copyright 1943 by T. S. Eliot and renewed 1971 by Esme Valeria Eliot, reprinted by permission of Harcourt Brace & Company.

Erikson, Erik H.: From ADULTHOOD by Erik H. Erikson. Copyright (c) 1978. Reprinted by permission of W. W. Norton and Company.

Farrell, Michael & Rosenberg, Stanley: MEN AT MIDLIFE, reprinted with permission of Greenwood Publishing Group, Inc., Westport, CT. Copyright (c) 1991 by Auburn House Publishing Company.

Finley, James: Excerpt from MERTON'S PALACE OF NOWHERE: A SEARCH FOR GOD THROUGH AWARENESS OF THE TRUE SELF by James Finley. Copyright (c) 1978 by Ave Maria Press, Notre Dame, IN 46556. All rights reserved. Used with permission of the publisher.

Finneran, Richard J.: "Vacillation," Part IV. Reprinted with permission of Simon & Schuster from THE POEMS OF W. B. YEATS: A NEW EDITION, edited by Richard J. Finneran. Copyright (c) 1933 by Macmillan Publishing Company, renewed 1961 by Bertha Georgie Yeats.

Finneran, Richard J.: "The Four Ages of Man". Reprinted with permission of Simon & Schuster from THE POEMS OF W. B. YEATS: A NEW EDITION, edited by Richard J. Finneran. Copyright (c) 1934 by Macmillan Publishing Company, renewed 1962 by Bertha Georgie Yeats.

Foster, Genevieve W.: Reprinted from THE WORLD WAS FLOODED WITH LIGHT: A MYTHICAL EXPERIENCE REMEMBERED, by Genevieve W. Foster, by permission of the University of Pittsburgh Press. Copyright (c) by University of Pittsburgh Press.

Fowler, James W.: SELECTED QUOTE FROM PAGES 186-187, 200, 201 from STAGES OF FAITH: THE PSYCHOLOGY OF HUMAN DEVELOPMENT AND THE QUEST FOR MEANING by JAMES W. FOWLER. Copyright (c) 1981 by James W. Fowler. Reprinted by permission of HarperCollins Publishers, Inc.

Fox, Matthew: From BREAKTHROUGH by Matthew Fox. Copyright (c) 1980 by Matthew Fox. Used by permission of Doubleday, a division of Bantam Doubleday Dell Publishing Group, Inc.

Fox, Matthew: SELECTED QUOTES FROM PAGES 43, 48, 51, 63, 64, 65 from THE COMING OF THE COSMIC CHRIST by MATTHEW FOX. Copyright (c) 1988 Matthew Fox. Reprinted by permission of HarperCollins Publishers, Inc.

Goleman, Daniel: From "Why Spiritual Groups Go Awry" which appeared in the May/June 1990 issue of Common Boundary. Reprinted by permission of Common Boundary, Bethesda , MD.

Gray, Charlotte: "Untitled", by Charlotte Gray. From FOR FATHER WITH LOVE published by Exley Publications Ltd. Reprinted by permission of Exley Publications Ltd, Great Britain.

Grimm, Jakob & Wilhelm: From THE COMPLETE GRIMM'S FAIRY TALES by Jakob & Wilhelm Grimm, grans. by Margaret Hunt & James Stern. Copyright (c) 1944 by Pantheon Books, Inc. Copyright renewed 1972 by Random House, Inc. Adapted by permission of Pantheon Books, a division of Random House, Inc.

Grof & Grof: Reprinted by permission of The Putnam Publishing Group/Jeremy P. Tarcher, Inc. from THE STORMY SEARCH FOR THE SELF by Christina Grof and Stanislav Grof. Copyright (c) 1990 by Stanislav and Christina Grof.

Happold, F.C.: Approximately 323 words (pp. 368-372) From MYSTICISM: A STUDY AND AN ANTHOLOGY by F. C. Happold (Penguin Books 1963, reviewed edition 1970) copyright (c) F. C. Happold, 1963, 1964, 1970. Reproduced by permission of Penguin Books Ltd.

Heinberg, Richard: Reprinted by permission of The Putnam Publishing Group/Jeremy P. Tarcher, Inc. from MEMORIES AND VISIONS OF PARADISE: EXPLORING THE UNIVERSAL MYTH OF A LOST GOLDEN AGE by Richard Heinberg. Copyright (c) 1989 by Richard Heinberg.

Hite, Shere: From THE HITE REPORT ON MALE SEXUALITY by Shere Hite. Copyright (c) 1981. Reprinted by permission of Knopf: New York.

Houston Jean: Reprinted by permission of The Putnam Publishing Group/Jeremy P. Tarcher, Inc. from THE SEARCH FOR THE BELOVED: JOURNEYS IN MYTHOLOGY AND SACRED PSYCHOLOGY by Jean Houston. Copyright (c) 1987 by Jean Houston.

Houston, Jean: Reprinted by permission of The Putnam Publishing Group/Jeremy P. Tarcher, Inc. from THE POSSIBLE HUMAN: A COURSE IN ENHANCING YOUR PHYSICAL, MENTAL AND CREATIVE ABILITIES by Jean Houston. Copyright (c) 1982 by Jean Houston.

Huxley, Aldous: SELECTED QUOTE FROM PAGE 255 from THE PERENNIAL PHILOSOPHY by ALDOUS HUXLEY. Copyright 1944, 1945 by Aldous Huxley. Copyright renewed 1973, 1974 by Laura A. Huxley. Reprinted by permission of HarperCollins Publishers, Inc.

James, William: From THE VARIETIES OF RELIGIOUS EXPERIENCE by William James. Copyright (c) 1936. Reprinted by permission of Modern Library: New York.

Jeffers, Robinson: From THE SELECTED POETRY OF ROBINSON JEFFERS by Robinson Jeffers. Copyright (c) 1938 by Donnan and Garth Jeffers. Copyright renewed 1966 by Donnan and Garth Jeffers. Reprinted by permission of Random House, Inc.

Johnson, Josephine: "Year's End" Copyright (c) 1995 The estate of Josephine W. Johnson. Reprinted by permission of the estate of Josephine W. Johnson.

Jong, Erica: "Living Happily Ever After" from MARRIAGE A KEEPSAKE. Reprinted by permission of Sterling Lord Literistic, Inc. Copyright 1977 by Erica Jong.

Jung, C. G.: From MEMORIES, DREAMS, REFLECTIONS by Carl G. Jung, rec & ed by Aniela Jaffe, Trans by R & C Winston. Translation copyright (c) 1961, 1962, 1963 by Random House, Inc. Copyright renewed 1989, 1990, 1991 by Random House, inc. Reprinted by permission of Pantheon Books, a division of Random House, Inc.

Jung, C. G. and M.L. von Franz, Joseph L. Henderson, Jolande Jacobi, Aniela Jaffé: From MAN AND HIS SYMBOLS. Copyright (c) 1964. Reprinted by permission of Carol Summerfield.

Jung, Carl: From ASPECTS OF THE MASCULINE by Carl Jung. Copyright (1989). Reprinted by permission of Princeton University Press: Princeton, N.J.

Jung, Carl: From TWO ESSAYS ON ANALYTICAL PSYCHOLOGY by Carl Jung. Copyright (c) 1966. Reprinted by permission of Princeton University Press: Princeton, N.J.

Jung, Carl: From THE COLLECTED WORKS OF C. G. JUNG translated by R. F. C. Hull. Reprinted by permission of Princeton University Press.

Kalweit, Holger: From DREAMTIME AND INNER SPACE by Holger Kalweit. Copyright (c) 1988. Reprinted by permission of Shambhala: Boston.

Kast, Verena: From SISYPHUS: A JUNGIAN APPROACH TO MIDLIFE CRISIS by Verena Kast. Translated by Norman Brown. Copyright 1991. Reprinted by permission of Daimon Verlag: Switzerland.

Keen, Sam: Excerpt from interview by Stephan Bodian as appeared in YOGA JOURNAL May/June 1991. Reprinted by permission of Yoga Journal.

Kipling, Rudyard: The poem "IF" from RUDYARD KIPLING VERSE, definitive edition, by Rudyard Kipling. Copyright (c) 1910. Reprinted by permission of Bantam Doubleday Dell: New York.

Kipnis, Aaron: Reprinted by permission of The Putnam Publishing Group/Jeremy P. Tarcher, Inc. from KNIGHTS WITHOUT ARMOR: A PRACTICAL GUIDE FOR MEN IN QUEST OF MASCULINE SOUL by Aaron R. Kipnis. Copyright (c) 1991 by Aaron R. Kipnis.

Kornfield, Jack: From "Mindful Living", an interview by Anne A. Simpkinson in Common Boundary, July/August 1993. Reprinted by permission of Common Boundary, Bethesda, MD.

Krishna, Gopi: From KUNDALINI: THE EVOLUTIONARY ENERGY IN MAN by Gopi Krishna. Copyright (c) 1970. Reprinted by permission of Shambhla: Berkeley, CA.

Kunitz, Stanley: "End of Summer" by Stanley Kunitz from THE POEMS OF STANELY KUNITZ 1928 - 1978. Copyright (c) 1979 by Stanley Kunitz. Reprinted by permission of Darhansoff & Verrill: New York.

Lawrence, D. H.: From APOCALYPSE by D. H. Lawrence Introduction Richard Aldington. copyright 1931 by The Estate of D. H. Lawrence, renewed (c) 1959 by the Estate of Frieda Lawrence Ravagli. Used by permission of Viking Penguin, a division of Penguin Books USA Inc.

Lawrence, D. H.: "Two Ways of Living and Dying" by D. H. Lawrence, "The Primal Passions" by D. H. Lawrence, "Healing" by D. H. Lawrence, "If You are a Man" by D. H. Lawrence, from THE COMPLETE POEMS OF D.H. LAWRENCE by D. H. Lawrence, Edited by V. de Sola Pinto & F. W. Roberts. Copyright (c) 1964, 1971 by Angelo Ravagli and C. M. Weekley, Executors of the Estate of Frieda Lawrence Ravagli. Used by permission of Viking Penguin, a division of Penguin Books USA Inc.

Laski, Marghanita: Reprinted by permission of The Putnam Publishing Group/Jeremy P. Tarcher, Inc. from ECSTASY IN SECULAR AND RELIGIOUS EXPERIENCES by Marghanita Laski. Copyright (c) 1961 by Marghanita Laski Howard; Renewed (c) 1989 by John Howard.

Lee & Hand: From A TASTE OF WATER: CHRISTIANITY THROUGH TAOIST-BUDDHIST EYES. Copyright (c) 1990. Reprinted by permission of Paulist Press.

Levinson, Daniel J. et al: THE SEASONS OF A MAN'S LIFE by Daniel J. Levinson, et al. Copyright (c) 1978 by Daniel J Levinson. Reprinted by permission of Alfred A Knopf Inc.

Maharshi, Ramana: From THE SPIRITUAL TEACHING OF RAMANA MAHARSHI by Ramana Maharshi. Copyright (c) 1972. Reprinted by permission of Shambhala: Boulder, Colorado.

May, Robert M.: From COSMIC CONSCIOUSNESS REVISITED by Robert M. May. Copyright (c)1991. Reprinted by permission of Element Books: Rockport, MA.

McGuire, W. & Hull, R.: From C. G. JUNG SPEAKING. INTERVIEWS AND ENCOUNTERS by W. McGuire and R. Hull. Copyright (c) 1977. Reprinted by permission of Princeton University Press.

Merton, Thomas: NEW SEEDS OF CONTEMPLATION. Copyright (c) 1961 by the Abbey of Gethsemane Inc. Reprinted by permission of New Directions Publishing Corp.

Mitchell, Stephen: Translation of The Sonnets to Orpheus by Rainer Maria Rilke. Reprinted by permission of Stephen Mitchell.

Mitchell, Stephen: From THE SELECTED POETRY OF RAINER MARIA RILKE by Stephen Mitchell. Translation Copyright (c) 1982 by Stephen Mitchell. Reprinted by permission of Random House, Inc.

Mitchell, Stephen: From LETTERS TO A YOUNG POET by Stephen Mitchell. Copyright (c) 1984 by Stephen Mitchell. Reprinted by permission of Random House, Inc.

Mood, John: From RILKE ON LOVE AND OTHER DIFFICULTIES by John Mood. Copyright (c) 1975. Reprinted by permission of W. W. Norton and Company.

Moore, Robert and Gillette, Douglas: SELECTED QUOTE FROM PAGES 13, 41 from KING, WARRIOR, MAGICIAN, LOVER by ROBERT MOORE and DOUGLAS GILLETTE. COPYRIGHT (c) 1990 BY ROBERT MOORE AND DOUGLAS GILLETEE. Reprinted by permission of HarperCollins Publishers, Inc.

Moyne, J. & Barks, C.: "Be Melting Snow" from OPEN SECRET: VERSIONS OF RUMI. Copyright (c) 1984. Reprinted by permission of Threshold Books, RD 4 Box 600, Putney, VT 05346.

Rilke, Rainer Maria: SELECTED QUOTE FROM PAGE 49, 89 AND 105 from SELECTED POEMS OF RAINER MARIA RILKE, EDITED AND TRANSLATED BY ROBERT BLY. Copyright (c) 1981 by Robert Bly. Reprinted by permission of HarperCollins Publishers, Inc.

BIBLIOGRAPHY

Agosin, Tomas. 1992. Psychosis, Dreams and Mysticism in the Clinical Domain. In Holligan and Shea The Fires of Desire.

Assagioli, Roberto. 1977. Psychosynthesis: A Collection of Basic Writings. Penguin: New York.

Barks, C. & Moyne, J. 1988. This Longing: Poetry, Teaching Stories and Selected Letters. Jelaluddin Rumi. Threshold Books: Putney, Vt.

Bergquist, William H., Greenberg, Elinor Miller, Klaum, G. Alan. 1993. In Our Fifties: Voices of Men and Women Reinventing their Lives. Josey-Bass: San Francisco.

Berry, Patricia, ed. 1990. Fathers and Mothers. Spring Publications: Dallas, Texas.

Berry, R. & Berry N., ed. 1992. The Spiritual Athlete: A primer for the inner life. Joshua Press: Olema, California.

Bly, Robert. 1977. The Kabir Book. Beacon Press: Boston.

Bly, Robert. 1981a. The Man in the Black Coat Turns. Doubleday: New York.

Bly, Robert. 1981b. ed. Selected Poems of Rainer Maria Rilke. Perennial Library: New York.

Bly, Robert. 1990. Iron John: A Book About Men. Addison-Wesley: Reading, Massachusetts.

Bucke, Richard Maurice. 1923. Cosmic Consciousness: A Study in the Evolution of the Human Mind. E.P. Dutton: New York.

Buechner, Frederick. 1982. Sacred Journey. Harper: San Francisco.

Bynner, Witter. 1944. The Way of Life According to Laotzu. Perigee Books (Putnam): New York.

Campbell, Joseph. 1968. The Hero with a Thousand Faces. Princeton University: New York.

Campbell, Joseph. 1977. The Portable Jung. Princeton University Press: Princeton, N.J.

Campbell, Joseph. 1988. The Power of Myth. Doubleday: New York.

Carruth, Hayden, ed. 1970. The Voice That is Great Within Us. Bantam: New York.

Chinen, Allan B. 1989. In the Ever After: Fairy Tales and the Second Half of Life. Chiron Publications: Wilmette, Illinois.

Chinen, Allan B. 1992. Once Upon a Midlife. Jeremy P. Tarcher: Los Angeles.

Chinen, Allan B. 1993. Beyond the Hero: Classic Stories of Men in Search of Soul. G. P. Putnam's Sons: New York.

Cirlot, J. E. 1971. A Dictionary of Symbols. Philosophical Library: New York.

Cohen, J. M. and Phipps, J. F. 1992. The Common Experience: Signposts on the Path to Enlightenment. Quest Books: Wheaton, Illinois.

Corneau, Guy. 1991. Absent Fathers, Lost Sons: The Search for Masculine Identity. Shambhala: Boston.

Courtois, Flora. 1986. An Experience of Enlightenment. The Theosophical Publishing House: Wheaton, Ill.

Cousinear, Phil, ed. 1990. The Hero's Journey: Joseph Campbell on His Life and Work. Harper & Row: San Francisco.

Dalai Lama. 1990. In Common Boundary. May/June.

deCaussade, Jean-Pierre. 1975. Abandonment to Divine Providence. Doubleday: New York.

de Chardin, Teilhard. 1960. The Divine Milieu. William Collins Sons & Co.: London, and Harper & Row: New York.

Edinger, Edward F. 1992. Transformation of the God-Image An Elucidation of Jung's Answer to Job. Inner City Books: Toronto, Canada.

Eliade, Mircea. 1954. The Myth of the Eternal Return. Princeton University Press: Princeton, N.J.

Eliade, Mircea. 1961. The Sacred and the Profane. Harcourt Brace: New York.

Eliot, T.S. 1943. Four Quarters. Harcourt Brace & Company: Orlando, Florida.

Erikson, Erik H. ed. 1978. Adulthood. W. W. Norton and Company: New York.

Exley, Helen, ed. 1982. Marriage a Keepsake. Exley: United Kingdom.

Exley, Helen, ed. 1985. For Fathers with Love. Exley: United Kingdom.

Farrell, Michael P. and Rosenberg Stanley D. 1981. Men at Midlife. Auburn House: Dover, Massachusetts.

Farrell, Warren. 1988. Why Men Are The Way They Are. Berkley Books: New York.

Ferrucci, Piero. 1990. Inevitable Grace. Jeremy Tarcher: Los Angeles.

Feurstein, George. 1991. Holy Madness. Paragon House: New York.

Fields, R., Taylor, P., Weyler, R., & Ingrasci, R. 1984. Chop Wood, Carry Water. Jeremy P. Tarcher: Los Angeles.

Finley, James. 1988. Merton's Palace of Nowhere: A Search for God through Awareness of the True Self. Ave Maria Press: Notre Dame, Indiana.

Finneran, Richard J., ed. 1989. The Collected Poems of W. B. Yeats. Collier: New York.

Foster, Genevieve W. 1985. The World was Flooded with Light: A Mystical Experience Remembered. University of Pittsburgh Press: Pittsburgh, Pennsylvania.

Fowler, James W. 1981. Stages of Faith: The Psychology of Human Development and the Quest for Meaning. Harper: San Francisco.

Fox, Matthew. 1980. Breakthrough: Meister Eckhart's Creation Spirituality in New Translation. Doubleday: New York.

Fox, Matthew. 1988. The Coming of the Cosmic Christ. Harper & Row: San Francisco, California.

Frost, Robert. 1971. Robert Frost's Poems. Pocket Books: N.Y.

Gallup, George. 1982. Adventures in Immortality. A Look Beyond the Threshold of Death. McGraw-Hill: New York.

Gassner, John ed. 1987 (1963). Medieval and Tudor Drama. Applause Theatre Book Publishers: New York.

Goleman, Daniel. 1990. In Common Boundary. May/June.

Goleman, D. & Davidson, R. eds. 1979. CONSCIOUSNESS: Brain, States of Awareness, and Mysticism. Harper & Row: New York.

Gordon, James. 1990. In Common Boundary. May/June.

Grof, Stanislav and Grof, Christina. 1989. Spiritual Emergency: When Personal Transformation Becomes a Crisis. Jeremy P. Tarcher: Los Angeles.

Grof, Stanislav. 1990. The Holotropic Mind. Harper: San Francisco.

Grof, Christina and Grof, Stanislav. 1990. The Stormy Search for the Self. Jeremy P. Tarcher/Perigee: New York.

Halligan, F. & Shea, J. 1992. The Fires of Desire. Crossroad: New York.

Happold, F.C. 1990. Mysticism: A Study and an Anthology. Penguin Books: London W8 5TZ, England.

Heinberg, Richard. 1989. Memories and Visions of Paradise: Exploring the Universal Myth of a Lost Golden Age. Jeremy P. Tarcher: Los Angeles.

Hillman, James. 1964. Suicide and the Soul. Spring Publications: Dallas, Texas.

Hillman, James. 1990. Lecture from conference: The Male Psyche: Men in the Consulting Room. April, 1990.

Hite, Shere. 1981. The Hite Report on Male Sexuality. Knopf: New York.

Houston, Jean. 1982. The Possible Human: A Course in Enhancing Your Physical, Mental, and Creative Abilities. Jeremy P. Tarcher: Los Angeles.

Houston, Jean. 1987. The Search for the Beloved: Journeys in Mythology and Sacred Psychology. Jeremy P. Tarcher: Los Angeles.

Hunt, Margaret & Stern, James, trans. 1972. The Complete Grimm's Fairy Tales. 1944 Pantheon Books. 1972 Random House.

Huxley, Aldous. 1945. The Perennial Philosophy. Harper & Brothers: New York.

James, William. 1936. The Varieties of Religious Experience. Modern Library: New York.

Johnson, Eric W. 1986. Older and Wiser: Wit, Wisdom, and Spirited Advice from the Older Generation. Walker and Company: New York.

Johnson, Robert. 1983. WE: Understanding the Psychology of Romantic Love. Harper and Row: San Francisco.

Jung, Carl. 1933. Modern Man in Search of a Soul. Harcourt Brace Javanovich: Orlando.

Jung, Carl. 1959. The Archetypes of the Collective Unconscious. Princeton University Press: Princeton, N.J.

Jung, C., von Franz, M., Henderson, L., Jacobi, J., & Jaffe, A. 1964. Man and His Symbols. Doubleday: New York.

Jung, C.G. 1965. Memories, Dreams, Reflections. Vintage Books: New York.

Jung, Carl. 1966. Two Essays on Analytical Psychology. Princeton University Press: Princeton, N.J.

Jung, Carl. 1969. The Collected Works of C. G. Jung, translated by R. F. C. Hull. The Structure & Dynamics of the Psyche, Collected Works, Vol. 8. Princeton University Press: Princeton, N.J.

Jung, C.G. 1989. Aspects of the Masculine. Princeton University Press: New Jersey.

Kalweit, Holger. 1988. Dreamtime and Inner Space. Shambhala: Boston.

Kaufman, Sharon R. 1986. The Ageless Self. New American library: New York.

Keen, Sam. 1991. Fire in the Belly: On Being a Man. Bantam Books: New York.

Keen, Sam. 1991b. Interview in Yoga Journal. May/June.

Kimbrell, Andrew. 1991. "A Time for Men to Pull Together". Utne Reader, May/June.

Kipnis, Aaron R. 1991. Knights Without Armor: A Practical Guide for Men in Quest of Masculine Soul. Jeremy P. Tarcher/Perigee: New York.

Kornfield, Jack. 1993. In Common Boundary. July/August.

Krishna, Gopi. 1970. Kundalini: the Evolutionary Energy in Man. Shambhala: Berkeley, California.

Kubler-Ross, Elizabeth. 1969. On Death and Dying. Macmillan Co., New York, N.Y.

Kunitz, Stanley. 1979. The Poems of Stanley Kunitz. Darhansoff & Verrill Literary Agency: New York.

Laski, Marghanita. 1961. Ecstasy in Secular and Religious Experiences. Jeremy P. Tarcher: Los Angeles.

Lawrence, D. H. 1931. Apocalypse. Viking Press: New York.

Lee, Chwen Jiuan A. and Hand, Thomas G. 1990. A Taste of Water: Christianity Through Taoist-Buddhist Eyes. Paulist: New York.

Lee, John. 1987. The Flying Boy. Health Communications, Inc: Deerfield Beach, Fl.

LeShan, Lawrence. 1966. The Medium, the Mystic, and the Physicist. Ballantine Books: New York.

Levinson, Daniel J. 1978. The Seasons of a Man's Life. Ballantine Books: New York.

Luccock, H. & Bretano, F. 1947. The Questing Spirit. Coward-McCann: New York.

Lukoff, D., Lu, F., & Turner, R. 1992. "Toward a More Culturally Sensitive DSM-IV. Psycho-religious and Psychospiritual Problems". Journal of Nervous and Mental Disorders, Vol. 180, 11, 11/92.

Lynn, David B. 1974. The Father: His Role in Child Development. Brooks/Cole: Monterey, California.

MacLeish, Archibald, ed. 1970. The Complete Poems of Carl Sandburg. Harcourt Brace Jovanovich: San Diego, California.

Maharshi, Ramana. 1972. The Spiritual Teaching of Ramano Maharshi. Shambhala: Boulder, Colorado.

Maslow, Abraham H. 1968. Toward a Psychology of Being. D. Van Nostrand: New York.

May, Robert M. 1991. Cosmic Consciousness Revisited. Element: Rockport, Massachusetts.

McGuire, W. & Hull, R. 1977. C. G. Jung Speaking. Interviews and Encounters. Princeton University Press: Princeton, N.J.

Merton, Thomas. 1961. New Seeds of Contemplation. New Directions: New York.

Mitchel, Stephen., translator. 1985. The Sonnets to Orpheus. Rainer Maria Rilke. Simon & Schuster: New York.

Mitchel, Stephen, ed. 1989. The Selected Poetry of Rainer Maria Rilke. Vintage International: New York.

Mood, John. Translations and Considerations. 1975. Rilke on Love and Other Difficulties. W. W. Norton & Co.: New York/London.

Moore Robert and Gillette Douglas. 1990. King Warrior Magician Lover: Rediscovering the Archetypes of the Mature Masculine. Harper: San Francisco.

Moyne, J. & Barks, C. 1984. Open Secret: Versions of Rumi. Threshold Books: Putney, Vt.

Osherson, Samuel. 1986. Finding Our Fathers: The Unfinished Business of Manhood. Free Press: New York.

Pinto, V. & Roberts, W., eds. 1977. The Complete Poems of D. H. Lawrence. Penguin: New York.

Rinpoche, Sogyal. 1992. The Tibetan Book of Living and Dying. HarperCollins: New York.

Roethke, Theodore. 1947. The Collected Poems of Theodore Roethke. Doubleday: N.Y.

Sandburg, Carl. 1970. The Complete Poems of Carl Sandburg. Harcourt Brace Jovanovich Publishing: N.Y. Saitoti, Tepilit Ole. 1980. Maasai. Abradale Press/Harry N. Abrams, Inc.: New York.Sheey, Gail. 1974. Passages. E. P. Dutton: New York.

Sinetar, Marsha. 1986. Ordinary People as Monks and Mystics. Paulist Press: New York/Mahwah.

Some, Malidoma. 1992. Talk given at the Mendocino Men's Gathering, Mendocino, CA.

Somé, Malidoma. 1993. Ritual: Power, Healing and Community. Swan/Raven: Portland.

Stace, W. T. 1960. Mysticism and Philosophy. Jeremy P. Tarcher: Los Angeles.

Stafford, William. 1991. Passwords. HarperPerennial: New York.

Starr, Irina. 1991. The Sound of Light. Pilgrim's Path: Ojai, California.

Stein, Murray. 1983. In Midlife. Spring Publications: Dallas.

Sullivan, Harry Stack. 1953. The Interpersonal Theory of Psychiatry. W. W. Norton: N.Y.

Thompson, Keith, ed. 1991. To Be A Man: In Search of the Deep Masculine. Jeremy P. Tarcher: Los Angeles.

Underhill, Evelyn. 1974. Mysticism. New American Library: New York.

Van Dusen, Wilson. 1981. The Natural Depth in Man. Swedenborg Foundation: New York.

Warren, R. & Erskine, A. 1955. Six Centuries of Great Poetry. Dell: New York.

Watts, Alan. 1958. This Is It. Collier Books, published by arrangement with Pantheon Books, a division of Random House. Macmillan Co.: Toronto.

White, John, ed. 1972. The Highest State of Consciousness. Anchor Books: Garden City, New York.

White, John, ed. 1984. What is Enlightenment. Jeremy P. Tarcher: Los Angeles.

Whitman, Walt. 1969. Leaves of Grass. Avon Books, a division of Hearst Corp.: New York.

Wilhelm, Richard, trans. 1962. The Secret of the Golden Flower. Harcourt Brace, Jovanovich: Orlando, FL.

Wilson, Bill. "Pass It On" Bill Wilson and how the A.A. message reached the world. 1984. Alcoholics Anonymous World Services, Inc., New York, N.Y..

Yablonsky, Lewis. 1990. Fathers and Sons. Gardner Press: New York.

Z, Phillip. 1990. A Skeptic's Guide to the Twelve Steps. HarperCollins: New York.